In the Shadow of Mandela

In the Shadow of Mandela

Political Leadership in South Africa

Alexander Johnston

I.B. TAURIS
LONDON • NEW YORK • OXFORD • NEW DELHI • SYDNEY

I.B. TAURIS
Bloomsbury Publishing Plc
50 Bedford Square, London, WC1B 3DP, UK
1385 Broadway, New York, NY 10018, USA

BLOOMSBURY, I.B. TAURIS and the Diana logo are trademarks of
Bloomsbury Publishing Plc

First published in Great Britain 2020

Copyright © Alexander Johnston, 2020

Alexander Johnston has asserted his right under the Copyright, Designs and
Patents Act, 1988, to be identified as Author of this work.

Cover design by Adriana Brioso
Cover image: A sculpture of former South African President Nelson Mandela
designed by artist Marco Cianfanelli, in Howick, South Africa.
(© RAJESH JANTILAL/AFP/Getty Images)

All rights reserved. No part of this publication may be reproduced or
transmitted in any form or by any means, electronic or mechanical,
including photocopying, recording, or any information storage or retrieval
system, without prior permission in writing from the publishers.

Bloomsbury Publishing Plc does not have any control over, or responsibility for,
any third-party websites referred to or in this book. All internet addresses given
in this book were correct at the time of going to press. The author and publisher
regret any inconvenience caused if addresses have changed or sites have ceased
to exist, but can accept no responsibility for any such changes.

A catalogue record for this book is available from the British Library.

A catalog record for this book is available from the Library of Congress.

ISBN: 978-1-7845-3953-5
ePDF: 978-1-7883-1770-2
eBook: 978-1-7883-1769-6

Typeset by Newgen KnowledgeWorks Pvt. Ltd., Chennai, India

To find out more about our authors and books visit www.bloomsbury.com
and sign up for our newsletters.

For Anthea, again and always.

Contents

Preface

One day during the febrile period between the unbanning of the African National Congress (ANC) and South Africa's first democratic election, a tense standoff developed at the campus gates of the University of Natal in Durban, where I was teaching at the time. Police in armoured vehicles wanted to enter the campus but a large crowd of (mainly) African student supporters of liberation movements, who were sitting in the road and singing guerrilla songs, barred their way.

The confrontation went on long enough for the students to decide they needed a leader. There were hasty consultations and in no time at all, one of their number was hoisted on the shoulders of some others and cheered by the rest of the crowd. His expression mingled pride and panic. The cheering gave him a little time to prepare something to say; at length, he could make himself heard. 'I am your leader!' he shouted, punching the air in exultation. 'You must tell me what to do!'

It would not be strictly true to say that at that moment I knew I would one day write a book on leadership in post-apartheid South African politics, but my interest in the subject certainly developed from then. The conception of leadership that caused the young student to speak as he did is one of the most powerful currents in the political culture of the ANC.

For a time, Nelson Mandela defied this cult and personified a different conception of the leader. British journalist Alec Russell recalls witnessing Mandela facing down a crowd of unruly young supporters who wanted weapons to fight supporters of the rival Inkatha Freedom Party: 'I am your leader', said Mandela, 'If you don't want me, tell me to go and rest. As long as I am your leader, I will tell you where you are wrong.' He stared the young men down and they shuffled out abashed.[1] One of the key themes of this book is how, in the leadership vacuum left by Mandela's departure, Thabo Mbeki and Jacob Zuma in their different ways grappled with the ANC's reasserted cult of the collective and tried to turn it to their own advantage.

The book was written and produced during another febrile period in South African politics, the last year of Jacob Zuma's presidency and the first year of Cyril Ramaphosa's leadership of ANC and his tenure as state president. It is a story of decline ending in tentative and ambiguous hopes for renewal. The ambiguities are multiplying daily as the book goes into production and while they may have been eased somewhat by the ANC's comfortable victory under Ramaphosa's leadership in the May 2019 general election, it is clear to all concerned how massive the task of restoring legitimacy to both state apparatus and party really is.

When Thabo Mbeki took over as ANC president and state president from Nelson Mandela, the challenges of reconstruction and development and of redress and nation-building were huge but the resources available to meet them were substantial. The Mandela era had given hope and momentum. Whoever stood after him at the head of government could count for the foreseeable future on repeat electoral majorities won fairly in open contest, bestowing the right to preside over a new polity regulated by a widely acclaimed rights-based constitution, on behalf of a movement that had won broad-based (if sometimes grudging) respect for tenacity and bravery in struggles on several fronts and a shrewd, well-timed conversion to forms of democracy that guaranteed broad-based support.

There was, on the face of it, a wide-open opportunity for what theorists call 'transformational leadership' to flourish but did not work out like that. This book addresses itself to how and why it did not.

In writing it, I have been fortunate to have the encouragement and support of Professor J. E. (Jack) Spence, my closest academic friend. My greatest debt of gratitude in this and all my other endeavours is to my wife, Anthea.

Part One

Leadership and post-apartheid politics

Introduction: Political leadership in post-apartheid South Africa: From the sublime to the ridiculous

When South Africans went to the polls in May 2019, it was a quarter of a century and five democratic elections since the first one in 1994. This is a considerable slice of time – five years more, for instance, than the gap between the First and Second World Wars. More pertinently, in 2019, South Africa has been a democracy for over 60 per cent of the number of years of apartheid rule, that is, between the National Party coming to power in 1948 and the release of Nelson Mandela in 1990. In short, South Africa now has a considerable democratic history, ripe for assessment in weightier terms than the more tentative interim reports, including those produced by the presidency,[1] that have appeared at five- and ten-year intervals to date. The question is what to choose to bind the subject matter together and make it interesting for readers.

One possibility is to interpret the post-apartheid period through the lens of political leadership. In a democracy with fixed terms for presidents and/or alternation of governments through the polls, history falls seductively into periods defined by incumbents, long or short depending on their electoral fortunes. In this way, it is hard to resist the logic that there was something distinctive about (especially) the Mandela years, the Mbeki project and the numerous and varied dramas of the Zuma years, and that what shaped this distinctiveness had a lot to do with the qualities, attributes and failings of the three individuals concerned.

We are in any case conditioned by both high and popular culture to understand the world in terms of a narrative arc or, more simply, storytelling. This is true of all societies. Thus, political leadership – especially where there are term limits – is subject to a narrative template. This consists of the following components: backstory and honeymoon; developing tensions and expenditure of credit; exhaustion and a lame-duck period as the term limit approaches; and usually, though not invariably, post-office rehabilitation (which is tentatively observable in current portrayals of Thabo Mbeki). South Africans of all political persuasions and at all levels of political discourse, from popular understanding to opinion making in the media to academic analysis, tend to put great weight on leaders and leadership as explanatory factors in politics. A typical recent example, an examination of the Zuma years, has it that:

> We are a country in crisis; a country that by virtue of a leadership void and a state apparatus that has badly lost sight of the principles of ethics, integrity and honesty is losing traction fast.[2]

One of the purposes of this book will be to explore why South Africans think and talk about political leadership so much and to what effect as well as whether they are overinvested in the concept and if so with what political results.

In South Africa, in common with other countries, discussion of political leadership conventionally focuses on the occupants of the highest political offices. South Africa has had three presidents who have served at least one full term of office since the country's first democratic election in 1994 and Ramaphosa, the fourth, is set to follow them.[3] As the first, Nelson Mandela served only one of the two five-year terms as state president allowed him by the Constitution. Indeed, this period in office was in some respects an honorific postscript to the period between his release from twenty-seven years in prison in February 1990 and the 1994 election. During this time, he held no other position than president of the African National Congress (ANC), like the state presidency a five-year term but without limit under the party's constitution as to how many terms could be served. Even this term came to him as a result of Oliver Tambo's incapacity. Without formal legitimacy for the exercise of political power outside his own party until the 1994 election, he commanded little in the way of material resources. However, despite lacking most of the assets commonly at the disposal of political leaders, he was, more than any other person, combination of persons or organizations, responsible for keeping together not only the liberation movement he led but also the whole country, during a time of acute crisis.

The subsequent elevation of Mandela's life story to heights of unprecedentedly reverential celebrity built on an image cultivated since his time in jail is a well-known story. This image contains elements as diverse as chairman of the board, tribal aristocrat and perhaps the greatest product ever of global celebrity culture – everybody's friend on Facebook.

An essential element of all this has been to see Mandela in terms complementary to the 'miracle' of South Africa's transition to democracy and to Archbishop Desmond Tutu's coinage, the 'rainbow nation'. In popular parlance this is 'Madiba magic', and in more elevated terms a recent academic collection defines it in terms of 'the politics of the sublime: something that transcends the structures, constraints and ordinariness of the present'.[4] Writings about Mandela, whether by journalists, commentators, academics or people who have known him in one capacity or another (however fleetingly), are liberally scattered with words such as 'bewitchment', 'rapture', 'infatuation' and 'enchantment' as well as invocations of quasi-religious experience. 'The politics of the sublime' sums it up well.

John Carlin's fevered take on white rugby supporters chanting Mandela's name at the 1995 rugby world cup final is a case in point: 'They were crying out for forgiveness and they were accepting his, and through him, black South Africa's generous embrace'.[5] Another one of the many to share the experience of coming under Mandela's spell was the über-political strategist Stanley Greenberg. He felt that Mandela was so fundamental to everything he had done in his own career 'that I was about to meet my maker' and 'I may have been working for Bill Clinton, the most powerful man in the world at that point, yet I still felt unworthy to be here as if I had not done enough to justify the meeting'.[6]

Yet 'the politics of the sublime' is the province not only of the humblebragger, the mystic and the star-struck. As tough-minded and critical an analyst as South African political scientist and historian Hermann Giliomee could join in agreement on Mandela's magical powers with the late Van Zyl Slabbert, leader of the liberal opposition in 'The Last White Parliament': 'Afrikaners were captivated by Mandela; he cast a spell that produced a state of charismatic bewilderment'.[7]

Since Mandela left office in 1999, South Africans have been brought down to earth from transcendence, enchantment and the politics of the sublime with many a bump. Thus, it is not only a cynic that might be tempted to think that the journey from Mandela to Zuma via Mbeki has been from the sublime to the ridiculous. On the face of it, it did not have to be like that. There was a wide open opportunity for a transformative leader in what for a period was dubbed 'the New South Africa'. The challenges of dealing with the legacies of colonialism and apartheid, as well as of the bitter struggles against them, were huge. But the resources available to the country's new leadership were substantial. They included repeat large majorities won fairly in open elections, conferring the mandate to preside over a new polity regulated by a widely acclaimed rights-based and justiciable constitution, at the head of a movement that had won broad-based respect for its tenacity and bravery in the anti-apartheid struggle and its shrewd and well-timed conversion to constitutional democracy.

Instead, the enchanted one left the stage early with scarcely a curtain call and in his absence the rest of the leadership cast shrank and froze in the icy glare of the challenges. The most obvious question raised by contemplation of leadership in post-apartheid South Africa is, 'what went wrong?'

Perhaps part of the problem was simply that enchantment is a difficult act to follow. Perhaps South Africans (cheered on by the rest of the world) had binged on enchantment, and disenchantment was the inevitable hangover. Thanks to his proximity to the great man and perhaps to his own psychological vulnerability, Mbeki suffered more than Zuma from the 'After Mandela' syndrome: the endless editorializing from commentators – both resident and fly-in and most of them white – about whether South Africa could hold together after the icon's retirement. The relentless drumbeat of speculation continued throughout the fourteen years between his leaving office and his death in 2013. As early as 1996, three years before Mbeki became president of the country as it became clear that the succession was his, the *Mail and Guardian* newspaper (despite its small circulation, a key opinion maker and then, as now, flagship publication of the liberal-left) ran a profile headlined 'Is Thabo Mbeki fit to rule?' with the avowed aim of 'probing Mandela's enigmatic heir'.[8] In fact the piece, especially as reread today, was balanced and neither scaremongering nor muckraking: however, the headline was ill-chosen, a good indication of the reach and potency of the Mandela effect, especially we may presume, on his successors.

Mbeki has been portrayed by commentators and biographers in many ways: a kind of sagacious Afro-Saxon with his (pre-1994) tweed jacket, his pipe, his degree in development economics from Sussex University and his fluency in the Eng. Lit. classics; an intimidating intellectual who could cow his ANC peers with knowledge and powers of reasoning (admittedly the bar was not set high); a driven centralizer, intolerant of debate and shared decision making, never mind dissent; an aloof and distant technocrat, out of touch with ordinary people's experiences and values; author of the '1996 class project' and betrayer of the revolution and the working class to neo-liberalism; a thin-skinned and haunted figure, adrift in a post-imperial world and cursed by the residues of racism and colonialism that still shaped all around (and inside) him. Yet little of this seemed relevant in the aftermath of his fall, as a paper Caesar submitting meekly to an evanescent populist rabble.

Now that a decent interval has elapsed since Zuma's alliance of insurgents ousted him from the leadership of the ANC in 2007 and then in the following year brought his second and final presidential term to a premature and ignominious end, a new generation of admirers has dubbed him 'Africa's philosopher king'.[9] With so much to choose from, it is no wonder that so many would-be chroniclers, past and present, have from beginning to end chosen to hedge their bets and dub him, 'an enigma'.

Zuma began by being seen (with only a few dissenters) as a charismatic populist, personally warm and jovial, rooted and comfortable in his own culture but inclusive and respectful of other's ethnic roots; befriender of Afrikaners (especially poor ones who were no threat to him); a man who could be all things to the Left, to minorities, to ethnocultural traditionalists, above all, at the head of a coalition of those disaffected by one aspect or another of Mbeki's trajectory in office.

All things considered, despite the dark residual clouds of his (successfully defended) rape trial and the matter of his outstanding corruption charges, Zuma received a mixed welcome to high leadership. This veered from the exuberance of the Left and populists (who thought they had captured him) to deep satisfaction from traditionalists who had felt marginalized and were alienated by the secular and metropolitan veneer of the new constitutional and social order and saw him as one of their own. On the debit side, the crude populism with which these supporters swept him into the leadership of the ANC gave rise to misgivings on the part of many who were not committed to his cause. However, with the benefit of hindsight, such misgivings as there were now seem surprisingly muted, at least as at first expressed.

The qualms were tempered in turn by wary optimism from many who were not his supporters. This was in large measure due to the calculation, even of sceptics, that here at least was someone better in tune with actually existing South Africa than Mbeki had been and, conceivably, as much in tune with what South Africa had become since 1994 as Mandela had been in his day. If South Africa had become cruder, more divided, demotic and volatile in the first dozen post-apartheid years, then perhaps someone with his down-to-earth profile would make a better job of managing its contradictions than Mandela the natural aristocrat or Mbeki the mandarin.

Zuma's reputation as a negotiator and peacemaker did much to reinforce this cautiously positive image. In South Africa's own negotiations, in Burundi's civil war (while he was deputy president and Mbeki's envoy), but above all in the KwaZulu-Natal violence between the Zulu traditionalist movement Inkatha and the ANC (and its surrogates), he was widely credited with the human qualities, cultural fluency and astute tactics useful in resolving conflicts, especially ones with ethnocultural dimensions.

However, the misgivings multiplied and intensified, slowly at first but quickening after the publication of the first of two reports by the Public

Protector (at that time Thuli Madonsela) into improper and unethical behaviour by and on behalf of Zuma. This was in the matter of the use of public funds to enhance a private dwelling for the president (March 2014). With the second (November 2016), relating to cronyism and corruption in the running of state-owned enterprises (SOEs), disquiet had become public disaffection, spreading beyond the ranks of the opposition and civil society activists. By this time too, a critical mass of court judgements had gone against Zuma. Some cleared the way for reinstating corruption charges against him, which had been dropped under dubious legal and political conditions in April 2009. Others set aside appointments made by him to public bodies, appointments that owed much to cronyism and protecting Zuma and nothing to the public interest.

By mid-2016, Zuma cut an incongruous figure: a postcolonial African Big Man leader transplanted, as if by time travel, into a quite well-functioning and robust constitutional democracy. Protected by what is routinely described as a 'praetorian guard' of compromised appointments to head the criminal justice and security agencies, presiding over a bloated cabinet which contained far more than its fair share of incompetents and sycophants, surrounded by economic illiterates and partnered in what was increasingly revealed as a project of cronyism and state capture by a carpet-bagging family of businesspeople from the Indian subcontinent, Zuma seemed to personify the descent from the sublime to the ridiculous in South African leadership as he made the transition in the eyes of his critics from affable but ineffective dancing king to a pound-shop Bond villain in his taxpayer-funded lair in Nkandla.

He showed himself to have little respect for the constitutional order over which he presided, but despite his best efforts to subvert and dilute it he couldn't choose the final ploy in the dictator's playbook and overcome it. On the other hand, the various defenders of the constitutional order (by late 2016 some of them were in his own party) could frustrate him but not get rid of him. This is because whatever else Zuma may have lacked as a leader, it was not a grasp of bread and butter ANC politics. His command of this repertoire – effectively, dominating the provincial branch structures that are the building blocks of power in the party – was enough to provide him with a favourable balance of organizational power in the period leading up to the ANC elective conference of December 2017.

This grasp of party dynamics meant that despite leading the ANC to the unprecedented loss of three key metropolitan areas, Johannesburg, Pretoria and Nelson Mandela Bay (Port Elizabeth) in the 2016 municipal elections, he had reason to believe himself able to determine the succession to him as ANC president or even to secure a third term for himself. Thus, the ANC approached its elective conference in a state of febrile gridlock: a leader beleaguered in the courts, pilloried in the media, hounded by demonstrations, potentially a serious electoral handicap for his party, yet strongly rooted in the state apparatus and party organization. The excruciatingly narrow victory of Cyril Ramaphosa over Zuma's nominee, his ex-wife Nkosasana Dlamini-Zuma, and the subsequent ousting of Zuma in February 2018, which brought Ramaphosa's elevation to the state presidency but cleansed neither the state nor the party of Zuma's influence, has only partly broken this deadlock.

Unsurprisingly then, South Africa's narrative of the post-apartheid presidency is conventionally seen as a chronicle of decline and decay: Mandela's dignified recessional and garlanded retirement followed by Mbeki's Ides of March and Zuma's long third act of deepening disgrace. However, rather than complete our understanding of the role of leaders and leadership in South Africa's politics and democratic prospects, this judgement opens up many issues and questions.

Some of them are familiar from studies of political leadership across political systems and cultures. For instance, a preoccupation of such studies is how much explanatory power to apportion to individual qualities (and lack of them) and how much to national contexts – institutional, cultural, organizational – as well as global economic and geopolitical constraints and contingent events. Unsurprisingly, the specialist literature on political leadership tends to accept that these elements interact but leaves wide latitude as to how this interaction may be depicted. A related issue is whether leadership trends and continuities can be detected as they have been in other political systems. For instance, the expansion of 'imperial' presidencies in the United States and 'presidential' prime ministerships in Britain that were followed by pullback as legislatures reasserted themselves (in the United States) or parties (in the UK). The alternative is that each individual presidency or prime ministerial tenure is a discrete case study and the preserve of the historian and biographer.

A historical survey and analysis of political leadership in post-apartheid South Africa has of necessity to run in parallel with a history of the ANC in these years. From the vantage point of mid-2019, these are both histories of decline, tentatively offset by hopes of recovery under Ramaphosa. There has been a widely perceived decline of leadership quality viewed by any measures, whether they are guided by standards of ethical behaviour, democratic principles of accountability and fidelity to other constitutional requirements and purely instrumental measures of competence and effectiveness in governance or simply public opinion and election results.

This perceived falling off has proceeded in symbiotic relationship with decline in the ANC's performance from the unrivalled party of government with a claim to moral leadership that was widely (though not by any means universally) accepted, both domestically and internationally, into a vehicle for patronage and corruption. This has caused it to acquire a rapidly gathering reputation for disappointed expectations and deepening disgrace and to make it a target for cynical ridicule. This in turn has been related to division into factional conflict that goes beyond mere competition over positions and between ideological agendas, both of which characterize political parties everywhere in the democratic world, to include endemic malpractice and manipulation in the ANC branches that are the building blocks of power in the party, not to mention intra-party intimidation and violence, including resort to faction-driven political assassination. The publicizing of these pathologies is not confined to the ANC's external critics; they have been recorded in the reports to the ANC's five-yearly national conferences of at least the last two party secretaries general and are aired with increasing frequency by other senior party officials.

It is the nature of this symbiotic decline that gives leadership issues in post-apartheid South Africa their defining quality. As is always the case in analysing interactive relationships of this sort, it is easy enough to observe that bad leadership and dysfunctional organization react with each other but very difficult to turn this somewhat bland insight into attributions of cause and effect.

Is the ANC in a mess because of bad leadership? This is probably the majority view in popular political consciousness in South Africa, especially among those that still support the party, though it is not by any means confined to them. Or has leadership declined because, rather than nurture 'good' leadership (however defined), the political and organizational culture of the ANC has enabled 'bad' leadership.

This problem of cause and effect is made even more difficult when one of the parties to the interaction – 'leadership' – is an abstraction that is notoriously difficult to define, made up of very many different components and leaving all attempts to bring some sort of rigour to discussion of it stubbornly reliant on large helpings of subjectivity. Even by the standards of social science, leadership is an elusive concept. To make matters worse, the ANC does have a concrete existence in its members and structures, but the extent, nature and moral grounds of its agency – its capacities to act as a collective entity – are neither self-evident nor unproblematic. This is true of all political parties, of course. It is always worth unpacking what it means to say 'party x decided that' or 'party y represents this'. However, the ANC's self-image has historically included a particularly emphatic claim to collective agency, including a myth of unity, a vanguard mission, a commitment to collective leadership and stubborn insistence that it possesses 'a soul'.

This, like so many features of the ANC and of the wider South African polity, dates from the years of struggle when the liberation movement was banned and its leaders jailed, in exile or tortured and murdered. In the years of high apartheid, the message disseminated by such pamphlets as could be distributed by underground cells and broadcast by exiled radio was 'The ANC lives! The ANC leads!' This worked as a defiant slogan but it (especially the second part) represented much more than that. It perpetuated an enduring two-faceted mythology about the organization, its relationship to its country of origin and its organizational sense of self. This mythology had far-reaching and far from simple implications for post-apartheid politics, leadership included, that endure to this day.

The first is that the ANC and not any representative individual is the leader of the country, and indeed it is the embodiment of the whole South African people, however defined. The second facet is that in a virtually mystical way, which is hard to reduce to practical terms, the ANC leads itself. This myth is very hard to deconstruct, not least because deconstruction is utterly anathema to all adherents of the ANC, whatever their persuasion or faction. The idea that the ANC can be reduced to the sum of its parts for analysis or any other purpose is abhorrent; indeed, for them it is literally unthinkable. Held in the hands for examination by an objective observer then, this myth tends to slip through the fingers.

The essential point, however, is that the elusive myth that the ANC leads itself is ripe for exploitation by the very leaders who ostensibly fall in with its requirements of self-effacement and professions of humble service at the pleasure of the collective. This cultural phenomenon is closely linked to the deeply rooted credo that the ANC has a soul (and it is very difficult to deconstruct a soul). This of course is a familiar political party motif, especially on the centre left where the post-apartheid ANC has tried to position itself, but rare on the right or the extreme left. It too is a cherished tradition, held in common across the ANC despite all other differences. For the uncommitted and the sceptical, however, the ANC's soul is a little like the Cheshire Cat in *Alice's Adventures in Wonderland*, which can appear and disappear at will, leaving only a disembodied and mocking grin.

What follows, then, is an attempt to audit and understand how Mandela's successor presidents dealt with the South African political, economic and social context as it changed in the wake of democratization, and how they took forward Mandela's and all the other legacies that haunted their present. Central to this context have been the myths, embedded practices, structures and cultural assumptions of the ANC itself, and this book will assess the place of leaders and leadership among them. Our starting point is that while the cumulative effect of all this historical baggage is the belief that the ANC leads itself and its 'leaders' are its servants, this mythology has the paradoxical effect of simultaneously liberating and constraining them, as they act in the organization's name.

1

The rediscovery of political leadership

Leadership in democracies is one area – perhaps *the* area – in which popular perceptions of politics diverge most from those of experts, defined for the most part as academic political scientists and historians. In popular discussions of politics and in popular media which both reflect and shape this conversation, it is established common sense that leadership is central to all political transactions and processes and that for individuals and parties in a democracy, good leadership is essential to success; however, 'good' and 'success' are defined in this context. In matters of voter choice and national security in particular, leadership is held to be a defining and determining quality.

As a result, it is unlikely that the average citizen of the average democracy today would be very surprised to hear that political leadership is coming to be taken more seriously than before in expert studies of politics. The more predictable reaction of the voter in the booth might be puzzlement that leadership was ever considered anything but central to our understanding of politics. He or she might even be unaware that according to Robert Rotberg, American historian and political scientist and a recent advocate of strengthened political leadership in South Africa, 'In recent years the study of the political leadership variable has been neglected in mainstream social science.'[1] Indeed, if this average citizen were ever to ponder the issue at all, this revelation might further erode his or her faith in experts.

This is not entirely fair. One of the reasons for the existence of experts, and among them academics, is to demonstrate to the average citizen the limitations of common-sense understandings of things, even to point out that common sense, about political leadership among other things, is not always common nor even reliably sense. At times, experts serve this salutatory function well. While interrogating common sense in the case of political leadership, there have been two principal sources for scepticism that have led to downplaying leadership as a central concept used to unlock our understanding of politics, though rarely of course for ignoring it completely. Such scepticism arises first from democratic doubts and second from intellectual reservations about leadership agency in politics. Some of the specific objections derived from these two sources pertain to all political systems and cultures, while several of them apply more to democracies than societies ruled in an authoritarian way.

Democratic doubts about leadership

The principal democratic doubt about political leadership is derived from the central insight that a defining and foundational quality of democratic theory and practice is distrust of personalist leaders' relationships with political power, what they bring to the exercise of it and what they may become once they are habituated to it. At its simplest, one of the key ways that democracy differs from authoritarian rule – whether by European dictators, communist party bosses, Latin American *caudillos* or postcolonial African Big Men – is in its attitude to leaders and leadership. It follows that one of the most important tasks for democrats is to devise ways of setting limits to the powers of leaders in order to ensure that the democratic polity is, in the words of John Adams (1735–1820), second president of the United States, the government of laws, not men. This has to be done, however, in such a way that leadership is not so disempowered that paralysis – or what today is conventionally termed 'gridlock' – is the result.

Typical constitutional and statutory constraints include, under the general rubric of the rule of law, a rights-based and justiciable constitution that is the supreme authority, the separation of powers including an independent judiciary, backed by instruments of accountability including term limits, free elections including direct or indirect election of the head of government, votes of confidence and impeachment. Such a regime of laws will generally exist in mutual support with constraints on leadership in democratic political cultures such as a free press and a critical civil society.

Not every democratic system has all of this constitutional and cultural apparatus, but most are required for a polity to be worthy of the name democratic. All of the provisions listed (except direct election for the president) were inserted into the 1997 South African Constitution. It would be a mistake to assume that they were put there solely to soothe the fears of liberals and racial minorities who (correctly) predicted massive electoral majorities for the ANC under open, free and fair elections and were concerned about the temptations of power that would go with such a mandate. There was enough nervousness about the African Big Man leader syndrome inside the ANC itself and, more pertinently, the wider 'progressive' civil society movement aligned in sympathy with it at the time of transition to democracy, for it to be a widely shared concern.

Two other democratic doubts help undermine the ethos of leaders and leadership in democracies and contribute to the belief that it should be kept in its place. Though they are more manifestations of particular political cultures, rather than of general democratic theory, and do not issue so much in legal and constitutional form, they are nonetheless politically important.

The first concerns the relationships between leaders and parties, the most characteristic institutions for aggregating and mobilizing interests and opinions in the development of modern democracy. The classic modern expression of these tensions in fact predated the emergence of parties as we have known them since the beginning of the twentieth century. Edmund Burke's speech to the electors of Bristol (1774) emphatically set out the case for the independent judgement of representatives. His constituents' wishes, said Burke, ought to have great weight with the representative and their opinion high respect; he should even and in all cases prefer their interests to his own.

> But his unbiased opinion, his mature judgment, his enlightened conscience, he ought not to sacrifice to you, to any man, or to any set of men living. These he does not derive from your pleasure; no, nor from the law and the constitution. They are a trust from Providence, for the abuse of which he is deeply answerable. Your representative owes you, not his industry only, but his judgment; and he betrays, instead of serving you, if he sacrifices it to your opinion.[2]

The tensions that Burke described in a much looser era of political representation have been carried over and sharpened into the era of mass political parties with both national and face-to-face local organization. They are the same in principle and tend to arise between the idea that leaders have a special relationship with and special accountability to those who mobilize to put them in leadership positions and the counterargument that they have to be guided, especially in a complex and diverse society, by a conception of the national interest which transcends and may conflict with the self-perceived interests of that support base. This base may in any case have fragmented and been captured by factional and unrepresentative special interests. Such has certainly been the case with the ANC in recent years.

Such tensions tend to be sharper where the head of government is indirectly elected. For success in a direct election, a leader generally has to attract a more diverse and/or bipartisan support and as a result his or her claim to represent the idea of national interest is more solidly based and the relationship with the party more ambiguous. A directly elected president has to go through his or her own party's selection processes and is accountable in some form or another to the party structures and members, however his or her own mandate from the broader electorate allows some breathing space. For these reasons, the conventional wisdom is that a directly elected president acquires the leadership by appealing to the party faithful and then retreats to the centre to be elected in national elections.[3] An indirectly elected prime minister or president lacks this asset and in theory at least is reliant solely on the party's mandate (though the need to appeal to 'floating voters' in closely contested elections may dilute it).

Until recently, these tensions were largely a question of relations between the leader and the legislators of his or her own party, which kept them among the elite of the political class and helped to dampen them. Now, in a much less deferential era, they have been exacerbated by a general tendency in democracies of broadening the process of electing party leaders to include a greater role for ordinary party members and easing the conditions of membership. This in turn has been forced by the perception that an unholy alliance between economic elites and a self-enclosed and out-of-touch political class has captured parties.

Such tensions came to a head in the British Labour Party in 2015, prompting the election of Jeremy Corbyn as leader and igniting a long-running guerrilla war between him and Labour MPs, in which the threat of 'deselection' of MPs or candidates deemed out of touch with the ordinary members and disloyal to the new leadership plays a prominent part, bringing uncomfortable echoes of the battle for control of the party in the 1980s between MPs and left-wing militants. Supporters of Bernie Sanders's unsuccessful bid for the 2016 US Democratic Party presidential nomination attributed Hilary Clinton's victory to capture of the process by party elites and bias in her favour. In both the UK and US cases, a general decline in party fortunes – attributable to many external factors – and chaotic conflict over leadership have acted upon each other in destructive ways. While there are no exact parallels in South Africa, there are strong echoes of these trends in the recent history of the ANC. The ousting of Mbeki by a populist revolt in his party in 2008–9 might even suggest that the ANC was ahead of the populist wave that came to the United States and Europe nearly ten years later.

A second and complementary source for a political culture of democratic doubt about leadership takes its inspiration from the romantic view of 'the mass as hero' and from the more down-to-earth historiographical movement, 'history from below' or 'people's history'. This approach seeks to construct historical narrative and interpretation from the perspectives of 'common people' rather than leaders and elites, especially from commoners who, defined by class, race, ethnicity and gender, had been hitherto 'hidden' in history.

As far back as 1935, Bertold Brecht's poem *A Worker Reads History* made a powerful statement of this point of view. It begins,

> Who built the seven gates of Thebes?
> The books are filled with names of kings.
> Was it the kings who hauled the craggy blocks of stone?

Brecht continues, ranging across many civilizations of the ancient world, including,

> Young Alexander conquered India.
> He alone?
> Caesar beat the Gauls.
> Was there not even a cook in his army?

And ends,

> Each page a victory
> At whose expense the victory ball?
> Every ten years a great man,
> Who paid the piper?
> So many particulars.
> So many questions.

This and many similar reminders of the dependence of leaders on a rank and file of workers, soldiers, peasants and others has helped warn against overplaying the role of leaders not only in the past but also in the present. This relationship strengthened as the alignment of history from below with the political left solidified, especially after the publication of English historian E. P. Thompson's hugely influential book, *The Making of the English Working Class*, in 1963. History from below has had an impressive foothold in South African intellectual life since the founding of the research group History Workshop at the University of the Witwatersrand (Wits) in 1977.

Intellectual reservations about leadership

Democratic doubts about placing undue weight on the role of leadership in democracy are combined with intellectual doubts about the explanatory power of the concept in history and politics.

In the first place, there was the recognition from the late nineteenth century onwards that as societies and economies become more complex and grow in population and wealth, especially in periods greatly affected by what we now call globalization, leaders' freedom of action is greatly curtailed by vast impersonal forces such as industrialization, imperialism and revolution, to mention only the most obvious of them. In real time, these forces were imperfectly understood by leaders of the day and sometimes not recognized at all. Rather than force leadership from the historian's agenda altogether – except in the case of the most dogmatic determinists – such developments have tended to relegate it to one among many causal and explanatory factors.

Good examples of this are debates about the origins of the First and Second World Wars. The origins of all wars provide exemplary material on how political leadership is treated in popular and historical memory, but arguably the First World War eclipses them all. This most minutely documented of historical controversies has been exhaustively ventilated in both popular and academically rigorous versions. A rush of studies published to coincide with the centenary of the war's outbreak in 2014 added to an already impressive back catalogue. This controversy has many dimensions – how far back should historians go in looking for the origins of the conflict? How inclusive should they be about contributory causes? What weight should be assigned to each? Where should responsibility or even guilt lie?

Common to all arguments on the subject of the First World War's origins, sometimes explicitly, sometimes implicitly, are attempts to assess the respective roles of contingent events and structural factors, among the latter being the 'impersonal forces' mentioned above as well as the institutional and geostrategic strait jackets leaders sometimes found themselves in. Contingent and structural factors are sometimes conceived of as rivals, sometimes in more sophisticated versions as interwoven. Depending on the explanatory balance of these factors in any given treatment, leaders tend to be portrayed as helpless flotsam, pushed around by great historical currents, or strategic managers of events who were nevertheless hopelessly outclassed by the combination of structural determinants and contingent events and, as likely as not, fatally hobbled by the residue of decisions taken by predecessors anything up to a generation before. Sir Lewis Namier set the tone for this kind of judgement with the title of his 1952 essay, 'Men who floundered into the war'.[4]

Recognition of the manifold obstacles to good leadership and of the ever-multiplying impersonal factors that could help explain any given historical event tended to move thinking about political leadership in two directions, sometimes at once. In one view, the experience of the First World War could be seen as a cautionary tale about the need for good leadership and, for a short time at least, the utopian belief that this could be better provided through international institutions rather than the nation-state with its individual leaders. In another view, all leadership, good or bad, was relegated as an explanatory variable in favour of forces beyond the control of decision makers.

As with the previous global conflict, historians have debated the roles of leaders of the democracies in the approach to the Second World War. In particular, 'appeasement' – buying time or even hoping to secure enduring peace by acceding to the demands of dictators – has been the subject of seesawing conflict between established orthodoxies and revisionist accounts. Critics of 'the appeasers' lay stress on their personal failings, including lack of moral courage, allegedly compounded by ideologically inspired strategic misreading of the comparative threats of Nazi Germany and Soviet Russia. On the other hand, their defenders emphasize contextual factors, including the balance of power in Europe and public opinion in the democracies, in order to argue that, in its day, appeasement was a rational response to the rise of the dictators, one which illustrated the limited room for manoeuvre possessed by the leaders of democracies.

While historians may extend more sympathetic understanding now to the leaders of the 1930s than they did fifty years ago, appeasement is still popularly understood as meaning enervated leadership and failure of resolve. Indeed, it has endured as a universal term of political opprobrium and one of the greatest clichés in the lexicon of political leadership.

One way in which purported lessons of the appeasement years broadened understanding of political leadership and added to scepticism about the role of office holders was the claim that whole governing classes, political classes and indeed entire national psyches were influential in determining policy. In the case of Britain, for twenty years after the publication of 'Guilty Men' in 1940,[5] until the emergence of revisionist accounts of the war's origins in the early 1960s,[6] popular and professional orthodoxies were based on the idea that a decaying political class badly misread and betrayed Britain's national interest. According to this interpretation, the personal failings of individual decision makers were essentially irrelevant; it was the decadence of the class from which they came and the fact that they were unrepresentative of a greatly changed Britain that made them incapable of leadership. This view represented useful political capital for the Left in Britain even after professional historians began to challenge it.

In the case of France, an enduring historical orthodoxy blames failures of leadership and policy in the interwar period, especially in facing the dictators, on the entire political class and, in some versions, the whole nation. One reason for this attribution of collective responsibility was the effect on national morale of the way the French army was 'bled dry' in the Western front battles of the First World War, especially Verdun in 1916. The lesson is that if leaders feel that the populations they represent are unable or unwilling to contemplate the risks and sacrifices necessary for vigorous policies, then their choices are greatly circumscribed and their prospects of leading – in any common-sense understanding of the term – rather than following, are greatly undermined.

However, the conduct of war by democracies seemed to point the way back to Great Man models of leadership. The war offered Churchill and Roosevelt the opportunity to show not only fighting qualities but also vision, as exemplified in the Atlantic Charter and preparatory diplomacy for the United Nations. The Great Depression had already done this for Roosevelt. However, this turned out to be a fleeting episode. It is remarkable that both were replaced by leaders quite unlike them, after Roosevelt's death and Churchill's electoral defeat – in itself a telling verdict on democratic leadership in peace and war. Despite their lack of 'Great Man' qualities, Harry S. Truman and Clement Atlee both continue to enjoy high reputations for effective management of colleagues and policies and for consensual styles. Both, for instance, are singled out for high praise in Archie Brown's recent critique of 'strong' leaders.[7]

In the post-1945 world, political leaders in Anglo-American democracies had two main concerns to address. One was managing international relations in a global environment shaped by the Cold War and the other was preserving, in broad terms at least, the domestic settlements represented by the New Deal in the United States and the creation of the welfare state by Atlee's government between 1945 and 1950. In Britain (and other colonial powers), another task was managing decolonization in an unfavourable political climate. Economic conditions were more favourable. The period of prosperity variously characterized as the 'long boom', the 'post war boom' and the 'golden age of capitalism' encouraged definitions of the character and tasks of political leadership that were broadly bipartisan, technocratic, non-ideological and secular, emphasizing above all the management of growth and employment.

This did not mean that there were no political differences between contenders in elections or differences in style and image. Indeed, for a short time, differences in style and image between Kennedy and Nixon were instrumental in defining politics, not only in the United States but wherever image makers could contrast (comparative) youth, verve and optimism with what could be portrayed as obsolete values and dark psychological complexities. However, to a large extent, managerial competence in dealing with issues of economic growth in an age of ideological compression came to define leadership in democracies. Despite this, leadership never went away as a subject of popular fascination; indeed, more and more media column inches and pages were devoted to the subject.

In the United States in particular, a rich tradition of closely observed studies of leaders grew up, pioneered by Theodore H. White, whose *Making of the President* books covered elections from 1960 to 1980. Arthur Schlesinger's 1965 account of the Kennedy administration, *A Thousand Days* was another landmark, while one of a different sort was Joe McGinniss's subversive account of the (literal) marketing of Richard Nixon in the 1968 presidential campaign, *The Selling of the President*. The Vietnam War also helped develop scrutiny, not only of presidents but also their advisers (and their advisers' advisers). David Halberstam's *The Best and the Brightest* (1972) was an indictment of the group mentality of a legion of advisers from academia and business who were responsible for political, strategic and military debacles in South East Asia.[8] Bob Woodward, of 'Watergate' fame, carried on the tradition of close examination of presidents, like Halberstam extending the scrutiny down the hierarchy of political, security and military decision making.[9]

Works in this recognizable if loose-knit tradition focussed overwhelmingly on presidential elections and wars, which meant that the less dramatic aspects of leadership went largely uncovered and a lopsided view of political leadership, indeed of politics generally, was usually presented. Domestic politics and policymaking do find a place in the weightier presidential biographies, however, sometimes to a fault. For instance, Robert Caro's biography of Lyndon Johnson has detailed treatments of Johnson's leadership roles in congressional politics in the four volumes (1982–2012: over three thousand pages) of a projected five that have so far been published.[10] While major historical works of this sort treat leadership roles and functions comprehensively (if not always systematically), the majority of popular accounts are selective, playing to presumed audience expectations of drama provided by war and election contests. However, many examples of this generation of leadership studies, both popular and academic, have things in common.

Two shared tendencies in particular are important in that they are both subversive of 'great man' myths of leadership, though often unintentionally so. The first widens the perspective to include layers and generations and hierarchies of leadership, thus diffusing responsibility for good and bad leadership (though mainly the latter) in much the same way that the 'Guilty Men' and other studies of appeasement did for an earlier generation. One of the by-products of this approach was to help inspire and give credence to ideas that advanced leadership theory, such as 'groupthink', that is the pursuit of consensus within enclosed leadership groups at the cost of suppressing constructive dissent and proper consideration of alternatives.[11] In general, such studies considerably complicated the questions: Who are leaders? What is good leadership? Indeed, what *is* leadership? However, this was for the most part without systematically addressing the implications.

The second tendency is to exaggerate the closeness of the observer to the leader(s), partly by formidable accumulation of detail and partly by purporting to recreate conversations and even thought processes.[12] In the end, whether by intention or not, the effect is to demystify or even debunk individual leaders and leadership. In some cases, of course (McGinniss's *The Selling of the President* was a notable innovator on this score), debunking is indeed the intention, but it is done not through satirical exaggeration but by plain (though selective) reproductions of fact, implicitly claiming greater credibility in this respect.

Over a long period then, the cumulative effect of democratic doubts, intellectual reservations and closely observed studies conspired to, as it were, put leaders and leadership in their place. Paradoxically, at the same time as leaders and leadership were being diminished in this way, scholarly attention came to be focused on what were perceived as two trends that moved in a different direction, led by political and societal changes in the 1960s and 1970s.

The first involved apparent accretions of leadership powers either through evasion of conventional restraints on executive action, particularly in questions of national security and the burgeoning use of discretionary ways of making legislation (such as statutory instruments in the UK), as well as the accumulation of bureaucratic resources to support and contribute to executive decision making. The term 'imperial presidency' was coined to describe the American version of this trend. The second development was media and political party complicity in concentrating attention during election campaigns on presidential, and in the UK, prime ministerial figureheads, with the corresponding diminution of focus on policies and political parties.

These developments forced academics and informed commentators to wrestle with apparent contradictions. At one level, leadership appeared to matter less in the face of structural, including geopolitical, determinants of history. At another, there were worries about the increasing concentration of power in the executive branches of democracies and also the excessive promotion of leadership image as the deciding factor in voter choice.

Reaffirmation of agency

However, these contradictory concerns were overtaken by a rediscovery of interest in political leadership, which received a boost from the turbulence in the soviet bloc from the mid-1980s and the fall of communist regimes in 1989–90. This generally undermined intellectual approaches to historical explanation that heavily favoured structure over individual agency and contingent events. Broadly speaking, this meant Marxist analyses of history in terms of determination by economic systems of ownership, production and resource allocation, along with social patterns associated with them. However, what was in the air had broader causes and was of broader import than the effects of the exemplary sight of the tide going out on discredited regimes, which in turn discredited their intellectual foundations. This was a generalized unease with grand narratives such as the class struggle or the destiny of nations, indeed of Whig versions of history and teleologies of all kinds, especially those that related the unfolding of some or other vision of progress.

The ebbing of these confident, causal narratives left a vacuum of explanation into which a rediscovered belief in human agency could slip. This intellectual sea change was exhaustively catalogued and theorized by postmodernists. Given that 'the death of the author' was such a postmodernist landmark, it is unlikely that postmodernists wanted to promote anything so vulgar as the rediscovery of leadership agency in history, though some of them might have appreciated the irony; but the change in the intellectual weather could in any case be easily sensed by anyone who had not the slightest intention of picking up a postmodern text.

Associated with the reaffirmation of agency in the form of political leadership was the emergence of a generation of leaders in both democratic and undemocratic countries from about 1980. While differing extensively in motivation and national situation, they were generally believed to have much in common and seemed to offer real-world confirmation of the turn to agency. The commonalities were often summed up in terms of their being 'transformative' leaders. As part of this broad generalization, in the case of the democratic countries, leaders were willing to lead against the conventional wisdom in their own parties. Thatcher moved away from ideological convergence and Blair towards it, but both went against the prevailing orthodoxy of their parties at the time. In the case of the undemocratic countries, leaders were associated with moves away from authoritarian dispensations and transitions towards democracy.

This earned for them all the reputation of being in some sense or another visionary rather than merely managerial; they took decisions that significantly altered the political status quo in their countries and that affected the geopolitical status quo. In addition, they were highly divisive, inspiring both adulation and vilification both at home and abroad. Among them were Ronald Reagan, Margaret Thatcher, Mikhail Gorbachev and F. W. de Klerk. The first two operated piecemeal and cumulatively, the latter two by dramatic gestures. The sense of their being linked as a generation is strengthened by the appearance of a chain reaction: Thatcher and Reagan acting in concert put Cold War pressures on the USSR, which hastened Gorbachev's reforms and the contraction of soviet geopolitical activity and influence, which in turn emboldened De Klerk to unban the ANC and other liberation movements, including the South African Communist Party (SACP). While this is broad-brush analysis, there is enough truth in it to embolden proponents of agency wielded by strong, personalist but still democratic leaders in historical explanation.

Having said that, it is important to recognize three limitations to the transformative agency of these leaders. The first is that leaders who acquire reputations for strong and transformative leadership do not come out of nowhere. They may in some respects be carriers rather than creators of a new ethos or vision for a country. Reagan is one example and perhaps Thatcher too. They emerged as leaders at a point when a sense of general crisis in Western countries, combined with perceptions of specific crises in their own, enabled a widening in what has come to be called the Overton window, signifying which policies could be permitted on the political agenda.[13] For the United States, the 'Vietnam syndrome' of failure in foreign policy, beginning with defeat in South East Asia in 1975 and culminating in humiliation in Iran in 1979, the economic fallout from the first and second oil price shocks (1973 and 1979) as well as the racial tensions and culture wars that were the legacy of the 1960s all combined to create the sense of malaise that Reagan attacked with his campaign slogan of rebirth, 'Morning in America'. For Thatcher's Britain, years of industrial unrest, stagflation and the 1979 'winter of discontent' created a sense of domestic crisis. Moreover, both Reagan and Thatcher could draw on senior advisers and on think tanks, some of which had been working, apparently thanklessly for years, for the policies that filled out their visions.

Tony Blair, who was a lineal descendant of this leader generation rather than a member of it, nevertheless shared some of its attributes. It is true that while Thatcher moved away from ideological convergence, Blair moved towards it, but both went against the prevailing orthodoxy of their parties at the time. Blair's claim to be a transformative leader attaches more to his party than to the country as a whole. Indeed, there was a strong measure of continuity between his Britain and Thatcher's, to the extent that one political history of the period characterized the New Labour Party as 'Thatcher and Sons'.[14] However, even on this restricted canvas, Blair had the way well prepared for him by historic enablers. Where Thatcher was enabled by a sense of national crisis, Blair's opportunity came from the crisis of his party. This was composed of internal convulsions – first a split that spun off the Social Democratic Party (SDP), then a struggle for control of the party with the extreme left-wing Militant Tendency – as well as years of unremitting electoral failure. Although Blair's personal leadership was important (especially in electoral terms), the project he headed – making the Labour Party a credible party of government – was a group undertaking.[15]

The second limiting factor on attributions of transformative agency to leaders applies to Gorbachev and De Klerk. Both were motivated less by visions of transformation than by projects of preservation. Both recall the character in Giuseppe di Lampedusa's classic novel, *The Leopard*, set in a changing Italy in the age of Garibaldi, who said, 'If we want things to stay as they are, things will have to change.' Moreover, their legacies are as leaders who did not dominate events but failed to control them. They set momentous changes in motion, but others capitalized. It would be an oversimplification (and unfair) to say that Gorbachev's legacy is Putin and De Klerk's is Zuma (though there are bitter detractors who would not hesitate to make this judgement); there are far too many intervening variables for that. However, their careers remind us that we have to see all leaders in perspective, even – or perhaps especially – those who have been elevated in popular mythology to the first rank of leadership.

A third cautionary note concerning the transformative agency of these leaders is that they are at the mercy of their own bad decisions. A case in point is Blair. With consummate political instincts and talents he dominated first his own party, then the electorate, the machinery of government and the opposition – to the extent that David Cameron, leader of the Conservative Party and prime minister from 2010 to 2016, modelled himself as the 'heir to Blair'. Yet Blair's reputation suffered a vertiginous fall as a result of his decision to attach himself and his country's armed forces – 'come what may' – to George Bush's invasion of Iraq. The way in which he (and his close associates) manipulated government agencies, colleagues, parliament and public opinion in the run up to an unnecessary war that had disastrous consequences raises interesting questions about the qualities of leadership in a democracy, especially the role of political skills. In this case, what were undeniably political skills of the highest order did not lead to good leadership outcomes.

It does not take long to become apparent that the more historical and contextual details are added to a group portrait of a generation of leaders, the more qualifications and exceptions to the features of the general profile are required. This is why, although leadership is such a powerful trope in popular understanding of politics, it is such an uneasy area for academic specialists. Nevertheless, approximately coinciding with the emergence of the leadership generation discussed above, an increasing number of political scientists attempted to address the phenomenon of political leadership systematically.[16] Gillian Peele, writing in 2005, noted both the previous suspicion of political scientists towards the phenomenon of leadership and 'the resurgence of interest in issues associated with leadership in the last 20 years'.[17]

Apart from the great political shifts of the late twentieth century and the strong roles in them accredited to political leaders, there were other forces pushing in this direction. Prominent among the seismic political movements during this period was the 'Third Wave'[18] of democratization in Southern Europe, Latin America, South and South East Asia, post-communist Central and Eastern Europe and sub-Saharan Africa. A movement away from authoritarianism on this impressive scale seemed to push leadership decisively away from its dubious associations with dictators, one-partyism and repressive regimes in general and made for a revived interest in its applicability as a central concept across a wide range of democratic forms. It also appeared to open up a wide range of opportunities and problems for new leaders and no shortage of opportunities for older democracies to offer them advice.

The complexities of new 'democratic' leadership and doubts about how far and how permanently leadership had moved away from authoritarian models soon emerged however. A case in point was the brief vogue in the West for 'new African leaders' in the 1990s, which showed up the balancing act in the West's relations with post-Cold War Africa, between 'democratic' leadership and 'effective leadership'. A conference held by President Clinton in Uganda with East African leaders in March 1998 was seen as sending a signal:

> That the United States is embracing a new generation of leaders in the region who care less about establishing full-fledged democracies than they do about developing their countries ... The unofficial standard-bearer for this group is Yoweri K. Museveni, a former guerrilla who rescued this Central African country from political chaos and economic collapse, but does not allow party politics. The others in the group include the Presidents of Eritrea, Ethiopia, Rwanda and Congo, the former Zaire.[19]

This report (based as it was on conversations with US diplomats) illustrates the flexibility of Western attitudes as to what constitutes 'good' and 'democratic' leadership in countries not their own. While it was an advance on propping up thoroughly despotic regimes in the Third World during the Cold War, this flexibility still left plenty of wriggle room for leaders, within which to maintain good democratic credentials. For a short time after he became president in 1999, Thabo Mbeki was numbered among the favoured 'new African leaders', but differences with Western governments over how to address the growing crisis in Zimbabwe after 2000 led to the coinage of the label 'rogue democracy' (by a *Washington Post* op-ed writer) to define South Africa's diplomacy under Mbeki's leadership.[20] For the rest of Mbeki's term the label enjoyed wide currency, especially in the United States, further revealing the twists, turns and nuances of Western attitudes to developing-country leaders and leadership in the aftermath of the Third Wave.

In the West itself, leadership in democracies has become a great simplifier in making voter choice more manageable at a time when political identification has become more fluid and less reliable. Policymaking in democracies where states assume broad responsibilities across complex societies and economies is correspondingly complex, presenting the citizen with a mass of information that is very difficult to manage, especially for the purpose of voting. This development also applies to South Africa. For instance, the ANC manifesto for the 2014 general election was 34 pages long, comprised 11,500 words and set out many hundreds of policy priorities and commitments for the following five years.

At the same time, thanks to increasing sophistication of political communication and image building, intrusiveness of the mainstream media and burgeoning of social media as well as increasing frankness of political memoirs all over the democratic world, voters know (or think they know) much more about leaders. This simplifies and dramatizes both choice and identification around the credibility of leaders and is a welcome relief from trying to interpret and weigh in the balance reams of statistics, technocratic argument and political promises.

Such developments have fed alienation and disaffection in Western democracies, a tendency that contributed to the election of Donald Trump to the US presidency in 2016. Not the least of his attractions stems from populist distrust of elites and preference for an apparently strong leader who can simplify complex issues and communicate directly (greatly aided by social media) without an intervening corps of expert technocrats, analysts and commentators getting in the way to muddy and complicate the message. It remains to be seen whether or not Trump's presidency will be an eccentric one-off or whether it will set a leadership template for the future.[21] Whichever is the case, it would be hard to dispute that the Trump phenomenon has helped to confirm the place of leadership on the popular political and theorists' agendas.

Another source of political leadership's newfound attraction for political scientists is that it is a concept well-suited to crossover with business, the military and indeed any other aspect of organizational life. Business and the military especially have produced much research on leadership (of varying depth and quality). This has made a critical mass of material readily available and suitable for comparative and crossover purposes.

All in all, the situation appears to be that of academic studies overcoming previous reservations in order to catch up and communicate with real-world, political developments and a wider world of popular understanding of them. This is generally in the hope of extracting some systematic information from this wider world of political practice and conventional understandings, feeding back some rigour and challenging some generally accepted perceptions.

Now that political leadership has been back on the political science agenda for a respectable number of years,[22] it is permissible to ask what political and other social scientists have made of it. Heavy weather appears to be the answer, since for many years practitioners have identified the same problems of definition and theory building. In 1987, Jean Blondel wrote, 'What is political leadership? There is in reality no generally accepted definition of the concept, a characteristic that seems to apply also to leadership in general.' In the previous year, Barbara Kellerman admitted,

> A source book for the study of leadership should begin with a simple definition of what political leadership is. The trouble is that no clear and widely agreed upon definition exists.[23]

In 2001, Howard Elcock confirmed that 'leadership is central to politics but its definition is elusive'.[24] More recently, a comprehensive survey of political leadership[25] (published in 2014) disarmingly opens with a chapter entitled 'Puzzles of political leadership'. It describes the study of political leadership as 'a slightly bewildering enterprise' in which 'puzzles abound and contradictory answers multiply'.[26]

Typically, academic writing on political leadership begins on a downbeat note. In the first few pages, sometimes in the first sentence of such works, due acknowledgement is paid to the difficulties (or even the impossibility) of finding a clear and succinct statement of the qualities and properties of political leadership. Such opening bids tend to be couched in apologetic terms that nonetheless display pride to be dealing with such an intractable, contested and yet undeniably essential concept. The impression given is that social scientists have belatedly and gingerly rediscovered agency in explaining and understanding politics; however, in quite properly trying to interrogate common-sense beliefs about political leaders and leadership, they expose their confusions, contradictions and in general the slim bases for holding them; at the same time, they have been hobbled by the difficulty of building theory or even robust and authoritative definitions that hold across the very great variety of political leadership situations.

The brief sketch earlier in this chapter of attributes of some of the 'transformative' leaders of circa 1980–2000 suggests some of the difficulties. So too does the issue of what constitutes 'good' leadership. Do we judge a leader by whether or not he or she is skilled and effective at doing what he or she sets out to do? Or should the onus of the assessment be on whether or not the ends are good in the ethical sense or in the sense of serving the general interest rather than sectional ones. In the South African context, these issues arise pointedly in the case of Jacob Zuma. Familiarity with South African politics also exposes the difficulties of objectively defining good political leadership. 'Good', or 'strong', political leadership is often a coded formula for keeping radicals in their place and not disturbing the status quo too much. This flimsy camouflage is typical of the everyday discourse of many South African whites (though it is true of classes and interests everywhere who have something to lose), and it was a significant contributor to Mandela's popularity with whites and scepticism about his legacy among radical Africans. However, with the growth of the black middle class in South Africa, this view of strong leadership is no longer the sole preserve of the previously advantaged.

To draw attention to the shortcomings of political leadership studies (something that its practitioners generously do themselves) does not mean that nothing of use can be gleaned from the burgeoning literature. It does suggest, however, that given the high degree of subjectivity about leadership and the very wide range of historical contexts in which it is practised, it may be better to take ideas and findings from it and apply them loosely, interpretatively and metaphorically from one situation to another, rather than try and find ways of making them fit snugly. One innovative and influential text suggests that leadership studies should be an 'interpretative affair' and not a scientific one: 'In other words the more "scientific" our methods of analysis become, the less likely we are to understand leadership because it is not susceptible to scientific approaches.'[27] The approach, then, should be that of an 'interpretative art, and indeed the practice of leadership itself should be understood as an amalgam of four arts: philosophical, fine, martial and performative.'[28]

Proceeding in this general spirit should not mean, however, a subjective free for all, with resort to the plain person's unreliable common sense and a myopic confinement to one parochial setting. The frame of reference for what follows in this book will be mindful of some of the ways in which inquiry and analysis of political leadership is shaped in the literature. Despite this, it will neither import nor aspire to create a model of political leadership that has pretensions to general application. However, if any reader with theory or model-building aspirations finds the book useful, that is all to the good.

The frame of reference is in the first instance democratic: little will be said in the pages to follow about outright authoritarian leaders and leadership, because whatever its peculiarities and deficiencies, the South African polity is still emphatically a democratic one. However, the relationship that has evolved between political leadership and democracy in South Africa is not a simple one. Indeed, some of the singular fascination for the observer of South African politics over the last decade has come from the spectacle, in Jacob Zuma, of a leader who consistently worked to subvert and manipulate democracy, without trying to overthrow it. Presumably, he knew the costs of doing so and that it was better for him that democracy should be enfeebled but not swept away. If he was to be the African Big Man that many of his critics feared that he aspired to be, then he had to be clothed in democratic robes.

The context of this study is South Africa with some reference to wider African conceptions of leadership and the experiences of leadership in other democratic countries. One line of discussion will be how political leaders and leadership have contributed to a pervasive sense of South African exceptionalism which has been such a feature of the country's political culture, sometimes with constructive but often with malign effects.

Several general points of departure come from the literature on leadership. The first is that leadership agency deserves the greater respect that it has been recently granted as an explanatory factor and that reductionist, structuralist versions were overdone in the past. Nevertheless, political leaders in South Africa, like their counterparts everywhere else in the democratic world, have had to interact with two contexts: the global and the national, and it is in this interaction between agents and contexts that patterns of individual and collective (as, for instance, in the ANC) are revealed as well as national characteristics of leadership and narratives of evolution (or declension).

In addition to the structuralist-agency contrast, several other standard dichotomies in the literature serve as reference points. Leaders are sometimes seen as operating in a functionalist mode, that is, in the sense of proceeding by a series of single steps, not necessarily all initiated at the apex of leadership (in democracies, the president or prime minister) but which may amount in time to something more (and often worse) than the sum of their parts.

This is contrasted with intentionalist leadership, which unfolds according to something more like a centrally directed plan. This may originate with the leader or, more likely in a democracy, be bequeathed by his or her party for delivery in whatever form the leadership finds feasible or desirable. Certainly, the official ANC version is of collective agency with an intentionalist will of its own, but whether this narrative survives scrutiny of actual leadership practice remains to be seen.

Similar dichotomies distinguish between transformational or *transformative* leaders and *transactionalist* leaders. The vogue for labelling leaders as transformational spread in the wake of the late-twentieth-century generation of leaders, which is discussed above. There are numerous definitions of transformative leaders and leadership: Robert Rotberg's emphatic endorsement, in terms rather like a portrait of a top-level sports coach, is tailored to South Africa:

> Transformational leaders are supreme motivators. They challenge settled expectations and demand new, higher levels of national and governmental performance … They drive a nation forward to new achievements, and to new views of itself. They instil pride … transformational leaders provide a sense of transcendence within the nation and among its peoples. Mandela did it magnificently.[29]

The last few words of this quotation are something of a giveaway; rather than drawing on a wealth of examples, Rotberg is generalizing hopefully from Mandela's life and career.

On the other hand, transactional leaders might govern well but from only a limited repertoire. They are incrementalists, 'business-as-usual politicians focusing on the mechanics of statecraft and on perpetuating themselves and their parties in office. They exchange mutual self-interests with their followers and hence are primarily engaged in transactions.'[30]

Another useful theme that has been developed in the study of political leadership is the principle that it is not only the highest public officials who exercise leadership. Post-apartheid South Africa has been reasonably well covered by biographies of presidents and aspirants. However, such biographies are a necessary but not sufficient resource for the study of political leadership. It is well enough established that leadership can be exercised by other political figures such as leaders of opposition and senior figures in the governing party. It is less obvious, but particularly important in the case of South Africa, that those who hold statutory but not political office as public servants can be leaders too, especially when they are adopted as popular heroes. Two-term (2009–16) Public Protector Thuli Madonsela is an obvious South African case in point, as are several prominent jurists, among them constitutional court judges and the present chief justice Mogoeng Mogoeng. The nature and especially the limits of such leadership are worth exploring. So too is the phenomenon of 'lost leaders' (Oliver Tambo, Chris Hani, Steve Biko, Van Zyl Slabbert and others), which is an important clue to the endemic nostalgia of contemporary South African political culture.

These insights about the breadth and depth of leadership roles, both formal and informal, lead in the direction of two other important developments in the literature of political leadership. They are not exactly countermovements, but they are certainly correctives to the more emphatic and exaggerated claims that are sometimes made for leaders and leadership agency. Acknowledgement of *followership* is one such corrective. Barbara Kellerman, whose name is closely associated with the development of ideas about followership, warns that focussing unduly on 'superiors' at the expense of 'subordinates' risks distorting the dynamic between them.[31] In this she is following James McGregor Burns who wrote in 1978,

> One-man [*sic*] leadership is a contradiction in terms. Leaders responding to their own motives appeal to the motives of potential followers. As followers respond, a symbiotic relationship develops that binds leaders and followers together.[32]

Despite the (deceptive) simplicity of this insight, it was underrecognized until taken up by Kellerman and others. While they tend to focus on relationships between leaders and followers, the latter understood as subordinates in the same corporation or political party as the leaders, followership needs to be seen in a much wider perspective in the case of political leadership in South Africa.

Throughout the whole of the post-apartheid period, political leaders in the ANC and government, echoed by civic and religious leaders, have expressed fears about the levels of deviance and social fragmentation among many of those they are responsible for leading. This is hardly surprising given the presence of endemic violent social protest, high levels of crime and corruption as well as low levels of social trust demonstrated in high levels of non-compliance with municipal payments and other forms of civic obligation. ANC leaders, 'from the point at which it became clear to them that the task of governing a country in the throes of transformation would fall to them, feared that they would inherit a population so morally compromised by apartheid and the struggle to overthrow it, and so deracinated by social change, that it might prove ungovernable'.[33] In this context, 'followership' takes on a dark meaning and an ominous presence. Fears of intractable, low-level ungovernability have not dissipated and are now compounded by the cynicism with which many South Africans of all political persuasions observe how morally compromised the leadership itself has become.

A second corrective to overemphasis on individual leaders, especially those labelled as some variant or another of a *strong* leader, is Archie Brown's recommendation of the virtues of *collegiate* leaders.[34] 'Strong leaders concentrate power in their own hands, dominate across the range of public policy issues and have firm control of the political parties to which they belong.'[35] Far preferable, with less danger of unfavourable outcomes, is a leadership style that is more collegiate, with leaders who are more modest and open to constructive presentation of alternative decisions by others, whether from colleagues or evidence-based expertise from outside.[36]

These considerations could scarcely be more germane to the study of leadership in South Africa, not only because the South African presidents clearly appear to be separable into these different categories – though their profiles may be more nuanced than the simple 'strong' and 'collegiate' ideal types. Arguably, more important however is the way that the myth of collective leadership has shaped and influenced perceptions and practice of political leadership in South Africa. This has been partly because of the ANC's organizational and cultural history and partly because of the use made of African traditional culture in the wider South African political culture. For the ANC, 'collective' has a much stronger and deeper meaning than simply 'collegial' in the sense of being open to advice, criticism and alternatives from close colleagues; the collective embraces the whole movement, past as well as present, in an ethos that can both confine and empower individual leaders. This is also given an ethnocultural cast by the insistence that there is a characteristic African mode of leadership.

In the South African context, then, a simple dichotomy between strong leaders on the one hand and collegiate leaders on the other is not enough. The distinction and relationships between leaders and led is an extremely sensitive and complex issue, and here a case could be made that the problem with leadership is not so much the myth of the strong leader but the myth of collective leadership. This, arguably, has been as great if not a greater source of dysfunction than the discontents with strong leadership that led to the overthrow of Mbeki.

That is, in post-apartheid South African politics, the vagaries of a culture of followership are as worthy of attention as the leaders themselves.

2

The South African context of political leadership

By context, what is meant here are all the factors that structure the operating environment of political leaders in South Africa. The context gives shape to the roles and functions that leaders have to fulfil, the resources and instruments that are available to them in discharging these functions as well as the limits – formal and informal – on their freedom of action. Out of these things, the context defines the challenges leaders face; or at least it offers the materials from which leaders, their advisers, colleagues, followers and any constituencies of demand and expectation with which leaders have to communicate can define them for themselves.

In all these things the context narrows down the range of available possibilities and choices, but it does not determine them. There is scope for different leaders to see different things in them, to emphasize some elements and downplay or ignore others or even to perceive the whole environment differently. It follows that leaders have some discretion in making choices, whether for the purpose of framing a vision or in reacting to contingent events. However, while agency is important, it is not agency in a vacuum. Unless we come to grips with the context it will be difficult to understand individual leaders, never mind to compare them and to think of leadership as a concept in any meaningful way. Of necessity, in engaging with the context it will be important to be selective and to aggregate themes and choose landmarks out of myriad factors. It will also be important to look for continuity and change in the environment, from immediate post-apartheid euphoria, over nearly quarter of a century of single-party rule,[1] to a situation that is now, arguably, much more fluid.

Historical legacy

The historical legacy of colonialism and apartheid is the most salient factor shaping South Africa's post-apartheid political context. Colonial dispossession and economic exclusion of indigenous people took place in stages over three hundred years, facilitated by state-building on racist bases, which reached its apogee between 1960 and the early 1980s, in the period known as high apartheid. Struggles against the various gross injustices involved in these historical movements were met with violent repression and generated violence of their own. The most obvious legacy has been substantial inequalities in the post-apartheid economy and society, which are clearly linked to race. Such clarity does not however extend to the principal challenge that this legacy bequeaths: how to achieve redress for injustices in a context of a constitution that guarantees equal rights and respects property (though protects it only in a limited and carefully calibrated way) while simultaneously reproducing the conditions of economic growth and development.

Lack of clarity also extends to the inescapable task of assembling policy priorities, on the assumption that not all issues can be addressed equally and at once. Is land hunger more important than unemployment? Who should benefit, in what way and in what order from redress measures? Political leaders would consider it suicidal to acknowledge openly that poor, rural people, aspirant bourgeois entrepreneurs and public service workers have claims that compete, never mind admit that some groups have more influence or bargaining power than others. However, such issues contain some of the great submerged policy, and hence leadership, questions of the post-apartheid era.

Political economy

The conditions under which modern political leadership has to be exercised in a democracy are unsparingly set out by John Dunn in *The Economic Limits to Modern Politics*: the requirements and possibilities of economic organization lie at the very centre of modern politics and prescribe the key problems which any modern political community must solve;[2] and, the workings of a global system of production and exchange impose a crucial range of constraints on modern political possibilities.[3] These fundamentals impinge sharply on political societies such as South Africa that combine late democratization with historical legacies of inequality and vulnerability to global economic conditions. In short,

> It is extremely hard to combine free political choice indefinitely with excessively palpable social injustice.[4]

There is a conventional narrative that relates the response of South Africa's post-apartheid presidents to these ground rules. In this account, Mandela played a crucial personal role in persuading the ANC of the importance of markets and investor confidence to South Africa's prospects; his credibility was enhanced, especially in his own party and among its supporters, by the fact that he could cite other African and post-communist leaders as having been influential in persuading him. Mbeki followed him in making fiscal prudence combined with incremental, targeted and rule-bound redistribution central to the policies of his administration. Under Zuma much of this was dissipated in the course of an exhausting war of attrition to wrest control of the National Treasury from guardians of financial rationality (or orthodoxy). Economic irrationality and short-termism in pursuit of crony and populist gambits characterized the prosecution of this war, which in turn defined the late Zuma period. These ploys, aimed at securing his personal fortunes – in more than one sense of the word – backfired in the face of a determined rearguard action symbolized by sacked finance minister Pravin Gordhan and which brought him down.

This narrative offers an economical and broadly accurate portrayal of political leaders' responses, in the South African context, to the central problem of contemporary governance. This is the choice and implementation of effective and politically viable economic policies. However, much remains submerged under it, including questions of which leadership miscalculations helped to determine that both Mbeki's espousal and Zuma's rejection of conventionally rational economic policies have been political failures. More specifically, what combination of inappropriate policies and political misjudgements ensured that however much they differed as leaders, both were authors of self-defeating policies?

Part of the explanation can be sought by considering the part played by populism in the interaction between politics and economic policy in post-apartheid South Africa. What is meant by populism here is popular sentiment in favour of drastic redistributive measures, which may not be economically sustainable under present global conditions yet which may acquire a political momentum of their own. Under such circumstances, they may throw off unintended consequences and inflict collateral damage beyond the economy itself, such as destabilizing racial hostility and violence as well as abandonment of constitutional democracy. The political fallout that followed Zimbabwe's accelerated land reform programme, including severe political repression at home and ostracism by investors and international financial institutions, represents a paradigmatic case.

Populism is generally understood to be driven by anger and frustration at inequality, poverty and exclusion and in part by anti-elitism and rejection of what technocrats insist are 'economic realities'. Such motivations are often mixed with extreme nationalism and/or racial, ethnic and tribal sentiment. In this sense, populist measures, even if initially driven by left or self-defined 'progressive' forces, which hope to control them, can be the gateway drug to economic irrationality, patrimonialism and Big Man, authoritarian rule. In South Africa, all these drivers of anger and volatile ingredients of identity politics are either visibly present or latent and close to the surface. They are combined with understandable feelings of entitlement among the majority of the population to redress for previous injustices. These ingredients of populist sentiment have presented the ANC and its leaders with a resource to be exploited, but they also represent an ever-present menace.

It has been a resource in several ways. It has been a useful threat to justify to business and whites generally such redistributive measures as the ANC government has felt able to undertake and also to extend redistribution's targets. Unsurprisingly, the 'pressure cooker' metaphor (closely followed by the 'ticking bomb') is the most widely used political figure of speech – by people of all persuasions and allegiances – in post-apartheid South Africa. In the ANC's warnings, there will be a populist explosion if its 'transformation' measures are not followed willingly and to the letter. It is also a useful mobilizing spirit, ideally controlled like a tap, for electoral purposes and for rhetorical scolding of 'white' media and business where deemed appropriate. In contrast, under Mbeki populism had an alternative utility: it was an expedient label used to discipline or even demonize unruly internal elements, in the party itself and in the wider Alliance, who threatened Mbeki's chosen image for the ANC, a 'disciplined force of the Left'.

The use of the label populism to define deviant tendencies was a favourite tactic of Mbeki's after the adoption of the 1996 Growth Employment and Redistribution (GEAR) macroeconomic policy. This disciplinary expedient of labelling and shaming came back to haunt him, since reaction to it was an important motivating and rallying factor in mobilizing the populist coalition that overwhelmed him in 2007–8.

In short, exploiting populist sentiment can serve a variety of interests: it can bind grassroots and leadership together, both for electoral mobilization and internal party struggles, as well as serve as a cover for cronyism and appropriation of public resources. However, it can also drive policy uncertainty and incoherence, undermine public finances and cause both political and economic destabilization. Populist sentiment has been a fact of the political weather that ANC leaders, whatever their dispositions, have had to navigate ever since the movement was unbanned in 1990, more especially since the party achieved power in 1994 and became accountable to an electorate that would not be patient forever about its socio-economic conditions. Under these circumstances, even if populism threatens to be a destabilizing choice, it may be hard to resist, since it is a choice permanently available to rivals outside in the political marketplace, including breakaways from the ANC such as the Economic Freedom Fighters (EFF), and to factions within the party and Alliance.

The Constitution

There was never any likelihood that the roles of the Constitution in post-apartheid South Africa would be confined to providing dignified background music and unobtrusive operating software for the newly democratic polity. The Constitution's principal characteristics – rights-based, justiciable and transformative – were an open invitation to activism. In addition, despite being the product of a negotiated settlement, many things on which it pronounced remained open to contest in a hastily improvised nation[5] and a divided, and in some respects, traumatized society. These things too would guarantee it not only an active working life but also a lively and controversial one. However, even a well-informed realist in the mid-1990s would probably have failed to predict the extent to which the Constitution would be propelled into the frontline of political conflict so that twenty years later, deliberations of the courts on constitutional matters would be a virtually daily spectacle and their judgements would be political landmarks that helped to determine the fate of leaders and possibly even parties. Two diametrically opposed views on how and why this has happened have themselves helped to escalate hostilities.

Critics of the government – including opposition parties and civil society bodies – claim that it has at times been careless of the Constitution and that the governing party holds values that are antithetical to it. They further claim that these things became systematic and explicitly subversive under Zuma's leadership, a charge that is supported by some court findings and reports of the Public Protector. Moreover, under both Mbeki and Zuma, parliament signally failed to hold the executive to account, due to the inertial weight of the ANC majority, its internal discipline as well as the loyalty and careerism of its members, which are higher priorities for them than their duty to the public interest, including the Constitution. Indifference and incompetence also contribute to the failings of the ANC majority in the National Assembly. This leaves recourse to the courts and to the Chapter Nine statutory institutions as the principal instruments at the disposal of an outnumbered opposition and broader civil society, for securing accountability and more broadly defending and developing democracy.[6]

By contrast, the ANC and the government have traditionally taken a strongly majoritarian line, claiming that the Constitution has been misused by conservative, liberal and populist interests, who, unable to attract significant electoral support or unwilling to solicit it, block or otherwise interfere with the ANC's legitimate popular mandate through the courts and in doing so frustrate the will of the people. In this way, the courts have been tempted into judicial overreach that constitutes a denial of genuine democracy. This was the line taken by Zuma's most convinced supporters, but his perceived delinquencies, notably in the 'state capture' and Nkandla issues, have motivated at least some in the ANC to rethink the question of judicial activism. At the same time, however, warning voices about judicial overreach have been sounded from sources outside the ANC, concerned at the frequency and some of the content of court proceedings aimed at curbing Zuma.

Despite this unease, circumstances have favoured the assumption of this role by the courts. By 2016, it appeared clear that a ruling party, which was hobbled by internal division and an organizational culture that was itself dysfunctional, could not effectively deal with the delinquencies and dysfunctions of its political leadership. Nor could the wider resources of the polity deal with them, parliament and the electorate included. The best that opposition parties and NGOs could hope for would be to take advantage of the Constitution's generous provisions for review by the courts. A typical route open to them, for instance, was to petition the courts to declare certain appointments irrational or that certain appointees were not fit and proper persons to hold office. Judgements of this sort could inflict sufficient cumulative reputational damage on the president, and by extension the ruling party, until either the party itself or parliament or, in the longer term, the electorate, would be motivated to hold the leadership accountable. Such judgements, however, also sometimes had the side effects of causing paralysis through suspensions and acting appointments pending long drawn-out appeals.

It is no coincidence that one of the main routes for attempting to hold Zuma accountable through the courts was by challenging the way he has exercised his powers of appointment. Presidential powers are extensive in this area and Zuma's exercise of them was all too vulnerable to challenge. As former deputy chief justice, Dikgang Moseneke put it,

> The vast powers of the national executive bring to the fore the debate whether the democratic project will be best served by a powerful central authority. Our courts have had to adjudicate challenges against the rationality of several appointments made by the president. It is self-evident that an appointment made by a deliberative collective is less

vulnerable to a legal challenge of rationality than an appointment by an individual functionary.[7]

Moseneke details the formidable array of presidential powers of appointment.[8] Presidential discretion stretches far beyond the nomination of close colleagues in cabinet and government: it reaches across virtually all statutory and quasi-state bodies, especially state legal and security organs and state-owned enterprises. Where there is a form of accountability – such as 'consultation' with the Judicial Services Commission (JSC) – this is in diluted form and further diluted by the political composition of the body in question, which is usually packed with ANC loyalists.

With what is probably judicious understatement, Moseneke comments on this 'remarkable concentration' of the president's powers of appointment: 'Much of the glowing talk about our constitutional architecture relates to fundamental rights and freedoms. And yet the manner in which public power is allocated within it is not always optimal for advancing our democratic project.'[9] This raises the obvious question: why did the exhaustive and closely argued negotiations leave such an obvious lacuna in what was such a widely praised democratic constitution? The answer lies in leadership. Moseneke offers an 'anecdotal account':

> At the time of the formulation of the final Constitution, whenever there was a dispute about who should appoint a public functionary, the negotiating parties were happy to leave the power in the incumbent President, Nelson Mandela. He, after all, will do the right thing.[10]

If this is the case, it is an example of an unhappy (and unintended) consequence of Mandela exceptionalism, adding an element of ambiguity to his leadership legacy.

Aside from these extensive powers of appointment, the Constitution's provisions regarding the president come from the conventional repertoire of democratic constitutional practice.[11] The president is charged with upholding, defending and respecting the Constitution as the supreme law of the republic: he or she assents to and signs legislation and, if necessary, refers laws back to the legislature or to the constitutional court; as head of the national executive, the president implements legislation, develops national policy, coordinates state departments and administrations and prepares and initiates legislation; he or she is elected by a simple majority of the House of Assembly and can be removed by a two-thirds majority of the house in a vote of no confidence, on grounds of serious misconduct or serious violation of the Constitution or of the law.[12]

However, as with all constitutions, these provisions for democratic leadership are embedded in the country's political culture and its political dynamics – especially affected by what the ANC, in a favourite usage, calls the 'balance of forces'. In this respect, the fact that the president is indirectly elected by the legislature has several effects. It means that up to now the president's links with and standing in the broader population have been of much lesser importance than domination of the majority party. Indeed, under the prevailing ANC mythology that the party was the embodiment of the electorate and indeed the nation, the distinction was in any case meaningless and to be president of the ANC and of the country was (in the eyes of the faithful at least) a comfortably harmonious state of being. As long as the ANC could be sure of a majority at or near two-thirds of votes cast, this myth could be complacently sustained and it was only with the unravelling of Zuma's second administration that it was seriously challenged.

This premium on domination of the party as the path to the highest political office has challenged presidential aspirants to devise ways of organizing power bases from which to capture and then lead the membership and structures. Both these centres of power are ideologically and sociologically diverse, as well as geographically dispersed, and the challenge has been rendered more complex by the post-apartheid conditions of rapid social change. As we shall see, Mbeki and Zuma approached this challenge in quite different ways: the former used the central state and its resources; the latter brought patronage-based factionalism and ethnocultural mobilization to bear on the provincial structures of the party.

Zuma was the first senior ANC leader to grasp that, thanks to an unintended consequence of the quasi-federal system that emerged from the constitutional negotiations, the truism 'all politics is local' applies with a vengeance to the ANC.[13] That is, the provinces do not have significant legislative or fiscal powers, but they are the conduits for the bulk of social expenditure. This makes them a major source of patronage powers – through appointments and tenders – which are at the disposal of whoever dominates them politically.

The political culture of the new South Africa: Six types of ambiguity

Lucian Pye's classic definition of political culture makes a useful point of entry to discussion of how South Africa's post-apartheid political culture has helped shape challenges of political leadership: 'The sum of the fundamental values, sentiment and knowledge that give form and substance to political processes.[14] Not unjustifiably, there were high initial hopes that democratic South Africa would develop a homogeneous political culture: the settlement that brought democracy was negotiated; the Constitution was globally acclaimed as a model of equal citizenship which both empowered and limited government; the ANC occupied the high moral ground because of the legitimacy of its electoral mandate and the sacrifices of its struggle; the unambiguous electoral endorsement that it received promised to ground the settlement in stability.

These hopes were already much diminished as Mbeki's first administration (1999–2004) gained momentum, and the temptation was to interpret the fissures that were appearing in terms of antitheses of race and ideology – black and white and right and left. However, a more insightful way of reading them would be as ambiguous readings of the same things: the nation, the settlement and democracy. Six types of ambiguity stand out; they are shaped not only by the legacies of apartheid but also, and importantly, by the disputed meeting between what the ANC brought home with it and South Africa as it actually existed.

An ambiguous settlement

Ambiguity over the provenance and the meaning of the negotiated settlement that brought democracy has been and remains a stumbling block to the development of a shared and inclusive political culture. The ambiguity is over whether the settlement represented a mutual achievement for which both sides deserved respect and even honour or a victory by the ANC over a cunning and recalcitrant foe and thus a legitimate cause for triumphalism. The negotiations were stage-managed from the beginning as a mutual achievement, but this quickly became quite difficult to sustain. Three issues contributed to this: the violence which continued throughout the negotiations, for which each side blamed the other; the deterioration of personal relations between Mandela and De Klerk (for which the violence was largely responsible); and the question of whether apartheid was a crime for which visible (though voluntary) gestures of atonement and material reparation were necessary or a mistake for which generalized expressions of regret and redistribution paid for by economic growth were sufficient.

Relief and elation at the eventual achievement of a settlement temporarily papered over the ambiguities, but these sentiments were not unmixed, depending on any given perspective, with senses of being cheated or triumphalism or fears for the future. The ambiguities were revisited in the various testimonies to the Truth and Reconciliation Commission (TRC), and they were deepened by the challenges faced by the ANC. Over the period since its unbanning, the ANC had to manoeuvre dangerous political shoals involved in negotiations with a still-powerful enemy, keeping intact but disciplining capitalism and the whites who largely owned it, ran it and profited from it, keeping populism on a leash – training but not defanging it – while at the same time establishing dominance in African popular politics and seeing off rivals such as Mangosuthu Buthelezi's ethnically based Inkatha Freedom Party (IFP). Delivering to the various constituencies involved in these tasks required ideological heavy lifting, flexible rhetorical footwork and appeals to both racial and non-racial identities.

As part of these dilemmas of positioning, after the settlement and the election victory of 1994, a priority for the ANC leadership became (and still remains) to demonstrate continuity and compatibility between founding documents, such as the Freedom Charter, the revolutionary rhetoric of the 1980s and the mixture of social democracy and constitutional and social liberalism that was the basis of the settlement. For good measure, revolutionary aspirations had also to be squared with the economic liberalism, modified by third-way social democracy, which was the initial direction of economic policy. In effect, the old dog of capitalism had to be coaxed or flogged into performing new tricks in the name of a revolution that had to be continually postponed and conceptually reworked. This agile reworking was sufficiently extensive for the commitment to anything recognizable in common-sense terms as 'revolution' on the part of those at the top could reasonably be questioned. Unsurprisingly, the spectre of betrayal was ever present.

In any case, it was never very clear under Mbeki what combination of socialism and African nationalism would contribute to the revolution: that depended on which part of the Alliance was expressing itself or which part of the Alliance any given leader was addressing. This confusion collapsed further into intellectual chaos under Zuma. As a result, the ambiguities of the settlement deepened: those who still believed in continuity with the revolution as historically understood felt betrayed and those who believed they had been protected from populist outcomes by the settlement constantly had their confidence in the future compromised.

In effect, these ambiguities resolved themselves quite early into a balancing act to be performed by the ANC leadership simultaneously to three audiences. These audiences believed, respectively, that the settlement was a negotiated coup to acquire the political power that would be a bridgehead to extensive and radical reconfiguration of the economy and society, probably requiring vigorous reworking of the settlement itself; the settlement itself provided the means to an evolutionary reconfiguration of society and the economy; the settlement now looked in retrospect more like a negotiated surrender leaving minorities at the mercy of undiluted, majoritarian African nationalism. In attempting to perform this balancing act, it was inevitable that the ANC leadership would look thoroughly devious from whichever direction they were observed and that, as their political credit ran out, they would be performing it above an increasingly threadbare safety net.

Managing the ambiguities of identity politics

Given the scale of colonialism's dispossessions and apartheid's exclusions and oppressions, it would be naïve to believe that race would die a natural death as a factor in South African politics. However, defining a legitimate space for acknowledgement of race in a democratic polity and under a constitution based on equal rights and non-discrimination has given rise to what is at best an uneasy coexistence of warring elements in the political culture.

In this way, the values of the Constitution are superimposed on blatant and deep racial inequalities: whites are equal compatriots in a citizen nation and at the same time the illegitimate beneficiaries of a legacy of conquest and racism; the ANC celebrates the citizen nation and has not only a long (though exceedingly ill-defined) history of non-racialism[15] but is also the embodiment and vanguard of a black nation (currently 79.2 per cent of the population[16]) that is uniquely bound together by past sufferings, whose psychic and material effects obtrude into the present and whose redress defines the central tasks of governance. These and other ambiguities coexist in a perceptual no man's land, which lies between two poles of the political culture. The first is the belief that honest acknowledgement of racial issues is an essential element of building shared citizenship and social cohesion, and the second is the belief that race is increasingly available for explicit strategic exploitation in the interests of political leverage and material advantage.

Several factors combine to ensure that this no man's land covers very extensive territory indeed. The first is the conceptual malleability of racism that can spin off subcategories such as 'Afro-pessimism' and shift shape so that, for example, concern over high crime rates if expressed by whites becomes racist criticism of a black government. It does not help of course that some criticism of the ANC's record in government is indeed explicitly and crudely racist. Although this tends to be confined to forums such as social media, it tends to taint by association more measured and objective criticism at a higher level of dialogue. Also unhelpful is the fairly widespread belief that, given the history of asymmetrical power relations between black and white, blacks are literally incapable of being racist about whites. Another source of difficulty in any attempt to address racial questions systematically is the chronic instability of measures relating to wealth, ownership and participation in the economy. The sharply disputed question of whether or not to include pension funds in measuring 'black' ownership of equity in the Johannesburg Stock exchange is a case in point, as are the technicalities of measuring land ownership and the 'once empowered, always empowered' issue in black empowerment.[17]

Despite these difficulties, the prevailing view in the ANC during the immediate post-apartheid years was that racial factors could be managed downwards by a variety of means, both formal and informal. It is probably true to say that in any case the party was not disposed to give such difficulties much thought or even perhaps to recognize them at all. In the first place, the ANC could reasonably claim that the Constitution itself was a major resource in dealing with racial inequalities, since it clearly recognized the need for measures to redress the legacy of racial inequality, including carefully calibrated and balanced endorsement of ('positive') discriminatory measures to do so.

Other hoped-for resources included the exposure through the TRC of the evils that racism could lead to, the demonstration effects of the ANC's own rhetorical commitment to non-racialism and educative measures by such bodies as the statutory Human Rights Commission (HRC) and NGOs such as the Institute for Justice and Reconciliation. A harder-edged approach involved legal injunctions against hate speech and ritual public shaming, indulged in at times by the HRC and by Mbeki himself, for instance when he exposed (in his 2000 State of the Nation address) a racist email circulated among previously anonymous whites. Raising the costs of racism to individuals in this way was also occasionally applied to prominent African personalities who made insulting generalizations about other races (usually coloureds and Indians), but they were much less likely to suffer public opprobrium and loss of position than when the racists were white.

More important than all of these, however, were race-based redress measures such as Black Economic Empowerment (BEE) and affirmative action. These would level the playing field of respect by raising the material and occupational status of black people. In general, however, the ANC paid far more attention to justifying these measures with reference to the racial gap in wealth, incomes and status than in giving thought to which black people should be empowered and affirmed and how the measures could impact on economy-wide measures, for instance of growth and employment. There is virtually no public indication that serious thought was given to including class as a factor in framing policy, thereby leaving the role of class as a major source of dissonance and ambiguity in managing race issues, especially as inequality among black people rose sharply at the same time as it declined between white and black.

There was a deeper confusion at the heart of the politics of race. For the ANC, the absolute article of faith that race has been central to shaping South African society and the economy is combined with the equally absolute rejection of the idea that the concept could have any ontological validity at all. On this shaky grounding, racial categories are assigned to all members of the South African population for the purposes of policies governing employment as well as selective access to government resources such as tenders and financing. It is important to note that these categories apply only to selected areas of (usually economic) activity and are not in any way compulsory or of general application. It is also possible to sympathize with the acute difficulties of democratic policymaking in the aftermath of racial tyranny. Nevertheless, how the ANC has chosen to address the politics of race points to ambiguities in what the party and its leaders represent.

Whatever their strengths and weaknesses, the means used by the ANC to cope with the politics of race at least reflect a commitment, unstable though it may be, to recognize and manage them. The same cannot be said for ethnic politics and 'the demon of tribalism'. It is scarcely surprising that denial of any differences, other than benign cultural ones between different African linguistic groups, has been (and remains) a staple of ANC rhetoric. From the very beginning in 1913, the ANC's self-perceived central task was to unite South African Africans in the face of the divide-and-rule tactics of colonial and, later, apartheid rulers. The Zulu chauvinism and separatism of the IFP under Mangosuthu Buthelezi, in the final period of the liberation struggle and the transitional negotiations, sufficed to give the ANC contemporary confirmation of this long-standing preoccupation. The numerous fissiparous examples of ethnicity in newly independent African countries were also a warning in their destructive effects. Despite these formidable and enduring incentives to proscription and denial, it is not surprising that tribalism has insinuated itself into the more relaxed political culture of democracy. Denial persists: tribalism has a subterranean, virtually occult quality (befitting the ANC's customary label 'demon') in official party discourse, but it is woven into everyday anecdotal exchange.

Perhaps because of this, and because of the salience of race in South African politics, the contemporary significance of tribalism has not yet received much extensive and systematic study,[18] although columnists and political analysts pepper their writings with references to it. Sometimes the issue breaks ground, as in a 2014 speech of Mbeki's, widely interpreted as an attack on Zuma, which warned of the encroachment of tribalism.[19] Certainly, it is not difficult to associate Zuma with neo-tribal expressions of cultural pride. He first made his mark in post-1994 leadership (having played a major role in the transitional negotiations) by successfully mediating an end to the regional civil war between the IFP and ANC in KwaZulu-Natal (KZN). He resolved the conflict partly by showing how comfortable he was in expressing himself in isiZulu and through Zulu cultural motifs as well as by showing respect for the Zulu monarchy.

Effectively, Zuma co-opted Zulu identity as a mobilizing resource instead of denigrating and fighting it as previous ANC leaders in the province had done. This was a mixture of unabashed personal identification (and enjoyment) allied to clever politics. For many African people, the liberation dividend included not only political rights but also recovery and enjoyment of traditional cultural identity free of the limiting and subordinating associations with the apartheid creations, Bantustans (or tribal homelands) to which the Afrikaner nationalist government had tried to confine African expressions of political and cultural identity. Zuma was astute enough to offer Africans the inclusive enjoyments of simultaneously being South African citizens and proud Zulus, while Buthelezi's offer was a chauvinist one, carrying strongly exclusive, separatist and militarist overtones. Having achieved all this, Zuma could extend this sense of shared cultural ease from himself alone to the ANC as a whole and from Zulus to all African language and cultural groups.

Some of the urban-based and modernizing parts of the ANC conspicuously failed to share Zuma's comfort with neo-tribalism and his facility with communicating in that register. Whatever the case, however, Zuma could take the credit for a major role in stopping the killing and, in the medium term, for opening up to ANC penetration those rural parts of KZN, South Africa's second most populous province, which had previously been no-go areas. These achievements were difficult to quarrel with. However, some diehard modernists may have sensed the threat of a classic political danger in Zuma's manoeuvres: whenever political leaders co-opt a powerful force for short-term gain, that force may, in the longer term, be difficult to manage or even perform a reverse takeover on them. Such was the threatened fate of the ANC in the peak Zuma years.

Zuma went on to use KZN as one of the most important power bases for his successful leadership bid and subsequent domination of the party. He also buttressed this by making a disproportionate number of appointments in government and across the public sector from this regional power base. Whether he did this following some master plan or by a series of improvisations, for what motives, and to what extent his exploitation of the ambiguities of identity amounts to ethnic or tribal mobilization in the service of political leadership, will be of central importance in later assessing Zuma as a leader.

Ambiguities of tradition and modernity

As it prepared to take power, the ANC and its leaders had to accustom themselves both to actually existing South Africa, which was more rural, traditional and socially conservative than it bargained for, and to a rapidly changing world of Anglophone globalization and post-communist, end-of-history liberal triumphalism. In this new world, the ANC's principal ideological inspirations – post-colonial as well as communist – were evaporating and the power structures that were built on them were collapsing. At the same time, unfamiliar domestic value systems and power structures – given the misleadingly neat label 'traditional' – had to be managed. As a result, the ANC had to adapt to the challenge of giving both modernization and tradition their due in the embryonic political culture and policy environment, while avoiding undue contradictions and disharmony between them. This task was not made easier by the fact that, in the context of the New South Africa, neither modernization nor tradition was internally coherent. Since the liberation movement was unprepared for this challenge, its response came in the form of improvised and opportunistic adjustments, rather than the unrolling of a holistic and harmonious worldview.

During the liberation struggle, both in exile and through its surrogates on the ground in South Africa, the ANC was a largely urban, internationalized and modernizing movement. In exile, it was influenced by Marxism-Leninism through the South African Communist Party (SACP), though other powerful influences were democratic socialism, Third World anti-colonialism, internationalist progressive solidarity and theories of uneven development.

Identity politics in the form of gender and sexual orientation issues were increasingly making themselves felt during the 1980s and the civil society movements that increasingly attached themselves to the liberation struggle were quick to press them on the ANC. Partly as a result, throughout the period of negotiation and transition, the ANC increasingly expressed itself in the language and values of constitutional and social liberalism, though not liberalism's economic versions. Grudging acceptance of some measure of economic liberalism appeared only gradually despite Mandela's early conversion away from nationalization. By 1996, Mbeki was using a modified, often coded version of the language of an emerging-market, political economy, much hedged around with revolutionary flourishes and nationalist qualifications. These did not spare him from the scornful accusation of being a 'neo-liberal'.

This barely coherent repertoire of metropolitan ideas not only had to be retrofitted to the ANC's history in the interests of a credibly continuous narrative, but it also had to appeal right across an entirely new territory of popular electoral politics, in which the electorate – mainly African – was much less homogeneous than the liberation struggle had made it appear. Moreover, it was not enough for the ANC to see itself as one competitor among several in an adversarial, multiparty electoral democracy, cherry-picking a coalition of interests to represent and accepting that it would face alternation in power, as the electorate was allowed to choose in its turn. On the contrary, it claimed to be the embodiment of both the new citizen nation, which included all minorities, and the African nation that was defined by its history of suffering and which underlay the citizen nation, giving it authenticity and meaning. The ANC's special mission was for the recovery and fulfilment of this nation. A mission of this sort required the ANC to establish permanent predominance in African popular politics, with registers of communication that extended beyond those who had already committed to it through the liberation struggle and were within the fold of the Alliance.

A first step in doing this was the incorporation of traditional leaders into broad association with the ANC (though not into the formal Alliance) through the lobby group, the Congress of Traditional Leaders of South Africa (Contralesa). According to the government department responsible for traditional affairs, there are eleven recognized kingships and around two thousand traditional leaders in South Africa (though there is no authoritative figure for the latter).[20] The association of many of these traditional leaders through Contralesa was accompanied by a less formal process of direct incorporation into the ANC of individual members of Bantustan elites, some at least of whom were chiefs, along with their networks of influence. This helped give the ANC better coverage of rural areas and delivered votes at election times. As we have already noted, a second sign of progress in this direction came after the 1994 election, with Zuma's diplomatic use of Zulu cultural identity to resolve conflict and to open doors in KZN for the ANC.

Contralesa, Bantustan elites and Zulu voters were fairly specific targets for ANC overtures to 'tradition'. What was also needed, however, was a more generalized sense of African authenticity, arising out of an adoption of African traditional values. The idea of a black nation conceptualized as bound together by a common history of suffering was not about to lose its utility. However, after the achievement of democracy, a national narrative that was more positive and oriented to the future was needed if a shared political culture was to be developed and the gap closed between the citizen nation and the African nation. The ANC was not alone in recognizing the need for this. Indeed, the movement to ground the Constitution and the new democracy in a loose association of African values was quite pervasive, though largely spontaneous and not centrally directed; its coverage was admittedly patchy, but it was quite inclusive. Inevitably, however, the ANC was the principal beneficiary.

This narrative is best understood as a series of oppositions between 'African' and 'Western' lived value constructions, along the following lines: communalism versus individualism and caring and cooperation versus competition; spirituality versus materialism and warm humanism versus cold rationalism; respect for the past including ancestors and tradition, however loosely defined, versus restless change and creative destruction that usually destroys more than it creates; forgiveness and restoration versus punishment that does not allow for context.

These oppositions were (and are) commonly summarized in one word, *ubuntu*, the African philosophy of common humanity. According to this worldview, *Umuntu ngumuntu ngabantu*, a person is a person through other people. The juxtaposition of Western and African, rather than 'white and black', left space for South African whites to include themselves and meant that the appeal to traditional values was not explicitly anti-white. However, the option to interpret the application of *ubuntu* to the new political culture in anti-white terms remained open in the event that whites did not respond wholeheartedly and in large numbers, which turned out to be the case. Those whites who did respond often looked opportunistic and insincere and even when sincere, some could look downright comic. The fact that, conveniently enough, the Western values highlighted as antithetical to *ubuntu* (especially individualism) were the liberal values espoused by the Democratic Party (later the Democratic Alliance (DA)[21]), then and now the main political home of whites and since 1999 the official parliamentary opposition, was a bonus for the ANC.

The ambiguities between traditional and modern came about as the result of the meeting between South Africa, as imagined in the constitutional negotiations for the purposes of improvising a new nation, and actually existing conditions on the ground, that is, in the hearts and minds of those who made up the new nation and the polity that expressed it. This requirement coincided with the ANC's self-perceived need to transform itself from a vanguard sect at the head of an inchoate mass movement, whose ties to the general population were much more complicated than its self-image as the country's hegemonic moral force would suggest, into the natural party of government, not only to meet the immediate challenges of transition but also in perpetuity.

Both these tasks required belief in the pretences that a coherent, unbroken and unproblematic reservoir of 'African tradition' existed, and that it could be applied smoothly to a complex and diverse country that was already modernized – albeit unevenly – across much of its society and economy. Neither of these things was true of course, and this would cause problems later, as would challenges to the legitimacy of such modernization as had taken place. However, the early years of the new political culture would show the ANC and its leaders that African tradition could be a considerable political resource.

The ambiguities of one-partyism in a multiparty democracy

Under the Constitution, South Africa has all the enabling attributes for a multiparty democracy, and to all intents and purposes adversarial multi-partyism is an official component of South African, democratic political culture. No serious and substantial political player *openly* espouses the one-party state as an aspirational ideal. Nevertheless, several factors have combined to give the South African polity features of both single and multipartyism. The former are so prominent – indeed overbearing – that it is commonplace to refer to the country as a dominant party state or a de facto one-party state.[22] What is also clear is that the dominant tendency of opinion in the ANC has been and remains more than comfortable with the fact of one-party dominance and desires both to prolong and exploit it. For the party as a whole, and for its leaders especially, this dominance has been a very useful resource, although the Mbeki and Zuma administrations deployed it in different ways, for different purposes and with different results. However, in the long term it has been a source of individual and collective hubris that has corrupted the state and weakened the party.

One-party dominance in the Mbeki/Zuma years rested on the outcomes of the five general elections between 1994 and 2014.[23] The ANC's lowest percentage in these polls (2014) was 62.15 per cent and its highest (2004) was 69.7 per cent. These victories in turn depended on a set of circumstances and of ANC attributes that came to be perceived as basic ground rules of the political culture. They began with the ANC's appropriation of the lion's share of the credit for South Africa's transition to democracy – the liberation dividend. However justified this was in the short term, it was translated into a collective ethos of entitlement to rule in perpetuity. This was reinforced by the implausibility of other parties' claims to be the authentic representatives of previously disenfranchised African people in the altered, post-struggle conditions of a free political marketplace. New parties that could not claim continuity with the struggle were out of the question. All the others that had been previously active were handicapped in one way or another. The Pan Africanist Congress (PAC) had been completely overshadowed by the ANC in the competition for recruitment and resources, both financial and diplomatic; its Africanist ideology was anachronistic and in organizational terms it was, in any case, terminally incompetent and incapable of self-management. Like the PAC, the various black consciousness (BC) groups had little to offer in a situation that called for accommodation of both minorities and an African majority (whose homogeneity was exaggerated by all, including the ANC) in a new nation. Their ideologies were wholly unsuited to governing a diverse population in a society linked to the global economy. In any case, most of the young BC talent had been attracted to and absorbed into the ANC during the last phase of the liberation struggle (1976–90). The IFP was tainted by ethnic chauvinism, separatism and collaboration with apartheid forces in the course of its civil war with the ANC. Despite its respectable showing in the 1994 election (10.5 per cent – concentrated heavily in KZN), the IFP was exposed as an isolated and parochial force with only niche appeal so that it could be neutralized at leisure, in part by Zuma's fluent ethnic diplomacy.

Continuity with the past and the challenges of quick and nimble reinvention were, of course, even greater problems for the legatees of white politics, the New National Party (NNP) and the Democratic Party (DP). Starved of credit by the ANC for his role in ending apartheid (except at occasional moments of high ceremony) and accused by many of his own support base of surrendering to unadorned, majoritarian African nationalism, F. W. de Klerk's status as a leader shrank. Concurrently, support ebbed away from the NNP, which came to seem ever more irrelevant and unprincipled as it sought to reinvent itself, first in coalition with the DP and then in 2004 by being absorbed into the ANC.

The DP's problem was not lack of principle but an excess of it. It was bad enough that it was vulnerable (however unfairly) to ANC accusations of defending white privilege as well as to other 'racial framing'[24] tactics, but in addition, the DP's strict adherence to liberal principles distanced it unequivocally from the conventional repertoire of redress measures in employment and other fields. By staunchly defending liberalism against nationalism (as it had under apartheid), the DP inevitably limited its appeal to African voters and initially at least, the ANC did not need to work very hard to dissuade Africans from voting for it. The DP's dogged adherence to liberal individualism alone was sufficient to put off even those African voters who might acknowledge the DP's opposition to apartheid and thus forgive its participation in the apartheid parliament. Nonetheless the DP was prepared to do what no other political party or grouping was willing or able to contemplate. It was prepared to embark on the long march of reinvention armed with self-belief, a combination of principle and pragmatism and a confidence in the future that, given where the party was starting from, was remarkable.

The march began with marshalling minority opposition voters and rump parties under its wing and renaming itself the DA in 2000. It then used this growing but still self-limiting support as a base on which to broaden its appeal to African voters. By 2015 it had a young African leader, Mmusi Maimane, and had modified its stance on affirmative and empowerment policies.

All these structural conditions and slow-moving developments allowed the ANC two decades of breathing space free from serious competition. Given that societies and economies – and hence politics – do not stand still and that there are time limits to the currency of past political credits, it may be surprising that the ANC's advantage lasted so long. This is partly due to those of the ANC's policies that were genuinely popular, reasonably well delivered (especially redistribution through social spending) and paralleled at the same time by responsible macroeconomic policy, all of which were supported by a reasonably favourable global economic environment. It was, however, also due to what the ANC made of its one-party dominance. In the short term, the choices involved in making good use of its electoral domination did not appear to be difficult. This is because the first election delivered a dream verdict and subsequent ones confirmed it: unchallenged supremacy, legitimized by free choice of the electorate and unsullied by resort to denial of rights, open repression or any other of the blatantly unsavoury means by which one-partyism is often pursued.

This was a priceless gift, but as it turned out, it was not enough for the ANC. Lacking any capacity to stand back and reflect on how to use it wisely; happy to bask in the liberation moment and to accept the benefit of the doubt that all but the most dogged liberal critics extended to it, the ANC took the gift of electoral confidence as an invitation to indulge legitimately the deeply ingrained one-partyism which survived the movement's conversion to constitutionalism. Thus, instead of searching for a synthesis of the ANC's own interests in an adversarial electoral system and the larger interests of developing South African democracy, it took up the invitation to fuse party and state in order to lay the basis for governing power in perpetuity. The principal vehicle for this was the policy of cadre deployment, through which the ANC sought to populate not only all nominally independent organs and structures of state – military, legal, state-owned enterprises and statutory bodies of all kinds – but also those of civil society and the economy, with ANC activists and supporters.

There was no single reason for this. Of the multiple motivations for using cadre deployment to fuse party and state, a key assumption was the quasi-Marxist notion that neutrality of the state is a bourgeois fiction designed as a camouflage to protect property and capital accumulation. Having swallowed many other bourgeois fictions to help ease the path to power, this was one that the ANC was apparently unprepared to stomach, conceivably because it was the most important obstacle to the achievement of unrestrained power.

Two other presumptions were closely related. The first was that in office the ANC would be forced to deal with a determined and well-resourced rearguard action by counter-revolutionaries inside the public service and linked to powerful interests outside it. Despite the (relatively) benign purge of white public servants that began immediately after the ANC formed the first post-apartheid government, using early retirement and other forms of leverage, a substantial white presence would have to be tolerated for a period, if only to ensure some continuity of capacity. Cadre deployment was a way of countering the presumed foot-dragging or subversion of policy that such legacy operatives might (*would* in the eyes of the ANC) undertake. The second presumption, less dependent on paranoid imaginings, was that tasks of the magnitude facing the ANC government could only be successfully addressed if the public servants charged with carrying them out were imbued with the revolutionary enthusiasm of ANC cadres. The culmination of all these worries and insecurities was the prospect of forming a government that was 'in office but not in power', disarmed in the face of 'white power' that was so deeply entrenched in the economy and society and so hegemonic in its values that only complete domination of the state and as much of society and the economy as possible could combat it.

There were ancillary motivations of course. One was to reward followers and open up opportunities for African people in the name of transformation. The subsequent history of the Zuma administration suggests that, for at least some, cadre deployment from the beginning provided a blueprint for plunder, especially when combined with affirmative action and extensive presidential powers of appointment. Arguably, the biggest mistake made by the ANC throughout this period was to allow overlap between the legitimate – affirmative action – and the illegitimate – cadre deployment.

Different combinations of these reasons were doubtless present in the calculations of all ANC leaders and followers. However, it is fair to say that they all subscribed to some version or another. That is because no policy of the ANC was defended with more vigour and conviction by the organization than cadre deployment and the fusion of party and state. That position remains to this day, even when the pathological effects of both have been laid bare in detail and only the most tentative self-criticism has emerged.

However, individuals and factions held onto one article of faith that has been common to everybody in the upper reaches of the ANC. This was the conviction that South Africa was and still is a country so fragile, so lacking in social cohesion, that without the ANC to guide it and lead it, to hold the balance between races, tribes, classes and factions of all kinds, it would simply fall apart in chaotic strife.

Doubtless for some, this lack of confidence in South Africa is no more than a cynical excuse for abuse of power; for others, it is a genuinely felt, dark and ever-present nightmare, amounting to a curious ANC-based variation on Afropessimism. It is not uncommon for ANC leaders to express this nightmare as an explicit choice: ANC rule or anarchy and barbarism. However, lack of trust in South Africa's resources for sustainable democratic development without open-ended ANC 'leadership' has not been confined to the ANC itself. Indeed, especially in the early post-apartheid years, it was quite widely shared, though often reluctantly and hedged with qualifications, by those who were not unaware of the dangers of prolonged ANC rule. One academic version confidently put the case:

> It is an inescapable conclusion, unwelcome to those who fear protracted one-party dominance, that a cohesive tripartite alliance, enjoying sustained and co-operative relations with opposition parties, offers South Africa the best hope of entrenching its highly imperfect democracy. The movement's popular reach and legitimacy help to render the majority's dire circumstances politically supportable, and its institutions ameliorate and contain the society's diverse conflicts. However, if the advertised benefits of a collaborative political order, marked by consensus and compromise within and between parties and institutions, are to be realised, this will require more open and democratic-spirited politics that the ANC is currently able to muster.[25]

Published at the beginning of 2003, when the ANC's dominance and Mbeki's domination of the ANC seemed to stretch unchallenged into the future, this is a fairly typical rationalization of both forms of hegemony, although it stops short of endorsing the fusion of party and state and it is hedged at the end with a coded warning about Mbeki's alleged authoritarian and intolerant tendencies. What such analyses do is usefully illustrate how widespread the doubts were about South Africa's democratic resources and prospects, and how the assumption that one-party domination was the remedy for the shallowness of these resources was not confined to the ANC. However, implicit in this prescription for stability is the problem of accountability and the problematic status of the opposition in how to achieve it. At a minimum, it is far from clear what was meant in the quotation above by 'enjoying sustained and cooperative relations with opposition parties'. This is a view of the Mbeki era that few in the DA (or for that matter any unbiased observer) would recognize.

Asymmetrical democracy: Accountability without opposition

Liberal democracies of the sort that South Africa was set up to be tend to operate on an assumption of symmetry. The axis of symmetry is electoral competition between political parties which, however much (or little) they differ in ideology, policy programme, support base and representative image, are organized in the same way and for the same purposes. These are to form a government or to hold the government accountable until such time as fresh competition may (or may not) lead to alternation in power. The outlines of such systems may develop through long historical evolution, as in mature democracies, or be purpose-built by negotiation, as in the case of South Africa. All of them, by recognizing political rights of various kinds (organization and expression mainly), allow for other means of conducting democratic politics. However, these are generally intended to be and conventionally regarded as ancillary supplements to the symmetry of the system's essential elements. They are the resort of single-issue groups or small numbers of politically aware people that cannot, or will not on principle, find a place in the symmetry of party competition; they do not constitute a central organizing principle that replaces the symmetry of contesting parties.

As social classes fragment and identities proliferate, political parties in mature democracies have lost traction and there is much disillusion with conventional politics, especially with politicians who behave as if they are entitled to power and on the part of people who feel left out or left behind. But although there is much more fluidity and the moral authority of symmetrical competition has been greatly undermined, it remains for the moment the backbone of mature democracy.

Adaptation, as in Emmanuel Macron's *La République en Marche*, or mutation, as in Donald Trump's rise to the presidency, as well as innovation in organizing method, as in Bernie Sanders's and Jeremy Corbyn's reinvigoration of left politics in the United States and Britain, have been the main responses so far to insurgent challenges to traditional symmetrical democracy. In all cases, however, they have so far left the essential premises of symmetrical electoral competition intact.

In contrast to mature democracies, South African politics in the post-apartheid period has had a very strong flavour of asymmetrical democracy. As an organizing principle, it has rivalled the symmetry of party politics and offered a parallel to and substitute for it. The coinage 'asymmetrical democracy' takes inspiration from strategic studies, in which asymmetrical warfare indicates hostilities conducted by sides that differ greatly in extent of power and/or in modes of power as well as strategy and tactics. It is the classic way of understanding irregular and insurgent warfare.[26]

The premise of asymmetric politics is that the ruling party cannot be held accountable, whether by being replaced in a competitive election or, through representative institutions, by a similar party or parties constituted for these purposes. Alternatives include discrediting the government through media exposure by investigative journalism, using the justiciable provisions of the Constitution to impose accountability through the courts or direct action through demonstrations, boycotts or other forms of civil disobedience. The magnitude and regularity of the ANC's electoral victories, as well as its hankering for one-partyism, have been factors in pushing South Africa towards asymmetrical politics, but they are not the only ones and arguably not even the most important. As the principal opposition party, the DA has not been intimidated or demoralized by the ANC's electoral hegemony. On the contrary, it has responded with vigour and energy in its use of parliamentary resources for holding the government to account and with long-term strategies for building its own support. Within limits, it has been successful at both and although it turned to using the courts to hold the Zuma administration to account, it came quite late to the tactic. That is, asymmetric politics has not principally been an outgrowth from formal party opposition, resulting from frustration with formal channels; although the DA now operates a successful synthesis of 'ordinary democracy' and the asymmetric variety, it has been a follower rather than a leader.

Asymmetric democracy in the face of ANC hegemony is encouraged by two significant features of the country's political culture and has advanced in three stages. The two features are first, distrust of opposition in general and in particular, its most successful manifestation, the liberal DA with its appeal to whites; second, distrust of formal institutions and the political class that operates them; and third, a hankering for direct democracy in participatory, activist forms of semi-permanent mobilization.

The three chronological phases may be described as follows: first, the ANC as its own opposition; second, a progressive movement, identified with but not part of the ANC, to hold the government to account through the courts, not so much for abuse of power but for failure to act quickly enough to realize the promise of socio-economic rights in the Constitution; and third, the spread of these tactics to opposition parties and a much broader civil society movement during Zuma's second and final administration in order to hold him to account for abuses of power amounting to state capture.

Pervasive distrust of opposition was influential in shaping South Africa's political culture in the early years of democracy. Its sources have a classic Third World and postcolonial ring to them. The first is that, in an ethnically diverse, materially unequal society with a history of repression, struggle and conflict, opposition is a source of disunity and fragmentation. This is an obstacle to the overriding priority, which is the creation of a single nation, whether citizen or ethnic, or, in the case of South Africa, an uneasy hybrid of both. It is particularly true of opposition that seeks a base in the majority African population. Residual opposition can be expected and even tolerated up to a point from minority populations whose life experiences and material interests differ (very substantially in the case of South African whites) from those of the majority. But opposition of this sort must be kept in its place and not violate the integrity of the majority experience, where it can only be destructive and based on false premises such as the delusions of tribalism or alien, profoundly un-African, ideologies such as liberalism.

The second source of distrust is that the tasks of government – reconstruction, development, nation-building, transformation of the economy and society to reflect the legitimate expectations of the previously excluded and repressed African majority – are not merely policy choices but also non-negotiable moral imperatives. Opposition, however conceived, is at best a futile decoration and at worst downright traitorous.

The third argument against formal, adversarial opposition is a cultural one. It is that the democratic transition should be an African one and not some mindless transfer of allegedly universal practices and principles to the South African context. This is a need that reaches deep below the surface of government and the phraseology of the Constitution to require the attachment of the majority of the population to the political culture. This view seeks to reinvent selected passages from the African past – notably the idea of democracy (and leadership) by discussion and consensus, without a role for adversarial opposition – and reinstate them in the African present.

It was not only opposition that attracted such distrust and lack of confidence. Distrust of 'bourgeois democracy' ran very deep in the wider liberation movement and not only in the parts of the ANC Alliance most influenced by Marxist ideas. The fear that a new and self-interested class might hijack the fruits of liberation did not need theoretical justification. What is more important, however, is that the liberation struggle held out the possibility in the minds of many people of a different and more authentic style of politics from that of a polity organized around formal institutions and structured, centrally managed political parties, operated by a political class of professional representatives and technocrats. South Africans are scarcely unique in the democratic world in their scepticism about political classes. Indeed, one of the great shaping forces in Anglophone and European politics in recent years has been the withering away of respect for and trust in political parties and their functionaries.

The liberation struggle affected more than minds and held out more than hopes. It gave to many South Africans the unique hands-on experience of alternatives to formal models of democratic politics (which were in any case unavailable to the great majority of them under apartheid). The struggle considerably broadened the range of people who could be called activists in South Africa. At the same time, it extended the range of activism – workplace, education, local government, consumer issues, local area defence and crime prevention – and the activist bodies – student representative and parent–teacher councils, shop steward structures, street committees – in which people could participate. What was unique about this, however, was that these were not fragmented, single issues; they were all unified as part of the liberation struggle. This was the key to the success of the United Democratic Front (UDF), which coordinated all these people, organizations (more than three hundred of them) and issues. Not only was all politics local politics, all local politics fed back into a single, national struggle. In this way, the UDF, as well as the trade union federation Cosatu, which in its early years was organized along the lines of grass-roots democracy, gave a glimpse of direct democracy's possibilities that stretched far beyond mobilization on single issues and offered a model of the whole democratic polity organized on a different basis from adversarial electoral politics.

It was a tantalizing glimpse, expressed in a comprehensive manifesto for empowering members and combating elitism in self-determining organizations.[27] This included collective, elected and recallable leadership at all levels; leadership knowledge and skills to be shared, not hoarded; mandates, accountability and report back; and criticism of and self-criticism by elites.

The great strength of this vision was that it was not some paper utopia but hammered out in grass-roots experience. Its great weakness was that the nature of this experience obviated any responsibility for government and after the advent of democracy its proponents never applied themselves sufficiently to how the vision might be adapted to coexist with the potentially clashing mandate of a democratic government, which had to manage different constituencies and legitimately clashing interests. Nevertheless, although the movement for direct democracy was effectively demobilized, partly by its own confusions and contradictions and partly by the ANC's effective use of its moral authority and ruthless drive to dominate all post-apartheid political space, the myth of direct democracy did not go away and, suitably adapted to the new constitutional order, reappeared later to challenge the ANC's supremacy in its most degenerate form under Zuma.

It is difficult to assign with confidence the relative contributions to asymmetrical democracy of several strands of causation: demoralization at the ANC's de facto one-party domination and despair at the prospects of electoral competition; principled rejection of the rules of the party-political game combined with measured acceptance of the ANC's moral authority, tempered by well-founded suspicion of the motives and capacities of those who were its custodians in government (at all levels). For whatever combination of these reasons, however, the pursuit of accountability without formal opposition gave South Africa's democracy one of its most characteristic features in the post-apartheid era.

The first phase, the ANC as its own opposition, lasted from 1994 until the early years of Mbeki's first administration (1999–2004). This should be distinguished from another source of ambiguity, the tussle over economic policy between Mbeki and the left-leaning components of the Alliance, Cosatu and the SACP, which was nothing less than a contest to define the direction and indeed the very nature of the ANC. This came later (from 1996) and will be dealt with below. Effectively, this brief earlier period saw one version of what was to be a recurrent theme in the ANC's life cycle (or as some would have it, its death spiral). That is, the belief that the ANC is a self-sufficient and self-correcting system, capable of homeostasis in the face of external change. In this way, one-partyism could be reconciled with democracy. It was a symptom of the extraordinary self-confidence fostered by the liberation moment that sufficient numbers of the first generation of ANC members of the National Assembly believed in this unlikely hybrid form of democracy to give the idea passing and partial credibility. They believed that they could be principled though loyal watchdogs and use the committee system of parliament as a viable check on the executive, which, in the spirit of intra-party democracy, would be sensitive to their concerns and obedient to the dictates of the Constitution, which they had helped to frame.

However, it did not work out quite like that. The principal reason for this was that the policies that were most likely to lead to the abuse of power – chiefly those designed to fuse party and state – were so broadly accepted across the party that the idea of the ANC holding itself accountable was so internally incoherent that it could neither achieve much nor last long. In addition, presidential power and party discipline as interpreted by Mbeki – first as deputy president and leader of government business and later as president – speedily curtailed the independence of electoral representatives on which the fantasies of self-correction rested. The fairly quick passing of the 1994 generation of MPs as they moved to government posts or lucrative private-sector deals, to be replaced by a considerably less talented and principled intake, also helped shorten this brief experiment in democratic fiction. Indeed, the two trends were related; the shrinking space for independence and initiative was a push factor in motivating exit and turnover. However, despite its thin achievements and fleeting life, this attempt at self-regulating corporate probity has passed into the mythology of the ANC as a golden age, to be revisited as the fragmentation of the party began in earnest during Zuma's second term.

The second phase, that of guerrilla democracy, may be viewed as a logical progression from the failure of the ANC to provide its own opposition. Landmarks in its development were the formation of the Treatment Action Campaign (TAC) in 1998 and Section 27 in 2010. The TAC is an HIV/AIDS activist organization, and Section 27 is named for the section of the Constitution which establishes citizens' rights to healthcare, sufficient food and water and 'appropriate' social assistance if they are unable to take care of themselves. This form of civil society activism, of which the TAC and Section 27 are leading examples among many, usually law-based, organizations, tends to see itself as a kind of purifying and standard-setting corrective to the current institutional form of the ANC. Its main points of reference, however, are the traditions of the organization itself, albeit very loosely defined and generously interpreted.[28]

Activist mobilization and direct democracy are key points of this interpretation. Attitudes towards conventional politics and formal institutions from this quarter are at best wary and at worst disdainful. Mobilization is important, but appeal to the Constitution through the courts has been the principal and most successful tactic. Landmark successes in this respect were the constitutional court cases, *Republic of South Africa v. Grootboom* (2000) and the *Minister of Health v. Treatment Action Campaign* (2002), in both of which the court vindicated civil society pressures on government to realize the promise of social rights in the Constitution.

This is a purist approach. It regards political parties as divisive, hypocritical and the camouflage for selfish interests and elections as remote, infrequent and essentially demobilizing events. It radically reconceives politics as a series of bilateral confrontations with government – whose essential legitimacy in power is simply taken for granted – strictly confined to the rights specified in the Constitution. As a result, asymmetrical politics lacks a broader context of policies for economic management and growth, which constitute the only way to accumulate the resources for redistribution and thus to realize the Constitution's promises. The result is that civil society has nothing of any interest to say about the economy. Trade unions are the exception of course, but what they have to say is largely confined to the inner chambers of the ANC Alliance. It is in any case debatable whether or not unions – certainly Cosatu unions – can be meaningfully considered as part of civil society, given Cosatu's self-imposed yoking to the ANC Alliance and the substantial erosion of whatever independence it previously had during Zuma's two terms as president of the ANC and of the country.

A third phase in the development of asymmetrical democracy stems not so much from a rejection of party and electoral politics but more from a recognition of their limitations in the face of the ANC's preponderance of power. In this sense, court cases on constitutional matters are not so much an alternative to conventional opposition but a supplement and extension to it. The DA and bodies associated or in sympathy with it, such as the Helen Suzman Foundation, turned increasingly to the courts in the face of Zuma's abuse of power, including a campaign of legal process to have the corruption charges against him – dropped in 2008 – reinstated. In most instances, the courts vindicated them.

Comrade, citizen and consumer: Ambiguities of followership

Confronted by the democratic possibilities of 1994, which were new, but at the same time heavily conditioned by long history and recent experience, South Africans were faced with more than one possible democratic identity. The choice of how to be democratic was rarely if ever a matter of conscious deliberation, more a question of intuition, reflex and instinct. Moreover, the democratic identities on offer did not have to be exclusive; in fact, the more they could be harmoniously combined, the better democracy would probably work. These are important qualifications but, nonetheless, juxtaposing these ideal models of democratic identity and acknowledging their differential weight in the post-apartheid polity is helpful in explaining the ambiguities of followership in South African democracy. These in turn are expressed in a paradox: for a political system that enjoys a very high degree of legitimacy and regularly reproduces decisive majorities in free and largely fair elections with relatively high turnouts, South Africa also exhibits high levels of localized dissent, expressed in protests that are often violent and enacted by the very people who contribute to the decisive electoral majorities.[29]

The comrade ethos sees democratic politics as a continuation in the same spirit of pre-democratic struggles; whether or not the means can remain the same is a grey and shifting area of communication between leaders and led. The primary political identity that goes with this ethos emphasizes past bonds forged in shared action (or at least identification with them), guided by ideals of sacrifice and selflessness. These are often expressed in appeals to military-type discipline and military metaphor: 'we were in the trenches together' is one such pervasive trope among many in post-apartheid politics. Its use extends far beyond those who have seen military service, regular or irregular, to encompass the entire political class and those who identify with it. Such bonds are exclusive and immutable; they trump the inclusiveness of citizenship and, frequently, the values of the Constitution. Democratic politics is not a matter of individual choice; the individual does not choose a party and its range of policies from several alternatives. The cause chooses the individual and the party is the embodiment of the cause, expressed in heroic terms of mobilization, the wholeness of the people, the politics of the will and eventual victory. Most importantly, the comrade ethos carries with it the expectation of fraternity, which is assumed to survive all possible political, social and economic changes. Another essential component is the conviction, taken over enthusiastically by the ANC from the wider Marxist-Leninist world, that political competitors and adversaries are enemies of the people.

This was an essential survival manual for ANC and other liberation movement activists in the face of repression, exile, prison, torture and death. Perhaps, it was the only viable one under the circumstances. However, its application to democratic politics is problematic. Expectations of fraternity are difficult to extend from a core of activists to the more than 60 per cent of the electorate that generally has voted for the ANC. They are difficult to sustain (in any sense of literal and general application at least), even in the activist core, in the face of suddenly opened opportunities for social mobility, which, at the same time, are very unevenly distributed so that they favour educated elites and political insiders. The leftist aphorism, 'Rise with your class, not out of it', makes sporadic and increasingly forlorn appearances in the rhetoric of ANC Alliance battles. Vexed questions concerning the nature of representation, which have immemorially plagued democratic theory and practice, arise, only for them to be fudged or shelved. Central to these is the problem of the remoteness of political classes from electorates and activist bases. New hierarchies of managerial and technocratic governance confront histories of mobilization, visions of direct democracy and expectations of fraternity. It did not help that the first generation of technocrats was made up for the most part of former comrades. Technocratic management is not always plausible as a medium for heroic causes. Comradeship is difficult to square with compromise and with constitutional and legal principle. In short, the comrade ethos has an absolutist quality that sits uneasily with gradualism, compromise and individual choice.

These confusions and contradictions have presented ANC leaders with painful dilemmas over how to use the comrade ethos. In the first place, it would be difficult to dispense with it, so deeply ingrained is it into the movement's history. It has also been an indispensable tool so far for mobilizing electoral support. Yet at the same time, it is so blatantly contradicted by the differential distribution of liberation's economic and status rewards that deploying it gravely risks credibility and fuels the endemic tendency to feel betrayed that marks post-apartheid politics. Moreover, however useful it may be to perpetuate myths of comradeship and fraternity at election time, their implications can be an irritant in the actual business of governing. This was one of the major sources of friction of the later Mbeki years. As a result, the ANC leadership is perpetually poised between mobilizing and demobilizing its support base.

The most inclusive democratic identity is that of citizen. The citizen's principal affiliation should be with his or her fellow citizens, while the principal citizen allegiance should be to the spirit as well as the letter of the Constitution. Subsidiary allegiances and affiliations are, of course, not only permissible but also inevitable and desirable. If the Constitution were all, then politics would be static and bloodless, without the spark of conflict that sets things in motion and ignites the arguments that provide choice.

There are two signs that the democratic identity of citizen remains only weakly developed in South Africa. The first is the uneasy and unstable relationship between comrade and citizen identity in ANC discourse and practice. 'Comrade' does not always trump 'citizen', but it does often enough to be a matter of concern, as some (though not all) ANC leaders hop from one register to another, according to the needs of the moment and the assumed temper of the audience. The second indication of undeveloped citizenship is not directly political but refers to relatively weak social compliance with norms of obligation such as payment for municipal services and television licences as well as the requirement for drivers to be licensed. Very high levels of crime and corruption are other measures. Governments, ever since Mandela, have bemoaned a tendency of South Africans to think of the Constitution in terms only of rights and not of duties owed both to the state and to each other. They point to the danger posed to the country's integrity by lack of social cohesion. This is a catch-all label, much used in official government discourse, for deviance, non-compliance, crime, corruption, racial and xenophobic hatred, violent protest, gender abuse, substance abuse and other manifestations of anomie and social decay. This is underscored by a lack of fit between demotic values and those of the Constitution, for which there is abundant survey evidence.[30]

There is a third conception of democratic identity, which is that of consumer. This self-understanding frees the individual from lifetime commitments based on grand narratives of value and project, as well as bonds of shared experience, and enables choices based on different criteria. These criteria emphasize political choice based on measures of managerial and technocratic competence, personal integrity and workable policies in governance. An appeal for support by a party or leader on these bases carries with it the (usually implicit) understanding that such support will be conditional on performance. At least, some ANC leaders are mindful of the dangers of complacency and of appearing to suffer from the arrogance of entitlement, so consumer appeal along the lines of these criteria does find its way into the party's electioneering often in the form of promises of 'delivery'. At the same time, the ANC fears that this kind of appeal risks reducing political relationships – between state and citizen, party and voter – to a host of individual, self-interested transactions, a dangerous minimum for a developing and still fragile democracy situated in a fractured nation.

These confusions of democratic identity are symptomatic of the ANC's continuing condition of being a hybrid of democratic political party and national liberation movement. The liberation movement ethos is still potent, but its days are visibly numbered, as the ANC's loss of control of the main urban centres in the 2016 municipal elections seems to indicate and the drop in percentage share of the vote in the May 2019 general election tentatively confirms. Losing the aura of inevitable victory and absorbing the lesson that voters can choose another party should be a powerful motivation for renewal; however, whether this will be in the direction of doubling down or scaling back remains in the balance at the time of writing. It is not clear whether the ANC will attempt to recover the old liberation movement élan or complete a transition into something attuned to the more modest ambitions of genuine electoral competition as well as the possibilities of coalition and even opposition politics. This is one of the principal challenges facing Cyril Ramaphosa as leader both of the ANC and the country.

The ambiguities of the ANC: Is there any 'there' there?

It should be clear by now that some of the ambiguities in South Africa's political culture that have been described so far centre on the ANC. This is only partly true of the ambiguous settlement that was the starting point of post-apartheid politics; the self-interested interpretations of other stakeholders have also contributed to what is, up to a point, a legitimately contested base for the development of democratic politics. Other ambiguities of race and identity politics; of one-partyism in a multiparty democracy; and between tradition and modernity can be more directly and exclusively attributed to the nature of the ANC.

There are various ways to understand the nature of political parties – or in this case, the hybrid of political party and liberation movement that is the ANC. These include the following: core beliefs; organizational culture, including how leaders, activists and supporters interact to maintain shape and discipline; ways of reproducing and mobilizing support; inward understandings and outward projection in political messaging of the party's meaning and purpose; habitual reflexes in response to unfolding events and changing structural features of economy and society; styles of governance, such as policy and law-making, as well as wielding executive authority. These and other characteristics of political parties might offer intellectual tidiness but risk over-compartmentalizing and imposing too much order on what, in the case of the ANC at least, is a sprawling and untidy phenomenon. Bearing this in mind, these categories will serve as suggestive guidelines rather than a rigid template.

There are, of course, classic difficulties in understanding the nature of individual political parties and movements. These begin with how much to take the parties and their leaders at their own words and how far to go in understanding them in their own terms. In addition, all political parties in democracies are coalitions to some extent or other, which means that they practise the politics of internal compromise, making it difficult sometimes to discern an essential and unambiguous nature. They are all mixtures of principle and pragmatism (sometimes heavily tilted towards the latter) as well as of strategy on the one hand and (by necessity) opportunism and improvisation on the other. All these reservations apply in the case of the ANC, but they are greatly exceeded by other complications, which arise from the ANC's singular history and aspects of its culture.

In the first place, not only does the ANC already occupy a wholly disproportionate amount of political space in what is an open, constitutional democracy with wide freedoms of political expression and action, but one of its central characteristics throughout the post-apartheid period is that it has nursed ambitions to occupy all the rest. Its pretensions have included the following: to embody the nation (or more accurately both the multiracial citizen nation and the racially African nation); to fuse party, itself and the state; to monopolize the moral high ground in recent history and in contemporary society and politics, to the exclusion of all other sources of value; and to rule in perpetuity (or in Jacob Zuma's much-quoted words, 'Until Jesus comes').

To harbour monopolist ambitions on this scale in a complex, diverse and rapidly changing society and economy under a democratic constitution, without recourse at the same time to the apparatus of political repression that supports authoritarian monopolism, puts at risk all hopes of ideological and organizational coherence. Instead, ambiguity is piled upon ambiguity in a carnival of improvisation in order to appear to be all things to all people.

This interpretation raises some obvious questions. Why and how has the ANC acquired these ambitions? How has it attempted to realize them? What have been the results for the party itself and for the country?

The first possibility concerns the ANC's relationship with the nation. In one version, it embodies an already existing nation; in another, it is the only entity with the moral authority (as the representative of the previously excluded and repressed majority), as well as the political weight, to harmonize the citizen and the exclusively African nation and bring a synthesis into being by achieving the equality between black and white that is the only sound basis for nation-building. In this conception, a sense of mission tends to be combined with expectations of entitlement. The latter are based on the ANC's self-image, comprising its contributions to liberation and democracy, including the individual sacrifices and heroism of some of its members, the corporate durability of the organization itself under the extreme stresses of the struggle against apartheid and the compromises it was prepared to make in the interests of a transition to democracy, which was shared across formerly warring parties. Closely related to this is the belief that, in apartheid's traumatic aftermath, South Africa was so fragile that unless the ANC occupied the maximum political space possible, race war and/or balkanization were distinct possibilities.

Unsurprisingly, there are those who are sceptical of how completely this self-image captures the essential nature and the ambitions of the ANC. Even when they are prepared to concede the credibility of some of it, they discern darker forces behind the ANC's insistence that it must be everywhere and everything. For some critics, it is characterized by an inbuilt, ideologically determined drive to domination in the interests of state-led social engineering, one among several quasi-soviet tendencies acquired via the SACP in exile. For others, the motivation is race-based nationalism while still others retrofit the narrative of self-enrichment by a patronage class, which has unmistakably emerged in the Zuma era, to the whole of post-apartheid history, as if this goal were the original motivating spirit for capturing power.

The banal truth is probably that each of these interpretations fits some of the moving forces within the ANC some of the time, but none of them fit all of them all the time. In short, while it was busy trying to be all things to all South Africans, the self-conscious leadership core of the ANC tended to overlook the fact that the movement meant different things to its members and activists at the same time. When it did grasp that this was the case, its members individually and collectively could do little about it. This is because the myth of the 'broad church' in which all could find a home and all differences could be resolved was one of the most important elements of the ANC's self-image. This myth has several sources, one of which is homage to the myth of African communalism and the humanist values that are habitually ascribed to it. Others are the pretensions to embody the nation and the fears of fragmentation that have already been cited above. However, the principal source for the broad-church myth is the ANC's most characteristic reflex, which is to incorporate different social and political interests and either absorb, adapt or suppress their ideological expressions.

This reflex was driven in large part by the ANC's weakness in the underground and exile years. Realizing that it could not easily afford to antagonize any group or interest that might conceivably have the same aim – in this case ending apartheid – it practised a form of popular-front politics that avoided confrontation and sidestepped contradictions. This tactic reached back even before exile, to resistance conceived as alliance politics with left-leaning organizations and groups based in white, Indian and coloured minorities. This was not without its difficulties, and the popular-front principle led to the breakaway of the PAC in 1959. However, it did the ANC no harm to have an outcast sibling in whom the darker sides of liberation politics – including spontaneous populist violence, inflammatory anti-white rhetoric and organizational incompetence – were conveniently highlighted, making the ANC look good by comparison. The intensification of the liberation struggle from the early 1970s, especially after the killing by police of hundreds of mainly young, African people in Soweto in 1976, encouraged an extension and a deepening of this broad-front policy. Many of the thousands of young people who went into exile in the aftermath of Soweto had backgrounds in the rival BC liberation tradition. This large-scale outmigration gave the ANC, with its well-established exile presence, the option of absorbing the BC youth directly, rather than having to develop some sort of front relationship with the BC groups.

The ANC's next phase of accretion was the crisis of the 1980s, sparked by resistance to reform apartheid and spearheaded by the UDF. How far the UDF was a surrogate for the ANC from the beginning and what role the ANC played in its genesis remain matters of historical argument. However, what is not a matter of dispute is that through the emergence of the UDF the ANC could considerably extend its reach among people who might have been sceptical of an appeal from undiluted African nationalism, either from a left standpoint or because they distrusted the closed organizational practices of exile leadership, or they were members of racial or ethnic minorities who feared African majoritarianism. In its short history, the UDF's identification with the ANC seemed to dispel these concerns and it established itself as something between a surrogate for and a cadet branch of the ANC. Having handled its relations with the UDF using characteristically ambiguous diplomacy during the struggle, once in power, the ANC absorbed it in much the same way that it had absorbed the BC recruits, while ruthlessly discarding the far-reaching principles of organizational democracy that had characterized it.

The ANC's most recent, and possibly its final, exercise of the characteristic reflex to incorporate came about as it faced the challenges of acquiring and then exercising governing power. In both its returned-exile and internal manifestations, the ANC was preponderantly led by activist revolutionaries returned from exile or jail, communists, industrial unionists and educated professionals who had led community resistance. This was a thin and narrow elite predominantly attuned to modernizing ideas of policy and governance in urban environments. Like all political and social organizations that need to expand quickly and to recruit in hitherto underexploited and unfamiliar territories, the ANC had to look for shortcuts:

> The quickest way to accomplish such expansion was through the incorporation of the elites and networks consolidated around homeland politics. The corollary to this was that in certain predominantly rural provinces the ANC's local leadership would re-enact the social relationships of established patterns of clientistic [sic] politics.[31]

As well as absorbing provincial and local small-town and rural elites, some with roots in the Bantustans and others newly emerging as patronage possibilities under the new regime became clear, the ANC entered into a formal relationship (though short of full Alliance status) with the traditional leaders' organization of 'progressive chiefs', the Contralesa. These chiefs were 'progressive' to the extent that they had thrown their lot in with the ANC, rather than serve under the flag of Mangosuthu Buthelezi. Otherwise, 'progressive chiefs' turned out indeed to be the oxymoron that it appears at first glance.

The effects of this history of accretion and absorption on the ANC's ambiguities of character and organization have been numerous and far-reaching. The broad-church character, especially taken to extremes as it has been in the ANC, means that bargaining and the contest between policy positions, which would otherwise take place in the wider polity where support is more transparently measured (in elections principally) and interests are more clearly exposed, take place in-house. In other political systems, formal coalitions and the 'supply and confidence' arrangements that enable governments to govern without absolute majorities tend to operate on transparent rules of engagement; in the ANC Alliance, things are much more opaque. The broad church also means that polarizing choices and confrontations, even trials of strength, which are sometimes necessary in democratic politics if stagnation and drift are to be prevented, are effectively ruled out. The regular addition of interests and ideological tendencies dilutes whatever there is of the host body's essential character and pulls it in different directions, between left and right, Africanism and non-racialism, tradition and modernity, guarantor of stability and revolutionary force. In the end, it becomes legitimate to ask whether or not there is any 'there' there.

Indeed, the accumulation of alliances, partnerships and fully absorbed elements brings a risk of reverse takeovers. Business and liberal critics used to worry about the 'left tail wagging the ANC dog'. In fact, other, perhaps less obvious sources of influence have been more powerful. The ANC used to congratulate itself on the political re-education of young BC sympathizers in exile in the 1970s and 1980s, steering them away from narrow Africanism into orthodox Marxism and non-racialism. In maturity and through the medium of position within the ANC itself, as well as through racially exclusive black business and professional bodies allied to the ruling party, the same activists, with the experience of navigating ANC networks for more than twenty years, have been able to lobby strongly for Africanist policy positions under the general rubric of 'transformation' to the point that the ANC's non-racialism, which in any case was always conceptually vague and unstable, has become even more shadowy and imprecise.

However, ideology is not the only basis on which competition for influence takes place. A constant theme in the politics of the ANC since 1994 has been the contest between the central party leadership and provincial power structures over management and direction of the organization and control of resources. One treatment of the influence of former Bantustan elites and traditional leaders in the ANC notes the wry quip: 'Q. What became of South Africa after 1994? A. It was colonised by its Bantustans.'[32] One underappreciated irony of the negotiations for democratic transition was that the ANC bitterly opposed full-blown federalism because it thought that 'white reactionaries' would be able to avoid the legitimate redistributive policy goals of a democratically elected majority national government from power bases in the provinces. As it turns out, the chief beneficiaries of the weak, quasi-federal system that issued from the settlement have been the

ANC's own clientelist provincial elites, and the damage to the ANC has not been from the triumph of the reactionaries, but through its own self-inflicted decline, due to the depredations of factionalists in the fiefdoms that provincial governments and ANC structures conveniently provide, through the means of fiscal redistribution from the centre.

The most generous verdict on the ANC's dominance is that by incorporating such a diverse range of social and economic interests and containing them within one political structure, the ANC gave the country stability and defused all manner of destructive tensions at a time when peaceful and democratic outcomes were not guaranteed. Even if this were the case, the gains came at considerable cost for the movement itself and for the country it claimed to embody and lead. It created an unwieldy and amorphous entity that is relatively easy to capture (as Zuma proved in 2005–7) but virtually impossible thereafter to manage and lead in any meaningful senses of these terms. By dominating so much of the public sector it became the career avenue of choice both for the talented and the not so talented, as a shortcut to economic survival in those large areas of the country where there was minimal economic activity and to wealth in those parts where wealth was concentrated. The passage was very short indeed from fantasies of rule by selfless technocratic *apparatchiki* – Mbeki's 'new cadres' – to gangsters who would – literally – kill competitors for positions in the party and the lucrative government tenders that go with them.

Holding the centre

The context of post-apartheid politics as described so far might seem a recipe for instability. In fact, however, there were considerable resources out of which the ANC could construct a centre and it could do so in what was, at least in the beginning, a fairly supportive environment, in which it could manage the sources of ambiguity outlined above.

In the first place, the moral authority of the ANC did not exist only in its own corporate self-image. There were real resources of authority independent of the formal constitutional mandate conferred by the electorate (which was itself considerable in size and force). These rested principally on what might be loosely labelled the liberation dividend, but they were buttressed from other sources. The ANC was credited (not least by itself) with suffering, sacrifice and stamina in getting to negotiation and with skill, self-restraint and capacity to adapt once there. The Mandela dividend was an essential part of the liberation dividend but, especially within the ranks of its own supporters, this was never an entirely individual currency, always shared with a generation of leaders. Once granted, these qualities supplemented with technocracy seemed to many a good enough skill set to take into the tasks of government, especially given that the bar had not been set particularly high by the National Party, the ANC's predecessors in government. This moral authority was enough to severely undercut the potential of opposition and contribute to the self-serving myth of the moral self-sufficiency of the ANC, its capacity to self-correct and where that failed, to rely on the resources of the Constitution. Above all, it contributed to the assumption of the inevitability of ANC rule.

On this basis, the ANC in government set out to construct the centre of South African politics, envisaging three principal components: a modernist vision of inclusion; a corporatist bargain; and an approach to poverty, inequality and redress for past injustice, based on fiscal and asset redistribution.

Modernization

The modernist vision has been the most important since it was the broadest-based; virtually everybody accepted it, whether or not they understand how to get there. The other components of the centre are closely related to and indeed dependent on it. It is the belief in the inexorable, one-way march of modernization expressed in a prosaic, everyday vision of people in formal housing in an urban area, sustained by a skilled, formal-sector job, preferably in a large industrial concern and complemented by trade union membership. In these ways, rights-bearing citizenship is complemented by economic inclusion and industrial democracy.

Not only was this vision desirable for the material benefits and security it would bring but also for the benign forms of self-discipline it would encourage and in doing so, organize and give shape to people's lives. This social-democratic vision of social cohesion had no truck with the irrationalities of identity politics and the disorderly indiscipline of populism. However the tasks of the new democracy were to be defined – reconstruction, development, modernization, nation-building – they were to be the province of professionals. This required the demobilization of activism and the ascendancy of a new, professional political class. This was to be composed of elected representatives, technocratic advisers and policymakers (planners, social scientists, engineers, medical professionals) who were often committed activists as well. It would also deploy cadres who, whatever they lacked in skills, were assumed to have the political commitment to provide the politics of the will to keep up the momentum of modernization. Activism of the sort that so many of the new class had practised to get themselves to their positions of power and influence in the first place was now looked upon as a needless luxury and potentially a restraining shackle on the forward movement of progress.

Corporatism

The second component of the centre ground was corporatism. South Africa's version is a weak form of the principle of the organization of representation through socio-economic groups and is generally referred to in South Africa as social partnership. The main, formal corporatist institution, the National Economic Development and Labour Council (Nedlac), is no more than a supplement to the main form of representative government and its mandate is narrowly defined. It is made up of representatives of organized business, organized labour, community and social organizations and government. Essentially however, it is only the tripartite relationship between business, labour and government – sometimes referred to as the 'golden triangle' in the days when people believed in such things – that counts. Its goals are very vaguely defined: 'strive to promote the goals of economic growth, participation in economic decision-making and social equity', and its main purpose is to act as a bargaining chamber in which social and economic policy can be debated and if necessary modified with business and labour before being passed by parliament.

Social partnership was intended to fill two gaps in South Africa's emerging polity. First, the constitutional negotiations had not attempted to frame a compact on the economy. Such a thing was not possible. Who would have participated? Who would have underwritten and adjudicated it? What aspirant government would have voluntarily concluded an agreement that would have compromised in advance its freedom to make economic policy? Nevertheless, the ANC (or at least the economically literate parts of it), which was that aspirant government, knew that it was not free to make economic policy in a vacuum and Nedlac reflected tacit agreement between it, business and labour that if consensus on the substance of economic policy was not possible and would in any case infringe on the prerogatives of democratic government, at least some sort of compact on process was desirable.

The second gap in South African politics was that there was no party of any electoral substance that shared the essential outlooks of business. Business was in any case anxious that it might be seen as part of any opposition grouping, however loose, to a party with an overwhelming popular mandate. As a result, business largely disowned the DP in the early post-apartheid years, in public at least. This did not mean that business was apolitical. From the 1980s through to the conclusion of the transitional negotiations, it had been very political. Big business, especially banks and mining houses, had been very active, first in the broker's role of helping to bring the government and the ANC to the negotiating table and second in wooing a reluctant ANC (and defiant Alliance) away from commandist economic policies that were being abandoned with indecent haste in many other parts of the world that had previously inspired the liberation movement's economic policies (such as they were). In the changed circumstances of democracy, it chose privileged bargaining rights rather than the marketplace of politics, a choice that suited its own increasingly cautious and defensive stances and chimed with the ANC's preference for acting as an arbiter of interests from a lofty position above that marketplace.

Addressing poverty and inequality

The third essential for a stable centre was a settled approach to the legacy of poverty and racial inequality left by apartheid. The one that emerged was shaped by the market view of economic common sense to which the ANC (though not the Alliance) was partly converted in stages between 1990 and 1996. This was conventionally summed up in the folksy metaphor, 'growing the cake' rather than radically dividing it, on the assumption that the more radical the division, the more likely the returns available for distribution would shrink. The strategy sought to balance the imperative of redistribution of state provision of services, opportunities, income and wealth, in favour of the black majority, not only with the conventional market understanding of the requirements for economic growth but also with concerns for the sustainability of the negotiated settlement and generally for political stability. In concrete terms, fiscal redistribution was constrained by concerns for macroeconomic prudence, prompted among other things by fears of inflation, excessive government borrowing and counterproductive levels of taxation. Asset redistribution was constrained by the need to compensate, in the case of land by buying owners out with government support or in the case of equity in companies, by the expedient of creating new, donor-financed shares. As we have already seen, the Constitution was also a constraint, not so much in granting an unrestricted right to property but through the general conditions under which rights could be limited and the specific conditions under which expropriation of property would be allowed, which are comprehensive and detailed. The founding principle of the supremacy of the Constitution and the justiciable principle, which allows recourse to the courts in the event of alleged violation of its provisions, also give protection against populist redistributive measures.

The success of this threefold approach to building a stable centre depended on several things. It depended on managing down identity politics in order to avoid distraction from the secular agenda of economic growth and social cohesion. It also required capability and integrity from the new political class in and around government. For social partnership to contribute to a stable centre, all three components, business, labour and government (including, crucially, the ANC and Alliance out of which the government was formed), would have themselves to remain coherent and stable. Above all, the centre would not only have to produce dividends in the shape of economic growth, but the distribution of the dividends would have to be sufficiently inclusive to appear credible and legitimate. These were very challenging conditions to meet and, in order to meet them, all participants in the system would have to show capacities for adaptability and self-correction.

The dissolving map of South African politics

The requirements for progressive, inclusive and transformative modernization have proved elusive. Each, as pursued by ANC governments since 1994, has had its own internal contradictions and failure to make progress in any one of them has tended to undermine the others.

Managing racial politics

There is much less optimism now (in mid-2019) about the prospects of managing down the influence of race in identity politics through a combination of symbolic nation-building (largely abandoned), exercise of common citizenship, material improvement in black people's lives and the disciplines of legal sanction and naming and shaming. A somewhat banal explanation for this is frequently offered along the lines that 'the country has failed to have an honest conversation about race'; usually without offering any substantial clue as to how the honesty deficit can be redeemed, who should be talking about what and what the likely payoffs from increased honesty might be, once a shared understanding of increased honesty has emerged. There is also the likelihood that 'honesty' in this context might be a quick route to being named and shamed in a deteriorating atmosphere of public exchanges, driven as they are everywhere else by the enhanced capacities to insult and be offended (often simultaneously) that are provided by social media.

Explanations citing the frustration of black people at continuing inequality, poverty and exclusion are more intuitively appealing, although some of the most determined lobbying for more radical transformation comes from people who have already done very well out of the process so far. Specific policy failures, including for instance land reform, help to raise the temperature. However, the fact that inequality between blacks is now a larger component of total inequality than white–black inequality complicates the issue, increasing anger and alienation, without in any way robbing inequality of its racial overtones.

Many whites believe they have their own frustrations, stemming from the powerful contradictions of experiencing subjective feelings of powerlessness and, among the most solipsistic of them, even victimhood, while at the same time being quite unable to understand how powerful, privileged and compromised they remain in the eyes of most black people. Defensiveness at feeling that they are held responsible for all the ills of the present as well as of the past combines with resentment at the individual and societal side effects of affirmative action and BEE polices, more especially the unintended ones of public-service dysfunction, patronage and corruption. Perceived injustices and threats that affect specific groups of (usually Afrikaans-speaking) whites add to the sum of frustrations. These include pressures to downgrade the role of the Afrikaans language at traditionally Afrikaans universities and the vexed question of whether or not 'farm murders' should be treated as 'ordinary' crime in a notoriously crime-ridden society, or a special category of hate crime, a racist (or even in some extreme versions 'genocidal') revenge strategy against isolated white farmers and their families.

In an evolving context where social media can increasingly escalate minor incidents of racial tension or abuse to national scandals, it is especially difficult to generalize about the state of interpersonal race relations. Anecdotally, incidents of this kind increased around 2015 or rather, thanks to social media, they were highlighted in a way they had not been before. A more useful generalization may be to suggest that in the past, especially under Mbeki, the ANC leadership could keep a fairly tight rein on how to define and when and how to highlight and exploit racism. It has now lost the prerogative of control or, perhaps more accurately, the leadership has fractured. As a result, the use of race and racism to gain political leverage has metastasized to the point where it is a weapon in internal ANC struggles. A case in point is the way in which the SACP's decades-old mainstay of disapprobation, 'monopoly capitalism', abruptly mutated into 'white monopoly capitalism' in 2016–17, as the rallying cry of the populist faction of Zuma supporters.

Modernization and neo-traditionalism

The emergence of neo-traditionalism under Zuma also complicated the straightforward march of modernism envisaged by the first generation of post-apartheid ANC leaders. This does not mean that Zuma alone put tradition on the agenda. As we have already seen, the ANC's imperatives of coming to terms with actually existing South Africa and broadening its reach to rural areas led to a close relationship with traditional leaders and on both grounds a way of harmonizing neo-tradition with secular modern politics and laws had to be found. However, while modernists would have preferred a co-opted relationship with the forces of tradition and a place for them in the post-apartheid polity that was more token than real, the emergence of Zuma as president of the ANC and then in 2009 of the country considerably emboldened the chiefs (and kings). The Traditional Courts Bill, setting out what was effectively a parallel justice system to that of the Constitution, was first drafted in 2008. It met considerable pushback from modernists in the ANC and civil society on grounds of accountability, gender discrimination and lack of fit with the Constitution. Since 2008, the bill has been redrafted, withdrawn and returned. In March 2019, the bill was passed by the National Assembly but had not been dealt with by the second chamber (the National Council of Provinces) before the May 2019 election. The envisaged synchronization of tradition and the Constitution is likely to remain a source of continuing tensions between neo-tradition and modernity, whatever the fate of the legislation.[33]

The new political class

The second requirement for building a stable centre was the capability and integrity of the new political class. Given the determination of the ANC to fuse the party and the state, this class greatly overlapped the public service, government and party. However, it is important to bear in mind (especially concerning developments in Zuma's second administration) that it would be wrong to assume uniformity in this class. It was no monolith and by Zuma's later years in power, fragmentation between those who had some idea of public interest and service and those who did not was clearly visible. Under Mbeki, the idea of the developmental state was adopted as the bringer of rational, technocratic modernization and inclusive economic expansion. This highlights the first problem of the new political class: the failure to develop a professional bureaucracy in more than a few isolated patches.

This central aim of the new government was signalled from the beginning in unambiguous terms such as those of a presidential review commission on the reform and transformation of the public service (1999), which recommended 'creating a professional public service under professional leadership and within a professional ethic'.[34] The reader of many subsequent reports and reviews over the following two decades is struck by a strong sense of déjà vu at both diagnosis and prescriptions. The diagnostic reports of the National Planning Commission (NPC, 2011) detail the failure to foster professionalism (which had in any case been documented in academic studies and in the presidency's ten- and twenty-year reviews), and the National Development Plan (NDP) summarizes the findings, noting that unevenness in state capacity leads to uneven performance in local, provincial and national government:

> The uneven performance of the public service results from the interplay between a complex set of factors, including tensions in the political-administrative interface, instability of the administrative leadership, skills deficits, the erosion of accountability and authority, poor organisational design, inappropriate staffing and low staff morale. The weaknesses in capacity and performance are most serious in historically disadvantaged areas where state intervention is most needed to improve people's quality of life.[35]

The NDP's verdict is tactfully worded. Race is not the only thing that is difficult to have an honest conversation about in South Africa. 'Tensions in the political-administrative interface' means senior appointments affected by factionalism and patronage while 'inappropriate staffing' is probably a coded reference to cadre deployment and poorly executed affirmative action. 'Unevenness' is another coded reference, this time to the fact that there are islands of excellence in the South African public service, notably in the National Treasury and the Reserve Bank. However, to single out these institutions for praise would be provocative in ANC political circles, given the level of ideological and policy contest in the ANC and Alliance over the role of the Treasury and the Reserve Bank in economic policy. The success of these institutions is in no small measure due to their record of successfully harmonizing the imperatives of affirmative action with those of professionalism and the public interest, unlike most other public entities where redress measures have been applied as a cover for patronage. The excellence of the Treasury and the SARB is a truly diverse excellence. Official reports generally decline to make this specific causal link, but overall they do acknowledge that the generally poor condition of the public service is partly attributable to the employment of 'inadequately skilled and inexperienced people from previously marginalised groups' and the 'unintended consequences of hastily implemented affirmative action programmes'.[36]

In the various reports of the NPC and presidency the general drift is clear enough, although often couched in coded and circumlocutory ways. It is as well, however, to note some specifics.

For instance, in his State of the Nation address in 2011, Zuma announced, 'In the health service this year we will emphasise the appointment of appropriate and qualified personnel to the right positions. We need qualified heads of department, CPOs, district health officers and clinical health managers.'[37] It took seventeen years from the ANC's first assumption of office, along with many media scandals involving the appointment of unqualified hospital managers as a factor in needless deaths at public hospitals, for this recognition of the importance of professionalism to make its way into government policy. It took a further three years for minimum competence requirements and professional qualifications to be put in place, for university courses teaching them to be set up as well as for hospital CEO posts to be readvertised and one hundred of them (some without high school diplomas) to be replaced by candidates with professional qualifications.

Official acknowledgement of corruption in the public service tends to blame individual failings rather than systemic failure due to misguided policies. For instance, the background paper on the public service for the *Twenty Year Review* states, 'The prevalence of corruption in some departments can be traced to the moral bankruptcy and lack of professionalism in the case of some individuals.'[38] Citing the police, the public broadcaster, state departments and municipalities as places where 'nepotism, cronyism, clientelism and other related cases of misuse of public resources' had increased up to its publication in 2014, the presidency report found that these developments had 'resulted in the erosion of trust between the state and the electorate'.[39]

The project of modernization executed by a technocratic class of professionals also required political direction by a class of 'cadres' who would lead by example in both the machinery of government and the wider ANC. The cadre idea was one of the ANC's gleanings from the wider world of Marxist-Leninist jargon and communist-party practice. Central to ANC ideology, but woefully lacking in its practice, the cadre concept adopts wholesale the communist language ('resolute', 'bold', 'tireless', 'unselfish') and from the same source, the ideal of a new and higher form of political consciousness, rigorous discipline and exemplary behaviour. Especially under Mbeki, the philosophies of the 'new cadre' and the 'new person' were relentlessly touted in ANC documents and completely ignored by the movement's body of adherents, to provide a striking example of Mbeki's delusions.

Despite this, the ANC has persisted with the myth of the cadre, suggesting that far from Mbeki being an isolated case, the movement as a whole was subject to mass hallucination on the subject of cadres. At the 53rd ANC national conference in 2012, where Zuma was re-elected for a second term as ANC president, he declared that the next decade would be 'The Decade of the Cadre'. In marked contrast at the same conference, in his organizational report, the ANC secretary general Gwede Mantashe reported the 'virtual collapse' of discipline in the movement as a result of institutionalized factionalism.[40] Between them they provided further evidence of the ANC's existence in a territory beyond the borders of irony.

Four years later, at the ANC policy conference (which is a precursor to the five-yearly national elective conference held in December) the secretary general's discussion document was unsparing: 'internal strife and factional battles over power and resources define the movement'; there has been a 'shift away from societal concerns and the people's aspirations to control over state power and resources'. Indeed, perhaps in an intentional echo of the Mbeki-era jargon, far from producing exemplars of 'the new person',

> These circumstances have produced a new type of ANC leader and member who sees ill-discipline, divisions, factionalism and in-fighting as normal practices and necessary forms of political survival.[41]

The discussion document went on to observe that 'four years into the decade of the cadre' very little progress had been made.[42]

The failure of corporatism

Hopes that corporatism would provide more than a platform for adversarial but rule-bound and consultative coexistence between business and labour, with government holding the ring, were central to the prospects of stability. This was a logical outgrowth of the system of labour relations that had evolved after 1979, when black trade unions won a measure of freedom to organize legally, as well as the roles that business and labour had respectively played in the pre-negotiation and negotiation periods in the 1980s and 1990s. However, with the removal of apartheid and the advent of democracy allowing new partnerships, new ways of doing things and new positions to defend, social partnership fell short of the new government's expectations. One problem was that the South African version of corporatism evolved into what was effectively a stalemate in which business and labour could each defend their core interests: prudent macroeconomic policy for business and for the unions, the inviolability of the labour-law regime which was put in place after 1994 to guarantee extensive employment rights to workers. However, neither business nor labour could persuade or force the government to adopt its favoured recipe for economic growth. This was a kind of elite pact, which had the consequence of ruling out radical measures from either left or right to address the situation of the 20–38 per cent of South Africans who were unemployed over the period (depending on whether the strict or expanded definition was used).[43] Whether this was intended or unintended is a matter of conjecture.

Part of the problem was the close relationship between the ANC and Cosatu in the Tripartite Alliance. This formal partnership undermined the government's credibility as a good-faith arbiter in the eyes of business and contributed to a strong sense of entitlement on the part of Cosatu. This sense of entitlement mingled with a distrust of government on part of the unions that was greater than the misgivings of business and was more corrosive of the corporatist model. The grounds for this mistrust included tensions over the direction of economic policy and the clash between Cosatu's ambitions and the government's determination to be master of its own policy house. The government and the ANC also resented Cosatu's apparent belief that it should have extensive privileges of access from being embedded in the wider movement, yet retain a large measure of independence to be critical of it. On its side, Cosatu, not surprisingly given the ANC's history of incorporation and co-option, feared being swallowed whole and losing all independence. Cosatu's tendency (which it shared with the SACP) to regard its own leaders and members as politically more sophisticated, better organized and committed than those of the ANC did not help. To a certain extent, this self-perception was valid since the ANC greatly depended on union commitment to mobilize votes at election time. This did not help either, contributing to Cosatu's expectations of entitlement and its corporate sense of being taken for granted between elections. All in all, alliance relationships existed in a parallel universe to the social partnership model, which both complicated and overshadowed the corporatist relationships.

However, the main threat to the viability of a corporatist framework came from the lack of internal coherence exhibited by all social partners. This was not immediately apparent and took some time to develop, but by the end of the second post-apartheid decade it was obvious that business, labour and the government could not be regarded as the building blocks of the economy and society which would collectively support the constitutional order and the ANC government's vision of modernization and progress.

In the case of business, it is likely that the ANC's crude imaginings of the commanding heights of the economy controlled by sinister cabals of (white) capitalists caused the government to exaggerate greatly the coherence and collective agency of business. Even in an admittedly concentrated economy such as South Africa's, business is an activity, not an entity. It is an activity, moreover, that contains strong behavioural attributes of both competition and collusion. These universal qualities of business are greatly exacerbated in South Africa by racial divisions. There have been several attempts to harmonize business organizations into a single, coherent representative body; all of them have failed, mainly because of the perception by black business and professional groups that their interests would be far better served by elite racially exclusive bodies with privileged access to the ruling party.

This does not mean that there is a strict black/white division. The fault line is rather between 'mainstream' corporate business, which is increasing racially diverse, and exclusively black organizations in which the definition of 'business' for purposes of membership is quite elastic and includes members of the professions and the higher reaches of state-owned enterprises. However, the division is real enough for the politics of patronage and state capture, which were increasingly exposed during Zuma's second term as state president, to be perceived frequently as a contest for control of the economy between two groups of capitalists. These can be labelled according to taste as 'white monopoly capital' (or mainstream business, irrespective of the race of its owners and managers) and insurgent black capital (or crony capital linked to the Zuma faction). Irrespective of how the divisions are perceived, however, it is clear that business has fragmented to the extent that any delusions about its potential to play a role in corporatist relationships are clearly exposed.

Fragmentation and conflict that is often violent have marked the decline of organized labour from a position in the immediate aftermath of the 1994 election where it appeared poised to play a pivotal role in post-apartheid politics. At this point, 'organized labour' effectively meant Cosatu, which, until it expelled its largest affiliate the National Union of Metalworkers of South Africa (NUMSA) in November 2014, accounted for about 60 per cent of the 3 million trade union members in South Africa. Through most of the period there were three other substantial federations, but Cosatu has been the only one with presence and influence in national politics. This has been by virtue of its numbers, its closeness to the ANC and the way labour legislation favours large numbers (in granting exclusive bargaining rights for instance). Cosatu's strong initial position, which was bestowed by its roles in the liberation struggle and the negotiation process, was rewarded with a comprehensive new legislative regime for labour relations that strongly emphasized worker rights. However, virtually from the beginning, decay, which hollowed out Cosatu and some of its member unions, began to take hold. Many of the generation that founded Cosatu and saw it through struggle and government repression left to go into government or business, the latter either to mainstream corporate jobs or to develop investment vehicles spun off from the unions themselves or, like National Union of Mineworker (NUM) founding general secretary Cyril Ramaphosa, to take advantage of politically connected BEE deals. Slower to take effect, but even more enervating, was the bureaucratization of the shop steward level. As part of the new labour regime, unions had won salaries and benefits (for instance, cars and mobile phones) for shop stewards and other union managers paid for by employers. These were supplemented by rake-offs from funeral insurance agents, payday lenders, mobile phone companies and other businesses eager to get preferential access to union members. These developments had two effects: they inserted distance between officials and workers, and they made elective positions sufficiently desirable for factionalism, patronage and at times violence (including assassination) to mark competition for office.

These largely subterranean developments were exacerbated by the visible politics of Cosatu, such as the tensions between being embedded within and independent from the ANC, as well as a long-running war of attrition between the Cosatu leadership and Mbeki over the latter's macroeconomic policy. Dissent and disaffection culminated in what turned out to be Cosatu's disastrous choice of playing a high-profile role in ousting Mbeki and helping drive Zuma's ascent to the presidencies of the ANC and then the country.

The combination of internal decay and outward political confusion was a powerful one and when it reached a critical point, from about 2010 onwards, the results were swift and drastic, centring on Cosatu's biggest affiliates, NUM and NUMSA. Another casualty was Zwelinzima Vavi, Cosatu's general secretary (1999–2015), who went from being Zuma's most vociferous champion in his struggle with Mbeki to becoming his most vocal critic.

The NUM was one of the unions worst affected by growing rank-and-file disenchantment with officials who were preoccupied with self-advancement and ANC politics and were thereby perceived to have lost militancy on the members' behalf. An insurgent, militant and fiercely populist union, the Association of Mineworkers and Construction Union (AMCU), organized increasingly large numbers of mineworkers, especially in the platinum sector. Violent competition with the NUM led to the wildcat strike (which was not led however by AMCU) at a Lonmin mine and the violence that saw forty-four deaths, thirty-four of them striking workers shot dead by police at Marikana on 16 August 2012. AMCU went on to lead the longest strike in South African history (January to June 2014), again on the platinum belt.

NUMSA, representing mainly workers in manufacturing and especially in motor manufacturing, was not only critical of Zuma but also of Cosatu's relationship with the ANC. Having resolved not to support the ANC in the 2014 general election and criticizing the Tripartite Alliance across a wide range of issues, NUMSA was expelled from Cosatu in November 2014, closely followed by Vavi in May 2015.

Declining membership due to competition from other unions and job losses in mining severely dented the credibility of the NUM, which had been the backbone of Cosatu since the federation's founding in 1979. Declining membership also meant declining resources, which meant sharpening the competition for office, which in turn helped set in motion the decline in the first place. To this was added ideological confusion stemming from AMCU's militant but non-aligned populism and NUMSA's ultra-leftism, which, among other things, put it at loggerheads with the SACP. The decline of the NUM and the expulsion of NUMSA confirmed and accelerated two related trends that were already in evidence – an increased weighting in Cosatu for public-sector unions and deeper involvement in ANC factional politics, plus shrinking space for a distinctive labour presence in the Alliance. Along with these symptoms of decline, the years 2010–15 put an end to any lingering belief that a unified, self-directed labour movement, close to but independent from the ANC, could be one of the building blocks of a stable centre in South African politics and society.

The continuing vexations of racial politics, coupled with the emergence of neo-traditionalism, the dysfunctions of the political class and the failure of corporatism to anchor the politics of policymaking across South Africa's various divides, all contributed to the failure of modernization to provide a stable centre for nation-building, growth and development. Together, these features of South Africa's recent history provide a necessary but not sufficient explanation for the dissolution of the familiar landmarks that were hopefully erected in the first post-apartheid decade. However, combining with all of them in complex relationships of cause and effect was the failure to grow the economy fast enough and consistently enough, as well as to share participation credibly enough to reproduce legitimacy for the evolving status quo.

Economic stagnation

Average growth between 2000 and 2016 was well below the often-quoted figure of 5 per cent, said to be necessary if South Africa was to deal decisively with poverty and inequality. For instance, the NDP states, 'Transforming the economy and creating expansion for job creation means that the rate of economic growth needs to exceed five per cent a year on average.'[44] From 2000 to 2016, South Africa's growth rate averaged 2.95 per cent; in three of these years (2005–7, at the height of the commodities boom), the rate exceeded 5 per cent; in each of the three years to 2016, it was below 2 per cent.[45] The shortcomings of past growth and the challenges of the future are best captured in the figures for inequality and unemployment.

According to the World Bank, 'The poorest 20 per cent of South Africa's population consume less than 3 per cent of total expenditure while the wealthiest 20 per cent consume 65 per cent.'[46]

From 2000 to 2017, South Africa's strict unemployment rate averaged 25.41 per cent, with a high of 31.20 in the first quarter of 2003 and a low of 21.50 per cent in the fourth quarter of 2008. Unemployment, measured by the expanded definition, was over 40 per cent between mid-2001 and mid-2004 and has been in the mid-thirties at all other times since 2000. According to a study by University of KwaZulu-Natal (UKZN) researchers, there is little to distinguish work-seekers (strict definition) from discouraged work-seekers (expanded definition), and the expanded definition gives a more meaningful picture of the South African situation. In the fourth quarter of 2016, unemployment for the whole labour force was 26.5 per cent, while for young people it was more than 10 per cent above that at 37.1 per cent. In absolute figures, there were 8.9 million unemployed by the expanded measure at the end of 2016, nearly three unemployed people for each member of a trade union.[47] In its Quarterly Labour Force Survey for the first quarter of 2019, the government statistics office calculated the unemployment rate at 27.6 per cent and the expanded rate at 38 per cent.[48]

Despite these brute figures of inequality and unemployment, it is undeniable that there is, as the ANC insists, a 'good story' to be told about post-apartheid South Africa: black people's shares of wealth, income, consumption and employment at all levels have risen, despite the high levels of both inter- and intraracial inequality. More than twice as many people had university degrees in 2011 than in 1995: more black people than white graduate from university every year. However, the relationship between employment and education and skills levels reveals that the good story is an 'insider' story of people with skills and social capital (including political connections), leaving many excluded. In the last quarter of 2015, 77 per cent of the 4.2 million adults who had tertiary qualifications were employed; 52 per cent of the 9.6 million adults whose highest qualification was a high school diploma were employed; and 34 per cent of 22 million adults who had not completed high school had jobs.[49]

An unforgiving context

There was a wide-open opportunity for a transformative leader in what for a period was dubbed 'the New South Africa'. The challenges of dealing with the legacies of colonialism and apartheid, as well as of the bitter struggles against them, were huge. But the resources available to the country's new leadership were also substantial. They included repeat large majorities won fairly in open elections, conferring the mandate to preside over a new polity regulated by a widely acclaimed rights-based and justiciable constitution, at the head of a movement that had won broad-based respect for its tenacity and bravery in the anti-apartheid struggle and its shrewd and well-timed conversion to constitutional democracy.

The context was unforgiving, however. Expectations were high and trust was low both inside the ANC and in the wider polity. The accumulated myths and practices of the ANC closed down space for leaders: the imperatives of consensual and collective leadership and initiative from below; the iron law of unity at all costs and the straitjacket of continuity with past pieties. Electoral success meant that there was no goad with which a leader might prod the faithful in the direction of change or even adaptation to the realities of governance and the global economy. This meant that there was very little space for a leader to craft a distinctive vision; what is more, the ANC's history and culture multiplied the tendencies, groupings and factions that would have to be brought on board to any leadership initiative.

As a result, the prospects of a transformative leader giving fresh meaning and purpose to and changing the direction of the ANC were greatly diminished. Yet, the ANC could not simply rest on the laurels of the past. When Mbeki succeeded to the leadership of party and country, his was not the kind of temperament that could dodge the challenge of creating coherence out of the broad church, which was in reality a sprawling and unmanageable accretion of syncretic theologies. The choice was to accept this challenge or to live with and maybe exploit the incoherence. Mbeki chose one way and Zuma the other.

Part Two

Leadership in the haunted present: Legacies and lost leaders

3

Possession and betrayal: Mandela's ambiguous legacy in South African politics

In 2009 when Nelson Mandela still had four years to live, Tom Lodge, author of a 'critical life' of Mandela,[1] wrote, 'It won't be long before the first fully revisionist biographies of Mandela appear and they will emphasise his political shortcomings and moral lapses.'[2] This was a reasonable prediction, but ten years later and six years after Mandela's death we are still waiting. In fairness, as Lodge himself acknowledges, much of what could be described as revisionism is already priced into existing versions of his life (including, as its title suggests, Lodge's own), thanks in large part to the 'confessional quality of (Mandela's) autobiographical testimony'.[3]

David Smith's overtly revisionist treatment (2010) is confined to the 'Young Mandela'.[4] In the assessment of one critic, 'for all its revisionist impulses' it 'simply deems to reproduce a familiar narrative trajectory – one that was essentially created by Mandela himself – and ends up leaving Mandela's iconic status intact'.[5]

What passes for revisionism on Mandela's legacy today has often been intellectually scanty and largely confined to posturing in the political marketplace. However, although so far there has been little to learn about Mandela himself, the contests surrounding his legacy are instructive about South Africa's political culture in general and about attitudes to leadership in particular.

There has been an ebb and flow to the Mandela legacy, according to the political needs of the moment, the audience and whichever advocate or critic is addressing it. However, two themes have dominated these contests: possession and betrayal. In some instances, the two are even combined.

One such instance is the Democratic Alliance's (DA's) attempted 'appropriation' of the Mandela legacy. This line of attack is best seen in two television campaign advertisements, flighted before the municipal elections in 2016.[6] In one, a young (probably single) African mother with an aspirational profile goes to vote, first shaking off the cynicism of a male neighbour about the value of voting, then ignoring the attempts of a group of ANC activists (again male) to intimidate and bully her. In the booth she hears the voice of Nelson Mandela expressing the dream of peace and work for all, whereupon she puts her cross in the DA box as the vehicle for realizing the dream she shares with the former president.

The second advertisement is a straightforward face-the-camera mini speech by DA leader Mmusi Maimane ('the Obama of Soweto'), dressed in post-Mandela, neo-African chic and putting forward the DA line that under Zuma the ANC grossly betrayed Mandela's values. The ad ends with the punch line, 'Honour Madiba's dream: Vote DA' (which was also the campaign poster strapline). Doubtless with tactical intent, the DA neatly deployed two of the most evocative cultural forces in South African politics, possession of Madiba magic and the idea of betrayal, both of them summarized economically in messages lasting, respectively, one and two minutes.

Unsurprisingly, the DA's raid on what the ANC regarded as its exclusive property was controversial. This was especially true since the DA had previous form in this area. In early 2013, there had been a bitter spat between the parties over the DA's use of photographs that showed Mandela with the DA's own icon, the late Helen Suzman, the liberal anti-apartheid parliamentarian and campaigner. The purpose of this juxtaposition was to counteract the ANC's crude racial stereotyping of the DA's 'whiteness' and its equally crude denigration of the role played by the opposition party's liberal forebears in opposing apartheid.

In reaction to the DA's campaign ads, the ANC national spokesman said, 'The DA displays a shocking form of arrogance and presumptuousness in claiming Nelson Mandela would endorse its organisation were he still alive', citing a quotation from Mandela (in 2000) that called the DA a party of 'white bosses and black stooges'.[7] The DA did not in fact claim that Mandela would endorse it; only that it now represented the values that Mandela stood for in life better than the current incarnation of his own party.

The ANC was not alone in its condemnation: The Royal House of Mandela said that the use of Madiba's voice was an attempt to 'lend credibility to a party which has made the preservation of white privilege its reason to exist'.[8] Less partisan commentaries on the affair bemoaned that the DA and the ANC were involved in 'a mighty battle for control of the past' which deprived South Africa of a vision for the future[9] and that voters should cast their votes based on who is best able to run municipalities: 'We should be making informed choices based on current conditions and not be coerced by sentimentality or blackmail.'[10]

Even without the DA's audacious raid on its territory, the ANC has struggled to come to terms with the Mandela phenomenon, both in his lifetime and with his legacy, and the struggle for possession is not only between the ANC and its rivals. It has become a struggle for possession of the legacy between the ANC and Mandela himself. This is because Mandela was an extreme case of quite a familiar phenomenon in democratic politics: that is, the leader who runs ahead of his or her party because he or she is more popular and more trusted by voters and particularly by the uncommitted than the party itself.

This was an enormous asset to the ANC and one that its leadership in exile and on the ground consciously cultivated. However, it set up tensions between the shared Mandela and the partisan Mandela:

> To the partisan eye he can be viewed as the distillation of all the ANC stood for; in the shared political arena he could be seen as a shining example of all it lamentably failed to be.[11]

Moreover, the ANC had reason to suspect the grounds for adulation of the shared Mandela; as with most things perceived by the ANC, there was a pronounced racial edge to this suspicion, though not without justification in this case. Although the shared Mandela broadened the base of the ANC's legitimacy at the crucial time of negotiation and the first ANC government, the effect was likely to be temporary and fragile. He was a living refutation of Afropessimism, an African even Afropessimists could trust and maybe even revere. However, it was only too clear that outside the ranks of the ANC itself, especially among whites and in the wider world, this was perceived to be *in spite of*, not *because of* his being an African nationalist. There was every good reason to suspect that the ANC's credibility dividend might diminish greatly with his departure from office then vanish altogether with his death. The extraordinary number of articles, columns and risk assessments commissioned to speculate on the 'When Mandela Goes' issue would have confirmed this to ANC leaders and followers and was doubtless a great cause of resentment to them. It did not help much that a very large majority of these assessments were cautiously optimistic about South Africa's prospects, largely dismissing speculative and scaremongering comparisons with Zimbabwe.[12]

One of the ways in which this resentment was expressed was in the form of counter-attack along the lines of 'the ANC created Mandela'. One particularly clear example of this was in an article written by Winnie Madikizela-Mandela in 2007. Emphasizing the need to honour Oliver Tambo, the ANC's last president in exile and Mandela's predecessor, she wrote,

> Of course he (i.e. Tambo) created Mandela ... It is not actually the men and women who sat in prison as such who made our country what it is

today. It was the sustained campaign and a deliberate decision was made
that Mandela would be used as a symbol of the ANC internationally, so
that people could focus on the ANC through this particular name …
The ANC has always been about the collectivity [*sic*] and centrality of
the leadership of the people's popular movement. As such, there ought
not to be individualism, which leads to autocracy. The masses will always
remove such a leader in whatever manner necessary, no matter how long
it takes them.[13]

At one level, this is no more than a version of the truth or perhaps a half-
truth. The ANC did indeed invest heavily in 'making' Mandela, though
perhaps through personal animus, Madikizela-Mandela goes far too far in
diminishing Mandela's own stature and contribution. The article, by virtue of
being written at all, signals the ANC's unease at how its 'creation' took on a
life of its own and threatened to dwarf its creator, but it does not address the
causes of this tension. Jacob Zuma provided more insight into this with his
response to the question, 'What was the most important part of Mandela's
legacy?' in the course of an interview on a Chinese television station.[14]

President Mandela was made by the ANC to be great – that is very
important to know. It is the ANC that is much, much more important
to many of us, including President Mandela. He was part of shaping the
policies of the ANC and the ANC has not changed policy. So its leaders
will always be there. But times are moving and Mandela's legacy will
always be remembered; not just Mandela alone … Oliver Tambo and
others. And we are sticking to what Mandela practised as the policy he
believed in and he believed in until … he departed this world.

Zuma's words point to the ANC's need to treat leadership – along with all
other aspects of its existence – in terms of seamless continuity. There is no
place for outliers, for the extraordinary or fresh starts. Past, present and an
unbroken mission into the future have to be in harmony if the unthinkable –
loss of power – is to be avoided. This is why all significant ANC occasions
and major speeches begin with a ritual recitation of ancestral leaders and
patrimony, reminiscent of the Old Testament in its insistence and probably
meant to carry the same liturgical quality and weight.[15] Another source of
this obsession with continuity is the ANC's self-image of a community of the
faithful with ties and obligations analogous to family and kinship. However,
it is also a party that in an electoral democracy has to reach out beyond the
boundaries of that community for legitimacy and support. A constant failure
of its organizational self-understanding is to underestimate the significance

for consistency and credibility of how these boundaries shift, as they expand and contract according to the movement's perception of the needs of the moment and the electorate's perception of the politics of the day. The shifts are in turn shaped by external events (the most obvious being elections) and the internal dynamics of Alliance and party, including ideology and competition between patronage-based factions.

Needless to say, this dual personality and the shifting boundaries between its two component parts are confusing for the ANC's interlocutors, opponents and interpreters. Mandela was able to straddle the duality between family of the faithful and bidder for support across the whole population, but since his departure, hopeless confusion between the ANC's two personalities has been a significant contributor to lack of trust in it.

These were not the only tensions surrounding Mandela's leadership and his legacy, about which there was enough ambiguity to add to the contentiousness. Some of the other tensions are part of the stock in trade of democratic politics everywhere, others more specific to the organizational culture of the ANC. When he was active, his importance as a vote bringer gave him a measure of autonomy and leverage unwelcome to other ambitious senior figures – a situation not unknown in other democracies. When he was gone – as the DA's ambush marketing made clear – his legacy could be used to hold his political home to account, although the DA might reasonably point out that such tactics would be useless if the ANC had remained without reproach when it came to being faithful to Mandela's values. The results of the 2016 municipal elections, in which the ANC lost control of three major metropolitan governments, suggest that many voters saw that it had not. Last, as Madikizela-Mandela's references to 'individualism', 'autocracy' and 'collectivity and centrality of leadership' illustrate (above), Nelson Mandela was very hard to assimilate into the organization's organizational mythology.

Tensions over Mandela's legacy have also followed themes of betrayal. This is not surprising since betrayal is part of the genetic makeup of contemporary South African politics. This is because for the last half-century South African history has proceeded from unrealizable absolutes (including Grand Apartheid and the National Democratic Revolution (NDR)) to ambiguous compromises through processes which, even when they emerged into a semblance of normality in semi-open negotiation after 1990, never lost the characteristics of clandestine warfare that had dominated liberation struggles since at least 1960. Even after complete normality was ostensibly achieved with the 1994 election and the formal passing of the Constitution through parliament in 1996, the shadow politics of security and intelligence agencies went to ground only temporarily, to re-emerge under Mbeki and Zuma.

Part of the reason why, despite the transition to constitutional democracy, these qualities have not yet been completely shaken off is the legacy of the last two decades of the liberation struggle when the ANC was thoroughly penetrated by double agents. For many of the first generation of the ANC that went into government, this was a defining feature of their political experience, whether, like Zuma, they were tasked with combating subversion inside the movement or whether they themselves had been accused in what was effectively an ongoing witch-hunt.

It is not surprising, then, that to this day one of the movement's stock reflexes is paranoia, whether real or simulated, about conspiracies against it, as a useful expedient for explaining away failure or fending off embarrassing criticism and investigative revelations in the media. Nor is it unexpected that compromised state security agencies and private security firms are increasingly used to spy on and destabilize rivals within the movement as well as other perceived enemies.

The absolutist heritage that was so much compromised by the negotiations and settlement came from both Afrikaner and African nationalists (both ANC and Black Consciousness) as well as from the socialist elements of the ANC Alliance.

The Afrikaner nationalists were schooled in apartheid ideology as a logical system of absolute classifications, exclusions and prohibitions; the long drawn-out and improvised retreat from this was attended throughout by suspicions and fears of betrayal, which survived apartheid's endgame into the new dispensation.

The Freedom Charter can be read in absolutist terms thanks to the simplicity of its mobilizing ideas. But the gaps between the simple rallying calls and the document's ambiguity as a specific platform for reordering society, the economy and the polity, all provide fertile grounds for feelings of betrayal, based on different interpretations of what constitutes fulfilment of the charter's pledges. Much the same can be said for the documents inspired by Marxism-Leninism, which provided guidance on strategy and tactics in pursuit of the NDR, another foundational document, which was incorporated into ANC ideology in 1969 and, in various updated iterations, remains the guiding vision to this day. At its simplest, the (mainly young) people who fought and made sacrifices during the 1980s were inspired more by the vision of insurrection, revolutionary seizure of power, destruction of the white state and overthrow of capitalism that was envisaged in ANC and South African Communist Party (SACP) documents than by the liberal constitutional state that emerged from negotiations in the 1990s.

Against this background, it is not surprising that betrayal haunts the South African polity. What is surprising is that it has so far made little inroads into the Mandela legacy. This is not for want of warnings that it would. 'By the late 1990s', according to historian Colin Bundy, one of the reasons that the powerful metaphor of the 'rainbow nation of God' had begun to fade was that while black Africans were proud of Nelson Mandela, they felt that 'he was too accommodating of white fears and not attentive enough to the scar tissue of apartheid's victims'.[16] If this were the case, there were no outward signs of any political significance as he left office. It was at the time of his death in 2013, by which time a new generation had entered extra-parliamentary politics, that the subject began to be canvassed. In two separate obituary pieces in the *New York Times* and the *Guardian*, prizewinning South African novelist Zakes Mda noted that there are 'black youngsters who are disillusioned with the "new" South Africa and hold Mandela personally responsible for betraying the revolution'.[17]

He added, 'There is an increasingly vocal segment of black South Africans who feel that Mandela sold out the liberation struggle to white interests'.[18] Bundy took up the issue again eighteen months later, quoting Mda and adding a quotation from a black South African journalist who reported feelings that 'Mandela was too preoccupied with white fears and not enough with black grievances and expectations of a better life ... from the outset, Mandela was too timorous'.[19]

Mda detects these discontents in young people expressing themselves on social media. Bundy quotes the Azanian People's Organisation (Azapo) Youth League president and the Pan Africanist Youth Congress (PAC Youth) spokesman, 'castigating' Mandela as a sellout and demanding that he apologize to black people. To add some perspective, however, in the 2014 general election, Azapo gained 0.11 per cent of the votes and the PAC 0.21 per cent.

What, in the light of this derisory evidence, should we make of the 'blame Mandela movement'? Not a great deal according to Mda and Bundy themselves. The former says that it is not by any means a groundswell (though vehement enough to warrant attention) and that the majority of blacks still 'adore' Mandela. Bundy calls the critique, 'poor historical explanation', personalizing a 'much more complex and plural accommodation by the ANC with capital'.

Why, then, should heavyweight commentators go out of their way to draw attention to such an insignificant phenomenon and give it column inches? Part of the reason probably lies in the anticipation – with excitement by some and apprehension by others – of the full entry into the political marketplace of a post-apartheid generation of young people, which is customarily dubbed with the evocative label, 'the born frees'.

Both historically and in the present, young people occupy an apparently disproportionate place in the dynamics of South African politics and, as a result, in the calculations of leaders. This is not surprising since young people loom large demographically. The census of 2011 recorded that 28.9 per cent of South Africans were aged between fifteen years and thirty-four years (the official definition of 'youth') and another 29.6 per cent were between zero and fourteen.[20] Young people are disproportionately affected by unemployment – the expanded unemployment rate for them is 48 per cent,[21] 10 per cent more than that measure for the general population – as well as by death from disease, especially HIV/AIDS, and from interpersonal violence (young men in particular).

In the mythology of the liberation struggle, great emphasis is laid upon the momentum generated by young people at crucial turning points: Nelson Mandela and his colleagues in the ANC Youth League (ANCYL) who, in the late 1940s, converted the ANC to a more radical programme of action; the young people who rose in Soweto in 1976 and, while many of them made the supreme sacrifice, shamed their elders as passive and acquiescent in their own oppression; they were followed by the 'young lions' who were the shock troops of the township rebellions in the 1980s. With the achievement of democracy, the impact of young people became more diffuse: inside the ANC, the ANCYL acquired a role as kingmaker for Mbeki and Zuma and within limits could express both militancy and lack of deference. Outside the boundaries of party discipline, the spectre of large numbers of unemployed, poorly educated, vulnerable and unorganized young people, concentrated in areas of high deprivation, was seen within the ranks of the new governing class and in wider society as a threat to the new order. For a time in the 1990s it was the subject of what some saw as a moral panic, a potential source of unfocused (indeed anarchic) destabilization.[22] Having subsided somewhat in the decade of (comparatively) healthy growth and the expansion of higher education in the 2000s, this sense of impending instability has returned, sharpened by the uncertainty of where the post-apartheid generation's political allegiances will lie and whether they will fit into or break the political patterns that were assembled, for the most part by the ANC, over the past twenty years. Such uncertainties have been multiplied by the emergence of the Economic Freedom Fighters (EFF) and the student-based 'Fallist' movement.[23]

Another possible reason why commentators have been quick to respond to signs that the Mandela legacy is being undermined by accusations of betrayal, no matter how fleeting, is that Mandela's political relationship to young people has been equivocal and in some respects ironic. He went from being the firebrand young radical who defied his more cautious elders in the

1940s to the austere patriarch who lectured the young lions on the need for discipline and in 1990 ordered the young militants who were prosecuting the war against Buthelezi's Inkatha in KwaZulu-Natal to 'Take your guns and knives and pangas and throw them into the sea'.[24] In the historical context of nationalist movements everywhere in the world, this is in fact a perfectly predictable trajectory and if it is ironic, it is only superficially so. However, knowledge of history beyond the parochial and an understanding of irony are both relatively rare commodities in today's South Africa.

Perhaps what the issue of betrayal and legacy illustrates most is the tendency of South Africans to overinvest in leaders, to fail to take into account the historical context in which they were working and to personalize blame when hopes and dreams collide with reality and are thwarted. Certainly there is an implicit consensus of this sort among commentators who have reacted to the alleged 'blame Mandela' phenomenon.[25] From this perspective, Mandela's 'appeasement' of whites should be seen in terms of the unlikelihood of any complete military and political victory for the ANC in the 1990s (and beyond) and the shared responsibility of a whole generation of ANC leaders for the negotiations, including Mbeki and Zuma for the early period and later Cyril Ramaphosa.

Other points might be added here. It is never very clear whether those who accuse Mandela of selling out would have had the ANC carry on the struggle to victory without negotiation, or whether negotiations should have been conducted differently. What kind of tactics? What kind of struggle? How much destruction would be acceptable to be able to dictate final terms to whites and avoid 'sellout'? Since a fair number of the accusers (to judge from quoted examples) were not yet born when the struggle was at its height in the 1980s, this does not add to their credibility. It is in any case difficult to frame any kind of meaningful debate on 'sellout' because where the ANC was insistent on what would replace apartheid (the Freedom Charter), it was and remains vague on what the charter actually means as well as opaque and convoluted about how to realize its promise (the NDR, Strategy and Tactics documents). In addition, one part of the Alliance can define a set of goals that another can deny and contest. As a result, the questions of who sold out what, when, and to whom are very difficult to address. Or at least they would be if anyone showed the inclination to tackle them at a level beyond labels and slogans.

In addition, these versions of the sellout argument ignore motivation – why did Mandela betray the revolution? And although it is largely about how whites got off lightly, it is notably unforthcoming, apart from the special (and extremely complicated) case of land, on the extent to which whites should be dispossessed, by what mechanisms and with what likely effects for good or ill. The likelihood is that no one who espouses the sellout position is remotely interested in these questions. That it is an emotional spasm rather than a considered political position does not, however, mean that it is irrelevant.

If there is a temptation to write off at least some of the legacy/betrayal issue as sloganeering by politically immature lightweights, the case of Julius Malema and the EFF is another matter. The EFF won 6.4 per cent in its first electoral contest (the 2014 general election), 8.3 per cent in the 2016 municipal elections (11 per cent in Johannesburg) and 10.79 per cent in the May 2019 general election. It plays a serious (if at times disruptive) role in parliament and in municipal government. If there is something in the *zeitgeist*, Malema is a better harbinger of it than the near-anonymous young people on social media. Addressing the Oxford Union in December 2015, he is quoted as saying,

> The deviation from the Freedom Charter was the beginning of selling out of the revolution. When Mandela returned from prison he got separated from Winnie Mandela and went to stay in the house of a rich white man, he was looked after by the Oppenheimers, Mandela used to attend these club meetings of those white men who owned the South African economy … The Nelson we celebrate now is a stage-managed Mandela who compromised the principles of the revolution, which are captured in the Freedom Charter.[26]

On his return however and in the face of criticism from many quarters, he backtracked, saying, 'A collective of the ANC compromised the Freedom Charter', rather than Mandela alone.[27] Mandela's role, according to Malema, was no more than that of an individual who had grown old and tired in the struggle and handed the responsibility on to the younger generation, represented by Malema himself.

The betrayal thesis has a much longer pedigree than recent dabblings on social media would suggest. Indeed, it has been the major preoccupation of the South African Left throughout virtually all of the post-apartheid period, both inside the Alliance (Cosatu and the SACP) as well as in supporting and ancillary forms, mainly academic. The focus has been less on Mandela and more on Mbeki. As we shall see, one of the defining themes of the Mbeki presidency, as well as the major cause of his downfall, was the politics of assault and counterattack between him and the Alliance Left over macroeconomic policy. This version of betrayal differs from the jejune populism and racial nationalism, discussed above, in lacking the latter's pronounced racial dimension and emphasis on dispossession. The 'fatal compromises', 'Faustian pacts' and 'elite bargains' that are the stock in trade of the leftist version are not in favour of 'whites' but of 'capital'. This keeps the Left's discourse precariously within the ANC/SACP commitment to non-racialism, though it is likely that few whites are impressed by this conceptual and semantic concession.

The academic writings that underpin this discourse are quite specific about what was given away in the decade between the unbanning of the ANC and the end of Mandela's administration.[28] Markers of the devil's pact include commitments to wholesale nationalization abandoned; a wealth tax on the 'super rich' not imposed; apartheid-era debt not cancelled; globalized free trade enthusiastically embraced; listing abroad by major South African corporations condoned; and the independence and inflation targeting mandate of the South African Reserve Bank (SARB) enshrined in the Constitution.[29] These were the overtures: the denouement was the adoption of the growth, employment and redistribution (GEAR package of measures that put South Africa firmly on the road of macroeconomic orthodoxy). While there is broad consensus on the left as to what the devil's pact consisted of, there is less clarity on the 'how' and 'why' of its conclusion. One version is that the ANC succumbed to a kind of 'project fear' on the part of local and multinational business and international finance institutions (IFIs). A racy iteration of this comes from Ronnie Kasrils, former underground guerrilla, senior SACP leader and deputy minister of defence in Mandela's administration.[30] Kasrils sees the evolution of ANC economic policy as a continuation of the liberation struggle and the war in the shadows. In 1993, the long-hatched strategies of business

> were crystallising in secret late night discussions at the Development Bank of South Africa. Present were South Africa's mineral and energy leaders, the bosses of US and British companies with a presence in South Africa and young ANC economists schooled in Western economics. They were reporting to Mandela and were either outwitted or frightened into submission by hints of the dire consequences for South Africa should an ANC government prevail with what were considered ruinous economic policies.[31]

It is worth quoting Kasrils at length because it is a version that has gained considerable traction from his colourful personality and large (for South Africa) sales of his autobiography and because it is typical across the demotic versions of the betrayal thesis, not only in its interpretation but also in its counter prescriptions. These amount to a combination, not untypical across the South African Left, of South African exceptionalism and the politics of faith and the will, couched in florid rhetoric. In Kasrils's words, 'We had lost faith in the ability of our revolutionary masses to overcome all obstacles,' as well as faith in the ability to defy the pressures of global capitalism, 'because the world could not have done without our vast reserves of minerals'.[32] It is also a leading example of the 'shared betrayal' rather than personalized version; a whole cohort of ANC leaders, including Kasrils himself, is implicated in what is effectively his generational *mea culpa*.

Other more academic variants variously attribute the devil's pact to the ANC's tendency to concentrate on political negotiations at the expense of 'technical' economic matters, which they left to 'experts' and which their leaders were ill-equipped in any case to deal with. This led to the ANC being outmanoeuvred as a consequence. Simple inattention ('we took our eye off the ball', according to Jeremy Cronin, cabinet minister and deputy secretary general of the SACP[33]) is another explanation, as is failure in the culminating years of the struggle to assess what the slogans of the Freedom Charter, not to mention what the content of the 'smash capitalism and state structures' school of economic thought might actually mean from the vantage point of a new government taking power in actually existing South Africa.[34]

Whether it was naivety or 'chickening out' (Kasrils) or 'taking our eye off the ball' (Cronin) that was to blame, only rarely does one other possible explanation get an airing, that Mandela and his advisers were genuinely convinced rather than duped that capitalism was a better option than a command economy. Patrick Bond, although he is the longest-serving, most prolific and dogged academic/activist opponent of the ANC's economic policies from a leftist point of view, does consider this a possibility: 'the key was the simple fact that an active choice for capitalism was being made by those moving toward power – a decision to embrace and celebrate capitalism, its present and ostensibly promising future.'[35] What is more, in a significant departure from most of the other critiques, Bond is prepared to hedge his explanatory bets between 'structure – externally imposed necessity – and individual agency', in concluding that Mandela jumped at the same time as he was pushed.[36]

On the other hand, Bond gets one thing squarely wrong: by no conceivable stretch of imagination could the attitude of any ANC leader from Mandela onwards be described as celebratory of capitalism's benefits. The accommodation with markets and business has always been portrayed as a regrettable and sometimes tragic necessity. If Mandela and Mbeki after him had shown the leadership mettle actually to advance beyond their own version of 'project fear' and actually argue the case for markets, then economic policies and outcomes might have been different.

The variations of betrayal that have attached themselves retrospectively to the Mandela legacy come with or without racial anger, take the form of either personal or generational blame and are expressed alternatively in auto-critique, rage from below or (more or less) dispassionate academic critique. They target naivety, technocratic deficiencies or lack of courage and willpower. So varied are they that it is tempting to conclude that they tell us more about the accusers than the accused. However all their indictments have one thing in common: none of them accuses Mandela and his technocratic advisers and political colleagues in the leadership, including Mbeki, of personal venality and the desire for self-enrichment. Looking back from the perspective of the Zuma years, to a time when ideology really mattered and leaders made choices on the basis of conceptions of the national interest, this gives them a curiously dated quality.

Again, with the benefit of hindsight, another take on the economic policy dimension of the transition years suggests itself, which does not appear in any of the conventional forms of the betrayal theme. There is no more insistent trope in the standard journalistic and biographical accounts of the political negotiations than the 'seduction' of the Afrikaner nationalists by the ANC. In these accounts, Mbeki, Ramaphosa and Mandela himself are credited with extraordinary powers of seduction.[37] There is obviously something in this – Afrikaners, for all the 'granite' clichés about their character, are a more romantic people than most – though the seduction theme is greatly overplayed in the interests of dramatizing, simplifying and adding human interest to a complex story. Be that as it may, it is possible that, in an ironic mirror image, while the ANC was busy seducing its interlocutors in the political negotiations, their leaders themselves were being seduced by big business, away from the spotlight and in the less formal economic encounters. Certainly this would help explain the two narratives of betrayal – those of whites who thought De Klerk sold them down the river and blacks who thought the same of Mandela and his colleagues.

It is not only from the viewpoints of populists, racial nationalists and the orthodox Left that Mandela's legacy is questioned. There is also liberal scepticism, some of which has been there from the beginning of the post-apartheid era, some developing out of disillusion with the post-Mandela trajectory of South African politics. This does not organize around the idea of betrayal as such, nor does it even necessarily accuse Mandela directly of personal duplicity; however, this approach to his place in history does judge him as an essentially misleading figure who put a gloss on a movement that was in reality very different from his own image and indeed his own core personality and beliefs. In this interpretation, following his release the ANC was never Mandela's organization, despite outward appearances, or if it was, this was only a passing phase before the movement reasserted its essential nature. That nature was fundamentally autocratic and propelled by paranoid one-partyism in the direction of wholesale, state-directed social engineering in the interests of racial nationalism. Anybody who believed otherwise was deceiving him or herself.

This is the view taken by Hermann Giliomee. Mandela's 'mesmerizing' influence and his disavowal of nationalization

> led to the mistaken conclusion that the ANC had discarded the idea of revolutionary African nationalism ... During the 1990s the ANC and SACP ostensibly retreated from many of their earlier commitments. However once political power had been secured their leaders made clear that they regarded the political settlement merely as a bridgehead for a comprehensive social and economic transformation.[38]

After 1996 (when Mandela was still president), the ANC did not trouble to conceal its intention to capture 'all levers of state power':

> However, by that point the myth of the ANC as a non-racial and democratic organisation had taken such hold that overt statements of intent tended to be ignored or discounted by Western public opinion.[39]

R. W. Johnson makes the same point: 'Mandela's warm personality and inclusive spirit were stamped indelibly on the nation's heart in those years but the realities of power suggest that his well-loved face was merely the mask of a very different regime.'[40]

A key moment in this interpretation was the speech Mandela gave as outgoing president of the ANC at the movement's fiftieth national conference in 1997.[41] The speech, the president's report on the state of the movement, was a fierce denunciation of everything and everybody that was not part of the ANC and for good measure included an enemy within. Despite its overwhelming electoral mandate and, at this stage, thanks to Mandela, its still generally positive global image, the speech portrayed the ANC as embattled and fighting for its life. In stark language, it described a threefold onslaught. The first was from a 'counter-revolutionary network' based on 'various elements of the former ruling group' intent on 'using crime to render the country ungovernable', subverting the economy and eroding the confidence 'of our own people and the rest of the world' in the capacity of the ANC to govern.

The second front of subversion included the media (which, 'set itself up as a force opposed to the ANC') and opposition parties, which contrived, in the terms of the speech, to be at the same time 'weak and pitiful' but also 'implacably destructive'. The traitorous third front was composed of 'certain elements that are supposedly part of our movement who have set themselves up as critics of the same movement', at the 'precise' moment when the ANC was faced with the determined opposition of the forces of reaction. This was generally understood to refer to 'progressive' NGOs loosely associated with the ANC, which took advantage of not being subject to its discipline to be critical of, among other things, signs of emerging corruption.

In this fantasy version of the realities of South African politics of the day, these Three Horsemen of the Apocalypse threatened the destruction of the ANC and all it stood for, past, present and future, at the 'precise' moment of its apparent triumph. The speech was out of character for Mandela, not only in its Manichaean sentiments but also in its wooden verbiage and employment of an apparatchik's formulaic vocabulary. Even in moments of anger – as in his contemptuous put-downs of De Klerk during fraught moments in the negotiations – Mandela had not spoken like this. The explanation appeared obvious: Mbeki (with the assistance of his ideologue-in-chief Joel Netshitenzhe) had written the speech to inaugurate formally his own leadership and to demonstrate the continuity that is so important to the ANC. R. W. Johnson's verdict is scathing: the speech 'saw the President treated like a ventriloquist's doll' in order to 'legitimate in advance the key projects of the Mbeki presidency'.[42]

Mbeki's imprint on Mandela's speech is clear to anyone who has read more than one of Mbeki's own, but this raises the question of why Mandela should cooperate in this way. Mandela's closing speech to the same conference (much more in his own voice) provides a possible answer: 'I wish to reiterate that I will remain a disciplined member of the ANC and in my last months in government office, I will always be guided by the ANC's policies, and find mechanisms that will allow you to rap me over the knuckles for any indiscretions.' This is of a piece with Mandela's consistent line, ever since his release[43] and even as he ascended the heights of global fame, that he was no more than one disciplined ANC cadre among many. This is fine as far as it goes, although Mandela was not always entirely convincing in the guise of this humble persona and there may have been times when his tongue was in his cheek. However, given that the ANC is an amalgam of influences including racial nationalism, communism and liberal constitutionalism, whose essential nature is difficult to pin down in any economical way, what does it mean for anyone, never mind Mandela, to say that he or she is a 'disciplined member of the ANC'? Which of the ANC's many avatars does she or he stand for? To say that Mandela's self-effacement raises more questions than it answers is at best an understatement.

On this question, the most radical deconstruction of the Mandela legacy from a liberal perspective turns on the long-running issue of Mandela's membership of the SACP. For something like fifty years, the question of Mandela's membership of the SACP was a matter largely for cold warriors and apartheid apologists and was met by firm denial: 'Mandela denied his membership of the communist party in his treason trial testimony in 1960 and at the Rivonia trial in 1964 (as did Walter Sisulu). This denial was repeated in Mandela's autobiography published in 1993 and perpetuated by Anthony Sampson in his authorized biography of Mandela published in 1999.'[44] Two books published shortly before Mandela died, independently penetrated this 'bodyguard of lies', establishing that Mandela had been a member of the SACP's central committee at the time of the turn to armed struggle in the early 1960s. Both the ANC and SACP confirmed his membership shortly after he died.[45]

The question is whether or not this information should be regarded as anything more significant than a historical footnote in the post-Cold War world and in a South Africa whose democratic constitution remains intact more than twenty years after its inauguration. For James Myburgh, it is indeed significant. It exposes the gulf between Mandela's statement from the dock in 1964 and the reality of ANC strategy, which was and remains based on the SACP's *The Road to South African Freedom* (1962 and incorporated into ANC *Strategy and Tactics* in 1969). Mandela's speech, certainly one of the most famous and influential political speeches of the last hundred years, is the foundation document of his image. In it he denies that he is a communist and professes profound admiration for the institutions of British and American democracy. For Myburgh, 'If one picks up the thread beginning with the falsehood that he had never been a member of the Communist Party the plausibility of much of what Mandela then says about his political beliefs then in his statement also starts to unravel. His expressed admiration for the institutions of Western government seems designed to mislead.'[46] Indeed, in this version, the purpose of Mandela from the trial statement onwards was to win over Western liberal public opinion to the ANC/SACP cause and to divert scrutiny from the actual (and unconcealed) intentions of their strategy documents: 'The statement thus arguably represents one of the greatest feats of political misdirection of the twentieth century.'[47]

Questions are left unanswered (indeed unasked) by this kind of interpretation. Was Mandela part of a conspiracy of deception to misrepresent the ANC/SACP axis and thus disarm De Klerk from a sufficiently vigorous use of his assets (threat of military force included) to push for constitutionally guaranteed power sharing and minority group rights? Was Mandela acting in good faith but shoved aside by Mbeki and other ANC leaders when the size of the ANC electoral majority became clear?

There are other problems. In some versions, the arguments verge on hyperbole. According to Myburgh, the commitment to the NDR is reflected in 'the innumerable laws passed by successive ANC governments enforcing escalating levels of racial discrimination against South Africa's racial minorities, and particularly its white minority'.[48] This is a version of the truth, but one that is quite without nuance or signalling of limits, which could give to anyone unfamiliar with South Africa a quite distorted impression.

In addition, this interpretation has little appetite for addressing counterfactuals. There is an unstated assumption in critical liberal treatments of the Mandela years that constitutionally enforced power sharing, group minority rights and/or a liberal society with some version of equality of opportunity (magicked somehow out of a patrimony of gross deprivation and exclusion) would provide a stable basis for reconciliation, democracy and inclusive economic growth. At the very least, these assumptions deserve thorough interrogation as to their political and economic prospects of sustaining South African democracy.

ANC practice and African leadership

A haunting refrain audible throughout the politics of the post-apartheid era is a praise song about a distinctive African tradition of political leadership, a legacy which has shaped an organizational culture of leadership peculiar to the ANC, as well as more general ideas about and attitudes to practices of leadership in South Africa. The two merge into one another – African tradition is one among several sources claimed for ANC practices – they share the same essentially collective roots and, as a corollary, the rejection of concepts of leadership that emphasize individual agency.

The myths of African cultural practice and traditions of ANC organizational behaviour work on leaders in two ways. They offer a resource that leaders can (indeed have to) use in order to legitimate themselves and build their images, while at the same time they set cultural parameters as to what is acceptable and what is not in leaders' behaviour and thus constitute standards by which leaders may be judged by an internal audience.

African political leadership

The influence of the African past on political leadership today has its starting point in the relationship between chief and people in precolonial societies:

The relationship was summed up in the saying common to all South African preconquest farming societies and is the key to their politics, that power was reciprocal: *inkosi yinkosi ngabantu* or *morena wamorena kabatho* – a chief is a chief by the people.[49]

Among the implications for leadership derived from this universal principle was that of consensual decision making on the basis of everyone being heard. This powerful myth is particularly celebrated in the lives and careers of Oliver Tambo and Nelson Mandela. Tambo's biographer, Luli Callinicoss, draws a direct line of influence from the traditional society into which Tambo was born to ANC decision making:

> The Amapondo, like many polities in Southern Africa, had a consensus approach to decision-making, a feature that was to become characteristic of resolutions passed in the African National Congress, particularly under the presidencies of Chief Albert Luthuli and Oliver Tambo. Between headmen and the community, as well as between the chiefs and the people, there was a balance of power. Consensus was the aim and method of reaching a decision. After a long discussion in which all the parties participated, the chief and his advisers would 'get the feel of the meeting'. Opponents of the plan were encouraged to speak out, because, as the saying went, 'people should not be like a stream that flows in only one direction'.[50]

Callinicoss's informants were fulsome in their praise of Tambo's style:[51] He was a traditional leader but the benign chief who listened; there was something of the *lekgotla*[52] where everyone comes in, and everybody has a chance to be heard; it is very democratic, consensus, not majority rule. For Jacob Zuma (one of the interviewees), the experience was 'amazing': the discussion was 'never haphazard', and 'by the time you had reached an agreement you had all agreed'. Zuma concludes, 'In his time, thorough as he was, in terms of discussing issues, we developed a culture in the ANC leadership of actually taking decisions by consensus.'[53]

The same ascription of influence to traditional African culture is customarily attached to Mandela's leadership values and style. Unlike Tambo who was a commoner, Mandela was of chiefly lineage and he spent from about the age of seven through to young manhood at the court of the regent of the Thembu royal house.[54] Throughout his formative years, he was exposed to the culture of the royal court: 'In particular, the regent's manner at court, where he would listen with regal impassivity to all sides of the argument, before finally deciding and pronouncing a decision left an enduring impression on Mandela.'[55] There is widespread agreement on this. Boehmer notes that

> the long-winded, yet wisely choreographed meetings in the chief's courtyard represented an important lesson for the young Mandela on how agreement between competing views might be achieved: how patrimonial loyalties and clan obligations might be weighted against each other ... all constituencies were heard and the leader paid heed to all.[56]

However, despite this consensus on the importance of consensus for the African leadership that influenced Tambo and Mandela, the literature on Mandela strikes a more balanced note than the sometimes-rapturous treatments of Tambo (for instance, that of Callinicoss). Bonner notes as one of three antimonies in Mandela's story the tension between his submission to party discipline and his 'individualistic tendencies', citing the times when he 'took initiatives that were profoundly controversial in the upper ranks of the ANC and had never been collectively approved'.[57] The most momentous of these was, of course, his decision in the late 1980s to enter into discussions with the South African government, while he was still in prison.[58]

For her part, Boehmer tactfully draws attention to the limitations of African conceptions of democratic leadership in contemporary settings by noting that retrospective constructions are subject to 'a certain amount of allegorical inflation, especially at a time, the mid-1990s, when the ideal of African social harmony carried a particular symbolic resonance'.[59]

For all the celebrations of African cultural influence on the leadership of Tambo and Mandela – and by strategic elision, extended to the ANC as a whole – there is something elusive about this hybrid of individual and collective agency. In the end, those (such as Zuma) who speak or write in these terms seem happy to assume that in this cultural paradigm something mysterious happens at a tipping point to produce a decision acceptable to all. Perhaps something exclusively African renders it unnecessary to explain the mystery. For those that are inside the culture, no explanation is necessary; for those outside, no explanation is possible.

Perhaps not. A more prosaic explanation may be that African people who were used to being treated with casual contempt by white power wanted to appropriate the approach of listening with respect as exclusively 'African', while it is in fact a familiar leadership strategy (both in its presence and its absence) to anyone with reasonably wide experience of organizational life in other cultural contexts.

Tambo was leading a self-selected elite of full-time revolutionaries whose accountability to, or even communication with, any community outside of themselves was very tenuous. The centralization of power that exile and underground existence dictated, which was regrettable to some in the ANC leadership and more than welcome to others, was mitigated by the saintly (and mysterious) qualities retrospectively attributed to Tambo and built into his myth. This leader aura was given the legitimacy of African cultural practice at a time when restoring African self-respect was a priority. What Tambo did for the closed circle of ANC activists, Mandela brought to the world, establishing continuity with Tambo, confirming the continuing relevance of African history and tradition and adding the weight of his own charisma and moral authority.

The symbolic resonance of African tradition was very important in the age of the elders, Tambo and Mandela. However, the scope was more limited for the next generation of leaders. In the first place, it would not be possible to transfer this kind of leadership from an essentially homogeneous and small-scale community dealing with a circumscribed range of issues, whether in an African village or a small, closed circle of revolutionaries, to governing a society that is much bigger in scale, more complex, diverse to the point of fragmentation and harbouring differences – even within the ruling party – that approach the irreconcilable. Mandela could do it because he confined himself largely to the soft (though still very difficult) macro issues of nation-building rather than the hard, technically demanding issues of evidence-based policymaking across the whole range of government. However, this was only possible in the short term. Second, there was the issue of harmonizing symbolic Africanism with the internal organization of the ANC, once the exigencies of exile and repression were removed.

In short, like the other myths and legacies that hovered over the democratic present and staked claims there, African leadership could be an asset for the new generation of leaders or a stick to beat them with. To capitalize on the former and avoid falling victim to the latter, the successors would have to find ways of making the claims of African leadership credible in the altered present, which also meant institutionalizing it.

The ANC's organizational democracy in theory and practice

To a degree that is unusual for a political party, the informal principles that supposedly govern how a leader should conduct him or herself have been conventionally spoken about as if they are set in stone. The best example of this has been the customary canon that potential leaders must not seek office but must always behave with complete passivity, other than denying all ambition except to be a humble servant of the movement, until the moment of being called forward to serve:

> 'It is a profound cultural practice within the ANC that individuals do not promote or canvass for themselves.' This, apparently is 'in bad revolutionary taste'.

This corporate view of leadership can be found in one of the few documents produced by the ANC on the subject, 'Through the Eye of a Needle?' from which the quotation above comes.[60] Although it dates from 2001, it is still invoked and it features prominently on Cyril Ramaphosa's personal website. Effectively, it amounts to a fourteen-page homily combining folksy self-help rules for aspirant leaders and stern but avuncular strictures on conduct and appeals to 'revolutionary morality', as if Samuel Smiles had been reborn as a communist party apparatchik.

A widening gap has developed between Through the Eye of a Needle's ritual invocation of ideal practices of leadership and what is actually happening on the ground. Leadership succession at the highest level bears no resemblance to prescribed cultural norms and at lower levels, squalid factionalism, not excluding murder when bribery does not work, is often the order of the day. Yet to a large extent the ritual parameters of leadership are still spoken of as if they have real meaning and substance.

It is possible, however, to feel some sympathy for those who have struggled to construct a leadership culture in the ANC because the organizational dilemmas of political parties and movements in democracies are easy to identify but hard to resolve. The problem is even worse for a hybrid entity such as the ANC, which insists on its 'democratic liberation movement' character[61] but in many respects has to organize itself and behave like a political party in a constitutional democracy and mixed economy, for instance in soliciting support from the uncommitted in elections and adjusting to the power of markets in the economy. Essentially, the universal problems of organizing democratic parties boil down to those of harmonizing top-down and bottom-up characteristics in terms of, for example, balancing freedom of expression with organizational unity and integrity; the need to have both direction and leadership by party elites and accountability to the grass roots; and the need to aggregate a single identity and programme from multitudes of bottom-up interests and demands.

The dilemmas are heightened by the knowledge that addressing them takes place in the shadow of what the political sociologist Robert Michels called as early as 1911, 'the iron law of oligarchy':

It is organization which gives birth to the dominion of the elected over electors, of the mandatories over the mandatory, of the delegates over the delegators. Who says organization says oligarchy.[62]

This idea is so intuitively plausible that political activists and ordinary citizens may feel no need for expert confirmation of it,[63] and suspicion between them and political classes is mutual and endemic to democracies. Elites fear the chaos of conflicting, unfeasible and poorly articulated demands from below, while the grass roots decry the preoccupation of political classes with their own careers and fortunes, as well as their dilution of principle in the interests of broad electability and compromises with forces, both local and global, beyond their control. Formally, the ANC resolves the dilemmas of organizational democracy in terms set out by another classic theorist of elites and political parties, French political scientist Maurice Duverger (1917–2014). To address the inevitability of elites in party organization, he recommended, 'Government of the people by an elite sprung from the people.'[64]

According to the ANC constitution, 'Its policies are determined by the membership and its leadership is accountable to the membership in terms of the procedures laid down in this constitution.'[65] Leadership positions are elective at all levels (branch, provincial and national). National leadership is composed of the so-called top six positions, president, deputy president, chairperson, secretary general and deputy and treasurer general, as well as the National Executive Committee (NEC), the highest organ of the ANC between five-yearly national conferences. The conference is the supreme ruling and controlling body of the ANC, with the power to elect leaders and determine the policies and programmes of the organization, and is composed of delegates, 90 per cent of whom are elected representatives of branches.

In other documents, the principle of collective leadership is stressed: 'The ANC has leadership collectives, instead of a single leader, at all levels,'[66] that is, the branch, provincial and NECs (structures and elective processes are mirrored at all levels). An element of ambiguity is introduced to this commitment to collective leadership by the treatment of the ANC president in its constitution. He or she does not have 'powers' but 'duties and functions'. These, as listed, are quite mundane and rather scanty, but on the other hand the president is defined in a rather open-ended way as 'the political head and chief directing officer of the ANC'.[67]

Formal organizational rules are one thing, organizational culture and practice another. There have been strong reasons for this commitment to collective leadership, but how it has been applied has varied from period to period. Among the reasons have been revolutionary solidarity and fears of both the 'Big Man' leadership syndrome and tribalism, both associated with a single, strong leader. The influence of pastoral, African communal ideals and rejection of competitive, individualistic and adversarial models of leadership associated with the West has also been strong. Collective leadership provided better cover for the influence of the SACP on the NEC, which was considerable in the exile years and, according to one account of the period, was additionally facilitated by Tambo's non-assertive leadership and his 'temperament that abhorred confrontation'.[68]

The adoption of 'democratic centralism' in exile was an attempt to reconcile the need for central direction with the movement's insistence that it is a bottom-up, collectively led organization. Given the association of democratic centralism with Soviet communism, first in its party dictatorship form and then with Stalin's individual dictatorship, as well as the strong influence of the SACP in the ANC exile leadership, this was a gift (one among many) to the apartheid government's efforts to portray all opposition to it in Cold-War terms. It could have been worse, however; even the ANC did not go so far as its Zimbabwean counterpart, ZANU-PF, in calling its supreme party body 'the politburo'. One way of looking at the adoption is the following:

> The 'democratic centralism' that the ANC has taken over from its SACP ally as an instrument of discipline echoes an idealised understanding of the governance of traditional African societies.[69]

In this view, all may speak freely before the leadership finds a consensus, based 'on the interests and values of the people' and which 'reflects and reaffirms an underlying societal unity'.[70] This is not a widely held view of democratic centralism. More common is the understanding that democratic centralism is the instrument of establishing and maintaining central control in the hands of leadership at times, such as the exile years, when there is a premium on discipline. Reviewing the ANC's history of organizational practice, Myburgh notes four periods: before exile when relatively loose discipline was tolerated in the interests of creating as broad a front as possible; much tighter central control in the exile years; reversion to greater openness after the return to legality and from overseas, as the movement sought to integrate the various elements (such as the United Democratic Front) that had grown up under its influence; and the reassertion (or at least the attempt to do so) of central discipline in the late 1990s.[71] An ANC document of mid-1997 exposes the tensions which democratic centralism is supposed to address.[72] It begins on a defensive note: 'Questions are raised as to whether we have become a movement which is top-down, elitist and lacking a climate for free, open and critical debate'.[73] In reply, the document, which was probably authored by Mbeki or someone close to him, defended the need for discipline and leadership from the centre and restated the key principles of democratic centralism: majoritarianism ('the decisions of the majority prevail' and are binding on all members of the ANC) and decisions of higher structures bind lower structures.

In reality, such principles tell us little about the actual working of the organization. About all that can safely be said is that if the movement was genuinely composed of cadres who heeded the exhortations that appear later in the document (and again point to Mbeki's authorship), then democratic centralism would indeed be democratic as well as centralist: 'Our cadreship and our leadership must strive for personal attributes such as commitment, dedication, loyalty, respect for others, modesty, incorruptibility and critical, independent thinking.'[74] Sadly, it is by now common cause inside the movement as well as outside that these paragons are in short supply. An unusually penetrating diagnosis by a senior ANC provincial leader in September 2016 illustrates how democratic centralism (or any other organizational principle) depends wholly on the prevailing state of the movement's culture and dynamics:

> Democratic centralism requires that all members and lower organisational structures must have confidence in the capacity of higher organisational structures to take grounded and politically sound decisions that are in the best interest of the organisation. When members and lower structures suspect that the best interest of the organisation is relegated to the backyard and factional interest finds pre-eminence they lose confidence in higher structures and this manifests itself in subtle, sometimes open, revolts against the decisions of higher structures. This can reach a degenerative state where the organisational integrity of the party hits the dust, as higher structures cannot issue authoritative values.[75]

Despite this, democratic centralism continues to receive ritual obeisance in speeches and documents as if it were a completely unproblematic principle of leadership and organization. It is a prime example of how the language of leadership has been narrowed, predetermined and reduced to formulae and templates that have come to bear increasingly less correspondence with reality.

Lost leaders

It is not only the political leaders who held government office during their careers whose legacy obtrudes into the political present. Thanks to the traumas of South Africa's recent history, the near ubiquity of betrayal as a political reflex, the tendency (of the ANC in particular) to obsessively seek legitimacy in continuity with the past as well as the prevalent tendency to invest heavily in leaders and leadership, South African politics is frequently touched by the 'lost leader' syndrome. In the South African context, lost leaders, among whose number we can count Steve Biko, Oliver Tambo and Chris Hani, were leaders in their own right but leaders of resistance who were prevented from leading in the aftermath of victory. Tambo was incapacitated by a stroke in 1989, months before the ANC was unbanned. Biko was murdered in custody by apartheid security forces in 1977 and right-wing extremists assassinated Hani in April 1993, at a time when negotiations between the Nationalist Party government and the ANC had broken down. The combination of the thwarted potential that apartheid's exclusions forced on talented black people and the violence of Biko's and Hani's ends makes the stories of these lost leaders particularly poignant.

Lost leaders, who by definition are untainted by the temptations, excesses or compromises of office, can serve several political functions: as a reference point for endangered or lost principles; a way of keeping thwarted dreams alive; a focus for anger with current leaders who can be fitted for the roles of usurper, accident of history or betrayer.

Distance limits the effects that lost leaders can have. Biko was murdered at a time when no African political leader could contemplate a life of anything other than resistance. It is beyond the realms of reasonable speculation how he might have addressed the challenges of wielding power or even, given his well-documented personal flaws, who and what he might have led if he had survived until the later stages of the liberation struggle. This distance from the realities of power politics allowed him the luxury of uncompromising positions – on whites as a homogeneous oppressor community for instance – which are an important part of his attraction to ultras in the greatly changed circumstances of today. He would have had to deal strategically not only with apartheid repression but also with the ANC, which would either have absorbed, marginalized or otherwise neutralized him. Whether or not the categorization 'Xhosa prophet' is a fair or useful one, he is certainly best seen as an inspiration – principally to a new and young post-apartheid generation – rather than a leader in a managerial and operational context.

In a sense, how he would have shaped as a political leader in a conventional way is beside the point. Although the power of the lost leader myth is counterfactual – things would have turned out differently if we'd had these leaders rather than the ones we did – the qualities of the lost leader are rarely interrogated in today's terms. Although lost leaders can be rallying points for change, paradoxically they remain stuck in the past. None of this means that

Biko would have been incapable of modifying his views, making strategic or tactical compromises or otherwise behaving like other political leaders; after all, both the ANC and the National Party government did plenty of these things in the 1980s and 1990s. However, if he had lived to do these things, then he would probably be much less of an inspiration.

Oliver Tambo is a lost leader in a truer sense than Biko in that for thirty years he was in a leadership position, one which required great resources of party management and diplomacy. Indeed, in terms of international relations his role was analogous to a president or at least a foreign secretary and his responsibilities were probably greater than those of his South African government counterparts. By 1990, the ANC had diplomatic relations with more countries than the South African government. It is no exaggeration to say that within the ANC itself there is a Tambo cult equal to or even surpassing that of Mandela, about whom, as we have seen, there is a degree of equivocation. Outside the party faithful, Tambo is not well known and perhaps this is an additional source of his veneration; the ANC does not have to share Tambo with the rest of the world in the way it does Mandela. Perhaps another reason for the cult is that it is not only the leader that has been lost, but the experience of a whole generation that can only be remembered but not recaptured. Callinicoss speculates that Tambo represented a generation's 'age of innocence':

> He seemed to have succeeded in interpreting for them the brave and dedicated new men and women that the liberation movement required. He affirmed the value of their lives. He symbolised the transformation of dreary, unfulfilled township lives into the pursuit of freedom for all.[76]

The main reason that Tambo is held in such high regard, however, is that he managed to keep the ANC from falling apart in exile and his status as a lost leader is derived from this: the belief that he would somehow have been able by exercise of his characteristic African style of leadership to manage the post-1994 strains in the Alliance and prevent the organizational degeneration of the ANC itself. Again Callinicoss speculates that for this reason he became 'an exemplar, called upon particularly in times of contested interpretations of the ANC'.[77] This was prophetic, since the ANC decreed that 2017 – peak Zuma – would be the year of Oliver Tambo. However, it would have taken someone unusually resistant to grim irony to witness with a straight face the spectacle of Zuma announcing the dedication.

The lost leader who has had the greatest resonance in post-apartheid South Africa is Chris Hani. He is the only one to have been taken up by a specific political grouping and used for focussed political leverage. In a sense, of course, Hani, by virtue of his leadership role in the ANC's armed wing Umkhonto we Sizwe (MK), his personal bravery and concern for the soldiers under his command, 'belongs' to the whole of the ANC. However, it is the SACP that has attached itself most tenaciously to his legacy. This legacy has several components: the charisma and military virtues already noted; his reluctance to abandon the armed struggle, which appeals to those who feel too much was lost in negotiations (especially the young who were not around at that time to pay the price of continuing the violence in one last push); his decision to relinquish ANC offices to concentrate on building up the SACP as a counterweight to the ANC; his belief that extra-parliamentary politics and direct action would need to be maintained, even if and when the ANC won a majority and became the government; and last, his warnings shortly before he was murdered that the ANC was vulnerable to the ideological and material corruption of power.

The range of possibilities to spin lost leader myths is illustrated by a euphoric celebration of the meaning of Hani's death published in April 2008, fifteen years after the event. It was written by Tokyo Sexwale, tycoon, sometime ANC leadership contender and government minister, eight months before the ANC national conference that elected Zuma, when Sexwale himself was briefly a candidate. Sexwale doubtless had his own agenda but his anniversary eulogy is typical of the ANC's collective funerary disposition in whose shadow each generation of leaders must dwell but which they in turn can exploit.

Sexwale writes of all the leadership qualities that were lost: 'Comrade Chris the nationalist, Comrade Chris the democrat, the freedom fighter, the scholar, the theoretician and the practitioner' – and the 'unapologetic' communist. Despite these losses, he was a leader even by virtue of his death, which had 'magnificent consequences': 'the crescendo, the final revolutionary push for victory – all unleashed by the manner of his death that April morning.'[78] Hani may never have wielded executive power but 'the legacy of this humble giant' was that he 'knew how to die a worthwhile death which breathed newness into the lives of many others'.

Tokyo Sexwale is himself something of a lost leader, victim (as we shall see) of Mbeki's use of underhand methods to neutralize potential leadership rivals. He had to content himself with becoming a Black Economic Empowerment rand billionaire, with interests in diamonds among other traditional South African paths to wealth. It is interesting to speculate whether or not such accumulation opportunities would have been available had the communist Hani he was eulogizing been a fulfilled rather than a lost leader.

However, what gives the lost leader myth special power in the case of Hani is a cloud of suspicion, on real or speculative grounds, surrounding his death.

There is no doubt at all who pulled the trigger and who supplied the weapon – in both cases, white, right-wing extremists. Despite this, Hani's death could be portrayed as convenient for both the apartheid state's security forces (if not for the government, embroiled as it was in negotiations with the ANC) and also for the ANC, to whom his competitive militancy and declaration for an independent role in the SACP was a potentially destabilizing factor in an already fraught negotiating situation. In one version, the plot was indeed a white extremist affair, but it became known to both the state's and the ANC's security forces who let it go ahead or even, without revealing themselves, helped it along.[79] By the time of his death, Hani was a major rival to Mbeki and, according to Johnson, Mbeki was 'the most obvious beneficiary of Hani's death'.[80] This led to 'quiet surmise, quiet allegations, entirely unsupported by evidence' which amounted to 'ritualised psychological warfare'.

> Whenever tensions arose within the tripartite alliance of the ANC, SACP and Cosatu, pitting the latter two against Mbeki, they would not only make a very public point of celebrating Hani, the lost leader, but would issue calls for a fresh investigation into his death, claiming that the full truth has yet to be revealed.[81]

Another country

The pull of the past is particularly strong on most South Africans; on the ANC in particular but whites are also drawn into its seductive orbit, especially to the remembered past of Mandela and the 'rainbow period'.[82] The haunted present shapes some of the strongest influences on South African followership; not only ancestor worship and laments for lost leaders but also the belief in South African exceptionalism that South Africans will always negotiate themselves away from the precipice and the belief that there is always time for another round in the last chance saloon. But there is also the dark shadow of betrayal, which falls across the present and corrupts the memory of past leaders.

For the ANC, nothing is more essential than to break with the country's apartheid past; but nothing is less possible than for it to break with its own past, which must be imported wholesale into the present and future. This is a major stumbling block to transformational leadership and, as we shall see, a major problem for Cyril Ramaphosa's 'new dawn'.

4

Mandela's successors: A framework for analysis

The principal lesson to be derived from historical and contemporary studies of political leadership is that we have to understand political leadership as the interplay of context and individual agency. Whether or not we incline at the end towards one or another of structure and agency as determinants of leadership practice and outcomes, it is as well to begin by being even-handed towards them both. This should lead us to explore how leaders managed the context in which they found themselves and how they perceived, defined and met the challenges arising from it. In this, their own resources include those of identifying and employing the instruments and opportunities that present themselves, whether embedded in the political system itself or arising from unfolding events. An approach of this sort should provide space for narrative, analysis, generalization and detail.

In terms of generalizations about leadership in South Africa, three things stand out. The first is to look for continuities and discontinuities spanning the whole post-apartheid period, including Mandela and his successors, looking back to Mbeki and Zuma and forward with what we have learned to Ramaphosa, while discounting Motlanthe as having been to short a time in office. No leader starts off with a clean slate and to some extent all democratic leaders have to be both stewards of continuity and bringers of and adapters to change. The ANC operates on a cult of continuity and unity (while at the same time claiming to be the vanguard of revolutionary change), but amid a fog of misinformation and denial there is actually much discontinuity. To put it at its simplest, the ANC of Zuma is not the ANC of Mandela (though there are liberal critics who would dispute this point). Was the ANC of Mbeki a staging post on this journey or simply another version with its own characteristics? Were the roots of Zuma's chaotic governance already present under Mbeki? Or did things veer wildly off course only after Mbeki's defenestration? The challenge, then, is to try to discern whether these discontinuities are random, cyclical or unilinear in the direction of decline and what roles were played by individual leadership, contingency, factors built into the country's situation and by the nature of the ANC and its Alliance. Analysis of this sort should be helpful in assessing the respective prospects of renewal or further decline.

While the continuity/discontinuity issue is focussed very much on the South African context, the other two potential generalizations arise from the literature on political leadership. The first of these is the structure/agency issue, or in everyday terms, whether or not leaders matter much. The trump card in the hand of the 'agency' advocates, which is played with such gusto by analysts such as Robert Rotberg, is Nelson Mandela. He, more than any other leader in recent history, is held to be the epitome of the leader who can make a difference and transcend – the word is liberally used of him both in metaphorical and quite mystical terms – the limits of his own historical context and the social and political structures round him. The sheer power and pervasiveness of the Mandela myth and mystique raises the question of whether he was – in leadership agency terms – a one off or even a 'black swan event'[1] and how and to what extent we can usefully think of leadership in agency terms in his aftermath.

Lastly, there is scope for generalization in the various ways the literature of political leadership attempts to categorize leaders. Two dichotomous classifications stand out: strong and consensual; transactional and transformational. The strong/consensual (or collegial) dichotomy is potentially useful in the South African context because the myths of African tribal leadership and ANC collective leadership are important in shaping cultural ideas of what appropriate leadership is and the shadow of the Big Man, postcolonial African leader also hangs heavy. In the same way that the collective is relentlessly emphasized over the individual, it is the movement that is presented as transformational and not the leader in the ANC's (and hence dominant) political culture. If a strong and/or transformational leader is to emerge again in the ANC, it seems that he or she will have to pretend to be something else entirely. All of this leads to dissonances, denials and obfuscations about leadership, which are interesting in their own right but do not make the task of the student of leadership any easier.

Entrances and exits

One potentially useful line of approach to studying leadership in any given context is to look at how leaders came to power, what the trajectory of their period in office was (in the sense of how secure they were and how well they could deploy the instruments and resources of leadership to achieve their goals) and in the end how they came to vacate office. Although Mbeki and Zuma were very different as individual leaders, their periods in office were similar in interesting ways. Given the ANC's electoral dominance over the post-apartheid period to date, as well as the ANC's insistence on the prime importance of unity in the movement, its leaders, in the dual roles of ANC and state president, ought to be secure; they ought to be able to expect the maximum of two terms (ten years) in both offices. In fact, both Mbeki and Zuma fell short, Mbeki by nine months and Zuma by fifteen months. However, this conceals an important truth in both cases. Their *effective* time in office was much less than would be suggested by the two objective conditions of their party's dominance and their own capacity to comfortably secure the party leadership – which both of them did twice.[2]

Mbeki became ANC president in 1997 and president of South Africa after the general election of 1999. He was re-elected ANC president in 2002 and of the country in 2004, apparently secure until 2009. However, from 2005 onwards, he faced a prolonged struggle for his political life in the fallout from his dismissal of Zuma from the deputy presidency. Having failed to secure either a third term as ANC president or the election of a sympathizer to that position at the 2007 ANC conference, he suffered the double ignominy, first of Zuma winning the ANC presidency and becoming the heir apparent to the state presidency and then of being 'recalled' by his party – that is fired – in September 2008, with about nine months of his term remaining. The story of Mbeki's presidential years, then, is of only one term of undisputed power and freedom of action, despite winning strong majorities in both national and ANC elections before the power struggle with Zuma sapped his leadership energy and momentum.

Zuma triumphed in the ANC presidential election in December 2007 and in the general election of 2009. By 2012, the coalition of the disaffected that put him in power had largely dissolved, but in 2012 he comfortably saw off a challenge to his leadership at the ANC conference and the ANC again won comfortably in the 2014 general election. Whether or not Zuma had much in the way of leadership capability or vision from the beginning is a moot point. Whatever the case, it became clear quite early in his second term, if not before, that his only real project was himself. Almost from the beginning he was beleaguered by escalating challenges, some coming to haunt him from as far back as the Strategic Defence Package (the 'arms deal', 1994–9) and others multiplying from his unconstitutional acts in office. His adversaries came from right across the political spectrum: the opposition, the courts and civil society as well as his own former supporters inside and outside of the ANC and Alliance. By 2016, he was fighting an increasingly desperate, rearguard action on all these fronts. At the December 2017 ANC elective conference, he failed to secure the accession of his favoured candidate and eight weeks later, he was gone.

Why, when so many conditions ought to have been favourable for long tenures in which leaders should have had the latitude to put their stamp on their party and the country, should both of Mandela's successors have become lame ducks so spectacularly and so early? These commonalities of presidential experience suggest that there is something larger than failings in the individual leaders at work – factors perhaps in the broader political culture and immediate organizational context in which both individuals were working. That in turn implies that biography, which may be necessary, is not a sufficient approach to understanding leadership.

It is possible of course that the explanation is counter-intuitive: that the ANC's dominance encouraged the belief that it would win no matter who was leader and it could dispense with the usual need for parties in electoral democracies to avoid public displays of disunity and internal bloodletting.[3] This kind of explanation would have to explore the apparent contradiction between the ANC's cult-like insistence on the idea of collective leadership and its simultaneous (though temporary) veneration of individual leaders.

Another possibility is that where leadership is concerned, the ANC has acquired a very specific character: relatively easy to capture but difficult – perhaps impossible – to lead in any of the conventional senses of leadership, especially that of harmonizing by force of will or persuasion a vision for the country and the party and harnessing it to a plan for action and for organizational discipline and integrity. The leader of the ANC is chosen by 4,000 to 4,500 delegates at the five-yearly national conference, out of a population (2018) of 57.73 million[4] and a party membership of something like 1 million. This allows a very narrow focus on securing the allegiance of a small number of people by fair means or foul. Especially if some of the means are believed to be foul (as they increasingly are), this gives ANC leadership succession the quality of a coup. Arguably however, its alliance and 'broad church' nature sets up such contradictions of ideology and of factional interests, exacerbated by cultural precepts such as collective leadership, that make it impossible to lead in any conventional sense of leadership as purposive direction. Another unhelpful characteristic of the ANC's organizational structure is the lack of synchronization between the ANC's and the country's electoral timetables. Both the ANC's elective conference and the country's general elections take place in five-year fixed cycles. However, the ANC elects its leaders at least sixteen months before the following general election. It is now standard practice for electioneering to begin up to a year before the elective conference, that is to say barely half way into the state president's term. The inevitable disruption is intensified if it is a second term and more especially if there is instability in the party, but it can be felt even in the first.

Other explanatory possibilities swing the balance of argument back in the direction of individual character and choice combined with the force of contingent events. Indeed for those who are of a literary persuasion, classic tragedy might be invoked. So instead of contextual factors, it was Mbeki's fatal choice for deputy president in 1999 of someone as compromised as Zuma that sprung a chain of events which would destroy both their careers. When that choice was made, the corruption allegations stemming from the arms deal and the rape trial were in the future; moreover, Zuma had substantial standing as the elected ANC deputy president. To that extent, it was not a completely irrational choice. However, the odds on future trouble could be calculated from Zuma's observable character traits, background, abilities and lack of governing experience. Presumably, Mbeki chose to gamble on his own powers of personal manipulation and control to be able to deal with any potential fallout. In any case, the conventional historical and biographical narratives of the period agree that Mbeki was already exercising these powers of manipulation and control by promoting Zuma as deputy ANC and state president, exactly because of these flaws. Because of them, so the narrative goes, Zuma would not be a threat to Mbeki, least of all as an ambitious successor-in-waiting. By the time Mbeki acceded to the presidency in 1999, these powers of manipulation and control had been accorded such extravagant public recognition that he may have made the mistake of believing his own publicity. He would be neither the first nor the last leader to do so if that were the case, nor yet the first to discover he had been too clever for his own good.

In its strongest form this line of explanation would have it that from 1999 and for the following twenty years the trajectory of high political leadership was set by the costly decision to appoint as deputy president a man so flawed and compromised that he would, before long, have to overthrow a sitting president – by a democratic, rather than by a literal coup d'état – and to become president himself in order to stay out of jail. A corollary to this is that once the aberrant case and historical accident that Zuma represents have worked their way through the political system, then some sort of normal democratic practice can be resumed. The counterargument to this is that the Zuma contingency arrived so early in the country's democratic history and distorted the fledgling development of democratic practice so thoroughly through manipulation of state institutions (especially in the security and criminal justice systems) as well as ANC organizational practices that there is no normal to go back to. Which of these versions turns out to be true will do much to determine the quality of political leadership in South Africa in the future.

Job descriptions

Something is needed to impose order on how these issues – structure and agency, continuity and discontinuity, styles and classifications of leadership, narrative arcs of entrance and exit – are to be pursued at the meeting point of individual leaders and national political context. One way of doing this is to draw up typical specifications of tasks expected of political leaders in a democracy, broad enough to be generic and narrow enough to fit the context of post-apartheid South Africa. In order to assess how Mbeki and Zuma managed the political context in which they emerged as leaders and met the challenges arising from it, they will be rated against three leadership functions.

In the first place, democratic leaders have to be representative individuals. One measure of success and/or failure and of how a leader reveals his or her style of leadership is whether and to what extent citizens and voters recognize themselves in a leader. This is by no means infallible and should not be taken too literally. A traditional way of understanding working-class, conservative voters in Britain has been through deference towards those believed to be 'natural' leaders, fitted by birth and special upbringing. Deference voting is motivated not by seeing yourself in a leader but in someone that you are unable to be. However, it is probably true that in a less deferential age and in a developing democracy in which nationalism and nation-building provide a substantial part of the political discourse, the role of representative individual is important. Citizens do not necessarily have to see themselves as they are in a leader (though it can be helpful) but rather what they aspire to be and a vision of what their country collectively could be. Deference has paid a part, it is true, in the dynamics of ANC leadership and followership – deference to the generation and individuals who sacrificed themselves in the liberation struggle, but there is a case for saying that this is becoming a wasting asset more quickly in South Africa than in neighbouring Zimbabwe.

A second role is that of party manager. Political leaders have to reproduce their own support within their party (in the case of the ANC this includes the broader movement and the Alliance) and that of the party in the country. Patronage is not the only way of reproducing support inside the party, but it is indispensable and a useful key to interpreting and understanding leadership type. It is an instrument that can be legitimate and functional but also pathological and disintegrative. Unhelpfully, it is very difficult to unravel the point at which these two personifications of patronage merge into each other in real time – although it may be easier to see in retrospect.

A third role is chief of policy and head of government business. There is wide scope for demonstrating leadership style in this role. At one extreme, there is the leader who stands aloof and leaves management to capable (or not so capable) subordinates but shares the responsibility for outcomes and represents the overall vision into which the various parts of government policy and business fit. At the other extreme is the micromanager who tries to combine the roles of policy architect and grand planner with, as it were, overseeing the installation of the plumbing. There is a certain logic in thinking in terms of a continuum that runs between these ideal types, both of which usefully connect with the world of everyday experience of management and leadership, although, as always with ideal types, there is the danger of toppling over into stereotype and loss of nuance. Certainly, there is an attractive case for contrasting Mandela (of the first, aloof type) and Mbeki (the micromanaging second) along these lines. Zuma presents a more unusual and hence far more difficult case. His lack of interest and capability in formulating, communicating and even understanding policy are legendary, as was his predilection for appointing ministers on grounds other than competence. These things are easy to identify, though much of the evidence has to be by inference from results rather than first or even second hand, as well as to deplore, but they will be much harder to explain.

Even if Mandela's successors can be satisfactorily assessed and compared with each other against these three leadership functions, there will be something missing. What seems to be required is a basis for overall assessment. One way to fashion this is to regard leadership in a democracy, especially in a late democratizer without a settled democratic history, as comprising the elements of inheritance, stewardship and legacy. Perhaps the central questions to be asked of all leaders since Mandela should be (and will remain for the foreseeable future) how will they be seen as stewards of the Constitution and how did they understand and manage the settlement of 1990–6, which produced it? Closely related to this are questions of political culture and processes. Did these mature and become more settled, or did they become less stable and more volatile under the tenure of each leader? Did democratic practices and institutions become more embedded or more endangered under them? Despite the way these questions have been framed, leaving open the danger that they are overemphasizing the roles of individuals, they don't exclude the possibility of counter-intuitive answers emerging from unintended consequences.

Part Three

Mbeki and Zuma

5

Mbeki

Mbeki: Path to power

There is a large measure of agreement concerning Thabo Mbeki's background and rise to leadership in the post-apartheid ANC in his biographies as well as the biographical treatments of him in general histories of the period.[1] He was, quite literally, born into the movement since both his parents were ANC and communist-party activists. His father, Govan Mbeki, was an ANC leader of Mandela's generation, an author (*South Africa: The Peasants' Revolt*) and political prisoner (1964–87), having been convicted at the same trial as Mandela. Thabo Mbeki's childhood was much disrupted by his father's political activities and the need for him to leave the family home at an early age to continue his schooling. Having begun his own career of activism early, he went into exile in 1962 (aged twenty) and did not return to South Africa until the ANC was unbanned in 1990 (when he was forty-eight). Educated at the University of Sussex (MA in development economics), he received some politico-military training in the Soviet Union and at an early age became close to the exile leadership of the ANC and the South African Communist Party (SACP) in various African postings and in London. His precocious rise was fuelled by his intellectual qualities and diligence. These were complemented by keen political instincts for intra-movement political manoeuvres as well as for the movement's diplomacy with international allies and backers (in which he came to specialize) and strategies towards its enemies and rivals.

All of these assets were recognized by his elders and superiors, none more so than Oliver Tambo, ANC leader in the exile years, who became his mentor and promoter and to whom he became effectively a political son. In the culminating years of the struggle, Mbeki was, after Mandela himself, the prime mover for negotiations to end apartheid rather than by armed struggle culminating in insurrection and overthrow of the white state, which was the official strategy of the ANC–SACP alliance until 1989. Backed by Jacob Zuma, he was the principal point of contact with South African whites, who could be cultivated and reassured regarding their prospects under a settlement negotiated with the ANC. This of course directly contradicted the message that whites were getting from Mbeki's colleagues both on the frontline and exile headquarters and helped to deliver key constituencies of them as supporters of those in the apartheid government who favoured negotiations and to undermine hardliners.

After its unbanning in 1990, the ANC was faced with three principal tasks. The first was to integrate the disparate elements that prosecuted the struggle into a coherent whole that could operate as a legal political party and also, at least until a settlement was reached, as a movement of mass mobilization. These elements included exiles, newly released prisoners, the armed wing Umkhonto We Sizwe (MK), the internal forces of resistance organized under the United Democratic Front (UDF), including trade unions and township youth. The second task was to settle the question of leadership succession, given that, of the leadership elders, Mandela was seventy-two years old in 1990, Tambo was seventy-three and in poor health and Walter Sisulu was eighty. The principal contenders were Chris Hani, since 1987, chief of staff of MK[2] and general secretary of the SACP from 1991, Mbeki himself and Cyril Ramaphosa, leader of the National Union of Mineworkers since 1982 and leading figure in the Mass Democratic Movement (MDM), the umbrella body for internal, above-ground resistance, including trade union federation Cosatu and the United Democratic Front (UDF). The third task was to conduct negotiations with De Klerk's National Party government in a way that combined an adversarial drive for victory with an understanding of the need for accommodation and compromise.

Mbeki was a key figure in all three of these tasks, but his progress was bumpy and not without setbacks. This was neither the enclosed world of exile intrigue nor the clandestine world of unacknowledged negotiation to which he had been accustomed. There was an element of free for all with unaccustomed participants such as the internal resistance of the UDF and the unions asserting themselves with their inconvenient views on accountability and transparency, and while intrigue certainly carried on, there was now greater openness: investigative journalists were eager to speculate and poke their noses into the ANC's business. While this was on the whole unwelcome to a movement that had been accustomed to secrecy and privacy (while at the same time being riddled with informers and apartheid agents), the media came to play a useful role in internal intrigue through its eagerness to accept leaks, tip-offs and briefing against rivals.

Mbeki's rise to this point had not been entirely effortless, but it had benefited greatly from Tambo's favour and tutelage. Now, not only were Tambo's powers greatly reduced by the stroke he suffered, but although he remained greatly revered, in operational terms the leadership had been substantially broadened, not least by the emergence of Mandela.

Despite having played a crucial role in making substantive negotiations a possibility through negotiations about negotiations, Mbeki was sidelined by what was effectively a coup when it came to the actual business of coming to a settlement with the National Party. Backed by the SACP and the left/progressive forces of internal resistance, Cyril Ramaphosa was given the task of leading the negotiations, partly because of his reputation as a trade union negotiator and partly because of the Left's suspicions that Mbeki would be too accommodating to white – and especially capitalist – interests. Although Mbeki (supported by Zuma) made something of a recovery by playing the pivotal role in defusing the threat from white right-wing forces and from Zulu separatists to derail the final settlement, the negotiations were widely seen to be Ramaphosa's triumph.

In terms of leadership succession, the rivalry between coevals Hani and Mbeki (both born in 1942) was something of a stalemate until the former's murder in April 1993. Hani had what Mbeki lacked. Both rivals had footholds in party elites, but Hani had popular constituencies in township youth and rank-and-file MK soldiers, which his militancy, dashing and outgoing style and personal bravery had won for him. He also had the prestige of education, perhaps not to Mbeki's level, but he also had the gift of simple and direct communication with which Mbeki was less well endowed.

Despite this relatively unpromising beginning, it took only thirteen months from the murder of Hani by reactionary white extremists for Mbeki to emerge as first deputy president in the initial post-apartheid government (a second deputy president was reserved for the National Party as part of the settlement) and a further seven months (to December 1994) for him to be elected unopposed as deputy president of the ANC. Hence, given the realities of South African electoral politics, the political culture of the ANC and Mandela's firmly expressed intention of serving only one presidential term, Mbeki would follow Mandela as president in 1999.

Again, there is consensus on how this happened. For Gevisser, a turning point was the coup that had installed Ramaphosa as negotiator-in-chief:

> It was [also] clear to Mbeki – or the people round him – that just as he had been sidelined by a small group of people rather than by the masses themselves, he would be elected to ANC high office not by the masses but by power-broking political elites within the movement: regional executives, alliance partners, auxiliary leagues.[3]

For Gumede, Mbeki's territory had been with barons of industry and diplomats rather than in Hani's townships, military bases and squatter camps: 'Not having a mass power base of his own he ran up credit with those that did' and courted influential leaders and factions.[4] In addition to working on the high officials of the SACP and Cosatu, he cultivated populist leaders such as ANC Youth League president Peter Mokaba – who became the spearhead of Mbeki's bid for high office – and Winnie Madikizela-Mandela. Both had reason to dislike Ramaphosa because he had been the instrument of discipline against each of them – on behalf of the MDM in the case of Madikizela-Mandela and of the ANC in the case of Mokaba – and he had been concerned neither to spare their feelings nor conceal his disdain. Both were vulnerable: Madikizela-Mandela for her history of surrounding herself with thugs who, among other things, had killed a young activist, and Mokaba, who had been interrogated in Lusaka in 1989 on suspicion of being an apartheid security branch informer. In both cases, Mbeki could offer rehabilitation in return for their support.

The new sources of support that were the fruits of this lobbying were important in securing election to party office, but the crucial leverage was provided by the exile grandees among whom he had originally built his career. It was their support that sealed Mbeki's rise when Mandela sought their counsel on whom to appoint as first deputy state president after the election victory of April 1994. Mandela wanted Ramaphosa, partly on grounds of the need for ethnic balance in the leadership and partly in recognition of Ramaphosa's undoubted talents. Ramaphosa's background was in the political and cultural heartland of Soweto and he was a thoroughly urban and detribalized figure, as befitted this metropolitan melting pot, a lawyer who had headed the country's biggest trade union, whose members were miners that came from every African ethnicity across Southern Africa. His parents were of the minority Venda people and this identification could be used to quell backstairs grumbling that the ANC leadership was overpopulated with Xhosas from the Eastern Cape, including of course Mandela and Mbeki.

However, the influential exile elders, including Walter Sisulu, Jacob Zuma, Treasurer General Thomas Nkobi – and perhaps most tellingly the known verdict of the recently deceased Oliver Tambo – preferred Mbeki. He was the known factor, against Ramaphosa the wild card, with his relatively recent adherence to the ANC and his associations with the unions and UDF and their alternative traditions of shop floor and community democracy.

Although he was the proverbial heartbeat away from the state presidency by May 1994, Mbeki was not assured of the succession, on the assumption that this would pass on Mandela's retirement. For this he needed the deputy presidency of the ANC, which would be decided a few months later in December 1994. He had been denied this post in 1991 when the top leadership took fright at the prospect of a divisive head-to-head battle between Mbeki and Hani at the conference of that year. This was a time when the movement was in too fragile a state to risk what might be a civil war on the brink of substantive negotiations to end apartheid. He was denied it again in August 1993 when, after Tambo's death, Peter Mokaba proposed that the National Executive Committee (NEC) should elect a deputy president without waiting for the conference. This was rejected, although Mbeki did become national chairman of the ANC at the NEC meeting, a hitherto honorific post that he was able to turn into a power base for further ascent.

In the event, however, the final stages of Mbeki's ascent seem to have come as much from Ramaphosa's abdication from the race as from Mbeki's striving. Denied the deputy presidency when, as we have seen, Mandela was prevailed upon to change his choice and give it to Mbeki, and preoccupied with the task of overseeing the finalizing of the Constitution (as chairman of the Constitutional Assembly, 1994–6), Ramaphosa did not oppose Mbeki either at the 1994 conference (for the deputy presidency of the ANC) or at the December 1997 national conference (for the presidency of the movement). Although he was elected to the NEC in first place at the 1997 conference, he resigned his political posts and went into business. Of course, by this time Mbeki had had more than three years in office as deputy president, the sole one after De Klerk's resignation in 1996. The administration was widely seen at the time as a dream team, combining Mandela's moral authority and soft skills of reconciliation and nation-building with the hard skills of building organizational architecture and policymaking which were customarily attributed to Mbeki. It is not a judgement that has worn well, but it was profoundly influential at the time.

Up to a point this abbreviated account of Mbeki's rise to the summit can be read as being within fairly typical parameters of leadership succession in democratic politics. There was a dash of ideological rivalry, a whiff of tribalism (balancing the ticket according to geography or origin is not unknown elsewhere) and there were strong differences of personal style. Different generations and constituencies were in play in a movement that was considerably more diverse in composition than many democratic peers, but there were strong unifying elements, notably the legacy of the struggle and the binding force of inferior status to which all people other than white had been subjected by colonialism and apartheid. Certainly, the shock of the contingent made itself felt through the murder of Hani and his removal from the succession rivalry, but given how fraught the circumstances were, the ANC and the other parties coped remarkably well in containing the aftershock. Indeed, given the surrounding uncertainty and violence of the period of negotiation and transition (and bearing in mind what the ANC would later become), it is noteworthy that the ANC succession rivalry was as civilized as it was.[5]

Mbeki's success – and this preceded his assumption of the presidency, beginning with his years as deputy president – meant that he was the one to lead the ANC in addressing the challenges it inherited by virtue of winning the first democratic election. These included establishing its own credibility as the party of government, building internal coherence and discipline out of diversity, remodelling the badly distorted economy that it had inherited, seeking cohesion in a shattered society and reorganizing a state apparatus that had been crafted to serve very different purposes from those the ANC espoused and giving expression to, while capitalizing on, South Africa's rehabilitation in the wider world.

'Unmandated Reflections' and warning signs

In short, Mbeki had to be a representative individual, party leader and focal point of government business. The surface normality of his rise to the presidency – give or take allowances for turbulent times and the faintly ludicrous ANC culture of denial that anything as vulgar as a rivalry was being played out before the country's eyes – helped to establish his credentials for these roles. However, there were warning signs, albeit buried in the kind of ANC documents that the general public and incurious journalists don't read. One of these was 'Unmandated Reflections', a memorandum authored by Mbeki when he was already deputy state president and circulated within the ANC ahead of the December 1994 national conference at which, as we have seen, he was elected unopposed as deputy president of the ANC.

The nine-page memo is divided into thirty-five statements in numbered point form, some of them divided into sub-points. The prose is muscular, staccato, declaratory and without any explanatory material or other support. It is very much in the style and form of a military situation report. It is entirely without the circumlocutions, florid decorations, literary references and intellectual obfuscations that mark Mbeki's later, if not mature, style. However, it is characteristic of his preoccupations and imaginings as he expressed them in many later documents and (although at the time it was unattributed) is unmistakeably his. It was subtitled as a discussion document on the tasks of the ANC in the new epoch of democratic transformation and dated 9 August 1994.[6]

The reflections have two main messages: first, there can be no such thing as democratic politics in South Africa, only covert war without end, waged by implacable enemies of the ANC (a possible alternative reading is that Mbeki believes that democratic politics *is* covert war without end); and second, all internal dissension (and even debate) within the ANC and between it and 'the broad front of democratic forces', the tripartite alliance as well as 'the civics, the student, youth, religious and other organisations', is the result of underground counter-revolutionary tactics of opposition parties and residual counter-insurgency forces of the old regime, all orchestrated by the 'white-owned media', which is dedicated to the destruction of the ANC. This 'analysis' is contained in Sections 16–21 of the document under the heading 'Strategy and Tactics of the Opposition', doubtless a deliberate echo of the title of the ANC's own venerable revolutionary blueprint, which is updated on a regular basis.

This message, then, effectively says, 'Do not be fooled by what appear on the surface to be legitimate democratic competitors in the political market place, all of them are instruments of all-powerful shadow forces that will destroy us from without and within if we allow them.' Of particular relevance to the document's timing and the question of ANC leadership are the following points, which list some of the counter-revolutionaries' tactics:

17.0.2. Splitting the ANC around the issue of leadership, with various comrades within the movement being set up against one another on the basis that they represent different competing tendencies within the movement and ensuring that such a leadership wrangle assumes precedence over all other matters of interest to the organisation;
17.0.2.1. (This will be of particular relevance to the forthcoming National Conference of the ANC.)
17.0.2.2. Ensuring that such a contest or contests at the top, is/are replicated at all other levels of the movement; and,
17.0.2.3. Encouraging tension among the leadership of the ANC through a press campaign aimed to incite inter-personal competition among this leadership.

Even competition for the leadership – a common enough and legitimate feature of democratic politics – becomes an epiphenomenon of the counter-revolution and its machinations. It is of course necessary to recall that three months after this document was circulated, Mbeki was returned unopposed to the second highest leadership position in the ANC. It is also worth calling to mind that when Mbeki's nominee for deputy president of the ANC, Jacob Zuma, was faced with a contest for the post at the 1997 national conference, his rivals all suffered damaging leaks to the press, most of them false but enough to knock them out of the race. Rumours surfaced that Tokyo Sexwale, premier of Gauteng (including Johannesburg), South Africa's richest province, was a drug dealer and that Mathews Phosa, premier of Mpumalanga, had been a spy for apartheid security forces. Both withdrew.

Winnie Madikizela-Mandela was more durable, but there was enough about her to her discredit that *was* true to make her vulnerable. Still, it took last-minute rule manipulation at the conference itself to see her off. Gumede notes that Sexwale's supporters 'muttered darkly that the damaging gossip had been deliberately planted from within the Mbeki camp, but nothing could be proved'.[7] Whatever could or could not be proved, it is unlikely that the dark forces of the counter-revolution inspired the leaks, that they were sprung from closer to home and that Unmandated Reflections was a classic piece of misattribution as practised by intelligence agencies.

It is not clear how widely the document was circulated. In October 2006, as the struggle between Mbeki and Zuma was reaching its height, an anonymous 'staff reporter' (who sounds however more like an ANC insider) wrote in the *Mail and Guardian*,

> *Unmandated Reflections* remained like a dirty family secret in the privileged possession of a few senior ANC leaders who feared its release would cause outrage in the ranks of the alliance. Those who did read it at the time were dumbfounded by the grave predictions.[8]

This may or may not be true: the piece carries no supporting quotations and refers to no sources, not even anonymous ones, which points to it being an insider rather than a journalist. At one level, the 'Reflections' can seem uncannily prescient in the way they predict the developing tensions in the tripartite alliance and the ANC. However, at another level, Mbeki knew what was going to happen because he was going to make it happen and was, in a ploy well known to rugby players, 'getting his retaliation in first'. According to Gevisser, Mbeki 'ascribes to "external counter-revolutionary forces" what was actually a manifestation of an internal contradiction within the post-apartheid liberation movement', but the purpose of the 'Reflections' 'is precisely to foreclose such analysis and deny it legitimacy by labelling it "counter-revolutionary" in and of itself. Mbeki knew, already, that the economic policies his government was planning to follow would not be popular with the Left'.[9]

R. W. Johnson has a different interpretation of 'Reflections', seeing it as an instrument to capture the allegiance of a constituency of racial nationalism in default of any other popular base, the others – the Left, MK, the trade unions, the ANC organization and Mandela's popular constituency all being spoken for:

> The only element unrepresented was the racial nationalism previously championed by the PAC, Azapo, the Black Consciousness Movement

and many Bantustan politicians. Mbeki moved quickly to make this base his own. The only possible threat to ANC rule lay in divisions within the African bloc – and what better way to unite that bloc than to seek a fresh polarization of the electorate by warning of threats from white plots, the return of apartheid and from a mysterious but ubiquitous 'third force'?[10]

Whichever interpretation one favours however (and it is not impossible to believe that with his 'Reflections' Mbeki was multitasking), the notorious memo set the tone for the numerous conspiracy theories based on fevered imaginings in the Mbeki era and on into the Zuma year. These not only poisoned the external and internal politics of the ANC but also polluted the prospects of genuinely democratic politics emerging. This does not mean that Mbeki single-handedly imported conspiracies into the ANC; they predated him and, as we shall see, endured once he was gone. But it has to be said that they seemed to come readily to hand as part of his leadership repertoire. Gevisser dismisses the subject with an implicit shrug and a rhetorical question: if Mbeki believed that the forces of counter-revolution were still ranged against him:

> Given his history and world-view and the unreconstructed nature of the country he now governed, mid-wifed into freedom by an accommodation with the oppressor rather than outright victory – how could he have believed anything else?[11]

Perhaps it is as well to leave the last word on Mbeki's ascent to Mandela, who made an unscripted departure from his farewell speech as outgoing ANC president at the 1997 national conference that had just elected Mbeki unopposed. He said,

> There is a heavy burden on a leader elected unopposed. The temptation is to use the power to settle scores, get rid of detractors, surround oneself with yes men. The first duty of such a leader is to allay the concerns of fellow leaders, to allow them to discuss freely within the structures. A leader must keep the organisation together – he can't do it without allowing dissent, or allowing criticism without fear or favour.[12]

He did add, 'Nobody understands that principle better than my comrade, president Thabo Mbeki. I have not the slightest doubt he is not the man who is going to sideline anybody.' But he did not then say why, if he felt so much confidence in Mbeki, he needed to labour the point about leadership's temptations at all.

Mbeki as a representative individual

Of all the leadership roles that can be identified in a democracy, that of being a representative individual is probably the most difficult to assess, partly because there are few, if any, concrete outcomes by which to judge success or failure. Even winning elections is an uncertain criterion because victory or defeat can depend on so many variables – the standing of the leader's party with the electorate being an obvious determinant that may have much, or on the other hand little, to do with the leader. In addition, the elements that comprise an image of a representative leader are viewed very subjectively – every citizen or voter has his or her own criteria and what is more, these may operate at a subconscious level. Together these criteria and ways of being a representative individual can encompass so many traits and qualities that this leadership function can grow to overlap all the others (party management, policy coordination, etc.) and threaten to obscure them in an overall impression. Lastly, the image of a representative individual is often a composite made up of positions between polarities especially when comparisons with other leaders are part of the making of the composite. These polarities can include strong/consensual; demotic/patrician; aloof/gregarious; and down-to-earth/ intellectual, but these examples do not exhaust the possibilities. Leaders can also project an image of inclusivity across class and ethno-racial boundaries or one that reflects more the lives and experiences of one of the groups that make up a diverse society. The leader may choose to situate him or herself at various points between these poles, shading the emphases according to purpose and audience. This kind of tactic may be good politics, indeed an inescapable part of the task of reproducing support in a democracy, but still leave the leader open to charges of inconsistency, hypocrisy, duplicity or even just being 'an enigma'.

Such considerations occur across most, if not all, electoral democracies but understandably there are national peculiarities. Four of these stand out in the case of South Africa. The first and most obvious is the range and depth of diversity of the citizen population. For the purpose of monitoring the effect of policies to address historical inequalities and injustices, the old apartheid classifications – black African, white, coloured, Indian and 'other' – are retained in official statistics. Black Africans now account for nearly 81 per cent of the population (up from 77 per cent in 1991) and whites for 7.8 per cent (down from over 11 per cent in 1991).[13] While black Africans are demographically and electorally dominant (since voting has so far closely followed racial lines), whites hold a disproportionately large share of the country's wealth and income, although intra-racial inequality – between newly affluent and newly middle-class blacks and those still excluded from meaningful participation in the economy – became an increasingly significant socio-economic and political factor from the early 2000s onwards. Economic inequalities are overlaid by patterns of life experience that are shaped and held apart by education, language, employment patterns, separate pools of social capital, kinship and class networks. Obviously, these patterns overlap in ways and to an extent that were undreamed of under apartheid; however, the convergences remain quite limited and in some respects cohesion is threatened, not only by old divisions persisting but also by new ones emerging (between whites and blacks over 'redress', 'empowerment' and other 'transformation' issues, for instance). One study of nationalism and identity in South Africa posed the provocative question, 'Do South Africans exist?' Another referred to a 'minimum nation and an identity of convenience' as characterizing the state of nation-building in South Africa today.[14] Under these unpromising circumstances, how should a leader represent him or herself? What, if any, are the common denominators of representation that can communicate a leader's claims to lead?

A second characteristic of South Africa's democracy is the hold that the ANC's conception of collective leadership has had in the political marketplace. In a democracy, there is always scope for lack of fit between personal and party followings and mandates. A leader may run ahead of the party or behind it in popularity, although if the latter is the case he or she may soon be dispensed with by colleagues fearful for electoral prospects. A leader might appeal strongly to party activists but be seen as divisive by the generality of the electorate. There are many possible variations. However, the potential for lack of fit is particularly strong in South Africa because the ANC has occupied so much political space and its collective ethos is relentlessly, indeed neurotically, dedicated to suppressing individual leadership in theory and rhetoric, while in practice, as we have seen in Mbeki's ascent, being obsessed with it in private.

Its ethos is collective in two senses. It has an internal dimension in that no individual has a pre-eminent claim to leadership, which tradition and the ANC constitution claim is vested in the so-called top six and the NEC, and devolved right down the movement to the humblest branch. 'Collective' also has an external sense denoting the ANC's claim to be the leading force in society. As a result of this, there is a very high degree of confusion between personal and party followings and mandates. This is exacerbated by the wholly spurious pretence that leaders, or potential leaders, have absolutely no personal ambition other than to humbly serve in whatever capacity the collective wisdom of the party deems suitable for them. Although nobody inside or outside the ANC has ever taken this seriously in practice, the pretence has nevertheless contributed to creating a shadow world in which individual and collective leadership followings – and hence the extent to which any ANC leader can be a representative individual – are chronically obscured.

The third peculiarity of South Africa's democracy to affect the question of the leader as representative individual is the Mandela legacy. This is the leadership function in which his shadow fell longest and deepest. By comparison, he left no great visionary or intellectual legacy and his influence as a party manager and policy chief was not profound; in terms of South Africa's representation to the wider world, his influence was striking but fleeting. Mandela's success as a representative individual effectively had a base of common decency and the kind of folk wisdom and ethics that transcend ethnic and racial boundaries of culture. It did not need to be labelled as *Ubuntu* (of which in any case most cultures have some sort of parallel code) or marketed as uniquely African. His genius was to draw on a common pool of values and instincts that all South Africans (indeed all humanity) are assumed to share, or ought to share, or can be persuaded by his example and its unadorned and unqualified communication that they, at least in the moment, *do* share.

Finally, there is another side to being a representative individual that is peculiar to the ANC: that is the question of the struggle profile. Struggle credentials play a part in conceptions of leadership in all liberation movements. In South Africa, the issue does not begin to approach the toxic extremes of Zimbabwe, where, throughout the bitterly contested elections of the 2000s, the military chiefs frequently stated that they would not recognize Movement for Democratic Change (MDC) leader Morgan Tsvangirai if he won office because he had not borne arms in the liberation struggle. However, struggle credentials are important. Mbeki did not lose his liberty for extended periods like Mandela, Zuma and many others; he did not lead soldiers in battle like Hani; he did not stand at the head of mass demonstrations and face down armed police or soldiers and call out capitalist bosses like Ramaphosa; he did not personify the individual and collective suffering of his people at funerals and other demonstrations of mass emotion like Winnie Madikizela-Mandela.

In a movement that prided itself on requiring that people serve where they are directed and in the roles for which the movement was the arbiter of suitability and utility and not the individual's own judgement and ambition, the question of struggle profile should be irrelevant. In any case, Mbeki had to bear his share of suffering and sacrifice. He lost a son and a brother to the cause, in both cases under unexplained circumstances, which precluded closure. In any case, his exile meant that he scarcely knew either of them, and exile is a kind of suffering in its own right. Nonetheless, the right profile is important and probably Mbeki was aware of this from an early stage. That is the implication of his principal biographer. According to Gevisser, although it is a matter of record that Mbeki expressed the wish to leave Sussex University at the end of his first year to join the ANC's military wing, 'he has, retrospectively, somewhat exaggerated the image of the radical activist forced against his will to attend a British university for a full four years'.[15] Indeed, by the end of his first degree, Gevisser reports Mbeki's then girlfriend as recalling that the only time she saw him 'devastated to the point of loss of control' was when he was told by the ANC in his final year that it was time for him to join the army.[16] Nevertheless, it was as the suave and wily diplomat who talked antagonists down and round, rather than face them down at the sharp end, that he made his career in the struggle years.

Intellectuals in politics

When leadership issues and choices emerged from the shadows, this led inevitably to Mbeki's claims being built in part at least around claims to be a representative figure, recognizable as an intellectual (and in the more exalted effusions of his acolytes and of journalists in search of a soundbite, a 'philosopher king'). In the light of South Africa's history, this claim to leadership had more demotic purchase (at least in the beginning) than it habitually does in more developed democracies where higher education is much more widely dispersed and intellectuals in politics do not, on the whole, enjoy high public standing. Under apartheid, the history of outright denial of meaningful educational opportunity to Africans, followed by expanded access that was very strictly regulated, monitored and controlled for dissent, meant that there was a high degree of respect among Africans for those who had acquired strong educational qualifications and especially for those who had acquired them on their own terms. On the foundation of his education and his strong track record of persuading antagonists by patient, dialectical probing rather than confrontation, a fuller image could be built of a figure who represented progress and reconstruction in the widest senses of the words, on the basis of rationality and modernity. It has to remain an open question to what extent this image was consciously built by Mbeki and his advisers and how much the ANC elders, the media and the citizenry saw what they wanted to see in him. Certainly, the British and English-speaking South African media went far, despite doubts and qualifications, to cultivate this image in the run-up to Mbeki's takeover from Mandela.[17] Quite clearly, they were motivated in large part by relief that the country would not have to deal with a firebrand populist or committed ideologue.

Although an intellectual image for a political leader carried more purchase in South Africa in the heady days of transition to democracy than it might have elsewhere, there are certain generic problems with intellectuals as political leaders. In the first place, there is a case for saying that cerebral bonds are more fragile than visceral, especially in a country where unresolved identity issues loom very large and democratic values and practices are not well embedded. If my claim to lead is because I am unlike you – no matter that it is also based on my claim that I will open the way for you or at least your children to become more like me – this has a good chance of being less durable than my claim to personify you as you have been and are now. In their own very different ways, Mandela and Zuma could claim to be much more grounded in this sense than Mbeki. Part of this problem is the ease with which intellectuals can be portrayed as elitists, remote from everyday life experience and concerns. It is after all not uncommon for political leaders' perceived strengths to be reinterpreted as weaknesses or negative traits under the pressure of (usually) internal party conflict: it is but a short step between being praised for strength of will and purpose to being castigated for being unbending and dogmatic and from being valued for cool analysis to being rejected as aloof and elitist.

In addition, intellectualism by its very nature invites competing ideas and disputation, which in turn opens questions of how a leader who bases a large part of his appeal on being an intellectual will deal with competition and dissent. Much will depend on how such management relates to aspects of his personality other than the strictly cerebral. Is he tolerant of criticism? Does he tend to the consensual or to the autocratic? Is he secure in himself or threatened and anxious? The quite unrealistic cultural expectations of the ANC and broader African mythology of leadership – that rejects 'strong' leadership's claims over community and comradeship, frowns on confrontation within the group and expects consensus on the way forward to appear by some kind of magic osmosis – are also unhelpful for a climate of robust confrontation between incompatible ideas on political and economic organization, ensuring a clear choice between them and boldly taking them forward in policies.

Thirdly, cleverness in conflict resolution, especially in a broker's role, requires generous helpings of what Jonathan Powell, Tony Blair's chief of staff who helped Blair negotiate the Good Friday Agreement in Ireland (1998), has called 'constructive ambiguity' and 'creative vagueness'.[18] Mbeki's role in pre-negotiations and in defusing the threat from the Afrikaner right and Buthelezi's separatists may not have been an exact parallel with Blair's in

Ireland, but it was analogous and it relied on some of the same principles and had some of the same features. These included playing on the suggestibility of antagonists who were keen to find a way out but became aggrieved when, after they had taken the exit indicated by 'constructive ambiguity', they discovered that it led out into the cold. Mbeki wasn't a broker; he was committed to the ANC cause. However, he was good at making people feel that he was helping them, like a good intellectual, to stand outside the issue, view it objectively and understand their own interests better. This kind of thing was all very well when it was practised on antagonists on the other side of a deadly struggle. It was another when it was an important part of his political armoury in dealing with his own party.

Fourth and last, intellectual claims to leadership require a core. Ideally, for solidly grounded and durable leadership legitimacy, dialectic process – cleverness in argument and persuasion – has to be in the service of a vision that is broad-based, coherent and clearly articulated. Vision is not essential in a leader's portfolio, especially in a country that is, so to speak, politically and economically a going concern. However, for an intellectual who also thinks of himself as a revolutionary and whose country stands on the brink of a new era, with new and untested institutions and massive problems of social, economic and political distortion and division inherited from the past, vision is much more important.

A revisionist vision

All four of these generic issues can bear upon intellectuals in positions of political leadership, wherever they may be. All of them duly affected Mbeki's presidency as it unfolded. However, it was the question of finding a core vision to explain and justify his leadership that was most pressing at the outset. As we have noted, politics in post-apartheid South Africa were riven with ambiguities and the ANC, thanks to years of accretion with and without assimilation, was a broad church without a settled theology. Intellectual qualities notwithstanding, it is arguable whether or not Mbeki was the man to bring coherence to all of this after-years of playing his cards close to his chest (or up his sleeve) and adopting identities of convenience, such as his membership of the SACP and of its central committee, allegiances that he sloughed off in 1990. What was required now was a vision that would not only inspire others but also arm him with autonomy and mark him with distinctiveness. This, under the conditions of open democracy, would require him to put his cards on the table. Even visions pitched at autonomy and distinctiveness cannot come out of nowhere if they are to be truly effective, especially in an organization so obsessively concerned with continuity and unity. However, the available materials, no matter how potent each one was in its own right, were unpromising as the basis of a package. There was the Freedom Charter, which had been inspirational in the days when the ANC was far from government but provided only the broadest of guides to what, more than thirty years down the line, were altered global and national circumstances in which to discharge responsibilities of governance and policymaking.

Much more detailed prescriptions were available in the form of the largely SACP inspired ANC ideological documents, including iterations of the National Democratic Revolution (NDR) and various strategy and tactics documents. These, however, were (and are) thoroughly alienating to anyone who is not completely immersed in the ebb and flow of the ANC's various party lines. They are partisan, Manichaean, frequently borderline paranoid and both ponderous in thought and muddy in expression. They had their uses for Mbeki but mainly as an instrument of party management and for imposing himself on the wider Alliance. For these purposes, he devoted considerable attention to planning and writing additions and new iterations to them, along with his main ideologist, Joel Netshitenzhe. However, they would not do as a source for a broad-based vision for the country. Apart from being designed for internal use and tailored for cadres and apparatchiks, they were party documents and could not be publicly claimed as his own.

The Alliance Left was a source of ideas and to some extent a strategic centre; but the SACP was still engaged in trying to rework its Stalinist past – flotsam to which it clung until the last possible minute as the soviet ship went down – into something relevant to the new world order. For its part, Cosatu seemed to want its cake and eat it – the privileges of access that the Alliance gave to it, combined with freedom of independent action. Not only did Mbeki think that the Left's policies were unworkable in a globalized world, but in any case if he positioned himself too close to them he would be in danger of losing his autonomy as leader and even of becoming the Left's prisoner.

What remained when these potential sources were excluded was the ramshackle architecture of the temporary nation that had been put together with generous helpings of constructive ambiguity and with the massive weight of Mandela's prestige behind it, in order to get the country and its people through the seismic period of democracy's establishment. This was composed of fidelity to the settlement, a belief in South Africa's exceptionalism, faith in the liberal principles and institutions of the Constitution, preoccupation with reconciliation between black and white and affirmation of the ANC's commitment to non-racialism. This would not be sufficient for Mbeki's own aims and those that he had for the country. These aims included the need to distance himself from Mandela and put clear water between him and the Alliance Left. Above all, it meant creating a basis of popular support broad enough to hold the country together but concentrated enough to give himself a durable base for the legitimacy of his leadership and a loyal following.

He needed these things to sustain him and win him time and autonomy for the struggle he knew was developing with the Left over his acceptance that South Africa would have to adapt itself to being a small, open, trading economy in a globalized world and, as a result, embrace free trade, (relatively) free movement of capital and a macroeconomic policy that emphasized monetary and fiscal stability. Another priority for which he needed time and space was to administer a sharp corrective to what he saw as a poorly thought through emotional attachment to the 'New South Africa', in particular complacency on the part of whites who had, in his eyes, neither addressed their responsibility for the past nor faced up to how they and the country would have to change in the future. What was needed was a harder, longer, but, above all, more honest route to reconciliation.

These purposes suggested the need for a new synthesis, one that would preferably not abandon wholesale the shaky foundations of the new South Africa but reassemble the construction that stood on them in what Mbeki probably saw as an artful project of renovation. In this way, fidelity to the settlement, the Constitution, reconciliation and non-racialism would be reaffirmed but made subject to stringent terms and conditions which pushed full realization of nation-building so far into the future that it was over the horizon. The fulfilment of these things would be subject to the achievement of two goals: first, a level of material well-being sufficient for African people to enjoy the rights and liberties of the Constitution, for, as every undergraduate student of political philosophy knows, under conditions of great material inequality, rights are differentially enjoyed by rich and poor; second, the restoration of African pride and, for the first time in history, the achievement of respect from others – especially their former and, in Mbeki's eyes, current oppressors.

At the core of Mbeki's revisionist synthesis, then, was the need for a vision that was inclusive, non-partisan and rooted in a version of the values that had brought South Africa this far but which acknowledged bluntly how far there was still to go. This vision had to recognize a special place for Africans as constituting the demographic and moral core of the nation, but this part of the vision should be neither parochial nor culturally backward-looking. At the same time, the vision should offer no comfort to recalcitrant whites while denying purchase for populists. It was an austere vision without immediate retail appeal for anyone.

The 'I am an African' and 'Two Nations' speeches

Mbeki expressed his core vision fairly consistently throughout his presidency but in an increasingly strident register as time went on. His most measured and complete versions were in the 'I am an African' and 'Two Nations' speeches, both of which came during his time as Mandela's deputy president.[19]

'I am an African' was praised at the time for its poetry, its imagery and its inclusiveness. It begins with invocations of Africa's topography, climate, flora and fauna. Although the place names are South African, the country itself is not named and there is already a sense of generic Africanness. The subject of 'I am' is, to begin with, an abstracted individual composed of the idealized life histories of all, native, settler, transported slave and immigrant, oppressor and oppressed, that compose South Africa's population past and present.

A turning point is reached when:

> I have seen our country torn asunder as these, all of whom are my people, engaged one another in a titanic battle, the one to redress a wrong that had been caused by one to another and the other, to defend the indefensible.[20]

The entanglements caused in trying to portray no one as alien while at the same time making a clear moral statement about the nature of the country's conflicted past begin to make themselves felt, and from then the speech lurches between the poles of inclusivity and partisanship. After some haunting and anguished passages on the conflict and its devastating human aftermath, including those 'who have learned to kill for a wage … like pawns in the service of demented souls', the subject changes again to 'the people who would not tolerate oppression' and 'the nation' that would not let fear cause the perpetuation of injustice as well as 'the great masses who are our mother and father'. It is the 'victory' of these masses who have acquired the right to formulate 'their own definition of what it means to be African' that is being celebrated in the occasion and the speech. Having acknowledged the Constitution, the words of the Freedom Charter 'South Africa belongs to all who live in it, black and white' (though without referencing the source), it delivers one of Mbeki's key messages:

> The dignity of the individual is both an objective that society must pursue, and it is a goal which cannot be separated from the material well being of that individual.[21]

Then the subject moves to Mbeki himself, 'It feels good that I can stand here as a South African and as a foot soldier of a titanic African army, the African National Congress.' This, with its associations of ubiquity and irresistibility, was a jarring note, especially for those already aware of the ANC's delusions of omnipotence and determined efforts to fuse itself with the state. But with the long perspective of hindsight on the ANC's subsequent history, calling the ANC a 'titanic' army strikes a grimly humorous not, given the Titanic's associations with hubris and disaster. However, the speech recovers its inclusive tone in wishing (somewhat bathetically) 'congratulations and well done!' to all who contributed to the Constitution.

Finally, in what is effectively a coda, the speech situates Africanness on the continent rather than in the country, 'I am an African. I am born of the peoples of the continent of Africa,' invoking solidarity and a common future.

If the intention was to make sure that no South African had to feel alien, then the speech may have been effective for many. But with its ever-changing individual and collective subjects and insistently non-specific bases of inclusion, it was easy to get the impression that everybody belonged but that whatever they belonged to was wrapped in 'a kind of heroic opacity'.[22] Ivor Chipkin asks whether or not the shifting subject (especially where it comes to rest on an unproblematic 'our') implies a hierarchy of African authenticity between indigenous and immigrant. Gevisser finds Mbeki's 'inclusive, hybrid and syncretic' Africanism less problematic, praising his 'act of appropriation that is identity politics at its most sophisticated' in assimilating the identity of his oppressor and using it to define himself.[23] Sophisticated 'I am an African' certainly was but at the expense of clarity. Unusually for Mbeki, the speech was not long-winded and convoluted. It lacked clarity, nevertheless, but it was the opacity that comes from brevity and being aphoristic; it was gnomic, in the sense of enigmatic and ambiguous. And to say merely that it lacked the common touch is to underestimate its distance from everyday concerns.

Perhaps in a sense 'I am an African' was Mbeki's 'Je vous ai compris' moment of creatively vague leadership. On 4 June 1958, three days after he had accepted the presidency of France under emergency conditions, General de Gaulle visited Algeria in an attempt to defuse the war of independence and settler revolt. From a balcony, he addressed a huge crowd with the opening words, 'Je vous ai compris' (I have understood you, implying that he was also listening). The response was immediate and ecstatic. All the warring groups, the Algerian insurgents, the army and the settlers, but especially the last, thought that he sympathized with them. In fact, he was not at all specific about what he understood, with whom he sympathized or that he would shortly make decisions that would inevitably take the part of one side or another (since they were incompatible). In similar ways, Mbeki's opaque inclusivity would shortly give way to a quite different conceptualization of who was who and what was what.

Alistair Horne's succinct verdict on 'Je vous ai compris' in his masterly study of the Algerian war could apply to Mbeki too: 'Such is the uncertainty of human communication.'[24] He might have added, 'in the hands of political leaders for whom constructive ambiguity is a way of life'.

In sharp contrast to 'I am an African', there was no ambiguity in 'Two Nations' speech. Addressing himself head on to the subjects of reconciliation and nation-building, Mbeki promised to be honest, however discomfiting, as a preamble to: 'We[25] therefore make bold to say that South Africa is a country of two nations.' One nation is white and 'relatively prosperous', its members able to exercise their right to equal opportunity. The second, larger nation, is black and poor, to whom the right of equal opportunity is merely theoretical:[26]

> The reality of two nations, underwritten by the perpetuation of the racial, gender and spatial disparities born of a very long period of colonial and apartheid white minority domination constitutes the material base which reinforces the notion that, indeed we are not one nation but two nations.

As a warm up to the bald statement of two nations, Mbeki had categorized all nation-building up to that point as dishonest; he went on to insist that the period of true reconciliation was open-ended and would be very protracted, that all significant inequality was race-based and there could be no other dynamic at work. As a seminar paper or an electioneering polemic, this would have been fine. As a statement of national political leadership, it was bad politics. In the first place, it was an inaccurate analysis. According to the foremost researchers on inequality in post-apartheid South Africa;

> Insofar as South Africa comprises a divided nation it is perhaps most accurate to see it in terms of three broad classes, not two racially defined nations: an increasingly multiracial upper class, comprising not just high profile corporate figures but much more broadly the professional, managerial and business classes; a 'middle' class of mostly urban, employed workers; and a marginalised class of outsiders, comprising many of the unemployed as well as workers in agricultural and domestic employment.[27]

This kind of framework would be much more honest as well as accurate and could still carry a powerful message about inequality based on class as well as race. But to adopt it would have had Mbeki veering dangerously close to the language and concepts of the Left. Moreover, it would have meant acknowledging that the African population was not an unambiguously united community and thus relinquishing the tempting prize of constituting all black people as his constituency. However, in order to avert the danger and grasp at the temptation, Mbeki had to reveal that he was not merely renovating the architecture of the settlement but tearing the whole building down. Moreover, by quarantining whites in a separate nation, he perpetrated one of the biggest ironies of the post-apartheid era. Negotiations and the transition to democracy were made possible because whites were persuaded to abandon their pretensions to separate nationhood and throw in their lot with a single, unified nation. The persuader in chief was of course none other than Thabo Mbeki, who then took an early opportunity to expel them from the single unified nation and for good measure brand it as a fraud.

Party manager: A Third Way in the Third World?

Before the controversy of Mbeki's HIV/AIDS dissidence and Jacob Zuma's insurrection eclipsed all other aspects of his presidency, Mbeki was frequently categorized as a 'Third Way' political leader with a mission to turn the ANC into a social democratic party. It was usually left wing or at least 'progressive' critics of Mbeki's espousal of 'neo-liberalism' that invoked this comparison and it was seldom, if ever, deployed as a compliment. William Mervyn Gumede provides a typical example:

> The ANC encouraged by Mbeki and his strategists would be shaped along social democratic lines not unlike Britain's New Labour Party, the German Social Democratic Party and the Swedish Social Democratic Party.[28]

Such comparisons by critics obsessed with neo-liberalism tend to concentrate solely on macroeconomic policy and leave out the project of one-partyism aimed at perpetual hegemony resting on a quasi-soviet fusion of party and state, as well as the unfolding agenda of racial nationalism, not to mention the paranoia of such documents as 'Unmandated Reflections' which was the first but not the last of its kind. These unconcealed attributes of the ANC under Mbeki's leadership made it about as unlike a Western European social democratic party as you can get without going off the democratic scale altogether.

However, if these inconvenient elephants in the room are ignored, then there are at least some superficial similarities. Like other third-way leaders, Mbeki was convinced that limitations on state power and policy autonomy in the global economy were enough to rule out socialism in one country and to require fundamental revision of approaches to economic development. Essentially, his approach was that the cause of reducing poverty and inequality can be served by the market, if a balance can be struck in a mixed economy between leaving the private sector free enough to generate growth and jobs (if not the latter then at least the former) and taxing and regulating it closely enough to fund public services and redistribute to those who are the collateral damage of capitalism's creative destruction.

The corollary to this group of convictions is that because they flew in the face of previous iterations of party principles and policies, to make them operational it would first be necessary to gain control of the party and to promote these policies, both inwardly and outwardly, in a coherent, single-minded and unified way. That is, third-way enterprises were projects of party control, renewal and reorientation. Although there was a basic similarity along these lines between Mbeki's position and that faced by Blair, there were enormously significant discrepancies, which shaped the leadership challenges in quite different ways.

In Britain, Europe and the United States, third-way projects were born of the need to make left of centre or progressive parties electable. When Blair's New Labour Party won the 1997 election, Labour had been out of office for eighteen years and had lost four general elections in a row, some of them humiliatingly. When Clinton won the presidency in 1992, the Democrats had over the previous twelve years lost three presidential elections in a row. When Mbeki took over the presidency in 1999, it was on the back of two crushing electoral victories in a row in favour of the ANC and the prospect of many more to come, especially with the aura of Mandela still shining its light on the political marketplace. Blair and other similar leaders had their hands strengthened immeasurably by the promise of delivering long-awaited political power if the party changed and the threat of continuing oblivion if it didn't. Mbeki had nothing like this in his gift and he could not even claim that the ANC's electoral popularity was due to his leadership; it was the movement's victory, not his.

Like Mbeki, Blair led a party in which labour unions had historically played a prominent role, but in the case of the Labour Party that Blair took over in 1994 they had been battered by years of attack from Thatcher's governments, devastated by deindustrialization and, thanks to public memories of the militancy of the strike-ridden 1970s (fuelled by an unremittingly hostile and predominantly right-wing press), ranked low in public esteem. By contrast,

Mbeki had to deal with a labour confederation that was the best-organized component of his party's wider alliance and which had played as important a part as any other part of the liberation movement in bringing the National Party to negotiation. The balance of power in the party and movement that Mbeki had to manage was quite different from that faced by Blair.

In short, the portrayal of Mbeki as a third-way leader does have a certain suggestive resonance and it had its uses for left-wing critique of his macroeconomic policy, but it does not stand up well to systematic examination in the light of his parallel and shadow projects, which are quite unlike the conventional social democratic agenda, and also of the different internal and external political circumstances of his leadership.

Another of the weaknesses of the third way comparison is that it treats the ANC as if it were, under Mbeki's leadership, an established political party with a settled history of organizing and functioning in a democracy that simply required remodelling. Unlike the new generation of social democratic leaders in established democracies, Mbeki's challenge was not simply to renew an existing model of ideology and political organization, a going concern that had temporarily broken down under the pressure of altered social and economic circumstances. Mbeki had, in effect, to create an entirely new party to operate under entirely novel circumstances – democracy – out of disparate elements (unions, SACP, UDF, the various components of the ANC itself – exiles, prisoners, soldiers), each of which had developed its own dynamic. What is more, he had to do this while paying tribute at all times to continuity with the past and to the unity, which in a central tenet of its collective self-belief had sustained it and carried it to victory. Homage to unity had, what is more, to coexist with tribute to the pluralist nature of the liberation movement, the broad-church nature of the ANC and the autonomy of the members of the Alliance, the nature of whose limits was a touchy subject to all concerned.

The shakiness of this edifice of belief is why the credo of unity had to be continually affirmed and why the idea of the ANC having a soul was (and is) so important. However, the basis of that unity – struggle against statutory racial discrimination backed by ruthless repression – was gone. It was quite correct to argue, as Mbeki himself did – that the economic and social legacies of that system and that struggle lingered and would do so for a very long time, that it was dishonest to pretend that they had magically disappeared or that they would gracefully solve themselves under the new conditions of freedom. The question for Mbeki's leadership would be how to reproduce the ideological and organizational unity required to address these malign legacies in ways that he, with the help of allies, was determined to define. This would have to be done under conditions of freedom and opportunity for the members and at a time when the associated bodies, particularly of the Left, wanted close access and influence but autonomy at the same time to press for their ways addressing those legacies.

As overall party manager Mbeki had to lead an organizational apparatus composed of members who, in theory at least, held an exalted status in the organization but whose quality, consequent on rapid and massive expansion of numbers after legalisation and when it became clear what a plethora of opportunities the ANC offered for advancement, was a constant source of anxiety to leaders; a party machine composed of elected officials at all levels and functionaries under them, though this conventional descriptive label dignified what was far from a well-oiled apparatus, and indications of organizational shortcomings amounting to chaos and fraud in some regions were soon to appear in the reports of secretary generals; public representatives at national, provincial and local levels; associate organizations, whether formally allied like the SACP and Cosatu or more loosely affiliated like Contralesa.

This functional breakdown was conventional enough and recognizable in other democratic polities, though each relationship within it posed its own challenges. What was less well recognized in Mbeki's time was that there was another breakdown, what might be labelled 'geopolitical' in that the demographic, political, economic and ethnic geography of the country made itself felt in shaping the ANC's organizational challenges. For instance, ANC electoral majorities and per capita party membership tend to be highest in provinces that have the largest African majorities, are least well-developed, poorest, most rural and most heavily marked by the legacy of apartheid's political geography of Bantustans. By contrast, the biggest metropolitan areas house the largest concentrations of people other than African; they are on the whole more developed and their populations, black and white are better educated and richer (though all metropolitan areas have large numbers of poor and unemployed people). As ANC leader, Mbeki had to deal with two strong gravitational pulls away from the centre: an ideological one towards the Alliance Left as an alternative centre of ideas and organization and another centrifugal force, but with a much more diffuse effect, towards multiple centres of influence, mostly powered by patronage, around locally powerful individuals in the ANC's provincial structures. Mbeki, as we shall see, was greatly preoccupied by the ideological dimension of party management and although he could see the threat to organizational integrity from the provinces and indeed moved decisively in his own terms to deal with it, he probably underestimated its importance and the likely consequences of his unilateral and uncompromising assertion of central authority over the provinces.

The Left, African nationalism and the young lady from Riga (1: The Mbeki years)

The cautionary tale of the young lady from Riga, 'who smiled as she rode on the tiger', carries a warning against unwise political alliances because, 'at the end of the ride, she was inside and the smile on the face of the tiger'. The warning is particularly relevant for parties and movements of the Left, which for tactical reasons ally themselves to nationalist counterparts in anti-colonial or other developing country struggles. Typically, they do this in order to capitalize on the wider and more visceral popular appeal of national liberation, especially in places where uneven economic development has limited the size of the industrial population that is a natural constituency for socialism. What such alliances should consist of and who should preside over them is a sensitive problem of political management, especially after national liberation has been achieved, nationalists are in government, political mobilization is open and competitive and (in the case of South Africa) the clandestine qualities of political organization that facilitated the SACP's entryism and obscured its relationship with the ANC are largely gone.

How should influence be distributed between the partners? What structures should give institutional form to the alliance? How much autonomy should the junior partner (usually the socialist component) have? How might expectations change when the oppressor is no longer in power (but not defeated)? When and on what terms is it necessary to bring the Alliance to an end? Issues of this sort were major preoccupations of Mbeki's presidency, both for Mbeki himself and the leaders of the other two members of the Tripartite Alliance, Cosatu and the SACP.

The Alliance was formed in early 1990, shortly after the unbanning of the ANC and the SACP, bringing to an end the long period of entryism and secrecy in which SACP members dominated the exile structures of the ANC.[29] Cosatu had been an open and legal organization since its founding in 1985 and though it had been subject to both legal and extralegal harassment (including violence) from the apartheid government and its security forces, it did not have the same clandestine history as the other two. Mbeki himself had been a member of the SACP, but he quietly left in 1990 after perhaps as much as a decade of growing disaffection based on his conviction of the unwisdom of the SACP's turn to insurrectionist tactics in the 1980s, a developing understanding of political economy that was confirmed by the collapse of the Soviet Union and a poor personal relationship with SACP general secretary, Joe Slovo.[30]

Each alliance partner is an independent organization with its own constitution, membership and programmes, goals and tactics. A succinct description written before the 1994 election gives a serviceable summary of the conventional rationale for the Alliance and the needs from and contributions to it of the three partners:

> The Alliance continues because of a happy coincidence of present political interests. The ANC needs the organisational skills, material support and membership of the country's largest trade union federation. Many of its best strategists and election prospects belong to the SACP and the party's reputation for militancy has given it a powerful base in the ANC's constituency. Cosatu needs a political organisation which can win the election for the constituent assembly and represent its interests in government. The SACP does not have enough popular support to be a powerful political force on its own, so it must remain in alliance with its more powerful partners and try to get them to incorporate its political and social objectives in their agendas.[31]

While this is an accurate enough snapshot of the Alliance as it stood in the 1990s and to some extent the bases for mutual cooperation and support described in it remained relevant thereafter, it does not deal with the basic tensions between the partners which were quick to show themselves in the second half of the 1990s. From then on, they consumed a substantial amount of the energies of leaders of all the partners. Cosatu and the SACP, in particular, have been engaged in perpetual heart-searching about the Alliance almost from the beginning, fearing that they (particularly the SACP) would be swallowed by the ANC, which was much bigger and, thanks to access to state power, much more powerful. For its part, the ANC wondered why the SACP and Cosatu tail should wag the ANC dog. In the 1994 election, 12.37 million people voted for the ANC; in the following year, the SACP claimed 75,000 members but 'perhaps the real figure, in terms of politically active membership is about a half or a third the official figure'.[32] At about the same time, Cosatu had a membership of perhaps 1.8 million, although in purely left-wing terms Cosatu's affiliates and members were as broad a church as the ANC was itself and it was far from a monolithic bloc.

Figures such as these shaped the Alliance relationships and fed resentments on both sides. However, the SACP and Cosatu felt that raw numbers did not tell the whole story. Cosatu felt with some justice that without the organizational skills and the committed work of its members the ANC would not get as many votes as it did, especially in later elections as liberation euphoria wore off somewhat. The SACP saw itself as a vanguard party, housing members with more highly developed political consciousness and (a subject of especial irritation to Mbeki) acting not only as the voice of the working class but also the conscience and custodian of value for the whole liberation movement. In this self-regarding respect, its relatively small numbers were irrelevant, perhaps even an asset; the spectacular growth in member numbers to the tens of thousands after the party's unbanning, albeit from a tiny base, was a source of regular debate between those who welcomed a mass base and those who worried about dilution of the party's vanguard qualities.

Tensions came to a head over the Growth, Employment and Redistribution (GEAR) macroeconomic policy, which was introduced in 1996. It has ever after been referred to on the Left as 'the 1996 class project'. Cosatu and SACP criticisms, both of GEAR's 'conservative' substance and the allegedly high-handed manner in which it was introduced, were sharply and publicly expressed. This in turn violated another of the ANC's procedural myths from the underground days, a corollary of democratic centralism, that criticism could only be expressed in internal forums. Despite being hopelessly unrealistic as an operating principle in an open democracy, it was a useful (and probably cynical) instrument of party management for ANC leaders and especially Mbeki.

Matters came to a head at the SACP's 10th National Congress in July 1998, when both Mandela and Mbeki addressed the delegates. Variously described at the time by words such as, 'tough', 'fiery', 'finger-wagging', 'ferocious', the two speeches were an unambiguous statement of ANC and government supremacy.[33] Mandela reiterated the government line that the policy was fundamental and not negotiable and that as long as he was leader, GEAR would remain:

> We fought and defeated one of the most brutal regimes in history. We have won the right to state our views freely and without fear. We are prepared to listen to our comrades. But I would give a warning that if Cosatu and the SACP leave the internal structures of the organisation and go public, and not only attack what we consider a fundamental policy of the organisation but ridicule it, they must be aware of the implications.[34]

The consequences were not spelled out as such but were widely understood to be 'toe the line or get out of the Alliance'.[35] Aside from the main message, two points of significance for assessing the development of ANC leadership in the early years of government should be noted. First, Mandela stressed the importance of the liberation struggle in achieving free speech, yet in the same breath he stated bluntly that free speech is only permissible (for 'comrades') in the controlled environment of ANC and alliance structures. The second point of significance is that for once there appears to be no ambiguity of authorship attached to the speech, and the words (and sentiments) were Mandela's own and not ghost-written by Mbeki. To judge from first-hand accounts, Mandela's warnings to the SACP came as an unscripted addendum to a courteous speech of acceptance for an award in the name of Chris Hani.[36] However having come to an end, he said that that had been a speech written for him 'by his masters' and now he would speak in his own words. It appears that although the Left holds Mbeki as the principal villain, there was more continuity in ANC leadership in the Alliance than the unions and communists have been prepared to acknowledge.

For its part, Mbeki's speech to the 10th National Congress was a classic of his style, which he used across his leadership from party management to confronting whites, liberals, Western governments and anyone else he felt needed putting in their place. Since it stands for so many other speeches, it is worth looking at closely as a component of his leadership repertoire.[37]

According to Mbeki, his Left antagonists mirror 'right wing critics' (i.e. whites, liberals, mainstream media) and wittingly or not serve the 'right wing agenda', which is to show that 'our government has failed as all other African governments have failed'; have not properly studied the relevant documents ('I'd like to invite delegates to study'); do not take into account the difficult situation faced by government policymakers ('Comrades appear to have forgotten' – the apartheid legacy, the global economy); have departed from traditional ANC ways of doing things ('This manner of proceeding, which is new to the Congress movement'); are acting like populists by indulging in 'fake revolutionary posturing', making irresponsible promises to 'our mass base'.

To add to the list of crimes, Mbeki (in a speech dripping with sarcasm) accuses the Left in *their* documents of 'being sarcastic'. It remains only to remind his antagonists of some or other classic of wisdom from revolutionary literature, often Marxism-Leninism, but sometimes (as in this case) from the canon of anti-colonial revolution. The aphorism, 'Tell no lies! Claim no easy victories', had wide currency in the liberation struggle (indeed across the Third World) to counsel patience in long struggles and it apparently gave Mbeki great pleasure to use the conventional wisdom and sacred texts of his opponents against them.[38] When Marxism-Leninism was the chosen medium of instructing his critics how they had strayed from their own path and didn't even know their own material, 'Ultra leftism' and Lenin on the 'infantile disorder of left wing communism' were favourite tropes of Mbeki and his acolytes.

The Left did not capitulate completely under this double-barrelled assault from Mandela and Mbeki; SACP and Cosatu spokesmen continued to voice reasoned opposition to the government's macroeconomic policy, albeit in a much more temperate register.[39] However, the attack underlined the determination of the ANC and government to be masters in what they saw as their own houses, which crystallized the unhappy choices facing the left components of the Alliance:

> To simply follow the ANC line would mean the complete submerging of the SACP's identity to become an appendage of the ruling party; to move outside would be to go into a wilderness where survival is not guaranteed.[40]

For the immediate future, the SACP and Cosatu veered towards the first of these unpalatable options until another option later presented itself, that of hijacking the ANC by installing a leader who would be beholden to them, by exploiting the contingency of the Mbeki-Zuma rift. However, this would not be for another six or seven years and for the moment, Mbeki, if his constitutionally anxious temperament could allow it, was entitled to a tiger's smile:

> Through a combination of outright political intimidation, ideological mysticism and the co-option of key ANC troublemakers and Cosatu/ SACP leaders into his governmental inner circle, Mbeki had largely succeeded in quashing genuine opposition and controlling the boundaries of debate.[41]

Co-option was probably the main key to coping with the Left.[42] It was easy enough to manage, especially since there were good grounds to justify movement of leftists into positions where the ANC and Mbeki himself could keep an eye on them. There had already been a mass migration of communists and trade unionists into parliament when the 1994 electoral list was drawn up and into government when it was formed after the election; with a massive skills shortage to cope with, the Alliance partners were obvious places to look and if individuals were not motivated by careerism, there were good grounds alternatively to see the move in idealistic terms of public service and patriotic contribution to reconstruction. The observant might have noted, however, that by the time of the 10th Congress in 1998 there had already been a countermovement out of parliament and government, with some individuals disillusioned and others squeezed out. Successful as it was in the short term, however, co-option failed to achieve two related things: it did not decapitate the Alliance partners who elected new (mostly) younger and more radical leaders; indeed in the case of the SACP, this had already happened before the 10th National Congress.[43] Additionally, since the general tendency was for the co-opted leaders to drift away from their constituencies, the strategy did not swing these constituencies behind Mbeki. Effectively, it was a repeat of the strategy Mbeki adopted when competing for the leadership of the ANC; since he could not or would not cultivate a critical mass of personal support, he tried to acquire one ready-made. This could work up to a point, but indirect, transferred loyalties are not so durable as those acquired directly and at the grass roots. Both these failings would come back to haunt Mbeki.

Behind the struggle over the nature and workings of the Alliance were at least three shaping factors: disagreement over the order in which growth and redistribution should take place and over the balance between state and market in securing the conditions for both growth and redistribution; the respective salience of class and race in South Africa's political economy; and the limits of pluralism in the ANC's internal democracy.

Although Mbeki was not alone in wanting to draw the limits of pluralism tightly and decisively – as we have noted Mandela was vocal and unambiguous on this count – he is generally seen as the main author and driver of increasing centralization in party management. It is possible to see a pattern, whether one approves of it or not, from demobilization – the assimilation and/or marginalizing of the UDF and other civil-society components of the liberation struggle – to depoliticization, in the form of discouraging Alliance partners from contesting the ANC's economic policy, in public at least. The rationale for this was along the following lines: government policy may be inspired from below (the ANC has a policy conference involving branch representatives a few months before the elective national conference) and performance may be accountable downwards. But policy has to be made possible in the real world by technocratic calculation free from political contestation on the part of what are merely semi-detached interest groups, not the heart and soul of the organization. This is what the Alliance partners are, no matter how closely aligned with the ANC they may be. This does, however, avoid the obvious question of where the exact location of the elusive heart and soul of the ANC might be.

In a sense, this is a variation on democratic centralism. An advocate of centralisation might sum up his case in the following way: 'We have paid our local and grassroots democracy dues by having even our highest ANC leaders elected by those who have been elected from below. The electoral chain goes right down to the humblest member. With that mandate we expect you to accept leadership from above and give leaders the space to do their job.' As the durability of the Alliance struggles suggests, this argument is harder to apply to the Alliance than to the ANC itself, since the SACP and Cosatu have their own leaders, elected by *their* members and are accountable to them. This means such struggles are not clear-cut and not only are they messy but in the end irresolvable, short of the left partners accepting complete assimilation or opting for complete independence. However, issues relating to pluralism and internal party democracy should have been far clearer within the ANC itself than they were (and remain) with the Alliance. This, however, turned out not to be the case.

Provinces: Central leadership and local democracy

The second of the two centrifugal forces Mbeki had to deal with as party manager also involved questions of pluralism, this time in the form of local democracy within the ANC itself. Although in theory the core ANC ought to be easier to manage than the Alliance, this proved not to be the case for Mbeki, because the central/local issues which were raised concerned one of the most troublesome features of the settlement, the provinces. How problematic the provinces would be was not easily predictable at the time. By the time the negotiations were complete and the Constitution put to bed, the ANC had bought into a somewhat complacent narrative about the provinces. In this narrative, reactionaries – the rump of Afrikaner nationalism, Zulu chauvinist separatists and liberals in thrall to federal conceptions of democracy – had all wanted to defend themselves against fundamental change by copying the machinations of colonialists and of apartheid's architects by perpetuating the balkanization of South Africa through versions of federalism. These were not the same. Some were relatively pure (inspired by German *Länder* and lobbied for by German *Stiftungen*), others bastardized, such as Buthelezi's monarchical and confederal fantasies. However in the eyes of the ANC, all were bogus, stalking horses for various racial and tribal interests who shared the aim of denying democracy and the aspirations of the African majority.

Fortunately, this narrative continued; the ANC's wily and hard-headed negotiators saw through all this and the result was a strong, unitary state with only homeopathic doses of local powers mainly in the form of disbursing amounts allocated by central government for social spending. That the provinces could *spend* what turned out to be very large amounts of money, but had only the most derisory powers to *raise* money, should perhaps have sounded warning bells in the ANC, but a greater priority was to ensure that the boundaries of provinces were drawn up to ensure that the greatest number of them would be won by the ANC and that the reactionary forces would be routed. The ANC duly won seven of the nine provinces in 1994, the exceptions being the Western Cape and KwaZulu-Natal. What this somewhat self-satisfied narrative failed to take into account was that the provinces might turn out to be a source of headaches for the ANC government, not from the machinations of reactionaries but from within its own ranks.

Central to these problems was not so much the overriding imperative that South Africa had to be a unitary state; it was rather that the ANC acted initially as if it believed that it had inherited one, rather than having to create one. Partly this was a result of the resistance myth, that the colonialists had conquered and subdued a single African people. In reality, conquest, settlement and state making in the nineteenth and twentieth centuries had operated according to an opportunistic and at times contingent dynamic of accretion at the expense of a diverse collection of discrete African peoples and state forms. Balkanization was certainly a preoccupation of colonialism and apartheid, but it was not superimposed on a single, pre-colonial African people and polity. Resistance to the imposition of inferior status and denial of rights, in the context of the centripetal force of economic development, may have created a single, though still diverse African people and the ANC's assumption of the leading role in the liberation struggle coupled with its post-transition electoral victories gave this unity a kind of expression. But the state form to accommodate this single people had to be built on the ground as well as in the pages of the Constitution.

Even when ANC leaders understood this principle, they were inclined to underestimate the extent to which it applied to the ANC itself. In short, some kind of balance had to be found between centralization, pluralism and local democracy in both the state and the party. In the central state there was a substantial amount of continuity with the old, white central state, now clothed in the language of rights and constitutionalism. But in both state and party, there was much less scope for building on continuity in relations between centre and periphery; the governance system of the old 'white' provinces had been discarded by the nationalist government even before the end of apartheid and the Bantustans had to be incorporated into the new unitary state. In the ANC itself, there was no history of formal, open, nationwide organization to build on at all and it turned out that it was not enough merely to declare that the ANC was a unified organization for it to become one.

The issue that threw centre-periphery relations into sharpest relief and overlapped both state and party was that of the office of provincial premier in those provinces where the ANC had won a majority.[44] To begin with, local democracy was respected by the principle that the ANC premier should also be the ANC leader in the province, that is, the elected chair of the ANC

Provincial Executive Council. Respect for local factors and loyalties did not translate into a completely 'hands-off' policy from the centre:

> In shepherding its preferred candidates into premierships, the national party involved itself in protracted negotiations with local and regional elements of the party. Efforts were made to fit the new premiers to some earlier involvement in their provinces.[45]

However, by August 1998, it was apparent to the ANC leadership and to Mbeki in particular that a more robust employment of central power was required. They were 'apparently shaken by provincial failures of self-management' and announced in that month that all future premiers would be 'deployed' by the national government.[46] This announced the intention of doing two things: shifting power decisively from the provinces to the centre and from the party to the government.

In the background, there were three sources of tension. The first was serious capacity and integrity problems, that is corruption[47] and incompetence in provincial government and party organization, that were detailed by various task teams and commissions[48] and by the office of the ANC secretary general. The second was the emerging reality that provincial leaders, thanks to the way elections for national office in the party were organized, and to the availability of provincial patronage, would become ANC power brokers, even 'kingmakers'.[49] Existing leaders would have to cope with this reality to ensure their survival and aspirant leaders pay homage to the provinces in order to rise to the top. The third source of tension was that in building nationwide membership and structures in both party and government, the ANC expanded its membership greatly, drawing in many veterans of Bantustan government structures who were unused to and not necessarily amenable to instruction in ANC codes, discipline and values, never mind those of the Constitution. Moreover and more importantly, they were less likely to be personally beholden to existing groupings in the party and wider movement. In short, in the provinces, leaders could build their own followings and be their own men and (more rarely in the early post-apartheid years) women.

The announcement by the NEC in August 1998 that provincial premiers would no longer have to be party chiefs in their provinces was followed in the next few months by Mbeki's removal of three of the seven ANC premiers. In practice, it is difficult to disentangle the motivations for this assertion of central control. Each of the three sources of tension between the centre and the periphery that were noted above interacted with the others and their causes and effects tended to overlap. As a result, the change could be seen in alternative ways: as a rational approach to modernizing the party and creating order out of chaos; in terms of Mbeki's desire to secure his continuing leadership against any possible provincial insurgency and more generally to ensure that the centre and not the periphery decided the succession; and as the centre's desire to curb the powers of provincial grandees in the interests of institutional coherence and integrity. There is at least some measure of truth in these explanations. However, in a political culture that conspicuously lacked trust and in which Mbeki, thanks to his developing wrangle with the Alliance over GEAR, was acquiring the reputation as something of an autocrat, it looked to many that this was a personal power grab and a denial of local democracy. This version became the dominant one and alternative nuances were lost for the purposes of practical politics within the ANC and Alliance.

What is certainly clear is that the centre's attempt to impose its idea of order on the provinces largely backfired: the resentment it generated was instrumental in fuelling Zuma's insurgent challenge to Mbeki in 2005–7 and the backlash against it ushered in an era of factional struggle within and between the provinces and between them and the centre. This era has lasted until the present and is by now thoroughly institutionalized.

The clearest example of a provincial leader at odds with the national leadership in the Mandela/Mbeki era was 'Ace' Magashule who, by the time the Zuma-Mbeki struggle reached its peak in 2007, had been the Free State leader of the ANC for over twelve years, despite the centre's many attempts to unseat him. He had been overlooked three times for the premiership by the national leadership and he was the cause of the provincial leadership being disbanded twice, by Mandela in 1996 and Mbeki in 2000.[50] In the wake of Zuma's victory, he eventually became premier in 2009. By 2017, he had seen out his second and final term in the position, using it, despite serious allegations and investigations of his involvement in corruption – as a springboard for election to a top six position – secretary general – at the national conference of December 2017. Whether he can survive the taint of corruption in the post-Zuma ANC remains to be seen at the time of writing.

During Mbeki's time as leader (which includes his period as Mandela's vice president), the ANC failed to find a balance between pluralism and local democracy on the one hand and on the other, the ideological and organizational coherence that is needed if parties are to sustainably win power under democratic conditions and more importantly to use it, again sustainably, for effective governance. This failure did not of course stop the ANC from repeatedly winning elections, but much was in its favour: the deference that came with the liberation dividend, racial nationalism and the peculiarity that the only effective opposition was disqualified in the eyes of the majority of South Africa's voters on the grounds of its historical provenance and the racial make-up of its leadership and core support. But these things were good only for masking the ANC's incoherence and buying time for its leaders to put it on a more ordered and sustainable basis. Instead, the opposite happened: a gradual but seemingly unavoidably entropic decline into ever-greater disorder.

How much of this can be attributed to Mbeki's leadership is difficult to say. He was not alone in wanting to modernize the ANC and put its organization on a more sustainable basis; those who supported him in this project were not merely his acolytes; Mandela was among them after all. Under conditions of late democratization, political underdevelopment and massively ambitious restructuring, it was not difficult to read signs of chaos into assertions of localism or ideological pluralism. When skills are catastrophically short and loyalties are suspect at the periphery, an obvious remedy is to vest more power where more skills are available and where loyalty is reliable, that is, inevitably, in the centre. In short, it is not difficult to make a case for rational motivations behind Mbeki's centralizing moves. However, his reputation for heavy-handed application of central power, driven by an inner-determined authoritarianism, contributed to his downfall and besmirches his legacy. It was a reputation that was well-enough grounded for opportunistic rivals and opponents, notably Zuma and the populist army that enlisted behind him, to exploit it to the hilt.

Mbeki as government leader

When the ANC took office in 1994, it was faced with formidable challenges of managing government business. These included making one unitary administration out of the many structures that under apartheid served the different 'population groups', with the overriding purpose of reorienting finance and function to serve the population as one; transforming the demographic profile of the public service; and organizing policymaking and delivery to satisfy the demands of technocratic rationality, while at the same time making good the ANC's somewhat ill-defined promise of 'people-centred' policymaking. Added to these were the universal problems of political leadership in a democracy of how to reproduce personal credibility and support both in the party and the country as well as for the party in the electorate.

It is important to note how inexperienced the top echelon of the ANC was in exercising power in a plural context. No one had been leader of the opposition or held a great office of state, as is customary for incoming leaders in the United Kingdom or, as is customary in the United States, been a senator, a state governor or indeed a public representative of any kind.

Moreover, only a very few had had the kind of experience in business or the professions which gives insight into an actually existing society and economy and how to function in the context of plural centres of power such as business, unions and civil society. This was not the fault of the individuals concerned; jail, exile and the underground were not their choice but the price they paid for challenging exclusion, persecution and repression. Some of course – Mandela being the best example – transcended their experience, but others did not and in general, the combination of inexperience and a fugitive background tended to reinforce an already ingrained tendency towards the values of a closed community in a hostile world, not to mention in some at least the prospect of substantial reward for sacrifices already made.

Both the challenges of reorganizing government and of reproducing political support fell largely on Mbeki. Although strictly speaking, he was as inexperienced at governing as the rest, he was better educated than most (his peers and rivals in this respect were mostly from ethnic minorities), his experience in exile was more cosmopolitan than most and involved closer contact with other democracies and familiarity with how they worked. Since it was known that Mandela would serve only one term and Mbeki, although deputy president, was not yet sure of the succession, the challenges of reproducing political support inside the ANC, but also credibility in the wider world of local and global business and markets, also fell on him. He met these challenges over more than a decade as either deputy state president or state president. As might be expected, his leadership developed over this time, but three approaches stand out.

The first was to attempt a fusion of party and state by using political appointments to notionally independent state, quasi-state or other statutory bodies, not in any covert and piecemeal way but as part of an openly declared and overarching strategic policy. The second approach was to centralize the business of government around two core departments: the National Treasury and the Presidency. This would serve the technocratic imperative on which he believed effective policy depended and he hoped would build for him a personal power base. Government structured in this way would also marginalize the Alliance with its (in his view) potential for populist destabilization and thus establish credibility with the markets. Lastly, he was prepared to manipulate state bodies, again mainly through appointments, to ward off political challenges to himself.

The second of these operating principles – technocracy and centralizing – comes from the conventional, contemporary repertoire of political management in a democracy; the other two do not. In the light of these features of his leadership, it is scarcely surprising that, as we have already noted, there is a conventional critical view of Mbeki's leadership that characterizes him as an authoritarian centralizer. Such criticism comes from more than one quarter. Liberals have tended to emphasize the party–state nexus and the manipulation of institutions in their critique, simultaneously approving of the technocracy, even or especially if it came at the expense of inner-party democracy. Criticisms from the Left have concentrated on the centralizing, technocracy and (in their own view) marginalizing of the Alliance while ignoring, condoning or applauding the party–state fusion and coming only belatedly and opportunistically (as part of the Mbeki/Zuma struggle) to condemning the manipulation of institutions. Indeed, after Zuma assumed the leadership, it took the Left until well into his second term to relearn the lesson that manipulation of state institutions and destroying their independence is reprehensible.

There is a superficially attractive but in the end rather lazy piece of folk wisdom that says if you attract criticism from all quarters then you must be doing something right. There is some truth in this in Mbeki's case, but as an assessment it underestimates his complex and tortuous approach to managing the structures and business of government.

Party and state

The National Party that governed apartheid South Africa was an ethnic party and the South African state was an ethnic party state. Viewed in the light of the horrors of the past and the spirit and the letter of the Constitution that was the bedrock of the new South Africa, a central challenge of the new dispensation should have been to establish clear lines of separation between party and state. Even a superficial acquaintance with the Constitution, for instance, in its inclusion of 'democracy supporting institutions', in Chapter 9, should have been enough to make that clear:

> These institutions are independent, and subject only to the Constitution and the law, and they must be impartial and must exercise their powers and perform their functions without fear, favour and prejudice.[51]

This is not at all how the ANC configured the challenge of overhauling, reorientating and rehabilitating the state. Two years after the Constitution was adopted, one of its principal ideology and strategy documents spelled this out clearly in what came to be known as its 'cadre deployment policy':

> Transformation of the state entails, first and foremost, extending the power of the NLM (national liberation movement) over all levers of

power: the army, the police, the bureaucracy, intelligence structures, the judiciary, parastatals, and agencies such as regulatory bodies, the public broadcaster, the central bank and so on. *This is not in contradiction to the provisions of the Constitution, which characterise most of these bodies as independent and non-partisan.*[52] (Emphasis added)

Attempts like this to harmonize the apparently incompatible, indeed diametrically opposed principles of cadre deployment and the independence of institutions make for confusion, uncertainty and lack of trust. This is especially so when they are spiced, as in the quotation above, with a brazenly Orwellian flavour, in the sense of 'doublethink', disguising, distorting or reversing the meaning of words. Cadre deployment was not Mbeki's creation alone. Indeed, there has been no more stoutly defended and apparently irreversible principle right across the Alliance to this day. However, as the party's chief ideologist and the principal architect of the new state, then it is reasonable to say that it was 'his' policy, though not his alone.

Matters have been made worse by the substantial overlap between cadre deployment and affirmative action in the public service. Altering the composition of the public service to better reflect the racial demographics of South Africa's population was one of the most important challenges faced by post-1994 governments. There were good grounds for this priority: redress for past exclusions and redistribution of opportunity; visible identification of the public service with the majority of the population and their home languages; and mutual confidence between an initially inexperienced government and the people, especially the senior ones, helping to make and implement their policies. However, racial transformation has been pursued, with only a few exceptions, as an overriding imperative on the unexamined assumption that changing its racial profile would by itself have beneficial effects on the service ethos, productivity and efficiency of the public service. It is true that policy documents and legislation include riders to the effect that affirmative action should not replace concerns for skills, capacity and performance. But all too often the policy has been driven through as a blunt instrument rather than managed with nuance and refinement, and it has frequently been motivated by individual and factional opportunism rather than principle. Especially where cadre deployment and affirmative action have fed off each other, artificially shrinking the skills pool and opening the way to patronage and cronyism, the combination has eroded public trust, producing profound cynicism about all public appointments and encouraging conspiracy theories about who gets what job. Much of this cynicism, it should be said, comes from people who have no problem in principle with the system; it is simply disaffection from within the system of the 'wrong cadres' who failed to get the advancement they wanted. Whatever the reasons, however, such cynicism has a toxic effect on democratic prospects.

Centralizing government

If the fusion of party and state was a shared, quasi-soviet project superimposed on a constitutional state, with Mbeki as its chief orchestrator, the move to centralize government was much more his individual creation. There was no template or formula for organizing the business of government under the new regime, and there is little evidence that the ANC had devoted much in the way of collective strategic planning to that end. As it happened there were suggestive forerunners in the late apartheid governments, which may or may not have influenced Mbeki, but at any rate they provide interesting parallels. P. W. Botha and F. W. de Klerk, admittedly under warlike, crisis conditions, both extended the powers of the presidency and downplayed the importance of their party in and out of parliament. In this way, the projects of 'reform apartheid' (Botha) and of negotiation (De Klerk) could be insulated from disaffected right-wingers. So successful was Botha in concentrating power that the right wing of the National Party was forced to defect and form the Conservative Party (1982) in order to express its opposition to 'reform', having been marginalized and frustrated by the drastic curtailment of internal party democracy. It is a strategy that Mbeki, either by emulation or pure coincidence, clearly wished to repeat with his left wing, even to the point of forcing the Left out of the Alliance to fend for itself.

He did not have the pressing justification of obvious security threats that the National Party elite had for the centralization of power, nor was he ever likely to have recourse to the militarization of the state, which was a key aspect of the apartheid government's strategy for concentration in the 1980s. However, it may be that by depicting elaborate conspiracies against the ANC government in documents such as 'Unmandated Reflections', he was trying to create a similar justification as a conscious tactic, rather than simply indulging in paranoid fantasies driven by inner demons.

Mbeki's centralization of the machinery of government focused on two institutions: the Presidency and the National Treasury. The first of these he saw as a strategic centre for evidence-based and, in the jargon of the era, 'joined-up' policymaking.[53] The roles of the presidency also expanded to include functioning as a means of coordinating, monitoring and evaluating the conventional machinery of cabinet government composed of line departments each headed by a responsible minister. The presidency developed under Mbeki first by amalgamating the deputy president's and president's offices, then by rapid and substantial expansion in personnel and resources. With these developments came broadened responsibilities and institutional subdivisions, including a powerful cabinet office and the Policy Coordination and Advisory Service. A full minister was appointed in the Presidency and the responsibilities of the deputy president were downgraded when Mbeki left the post.

At first sight, this programme of reorganization can seem no more than a rational response to the difficult tasks of governance in complex societies and modern economies and, in the South African context, a necessary focussing of scarce resources of human capacity. An increasingly technocratic bias in government was in tune with the spirit of the times in industrial democracies, although there were plenty of critics of managerialism and concentration of policymaking powers there to encourage Mbeki's own critics. However, the construction of the new Presidency coincided with the closure of the Reconstruction and Development Programme (RDP) office, an ominous coincidence for the Alliance Left.

The RDP was a manifesto for economic transformation, largely developed by the Alliance Left for the ANC's 1994 election campaign. Its central principles were public sector infrastructure spending to address massive backlogs in basic needs and redistribution of wealth and income leading to rising domestic demand to be met by local manufacturers. The RDP office was the coordinating linchpin working right across government to achieve the benign cycle of effects thus envisaged.[54] Mbeki clearly regarded it as an institutional failure for trying to be everywhere and ending up nowhere, beset as it was by skill shortages as well as scepticism and hostile bureaucratic politics elsewhere in government and oppositional lobbying from business and mainstream economists.

The closure of the RDP office in 1996 also coincided with the turmoil in the Alliance over the adoption of the GEAR macroeconomic policy and both contributed to growing unease about Mbeki's manner and style of leadership, including a manner of engagement that was more often scathing than engaging, relying less on the 'seduction' that his chroniclers were so fond of describing in his dealings with whites during negotiations, more on demolition by intellectual browbeating, backed up if necessary by political threat. His increasing reliance for the latter on what were popularly referred to as 'enforcers' in his immediate circle, who had the task of silencing critics within the ANC and wider Alliance, did not help these growing reputational problems. Prominent among these agents of coercion was the 'belligerent'[55] minister in the Presidency Essop Pahad who had been Mbeki's colleague and friend since their days at the University of Sussex in the 1960s.

Given the endemic lack of trust and the overtones of betrayal and conspiracy in South Africa's (and especially the Alliance's) political culture, the institutional and bureaucratic re-ordering of government based on the Presidency was predictably seen, particularly on the Left, as part of an autocratic and centralizing agenda that was antithetical to inner-party democracy. Despite the efforts of some critics to focus on 'systemic' issues in criticizing Mbeki,[56] to a large extent the alleged pathologies of his administration were seen in personal terms, despite the fact that they long preceded the serious doubts about Mbeki's judgement and, for some, his personality that emerged over AIDS and Zimbabwe. In this view, the remodelled Presidency had more to do with building a more reliable and trustworthy personal power base than Mbeki could count on in his own party, than with managerial efficiency and bureaucratic rationality. The second thrust of Mbeki's remodelling of the machinery of government was the emergence of the National Treasury as a kind of Weberian super bureaucracy at the heart of government. This was in some respects a more interesting and multifaceted development than the Presidency's rise and certainly less open to the kind of one-dimensional critical treatment it attracted.

The centrality of the Treasury to Mbeki's leadership is widely recognized:

In the 1990s and into the new millennium, the National Treasury was a key flag-bearer of central-state building. It helped to forge a unified state from the fragmented apparatus it inherited from the apartheid state, and achieved broadened capacities for intergovernmental coordination. It helped to forge a particular vision of a national state. The kind of hierarchical, technocratic coordination that Treasury undertook was central to Thabo Mbeki's approach to state-building.[57]

Like the Presidency, the National Treasury was created out of two pre-existing bodies, in this case the Departments of Finance and State Expenditure. Between them they were responsible for public financial management in the late apartheid years. In the peak years of the struggle (1983–90), security considerations predominated and the economic departments were weak in political reach and authority. By 1994, real per capita income had been declining for ten years. Inflation was running at 9 per cent despite very high real interest rates. South Africa's foreign reserves stood at less than one month's import cover. The fiscal deficit stood at a dangerously high 9 per cent of GDP.[58] By 2004, under the management of a unified National Treasury, all these indicators had improved dramatically. For instance, the deficit had remained well below 4 per cent since 1998. Prudent management cannot take all the credit – global conditions were relatively benign for the South African economy in those years – but it is widely believed, especially among business, markets and investors, that better fiscal management played a large part in recovery.

That this was possible depended on the Treasury being quarantined in a Weberian bubble, while in the wider world of bureaucracy, political appointments and racial representivity, both camouflaging growing patronage, factionalism and cronyism, were the dominant shaping forces. By Weberian what is meant here is a high premium on technocratic competence in recruitment and advancement, subscription to rational-legal authority, strong esprit de corps, public service values and relative autonomy from political pressures. These qualities were not confined to the Treasury but applied also to the South African Revenue Service (SARS), the South African Reserve Bank (SARB) and, to a lesser extent, the Presidency. What deepened and extended the range of the Treasury's influence, however, was that its technocratic credibility had very substantial political backing. This was in the form of Minister of Finance Trevor Manuel (1996–2009), who enjoyed a close relationship with Mbeki and had, moreover, a strong political foothold and profile in the ANC in his own right. In the light of these relationships, it would be a mistake to understand 'Weberian' in this context as 'non-political'. The point of the Treasury and its centrality to Mbeki's project was that it stood for a particularly decisive set of macroeconomic policy choices and was dedicated to upholding them: 'Treasury thus came to be the institutional embodiment of the macroeconomic paradigm.'[59]

Under Manuel, the Treasury developed processes and was armed with legislation that put this political backing to use. In 1998, it adopted the Medium Term Expenditure Framework (MTEF) approach to the budget process, which, by setting expenditure expectations three years in advance, greatly increased the Treasury's authority over line departments. The most important extension of the Treasury's powers came with the Public Finance Management Act (PFMA, 1999), which shifted responsibility for the legality and the outcomes of spending to spending departments at all levels of government, effectively trading the possibility of decentralized, financial management for greater accountability and transparency. As with Mbeki and Manuel's overall macroeconomic policy, the efficacy of the MTEF and the PFMA can be debated.[60] However, what should be emphasized here is that it was a key part of Mbeki's leadership in state-building and managing government business to treat the Treasury in a quite different way from most other parts of the machinery of government. Elsewhere, there was no more zealous exponent of cadre deployment and Africanization than Mbeki, but these things were relaxed in the case of the Treasury and a more gradualist approach to the latter was taken. This in turn has borne long-term fruit in producing a very high calibre of African senior appointments, but it was done in such a way that the political imperative of aligning the department's staffing with the racial demography of the country did not impinge on its technocratic competence in the short and medium term. Moreover, the Treasury was put to work right across government and down through the provincial and municipal levels with a wide remit to monitor, support and improve not only financial management, narrowly defined, but all kinds of bureaucratic integrity as well.

Inevitably, the role of the Treasury has been contested:

> The National Treasury is a pivotal institution in South Africa's governance landscape. Portrayals of the Treasury are often polarized: where some see an exceptional institution that stands 'head and shoulders' above other government departments and which has long held the line against reckless state expenditure, others see an elitist institution, which imposes top-down austerity and restricts a genuinely developmental agenda.[61]

Contested or not, however, the case of the Treasury suggests that the place of 'centralization' in Mbeki's leadership in the organization and management of government business is a lot more complex than critical caricatures of an 'autocratic' personality imposing itself on the structures of government and party dynamics would suggest.

So far, Mbeki's leadership has been treated largely as if he fell within the conventional canon of contemporary democratic leaders. It is possible to look at him as if the principal concerns of his leadership were how to organize the machinery of government to good effect with the resources available and how to manage the various interests and tendencies grouped within his own party, while juggling concerns for internal democracy with those of coherence, direction and momentum. Moreover, it is also possible to look at him as if in doing these things he would confine himself to the repertoire and limits of leadership in a plural, constitutional democracy. In the mid- and late 1990s when, as deputy president under Mandela, Mbeki began to exercise leadership in both government and party, he was, with relatively few exceptions, viewed in this way. This is partly because there was much that was familiar to observe: cajoling fractious party elements into discipline and applying rational-legal management to the business of government. These were familiar themes in political leadership; the fact that he was doing them in the context of building democracy and rebuilding government after apartheid added the excitement of the new to the comfort of the familiar. In addition, in the eyes of business, markets and Western media, he was on the right track economically, was facing down the Left and in any case there was always the reassuring figure of Mandela to signal that all, at least in the short term, would be well.

The exception was the one-partyism, exemplified by the cadre deployment that is profoundly subversive of plural democracy. However, as James Myburgh points out:

> Perhaps to its surprise, the ANC found itself pushing against an open door. The ANC met very little opposition in the appointment of party members to supposedly independent state institutions ... this policy was either excused or welcomed by many of the major English language newspapers in South Africa ... on the basis that it was enhancing democracy, for it was placing power – both symbolically and substantively – in the hands of the black majority.[62]

From centralization to politicization

It was not long after Mbeki became president, however, that disquieting signs began to emerge that under him one-partyism would triumph over constitutional values such as the separation of powers and that there was more to cadre deployment than the simple moral imperative of giving to African people what they had been denied for so long, a hand on the levers of power. More than that, it could be an instrument of executive manipulation of state agencies.

The first sign that all was not well came in the fallout from the strategic defence procurement package (1996–9), which became known simply as 'the arms deal'. Pan Africanist Congress (PAC) MP Patricia de Lille, who subsequently formed her own party, then joined the Democratic Alliance (DA) and became mayor of Cape Town, raised in parliament the allegations of whistle-blowers that ANC officials had receive kickbacks in the course of the deal. A special report of the auditor general in September 2000 flagged irregularities and the parliamentary Standing Committee on Public Accounts (Scopa) took up the matter. The chairman of Scopa, Gavin Woods, was an Inkatha Freedom Party (IFP) MP, but he worked closely with Andrew Feinstein, the lead ANC figure on the committee.[63] In Feinstein's insider account, which is largely substantiated by what was intensive media coverage at the time, senior ANC figures in parliament, including Deputy President Jacob Zuma and Speaker, Frene Ginwala, at first encouraged Scopa in its investigations of allegations of corruption but did a complete about face and waged a coordinated and aggressive campaign to enable Mbeki to refuse Scopa's recommendation that a special investigating unit specializing in corruption, under a judge, Willem Heath, be given a mandate to proceed further with investigations.

The Scopa affair, which ended with Feinstein's resignation and departure from parliament in January 2001, contained a number of Mbeki trademarks, including, according to Feinstein, a selective reading of legal advice he had received about whether or not to give a proclamation to the Heath Commission in order to do exactly the opposite of the lawyers' opinion; a letter purportedly from Zuma viciously criticizing Scopa ('malicious misinformation campaign intended to discredit and destabilise', which was in fact written by Mbeki);[64] and a broadcast to the nation in which he condemned allegations of corruption as nothing more than a campaign by hired (unnamed) 'enemies "of our country and our people"' to damage our image globally'. The affair began apparently in tune with the Constitution: the office of auditor general, which is established in Chapter 9 of the Constitution as a 'state institution supporting democracy', did its job of scrutinizing government expenditure; parliament, in the shape of Scopa, attempted to hold the executive to account. In a short time, however, Mbeki was declaring all criticism of the executive as 'subversive'. In this he was supported by the Cabinet, which, collectively dismissed, naturally 'with contempt', any possibility that either the arms companies – of all people – or ANC officials could be corrupt.

This was one-partyism in the sense of comrades closing ranks and was not yet manipulation of supposedly independent state institutions. Indeed, the auditor general, who had been appointed under the authority of the ANC, had done his job scrupulously and simply been squashed by the sheer political weight of the executive, supported by its huge majority in parliament. The only glancing mention in Feinstein's account to partiality of state servants is his own, somewhat naïve reference, as if it were the most natural thing in the world, to his consulting 'a sympathetic, senior, ANC-aligned judge'.[65] That Feinstein, the whistle-blowing 'good guy' of the ANC, should make such a casual (and unintentionally hilarious) reference to the political partiality of an eminent jurist indicates how deep the rot went and how acceptable it was assumed to be by Feinstein and presumably everyone else in the ANC. However, suspicions that Mbeki's handling of government was edging closer to abuse of power began to grow very shortly after the Scopa debacle, in April 2001. Moreover, an ominous sign for the future was that while in the Scopa affair Mbeki was able to carry the ANC with him, certainly the parliamentary wing of the party, the next contretemps, was much more divisive.

By this time, less than two years after taking office as president, Mbeki faced mounting criticism on several fronts: the arms deal; his policy of 'quiet diplomacy' towards Mugabe's increasingly violent authoritarianism in

Zimbabwe and towards the AIDS pandemic, which reflected his flirtation with AIDS denialists. His personal response and that of the government, which supported him, was angry and defensive, making increasing allusion to conspiracies, to the point that the label 'paranoid' began to be used of him with increasing frequency in the media and in political conversation. In early April 2001, Zuma issued a statement, apparently apropos of nothing, affirming his loyalty to Mbeki and denying that he planned to challenge him for the presidency of the ANC. Since the next election of top party officials was twenty months away, at the five-yearly party conference scheduled for December 2002, this was somewhat odd and in any case Mbeki was only in his first term as both ANC and state president and could reasonably expect to have second terms in both.

Zuma's pre-emptive self-abasement appears to be linked to an NEC meeting in March 2001 at which Mbeki had demanded to know the provenance of an anonymous pamphlet, 'One President, One Term'.[66] Later that month, a Johannesburg Sunday newspaper published an interview with the then minister of safety and security, Steve Tshwete, a prominent exile veteran and strong supporter of Mbeki. In the interview, he confirmed rumours that police intelligence units were investigating plots against Mbeki. Two days later, he named Cyril Ramaphosa, Tokyo Sexwale and Mathews Phosa, the former Mpumalanga provincial premier, as subjects of interest in the investigation. All three had previously had aspirations to leadership, and all were believed to have been sidelined by Mbeki and his supporters so that they would pose no threat to his grip on the party. All of them had left politics and gone into business, although all could claim residual popular bases. While Ramaphosa and Sexwale had left politics voluntarily, Phosa had been removed from the Mpumalanga premiership in a bitter ANC internal struggle, which saw him accused of corruption. The information that motivated Tshwete's investigation was provided by one James Nkambula, a former ANC Youth League leader in Mpumalanga who had been a key figure in ousting Phosa and, at the time of the 'plot' revelations, was himself facing seventy-seven charges of fraud and theft. The centrepiece of the plot's narrative was that the conspirators were going to frame Mbeki for complicity in Chris Hani's murder.

Nkambula was a hopeless witness; the allegations were fantastical; after six months (and an investigation that at best was cursory), Tshwete declared that there was nothing in the allegations and three years later Nkambula admitted he had lied and apologized.[67] Mbeki did his best to distance himself from the investigation and the accusations, but only his most diehard supporters believed that there was no connection between Tshwete and the president on the question of making Nkambula's allegations public: 'there is no doubt that he wanted them in the public domain, and that Tshwete was doing his bidding.'[68]

It is not possible to say whether Zuma's declaration of his immediate lack of ambition to rise to the presidency was a self-protective initiative or coerced by Mbeki. Whatever the case, it seems to mark the accelerating deterioration in relations between the two former close comrades. Already, downgrading the vice-president's status, including merging the two presidential offices in a single presidency, was a symbol of this. The conventional understanding in histories of the period is that Mbeki was convinced that Zuma – uneducated, polygamous and, in this and other cultural respects, too 'traditional' to exercise political leadership in a modernizing state and economy – was not a suitable candidate to follow Mbeki in the highest office and that he set about finding grounds to prevent such an eventuality.

Such interpretations inevitably rest on circumstantial evidence and reading of patterns in observable character traits and personal histories. What does seem clear is that it was around the time of the 'plot' that investigations of Zuma's role in the arms deal began in earnest. This in itself is enough to raise suspicions, since less than a year previously, Mbeki and his cabinet were adamant that there was nothing to investigate, never mind prosecute. The same was true of the principal instrument of investigations into Zuma, the head of the National Prosecuting Authority (NPA), National Director of Public Prosecutions (NDPP), Bulelani Ngcuka, who could also find no grounds in the suspicions thrown up by the auditor general and Scopa for proceeding against any individual or entity. It is on such suspicions and on pointed comparisons between the way Mbeki squashed the first allegations of corruption in the arms deal and his apparent willingness to entertain allegations against his vice president that Zuma's construction of a profile of victimhood was and is founded.

Enter the Scorpions and the National Intelligence Agency

The newly created (January 2001) Directorate of Special Operations (DSO), which was part of the NPA and fell under Ngcuka's overall authority, took up the task of investigating Zuma. Known as the Scorpions, the DSO combined criminal intelligence, investigation and prosecution, and the unit was seen as a multidisciplinary response to increasing corruption, organized crime and complex, 'white-collar' financial crime. Zuma was not slow to develop the intuition that he was being singled out from among a senior ANC cohort in which there were relatively few spotless records. Indeed, according to the *Mail and Guardian*, Zuma's supporters' main defence was the following: 'His financial indiscretions are relatively minor and almost no cabinet minister would survive with their reputation intact under similar scrutiny.[69] This perception was strengthened in his and the minds of his growing number of supporters, by the Scorpions' heavy-handed tactics, which included blatant departures from the rule of law and manipulation of the media. Raids and unlawful confiscation of documents, leaks and briefing against Zuma, as well as tip offs about the 'Hollywood' raids to a receptive press audience, were among the questionable tactics apparently designed for shock value and intimidation. Clinching evidence, in the eyes of the Zuma camp at least, that this was vendetta rather than a legitimate investigation, came with a briefing for journalists hosted by Ngcuka in July 2003 at which he intimated that there was a 'prima facie' case against Zuma but insufficient evidence to be sure of a conviction. It is hard to think of a legitimate reason why this should have been launched into the public domain with such fanfare. The fact that the briefing was restricted to African journalists and editors only was not exactly a smoking gun, but given Mbeki's views on the evils of 'white media' it pointed in his direction.

Further and stronger evidence that state institutions were being captured and used for factional purposes came in the second half of 2005, with the 'hoax email' affair. It also seemed to indicate that serious as such a development was, it also had a strong element of farce. By this time Schabir Shaik, Zuma's close friend, struggle comrade and 'financial adviser', had been convicted of corruption and sentenced to fifteen years in prison (June 2005). The judgement had made much of the close relationship between the two men and heavily implied that it was a corrupt one (though the judge was widely misquoted by the media). Mbeki removed Zuma from the deputy presidency two weeks later and he was charged with corruption shortly afterwards. The case was struck from the roll in September, though not permanently, on the grounds of the prosecution's lack of preparedness.

It was at this point that the origins of the convoluted affair of the hoax emails were exposed. They lay with the National Intelligence Agency (NIA), which was responsible for monitoring internal security threats and for domestic counter-intelligence (foreign intelligence was the responsibility of the South African Secret Service, SASS).[70] In October 2005, Saki Macozoma, former political prisoner, ANC MP, senior civil servant and wealthy Black Economic Empowerment (BEE) businessman, complained to the minister of intelligence, Ronnie Kasrils, that he was under heavy-handed surveillance, probably by an official agency. Kasrils and Macozoma were both strong Mbeki supporters.

Kasrils ordered an enquiry by the inspector general of intelligence, which uncovered an unauthorized project instigated by the director general of intelligence, Billy Masethla, into security aspects of the Mbeki-Zuma conflict. Surveillance and illegal wiretapping had been part of the project. Also uncovered were seventy-three pages of transcripts purporting to be of chat-room interactions and email messages between a large group of pro-Mbeki conspirators who were prosecuting a campaign of subversion to destroy Zuma. The 'conspirators' included Ngcuka, his successor as NDPP, Vusi Pikoli, Macozoma, senior Scorpions officials, white opposition politicians and white editors and journalists. There was a pronounced racial and tribal dimension to the alleged interactions (Zuma was nicknamed disparagingly 'Zuluboy'). Extracts from the transcripts, published in the *Mail and Guardian*, revealed them to be amateurish, concocted fantasies, woodenly scripted, completely lacking in conversational fluency and authenticity, all of which was obvious to anyone who had ever had even the most superficial contact with the alleged conspirators. Masethla and two other senior NIA officials were suspended in November and Masethla, who was blamed for the hoax, was sacked in March 2006.

Although the affair strikingly illustrates the increasingly deranged world where politicized state agencies met ANC internal politics, it was and remains quite difficult to interpret. It could have been an amateurish attempt by Masethla to discredit Mbeki and his supporters or it could have been a double deception aimed at discrediting an innocent Masethla. Why this should be so is hard to see, since Masethla had been a trusted Mbeki aide, brought into the Presidency in 2002 as a personal security source for Mbeki. Equally, it is hard to see why and when he defected to Zuma's side or why Mbeki and/or his acolytes should have seen the need to neutralize him. Certainly, he proclaimed his innocence in frequent, often tearful, interviews and portrayed himself as a martyr. He fought his dismissal through the courts but eventually, when the case reached the constitutional court, perhaps the last bastion of sanity in a politico-legal world that was spinning out of control, its judges did not share his version of events and dismissed his claims.

The inspector general's report received a mixed reception in the ANC and the affair deepened divisions in the party and the Alliance. Perhaps that is all it was meant to do; but to whose benefit and at whose instigation – though the evidence points to Masethla – is not clear to this day. Given that there was no follow-up inquiry after Zuma became president, it might be reasonable to assume that the malfeasance came from his side – had it been from Mbeki's, it is likely that the affair would have been remorselessly exploited.

The pattern that began with the 2001 plot saga and continued with the hoax email affair persisted during the parallel development of Zuma's rape trial in December 2005, before, during and after which the Mbeki and Zuma camps made accusations and counter-accusations of dirty tricks.[71] It was further advanced by the so-called Browse Mole report in May 2007, as the Mbeki/Zuma conflict reached a climax.[72] According to the author of Browse Mole (a journalist turned Scorpions operative), the head of the Scorpions, Leonard McCarthy, commissioned the report in early 2006.[73] One draft out of three was leaked by fax to Cosatu – by this time firmly in Zuma's camp – on 7 May 2007. The report concluded that domestic and international 'elements' were supporting, financing and manipulating the Zuma campaign, thus constituting 'a threat to the integrity of the South African state'.[74] For once, it was not Western but African 'elements', governments (with that of Angola allegedly at the centre) who were 'apparently alienated by South Africa's perceived pre-eminence in the African Union and New Partnership for African Development (NEPAD – Mbeki's flagship project)'[75] that were providing finance and support for Zuma's campaign to oust Mbeki. Domestically, 'elements' in the security and intelligence services 'appear to be considering the subversion of the apparatus of state in support of a Zuma presidency'.[76]

This piece of the pot-calling-the-kettle-black is clear enough evidence of the divisions in the state security establishment, and the fact that Browse Mole, a project of the Scorpions, was leaked to the Zuma camp suggests that the divisions were not only between security agencies but also within them. According to its author, Browse Mole was a combination of his open-source research and material handed to him by McCarthy, which had come from freelance, ex-intelligence operatives with backgrounds in apartheid and Western security agencies. It was certainly of a higher quality than the hoax conspiracy transcripts, combining material that was in the public domain with information and inferences that may or may not have been accurate but could be linked to material that was genuine. At any rate, the document was not outrageously implausible. Whatever its status, however, the effect of its leak was to dramatically discredit Mbeki and boost Zuma, then later to seal the fate of the already under pressure Scorpions, who were disbanded over the protests of civil society, at the insistence of the ANC under Zuma's leadership.

The final twist in the security establishment's involvement in the Mbeki/Zuma struggle came with the leaking to Zuma's legal team of taped phone conversations between McCarthy and Ngcuka, discussing the timing of the corruption charges against Zuma. The tapes were legally acquired by the NIA when it was investigating Browse Mole, but they were illegally handed over to Zuma's lawyers. The *Mail and Guardian* named a senior NIA official as the source who handed over the tapes.[77] The then acting NDPP, Mokotedi Mpshe, used this evidence of 'a political conspiracy' against Zuma to drop all charges against him in April 2009.

Making sense of Mbeki

Along with the AIDS and Zimbabwe debacles, this sorry tit-for-tat saga of bizarre and amateurish conspiracies in and around the ANC, the criminal justice system and the intelligence agencies left an indelible stain on Mbeki's leadership years. Only a few who were immune from the incurable optimism of post-apartheid South Africa, and were prepared to risk being branded as Afropessimists or racists, predicted at the time that the conspiracies would spread and deepen when Zuma took over.

The reputational stain persists despite the fact that at least some of it depends on the bizarre contingency of a judge's gratuitous comments on 'political interference' in the case against Zuma as pursued by the NPA during Mbeki's presidency. Many retain the vague impression that the judge thought Mbeki was up to no good. Fewer remember the withering reversal of that judge's findings by the Supreme Court of Appeal.[78]

However, smoking gun or no smoking gun, there was enough circumstantial and character evidence to make sure that the stain remains. In doing so, it tends to obscure larger issues of summarizing Mbeki's leadership. The following remarks on Mbeki's tasks and how he went about them are of course speculative. It is not yet part of the ANC's political culture for former leaders to publish revelatory memoirs. Nevertheless, a case can be made that they chime with what was observable during his terms of office.

Mbeki's initial tasks were to make space for himself to be a leader in something more than nominal terms and to bring organizational and ideological coherence to the movement and political party he led. Success in these tasks would arm him to right centuries of historical wrong to African people in a way that filtered populist demands to make them realizable in what Mbeki perceived to be the real world. He would not be able to do these things unless he made a clean and irrevocable break from 'rainbowism' and the politics of reconciliation. This would also have the collateral dividend of putting clear water between himself and Mandela.

What he could not make a clean break from was the liberation movement's past. This was awkward, because it faced a new embodiment and new tasks in a new world where so many things that had given it meaning, comfort and sustenance were disappearing or no longer relevant. Its past could not be a blueprint for the future, but this could not be admitted.

Mandela set about his tasks by leading from the front, using his endowment of personality, the aura so assiduously cultivated for him by the ANC and the crisis conditions in which he exercised these powers. Even so he had to wrap up his initiatives in pieties of submissiveness to the collective.

Mbeki too aspired to lead from the front. However, he had less compunction for the pieties and fewer soft skills to bring off the synthesis of paying tribute to the past while demanding that the present must be faced. As we have seen, he tried to lead by centralizing organisation and management in both the party and state, while ambitiously trying to fuse the two. He was frustrated by two things; first, he did not follow through with sufficient ruthlessness in his centralizing initiatives and second, he had no feel for democratic politics.

As we have seen, the conventional critique of Mbeki has him as an authoritarian centralizer. There is some truth in this charge but most, if not all, iterations of it miss an essential point. Instead of using too much central power, he used too little. Centralizing power, especially over the provincial structures of the ANC and government, should have meant following through to fire people who were useless, jail those who were corrupt and replace both categories right down through the apparatus of party and state with people who were competent and honest. This, obviously, would require drastic changes in the way the ANC made appointments. Instead, Mbeki appeared to believe that simply changing men and women at the top in the province for appointees that were beholden to or otherwise loyal to him would put the party on a more sustainable basis. If he was an authoritarian centralizer, he was a remarkably half-hearted one. At least, this failing cannot be attributed purely to Mbeki's individual character failings. Such feebleness is a hallmark of all ANC leadership (even Mandela was subject to it) at all times and at all levels. Perhaps, it is something to do with the movement's comrade ethos; perhaps, it is something to do with Ubuntu.

At the end of the day, Mbeki had no feel for democratic politics. This is not surprising because his position as deputy state president was assured even before he had participated in an open, free election. He had had no democratic apprenticeship. Up to that point, politics for him had been conspiracy, negotiations and elite pacting, all of them considered by him and his colleagues as war by other means.

Arguably, this wasn't his fault. Apartheid had denied democracy to Africans and they had to fight a war to get access to it. However, this undeniable truth didn't stop Mandela from slipping apparently effortlessly and with instinctive grace into both the hard and soft roles of democratic leader. Arguably, being in this long shadow was part of the reason for Mbeki's apparent discomfort with democratic politics. Certainly, he never seemed to be able to abandon the heritage of conspiracy and war. Resentment at being in Mandela's shadow may have been reinforced with suspicion of retail politics as being inauthentic, too tainted with the personal and pathologies such as individualism, materialism and tribalism, which he seemed determined to hold at arm's length. He was also motivated by a sense of entitlement, conferred by the liberation dividend and the ANC's apparently indestructible majorities, to be left alone to get on with the serious policy-driven business of political management. To judge by his attitude to the Left and to the loose collection of progressive organizations that were associated with the ANC in the last years of the struggle and the first few years of democracy, mobilizing politics and asymmetric democracy were anathema to him. They had served their purpose in the struggle and now they had had their day and should get out of the way of the chosen instrument of the people's will.

This narrow view of what democracy is and can be (allied to his intolerance of dissent and opposition from wherever they came) amounted to a tin ear for democracy's melodies, rhythms and harmonies. As with his lack of ruthlessness with incompetents and miscreants, it not only frustrated him but also motivated legitimate dissent to turn into revolt against him.

6

From Mbeki to Zuma

There is a case for arguing that after Mandela the ANC's relationship with its leadership has been shaping up to look rather like that of the Tory (Conservative) party in Britain. That relationship has been described in the well-worn phrase, 'dictatorship tempered by regicide'. As a recent version puts it,

They cower before the leader until they decide to kill him or her.[1]

The leadership transition from Mbeki to Zuma certainly seems to fit this metaphor and narrative frame; the ousting of Zuma at the hands of the newly elected Ramaphosa between December 2017 and February 2018 also conforms to the pattern of a culture of submissiveness followed by a putsch. Time will tell whether this is becoming the ANC's established way of doing things or whether the era of Mbeki and Zuma will be remembered as a time of troubles, like a medieval kingdom, before peace ends the jockeying for power. Whatever the case, the events of the last ten to twelve years have not gone according to the ANC's self-penned script for deciding leadership matters. This envisaged a united movement, deciding the succession by means only slightly less mysterious and holy than the College of Cardinals choosing a new pope, before instructing the heir apparent to take up office. He or she would accept in the name of humble service at the pleasure of the movement, having long ago abjured all personal ambition. If this thoroughly unrealistic template for succession ever had any chance of corresponding with reality, the Mbeki-Zuma conflict killed it off.

A coalition of the disaffected

Mbeki provoked a wide range of grievances and gave grounds to many individuals and groups in the ANC and the Alliance to feel that they had been marginalized or unjustly treated in one way or another. The cumulative effect was the impression that he was taking the movement and the

Alliance in directions that diverged from their traditions and purposes or, as some claimed, the ANC was losing its 'soul'. Key to the discontent was the centralization of power through disciplining the ANC in the provinces, creating an 'imperial presidency', suppressing internal debate and dissent and empowering a small group of advisers and associates close to Mbeki, who had neither traction in the wider movement nor substantial talents other than loyalty to himself. Inevitably, of course, many of these could be read in a more favourable way as necessary actions to modernize the ANC and fit it to face the challenges of government in a fractured society and a rapidly changing global economy.

Whatever substance Mbeki's justifications had, however, in delivery they often had a whiff of casuistry and chicanery about them. A penchant for quoting Leninist texts to the Left and accusing them of being 'objectively' counter-revolutionary were favourites, when a simple exposition of the facts of political and economic life at the turn of the twentieth century might have been more effective. There was usually a sense that point scoring was as important as persuasion, perhaps more so, especially points scored with reference to the ANC's own sacred texts. Tellingly, when others weighed in to support the contentious strategies of party management, they tended to be underlings who owed their position to Mbeki, rather than commanding figures in the party. Some of them, Minister in the Presidency Essop Pahad, for instance, seemed even more eager than Mbeki to wound rather than convince by strength of argument.

Specific concerns of the Alliance Left were added to these general worries about how Mbeki's leadership was managing the party and the government. To his critics, the abandonment of the Reconstruction and Development Programme (RDP)˙ and the 'embrace of neo-liberalism' were not merely the adoption of macroeconomic prudence in the interests of stability and growth nor even simply capitulation to domestic and global markets (though this was a key accusation), but in the eyes of the Left's ideologists, Mbeki's macroeconomic policies laid the foundation for policy instruments with a larger purpose. This was a 'class project', the creation not only of a black middle class as defined in terms of income distribution and professional and managerial occupations but also a class of state-aided 'entrepreneurs' who would challenge existing white business classes for the 'commanding heights' of the economy. The reversal of land redistribution policies from the goal of empowering subsistence and small-scale farmers to creating a class of African commercial farmers and, in particular, the Black Economic Empowerment (BEE) policies that made small numbers of Africans very rich, both stood out as examples of narrow rather than broad redistribution and empowerment. Such initiatives clearly demonstrated that for Mbeki, racial rather than class imperatives guided policies for redress. This was anathema to both liberal and left critics, albeit for different reasons, and it also prepared fertile grounds for populist sentiment on the part of those 'outsiders' who were not favoured.

At the same time, the GEAR policy package brought in measures of fiscal austerity that constrained employment in the public sector and also included proposals for selective privatization of state-owned enterprises (SOEs) and labour law changes to make the employment regime more 'flexible' (the latter two policy directions both frustrated by union opposition). In sum, all these things amounted in the eyes of the Left to an agenda that short-changed the poor and was anti-worker.

Mbeki could at least claim the support of substantial figures within the ANC for his macroeconomic policy. Two exceptions to the general rule that his supporters tended to be from his own entourage were Trevor Manuel, minister of finance throughout Mbeki's two administrations (and before that, for the last three years of Mandela's presidency) and Alex Erwin, minister of trade and industry (1996–2004) and minister of public enterprises (2004–8). Both were genuine figures of substance in the ANC. In office, Manuel had intellectual and political conviction and conducted himself with authoritative self-confidence; under his leadership, the Treasury became a real centre of excellence. He was voted into first place in the National Executive Committee (NEC) elections at the 2002 ANC conference. Erwin was a trained economist and one of the most important founding and moving spirits of the trade union movement as well as a senior South African Communist Party (SACP) member. However, there were limiting factors to their influence. Both are members of racial minorities and both came from United Democratic Front (UDF) backgrounds rather than the ANC proper. Manuel's history on the NEC illustrates the instability of this measure of standing; he was first in 2002 and, in line with the slump in Mbeki's popularity, fifty-seventh in 2007. Indeed, especially in the Mbeki era, individuals did not receive cabinet posts because of their standing in the party as measured by NEC position; they were voted into high NEC positions because they were already cabinet ministers. Erwin's conversion from neo-marxism to 'neo-liberal' economic policies, in which he was, vis-à-vis Mbeki, more catholic than the pope, left him in the eyes of the Left without credibility and with the odour of apostasy clinging to him. Moreover, their support for Mbeki was largely confined to macroeconomic policy, rather than to matters of party management.

Mbeki was not the only political leader to try to remodel and reorient his party in the light of changing global and domestic social and economic conditions. We have already noted the superficial and in some ways misleading comparisons that his critics liked to make with Third Way leaders in Anglo-American polities. But again, as we have noted, Mbeki did not have the leverage of leaders who headed parties that had endured a succession of electoral defeats. If anything was certain in the medium term of post-apartheid politics, it was that the ANC would win elections whoever the leader was. He could not even hope that backing from outside the ANC might balance his growing unpopularity inside it. Mbeki subscribed as much as anyone else in the ANC to the view that it was an entirely self-sufficient world, outside of which, nothing and nobody mattered. This, perhaps, was the single greatest change from Mandela's leadership to his and it turned out to be one of the most important characteristics that Mbeki and Zuma (in their different ways, of course) had in common. It was less to do with Mbeki as an individual, though his personality helped, and more a case of the dominant ANC culture reasserting itself after the Mandela interlude. In any case, by treating all shades of interest and opinion in wider society other than approved ANC ideology as potentially, or actually, subversive or 'counter-revolutionary', Mbeki clearly signalled that he had no need to create a plural support base either for himself or the ANC across society. As for whites, he coldly informed them that they were on probation, not only as to their acceptability within a new South African nation but also for re-entry to the human community itself. Mbeki implied, despite his habitual recourse to 'we', that he alone would draw up the criteria for acceptance as well as be the judge of whites' due performance on them.

These differences and grievances were enough to motivate a growing coalition of the disaffected and leave Mbeki isolated in its face. Two matters helped give the coalition momentum and bind it together, as well as crucially distancing Mbeki from potential sources of support among people who were happy enough with his macroeconomic policy, were unimpressed by the Left and relieved and content to see the ANC disciplined and managed. The two issues were AIDS and Zimbabwe.

HIV/AIDS and Zimbabwe

The story of Mbeki's catastrophic mishandling of the AIDS pandemic in South Africa is well documented: the refusal to provide Nevirapine, the drug that reduced the incidence of mother-to-child transmission of the virus, until forced to do so by the constitutional court; the public humiliation of Mandela at an NEC meeting in 2002 when he questioned government policy on AIDS; the appointment of and continued support for a minister of health who sponsored beetroot, spinach and olive oil as AIDS treatments rather than antiretrovirals (ARVs); the 343,000 deaths that could have been prevented between 1997 and 2007 if the national government had used ARVs at the same rate as the Western Cape government, which defied national policy;[2] and, above all, Mbeki's dalliance with AIDS dissidents that constantly attempted to frustrate the efforts of the medical establishment to put life-saving policies in place. Explanations for Mbeki's behaviour generally feature his obsessive desire to refute racist stereotypes of allegedly promiscuous (and rape-prone) African males, to confront Afropessimism generally, his outrage at the power of the Western pharmaceutical industry and his insistence that the pandemic was fuelled by socio-economic factors rather than behavioural ones.

The flavour of these driving concerns is best conveyed in an unattributed 114-page paper, which was distributed anonymously before an NEC meeting on AIDS in 2002. Gevisser says that in interviews for his biography Mbeki 'declined to confirm' that he was the author but said that it was an accurate reflection of its views.[3] In the introduction, it states:

> that the HIV/AIDS thesis as it has affected and affects Africans and black people in general, is also informed by deeply entrenched and centuries-old white racist beliefs and concepts about Africans and black people. At the same time as this thesis is based on these racist beliefs and concepts, it makes a powerful contribution to the further entrenchment and popularisation of racism.[4]

The paper goes on to subscribe to, in Gevisser's words, 'a version of African nationalism that described AIDS doctors as latter-day Mengeles, and the black people who subscribed to the orthodox scientific approach as "self-repressed" victims of a slave mentality'.[5]

It is also possible that Mbeki was motivated by a central aspect of his claims to leadership: the role of being an intellectual in politics. It is easy to imagine him inspired by Vaclav Havel's much-quoted words on the public duties of intellectuals:

> The intellectual should constantly disturb, should bear witness to the misery of the world, should be provocative by being independent, should rebel against all hidden and open pressures and incantations, should be the chief doubter of systems of power and its incantations, should be a witness to their mendacity.[6]

Whether or not he was influenced by Havel, such a worldview is clearly visible in Mbeki's stand against medical orthodoxy – a system of power in its own right, lumped together by Mbeki with the pharmaceutical industry, as well as Western racist imperialism – and his rebellious independence in taking it on. However, the irony is that he was himself the personification of a system of power, one in which he had worked to suppress parliamentary and party accountability and substitute loyalty to the party line – which, in the case of the AIDS policy and much else, was his line. He was at the head of a system of power that had a responsibility for the lives of millions of people and, at the same time, he was in a position to outrank the medical establishment and deny validity to its expertise-based plans to save lives. This he could do at least temporarily until the pressure of civil society, the courts and from within his own party made him give way, an initial stance and a forced retreat from it, which were both ruinous to his credibility. The idea that in such a position of power and responsibility he could take on the roles of questioning outsider and rebellious underdog was wholly preposterous. He wasn't speaking truth to power; he *was* power personified.

The struggle over AIDS policy presented another irony. An essential element of Mbeki's self-presentation as a leader was as the responsible adult, the grown up in a room full of irresponsible populists and ultra-leftists. In economic policy, where he had some claim to knowledge and training, he stuck to this: nothing could have been more orthodox than his macroeconomic orthodoxy. In medical science, however, where he had no expertise at all, far from being the responsible adult, he was an intellectual cowboy, playing with the life and death of his people on the frontiers of bad science and quack medicine, for reasons that were at best quixotic and at worst the product of a twisted racial obsession. With the benefit of hindsight, Mbeki on AIDS appears – another irony – as an early forerunner of the right-wing populist distrust of 'experts' which has become so much part of contemporary Anglo-American politics. Except, of course, where he considered himself as an expert in his own right.

Mbeki's handling of Zimbabwe, although it did not have the same life and death implications for South Africa as his stand on AIDS, also helped undermine his credibility at home. His support for Mugabe has often been portrayed as motivated by fear of repercussions for the ANC in the event of the Movement for Democratic Change (MDC) successfully challenging Mugabe and ZANU-PF. The prospect of a secular post-nationalist movement, which was moving on from struggle pieties, ousting an incumbent liberation movement was the stuff of exile generation nightmares. This interpretation simply confirmed the Left's (and not only the Left's) fears of the 'Zanufication' of the ANC into systemic corruption and authoritarian personal rule and more specifically that Mbeki might emulate Mugabe in finding ways to prolong his time in power. In this way, Zimbabwe engendered a self-perpetuating spiral of mistrust between Mbeki and his critics; Mbeki's policy prompted cries of 'Zanufication' from the Left, which in turn fuelled Mbeki's fear that post-nationalist politics were infiltrating across the Zambesi and, if unchecked, ANC hegemony in South Africa would be the next domino to fall. If this was indeed the case, it meant that Mbeki underestimated the Left's credulity and overconfidence in assuming that it could continue to ride the nationalist tiger, in the shape this time of Zuma, rather than striking out on to create a new post-nationalist world.

All of this was accompanied by a deep sense of shame, expressed best in civil society, parts of the Alliance and the media, mirroring the shame over AIDS, at the government's supine response to well-documented human rights violations and election rigging in Zimbabwe, which amounted in critics' eyes to complicity. A particularly low point came when Phumzile Mlambo-Ngcuka, minister of minerals and energy affairs, led a SADC monitoring delegation to the Zimbabwe elections in March 2005. The verdict: 'a peaceful, well-mannered election, which reflects the will of the people' was met with derision and incomprehension. Three months later, Mbeki rewarded Mlambo-Ngcuka by appointing her deputy president in the wake of Zuma's dismissal from the post.

'Gradually, then suddenly'

Formidable as these points of grievance and disagreement were, and exacerbated by Mbeki's far from collegial leadership style, it was not a foregone conclusion that he would be challenged over the succession, never mind overthrown and removed from office.[7] By some conventional economic and social measures, his second term had been at least relatively successful: in the four years leading up to the ANC's elective conference in 2007, economic growth averaged 5.2 per cent,[8] forecasts of banks and rating agencies were for around 4.5 per cent annual growth in the medium term, business confidence was high and portfolio and direct foreign investment were healthy.[9] Poverty and unemployment were still high, but an extensive system of non-contributory social welfare payments was expanding. In 2005, the government announced a development plan to address the 'binding constraints' on faster growth. Despite Mbeki's suspicious and sometimes hostile attitude to markets, the plan, the Accelerated and Shared Growth Initiative for South Africa (Asgisa), had been developed in consultation with business organizations and it was paired with a business-government plan for skills development, the Joint Initiative on Priority Skills Acquisition (JIPSA). Learning its lesson from the introduction of GEAR, the government claimed that there had been wide consultation with communities and civil society before the plan was finalized. Instead of angrily rejecting established 'Western' expertise as he did on AIDS, Mbeki sought it out in the form of a panel of Harvard economists who visited South Africa, wrote papers and made recommendations. At least some of the recommendations survived into the plan.[10]

At one level, it seemed clear that it was on economic indicators such as those that Mbeki wanted his government to be measured. However, they were the fruits of an approach to policymaking that was so different from the AIDS issue that the government appeared to have two leaders: one was a rational technocrat who was consultative, believed in partnerships and was open to policy based on evidence and best practice; the other was a race-obsessed loose cannon and a contrarian pseudo-intellectual. The sense of instability communicated by Mbeki's divided leadership self was palpable; yet, provided that observers focussed on the relatively encouraging economic performance, there would be no sense of crisis, and the growing disaffection could be regarded as a purely internal matter. Unlike what was to follow with Zuma, there was no broad-based movement in wider society to unseat Mbeki. Opposition was an in-house affair, confined to the Alliance.

Even the internal movement against him appeared containable until quite late in the day, largely because of an apparent dearth of alternative leaders to put at the head of the disaffected. The principal, early source of discontent was the Left, but the chances of the Left finding a leader from within its own ranks were remote. As the struggle generation of the Left was neutralized by generational change, co-option into government and/or Mbeki's inner circle, the wider public sector or even the private sector, a new generation of younger leaders emerged, elected into office on an explicitly anti-Mbeki ticket: Blade Nzimande and Jeremy Cronin in the SACP and Zwelinzima Vavi at the head of Cosatu. However they led their niche fiefs in the Alliance, their responsibility was to the special interests of their members and, in any case, they had neither the struggle nor the African nationalist credentials to rise in the ANC. As we have seen, Mbeki laid waste to the list of potential heavyweight contenders such as Tokyo Sexwale, Mathews Phosa and especially Cyril Ramaphosa, removing them from contention by fair means or (mostly) foul.

If all of this had been engineered to ensure a smooth transition to a candidate of Mbeki's own choice, then one crucial element was missing: a candidate of substance. What had evolved, either by over-elaborate machinations on Mbeki's part or by a series of unfortunate events, was not a well-oiled machine, but a vacuum. Like all successions, the passing of the ANC leadership, and with it the state presidency, as long as the ANC maintains its electoral hegemony, can be managed. However, one part of it cannot, and that is the timing. As we have seen, there is an inexorable timetable set in motion by constitutional provisions limiting the state presidency to two terms for any individual and for fixed-term parliaments of five-year duration. This is compounded by the ANC's own timetable of five-yearly elections of its president and leadership group. The awkward synchronization between ANC elections and general elections means that a successor has to be elected when a second-term president still has close to one-third of his or her final period in office to go, and succession politicking threatens to absorb as much as half or even more of it. Another lack of fit is the fact that there is no term limit on the presidency of the ANC. This means that theoretically an individual can serve two terms as both ANC and state president and go on to a third in the ANC post. Such an outcome – 'two centres of power' – would be at best untidy and at worst a recipe for a bitter and destabilizing power struggle over where the true centre of governing power lies, with the risk that either the state president or the party leader would be a puppet. The potential is also obvious for the creation of 'two centres of power' to be seen simply as a way of circumventing the two-term provision and subverting the Constitution.

It is no wonder that the ANC clung for so long to its wistful mythology of a frictionless succession, bestowed on candidates who are superhumanly devoid of any ambition other than to serve a supernaturally united party.

An obvious solution is for the vice presidency of the ANC and the country to move in harmony with the two presidencies. If the vice president of the ANC and the country is always a fit and proper person to become state president and is recognized as such across all the ANC's constituencies and sub-brands, then all will be well. For this to work, however, the choice has to be made up to ten years in advance, nothing has to change in that time, the two individuals must remain in harmony and the heir apparent must be content with an apprenticeship of as much as ten years in what is not, in common with polities throughout the democratic world, a particularly rewarding post. Every one of these problematic issues came together in the person of Jacob Zuma.

It is important to bear in mind that Mbeki was defeated in his efforts to manage his own succession, was replaced by Zuma and removed unceremoniously from office, not by a man but by a cause. Initially, Zuma himself was an unlikely candidate for the highest office. Despite widely acknowledged positive human qualities, he was disqualified in the eyes of many by his lack of formal education, rootedness in demotic culture, complete lack of distinctive vision or grasp of policy and not least by the shadow of corrupt dealings that hung over him. It is a matter of history now that all of these, except the last, were spun to his advantage in the eyes of a large constituency of the ANC faithful in the course of his struggle with Mbeki and for at least a honeymoon period thereafter. However, without a cause to put him at the head of and, arguably, the need to rise to the top in order to stay out of jail, he would never have been in the running.

The cause was the cause of all those who were disaffected by some aspect or another of Mbeki's policies, leadership style and management of the ANC. The label 'coalition of the disaffected' is the standard way of describing the vehicle of the cause. It follows that, given the broad front on which Mbeki managed to alienate people, this was a very diffuse cause. While hard to pin down, other than by identifying key elements such as the Alliance Left, what held it together more than anything was a powerful but formless desire to take the ANC and the Alliance back to one or other version of the past. This is one of the ANC's most potent reflexes. Even Mbeki in all his attempts at innovation felt constrained to corset them in the movement's history and the language of its sacred texts: his ideological jousts with the Left had at times an almost Talmudic quality about them.

The past could mean anything from the past of the Freedom Charter, the RDP, of the intellectual dominance of the SACP in exile, the leadership of Tambo or Mandela, the ethos of comradeship rather than technocracy, the direct democracy of the UDF or of the shop-floor movement in the unions, the greatly mythologized (and exaggerated) period of open debate and freedom to criticize in the early and mid-1990s and an even more distant past of an authentic, demotic Africanness. It mattered little that the past meant different things to different people: what has mattered (and continues to matter) to the ANC is to have a leader to take it back to the past, not to get it to face the future – which was, for all his flaws, what Mbeki tried to do. Indeed, it is probably Mbeki's efforts – however flawed – to make the ANC fit-for-purpose in the contemporary world that, above all, provoked this retro reflex. Zuma was a convenient figurehead in whom different versions of the past could be seen if the observer tried hard enough and, for those inclined to *realpolitik*, his very lack of political, as distinct from personal, qualities could make him a leader to be manipulated. Above all, he was not Mbeki.

He was not the Mbeki whose election slate triumphed at the ANC conference in 2002 and who delivered the ANC's biggest electoral victory yet in the 2004 election. Mbeki's defeat and fall were all the more shocking for this background; but the roots of disaffection went deep, despite being hidden by a culture of submissiveness. There was something in Mbeki's fall of the quality conveyed in a much-quoted exchange from Ernest Hemingway's *The Sun Also Rises* (1926): a character is asked how he went bankrupt: ' "Two ways," said Mike, "Gradually, then suddenly" '.

Three interlocking dramas

The struggle between Mbeki and Zuma played itself out in three interlocking dramas. The first, led by the Scorpions, centred on the criminal investigation of Zuma on suspicion of corruption in the arms deal, followed by a war of attrition in which it became customary to refer to the 'Stalingrad' tactics of Zuma's legal team and of fluctuating fortunes in the courts. This lasted from 2003 until 2009, when charges against Zuma were dropped, although this turned out to be a hiatus rather than final closure.

The second drama was much shorter in duration (November 2005–May 2006), but in some respects it was the pivotal phase. This was when Zuma (then aged 63) was charged with the rape[11] of the 31-year-old, HIV-positive daughter of a deceased struggle comrade of his. He was brought to trial in December 2005 and acquitted in May 2006.

The third front in the struggle was political jockeying in the ANC and Alliance. The principal turning point came when Mbeki relieved Zuma of his post as vice state president in June 2005, shortly after a close associate of his, Schabir Shaik, was sentenced to fifteen years in prison on corruption charges. However, the ANC's National Working Committee – the body responsible for the day-to-day leadership of the movement – refused to remove him from the deputy presidency of the ANC, thus giving him an effective base from which to fight back. It was from this point that the coalition of the disaffected began to build momentum behind Zuma, as an alternative leader to Mbeki.

As we have seen, investigation of Zuma for corruption became a matter of public and internal ANC controversy with Ngcuka's notorious announcement (August 2003), backed by the minister of justice, that the NPA had a prima facie case against Zuma but not enough evidence for a successful prosecution. It was, however, the conviction of Shaik in June 2005 that led to Zuma's dismissal and renewed efforts to prosecute him. A pattern emerged of delaying tactics on the part of Zuma's team (over access to documents in particular) and on the side of the Scorpions, raids and other ploys that skirted or crossed the boundaries of legality. Zuma was charged in October 2005, with the trial set for July 2006, but the charges were struck from the roll in September 2006 when the judge said that the state's case had gone, 'from one disaster to another'.[12] In November 2007, the NPA was successful in appeals against a previous, inadmissible ruling against some of the Scorpions' search-and-seizure operations, and on 28 December, eight days after Zuma had been elected ANC president by the national conference at Polokwane, charges of racketeering, money laundering, corruption and fraud were again laid against him. The hearing began on 4 August 2008, but on 12 September,

Judge Chris Nicholson ruled the charges unlawful on procedural grounds, while, at the same time, observing that political interference in the criminal justice processes had played a part in their being brought in the first place and in the way they had been subsequently handled.[13]

This finding was politically explosive, leading directly to the ANC's 'recall' of Mbeki from the presidency, ignoring the formality of having parliament, through the medium of the ANC majority, doing the job, and his replacement by Kgalema Motlanthe, who had been elected ANC vice president at Polokwane. The detonation however did not dispose of the matter of Zuma's alleged corruption, especially since Nicholson had carefully left open the question of his guilt or innocence. The NPA, joined by Mbeki, who, despite not being party to the original case, felt understandably that Nicholson had impugned him without any right of reply, took the ruling to the Supreme Court of Appeal (SCA). In January 2009, a full bench of the SCA not only set aside the ruling but also did so in terms so scathing as to seriously damage Nicholson's credibility and destroy his 'political interference' thesis.

According to the SCA, Nicholson was operating, 'according to his own conspiracy theory', had 'overstepped the mark' and 'failed to comply with basic rules of procedure'. The inferences of political interference were marred by 'a complete absence of hard facts', simply took Zuma's allegations at face value and relied on 'newspaper speculation'. In sum, they were 'gratuitous and not based on any evidence'. Specific allegations in Nicholson's ruling about the National Director of Public Prosecutions (NDPP) and about Mbeki were 'not only irrelevant but gratuitous and based on suspicion rather than fact (and) may well be vexatious and scandalous'.[14]

However, even such an apparently definitive ruling could not ensure that Zuma would have his day in court. As we have seen, the leaking of telephone transcripts made by the National Intelligence Agency gave the acting NDPP Mokotedi Mpshe (2005–7) the opportunity to drop the reinstated charges on 6 April, sixteen days before the general election that installed Zuma as president of South Africa. Even this did not exhaust the apparently endless resources of the South African legal system, which allowed the opposition Democratic Alliance (DA) to challenge Mpshe's decision; then seven years later (April 2016), the Pretoria High Court found that the decision was 'irrational' and ordered that the charges be reinstated. By mid-2018, Zuma's and the NPA's appeals had failed and the hearings were at a preliminary stage.

A summary of the proceedings in Zuma's corruption investigations and trials makes it clear how and why political conflicts and legal proceedings have become so intertwined in South Africa as well as how central judges, trials and appeals up the hierarchy of courts have become to South African conceptions of democracy. The Constitution and the system of courts provided a reasonably stable process for the Mbeki/Zuma contest to unfold and still does in the case of the corruption charges, but dramatic reversals, such as the Nicholson judgement, followed by its devastating rebuttal by the SCA, create unstable expectations of the legal route and help to suggest that, since it is something of a lottery, it is a good idea always to buy a ticket. Inevitably, such instability also motivates interested and ill-informed parties to call into question the impartiality of the courts. For example, Nicholson had an honourable history of anti-apartheid activism and SCA deputy-president Louis Harms was an 'old order' judge. Harms's name was attached to the judgement because he wrote it; however, he did so on behalf of a unanimous full bench, on which three out of the five were post-1994 appointments and the other was appointed in October 1993. However, such details were not of interest to excitable crowds on or off the scene.[15] This instability also contributed to the febrile atmosphere surrounding the court proceedings. Zuma's supporters behaved like the audience at an Elizabethan theatre, booing and cursing judges who gave 'wrong' decisions and cheering those who gave the 'right' ones. This was not, however, good-natured fun but a deliberate attempt to intimidate and undermine the 'wrong' judges with threats of violence and wild rhetoric about killing and dying for Zuma. Since several of the judges were white, there was a pronounced racial overtone to Zuma's support: a 'bad judge' was also a 'bad (and racist) white man' and a 'good judge' was a 'good white man'. Such judgements were of course reversible according to variations in the verdicts.

By contrast with the corruption charges, the rape case was speedily and conclusively settled with an acquittal. The court found the young woman to be an unreliable witness, partly because her past history included having made multiple accusations of rape, and accepted Zuma's defence that intercourse, which he acknowledged, was not only consensual but, in his version, took place at her initiative. In this instance, Zuma had had his day in court and been vindicated. The case was notable for the expressions by his supporters of hypermasculinity, ethnic solidarity – Zuma based his defence partly on interpretations of Zulu traditional culture – and diffuse populist anti-elitism. These were aggressively displayed in brazen attempts to intimidate the court and frighten the young woman and her supporters. They also helped broaden Zuma's support base beyond its largely leftist core, not all of which was comfortable with Zuma's conduct and his rationalization of it, while at the same time confirming in the eyes of Mbeki supporters that Zuma, guilty or not in the eyes of the law, was not a fit person to lead the ANC or the country. Zuma's own belief that there was a conspiracy against him was greatly hardened by the case, which he believed to have been a 'honey trap' concocted along lines familiar to intelligence services throughout the world, both real and fictional. He exploited this conspiracy theory extensively in the aura of victimhood that he created as an increasingly important part of his appeal.

Amid the see-sawing legal fortunes and swirling speculations about conspiracies and factions in captured and divided state institutions, the denouement of the events set in motion by Mbeki's dismissal of Zuma in 2005 was brutally short and simple. In just over two years, concurrently with the rape and corruption charges, Zuma and the coalition of the disaffected turned the tables on Mbeki and won a sweeping victory at the ANC elective conference at Polokwane in December 2007. Mbeki stood for a third term as ANC president and lost heavily to Zuma. The result was foretold by the provincial nominations in November.[16] They showed that Mbeki would take four provinces to Zuma's five, but that the votes would split approximately 60 to 40 per cent in Zuma's favour. This was very close to the result at the conference showing that the support for each candidate held firm. Compromise candidates such as Cyril Ramaphosa and Nkosasana Dlamini-Zuma received only a derisory handful of votes so that rather than stand aside for one who might have had a better chance against Zuma, Mbeki continued to work until the moment of defeat to try and detach enough of Zuma's delegates to cling on to his position.

Although Zuma was apparently content to allow Mbeki to see out his term (he was widely quoted as saying that it is a waste of energy 'to beat a dead snake'[17]), Nicholson's intervention gave the ANC – many of whom were worried about the 'two centres of power' – the excuse to be rid of him.

Explaining Mbeki's downfall

A reversal of leadership fortunes so complete and apparently so swift is not easy to account for. The difficulties lie not so much in lack of potential contributing factors but in ordering them and relating them to each other. Mbeki's reported character traits – aloofness, hypersensitivity shading into paranoia, lack of collegiality and so on – have been generously cited by his biographers and also in more ephemeral accounts. Some glaring political errors may also be noted. Ngcuka's 'prima facie case' statement in 2003 is very difficult to justify on any grounds. Even elementary political prudence should have given pause, and it is hard to believe that Ngcuka would make it without Mbeki's agreement, if not direction. The appointment of Mlambo-Ngcuka to replace Zuma was an outrageous and gratuitous provocation – she was after all the wife of Zuma's would-be nemesis and to all appearances she was completely dependent on Mbeki's patronage for political standing.

Given the dearth of talent in the ANC, it was most unwise of him to drive out what substantial talent there was, since this left him with no one credible to promote in the succession. He obviously had learned nothing about how to foster talent from his long and richly rewarding apprenticeship with Tambo. Ironically, by clearing others out he cleared the way for Zuma, whom he then had to frustrate. It is not clear whether Mbeki's bid for a third term as ANC president stemmed from an inner drive to prolong his own power or because his maladroit draining of the talent pool left only this as an improvised option for the succession. The balance of critical opinion seems to be with the former, but it is a judgement that rests, inevitably, on assumptions about character.

Another alleged political error was to underestimate the force of ethno-tribal factors in the ANC:

> The ANC's ethnic balancing act was clumsily undermined by Mbeki's second-term cabinet reshuffle, which resulted in 13 Xhosa-speakers taking up places in the cabinet. Meanwhile he fuelled suspicion that non-Xhosa leaders need not be treated with the respect that their seniority demanded.[18]

It may be a moot point to what extent finely tuned tribal head counting of government posts plays a part across the whole polity in calculations of support for political leaders, but there is no gainsaying the same author's point that 'some ANC activists in KwaZulu-Natal live in a fantasy world of their own in which ... Jacob Zuma is the victim of a tribalist plot'.[19]

Alternative explanations to the strictly personal combine the personal with the structural. In such a wider view, the nature of the ANC was changing, reflecting hard-edged materialism and rapidly increasing inequality among black people in wider society. This was a factor making for discontent with Mbeki that was complementary to resentment at the movement's organizational centralization and some of the blame could be laid at his door. Some measure of increasing inequality was inevitable anyway under conditions of expanded opportunity and rapid social mobility – for some – in a mixed economy. However, Mbeki's narrowly focused BEE policies and their dimension of at best political connectedness and at worst cronyism made sharply rising inequality all the harder to bear for those who felt, usually with good reason, excluded from the fruits of liberation. Ironically, no one lamented this materialism more than Mbeki himself; he railed against its destructive effects in shrill jeremiads and strident calls for a return to prelapsarian moral purity. No one listened, partly because he did not seem to grasp how his own policies were stoking the things he castigated, although everyone else did.

A line of explanation that is emphasized less than either a focus on the leadership candidates or discontents in wider society is one that looks at the mechanics of choosing the leader.[20] In 2007, the ANC claimed a little over 621,000 members. This was 5.7 per cent of the South Africans who voted for the ANC in the national component of the 2004 general election. Fewer than 4,000[21] branch delegates comprised 90 per cent of the voters at Polokwane (the other 10 per cent came from the Youth League, the Women's League and other affiliates). That membership grew from 401,454 in a 2005 audit to the 2007 figure of over 621,000. This means that the organization expanded in spectacular fashion between Zuma's ousting from the vice presidency and the Polokwane elective conference. Whoever could influence this membership best – and it was still only less than 6 per cent of ANC voters – would have a majority of the less than 1 per cent of members who would decide the succession. The new members were predominantly rural. Moreover, four audits over the ten years, from 1997 to 2007, revealed that membership of the ANC was cyclical, with considerable additions before provincial elective conferences followed by sharp declines.

While this is not conclusive evidence of a causal relationship between growing rural membership and Zuma's successful challenge, it is at the least an interesting coincidence. Nor does it necessarily show that Zuma and his supporters embarked on an early programme of recruitment, with an eye to taking on Mbeki at Polokwane, but it does point in that direction. Certainly, one of Zuma's most enthusiastic backers, Cosatu secretary general Zwelinzima Vavi, did urge the unions to 'flood the branches with members' to get rid of Mbeki. Unions have traditionally been the best-organized element of the ANC and historically have been the mainstay of getting the vote out in general elections. However, given the predominantly urban background of union members and the fact that the new members were predominantly rural, Cosatu's influence on the wave of recruitment may not have been decisive.[22] The expansion is unlikely to have been spontaneous however and traditional leaders and the structures associated with them may have been more likely recruiting agents. Whatever the exact mechanics were of putting together the electoral college that went to Polokwane, the suspicion is that Mbeki was too often out of the country and too consumed by the tasks of the African Renaissance, defending Mugabe by stealth, telling the world the 'truth' about AIDS, putting Western leaders in their place and firing scorching missives at 'racist' whites to attend properly to grubbing for votes in dusty places. It did come to that, but grudgingly and late in the day. Gevisser describes a visit to his mother's homestead in the Eastern Cape two months before Polokwane, but adds the comments of 'one of Mbeki's oldest comrades'.

> Can you believe that this is the man who once upon a time refused to pander to ethnicity to such an extent that he wouldn't even visit the Eastern Cape? Now there he is playing the Xhosa card. JZ and the Zulus versus Thabo and the Xhosas. Isn't that what we fought against all our lives?[23]

It is a comment that serves well as an elegy for the old ANC's failure to understand actually existing South Africa as well as a fanfare for the entry of Zuma's ANC. It even gets the dynamics of the contest wrong and should serve as a corrective for those who superimpose simplistic ethnic and tribal labels on ANC politics. If it really had been Xhosa versus Zulu, Mbeki would have won the Eastern Cape by a big enough margin to win the day overall. As it turned out, in a poignant irony given Mbeki's history of closeness to Tambo, the O. R. Tambo region of the ANC, the biggest, not only in the Eastern Cape but in the country, cast its votes for Zuma: 'In the end Mbeki won the Eastern Cape only by 51 per cent to 49 per cent. His lack of a solid regional base was fatal.'[24]

However it is explained, the passing from Mbeki to Zuma posed many questions for contemporary observers. Was there a conspiracy to subvert state institutions and if there was what would Zuma do about it? Would he clean up or treat his predecessor's gambits as a useful precedent? How would he manage the motley coalition that propelled him into power? Would he try to draw them together in a new ANC synthesis or handle them like a ringmaster in a circus?

These and other questions revolve around the issue of how much continuity there would be in style, vision and policy. Or would leadership matter less because the ANC would reassert itself after the Mandela aberration and now the Mbeki deviation? These issues will be pursued through an examination of the Zuma presidency and in an attempt at a concluding comparative resolution. But first it is worth noting the remarks of an astute outside observer of the ANC at the point of Mbeki's exit. In 2008, Tony Leon, the former leader of the DA (1999–2007), believed that politics had changed and that 'the arrogant assumptions of the past had been challenged'. He had this to say:

> The ANC cadres and MPs are unable to go back to their meek ways. The media and judiciary have also flexed their muscles after a fairly long

slumber during the Mbeki presidency. This is likely to continue and our democracy will be the better for it.[25]

In the short term he couldn't have been more wrong, but in the *longue durée* of the Zuma years and the coming of Ramaphosa, he may have turned out to be right.

7

Zuma from 2009 to 2017: A narrative of decay

The *Mail and Guardian*'s annual 'Cabinet report card' is, in the newspaper's self-estimation, 'a respected barometer of government performance'. In 2000, it graded Zuma, then deputy president, at B– (one of eight out of twenty-eight graded ministers to receive a B– or above) and had this to say about him:

> The surprise package of the Mbeki Cabinet, Jacob Zuma has emerged on to the national political scene with something of a bang and clearly he is a heavyweight in the government. He has improved as a stand-in for the president in Parliament and his approach usually generates warmth even among opposition MPs. … Within the presidency Zuma is seen as something of a gem. The hardworking ANC and Mbeki loyalist provides the president with solid backup whenever needed and he is not given to rocking the boat.

The assessment concludes warmly: 'Zuma is taking on the mantle of leader of those in the government and ruling alliance *who still believe the struggle for liberation was also a struggle for efficient and incorrupt delivery*' (emphasis added).[1]

By 2016, in the *Mail and Guardian*'s estimation, Zuma was so low that it could not award him a grade at all, not even an F for 'Fail': 'You have to hand it to President Jacob Zuma; he has a talent for finding new lows to achieve.' In 2015, prompted by Zuma's firing of respected finance minister Nhlanhla Nene, then in the course of a weekend replacing his replacement with former finance minister Pravin Gordhan, it labelled Zuma's performance as 'governance by farce, at the highest level, and with terrible repercussions. It was, we believed, as bad as things could get.'

In 2016, however, things got worse:

> In 2016, Zuma did a worse job as president by every important metric. He damaged South Africa politically, economically and socially. He now

stands accused not only of corruption in his own dealings but also of selling our sovereignty by allowing the state to be captured. But, because of his own delaying tactics, he remains untested on both counts.[2]

Even allowing for a touch of post-liberation naivety and progressive solidarity in the newspaper's 2000 grading and for the fact that fifteen years is a long time in politics, this is a spectacular fall from grace, which presents difficult explanatory challenges. As a first step towards meeting them, a thematic summary of decline and a chronological summary of events would be useful before proceeding to a more detailed discussion of Zuma as head of party and government.

State capture

The salient feature of Zuma's two presidential terms has been the development of a pattern of governance that has come to be labelled 'state capture'. This term generally means a situation in which state officials and politicians who control them grant privileged access to public goods and rents, generating advantages to favoured individuals in ways that undermine the credibility and integrity of state institutions and waste public resources.[3] Certainly, this happened in South Africa under Zuma. State resources, mainly through the medium of government procurement and especially contracts with state-owned enterprises (SOEs), were diverted to enrich politically connected people including the Gupta family and through them, Zuma's own family. However, there has been another purpose and focus for state capture under Zuma: the subversion of the police and criminal justice system to protect him from further legal proceedings arising from the corruption charges that followed the Arms Deal investigations. Court proceedings to reinstate the charges that were dropped in 2009, though moving very slowly, had Zuma on the defensive virtually from the beginning of his first term. His aim was at best to quash the charges altogether, but a more likely route to success was to stall matters until a political escape could be found, such as the granting of amnesty by a successor who would either be sympathetic or have his or her hands tied by pressures of party unity.

If enrichment and self-preservation were the main ends of Zuma's state capture, the principal means were the president's extensive powers of appointment, not only to the cabinet and core offices of government but also to state, quasi-state and those bodies that are (in theory at least) statutorily independent. Key points of focus in this respect have been the boards of SOEs plus the headships of various police agencies and the National Prosecuting

Authority (NPA). However, questionable appointments in the criminal justice system that were made to protect him merely led to the opening of another front in the ongoing politico/legal war of attrition as court challenges to them were mounted and it was this axis of resistance above all that led to his downfall.

African National Congress unity

A second theme of the Zuma years was exposure of ANC unity as a myth that could not survive the pressures of governing and of rapid social change. This prompted the partial fragmentation of the ANC monolith, which happened in two ways. The first was through breakaways to form rival parties, thus creating a more diverse opposition; the Congress of the People (COPE), mainly composed of supporters of Mbeki and concentrated in the Eastern Cape, broke away in the aftermath of the Polokwane conference in 2007 and the Economic Freedom Fighters (EFF) was founded by former ANC Youth League (ANCYL) leader Julius Malema in 2013 after he had been expelled from the ANC (2012), having gone quite quickly from being Zuma's most rabid supporter to his most extreme critic and would-be nemesis. The other route to fragmentation was through the breakup of the coalition that brought Zuma to power and the subdivision of the ANC and the components of the wider Alliance into pro- and anti-Zuma factions, thus weakening all of them. This tendency was most marked in Cosatu, which began to disintegrate (for a variety of reasons of which Zuma was only one) from about 2012. A parallel development to the ANC's fragmentation was Zuma's successful construction of an alternative foundation for staying in power, based on patronage and astute (some say corrupt) party management, mainly through manipulation of ANC branch membership, especially in KwaZulu-Natal (KZN). During this time, the ANC's profile became more clearly that of a party based predominantly though not exclusively on support in rural areas and from people with rural roots, whether or not they actually live permanently in rural areas. However, it is not easy to determine the extent to which Zuma's continuing hold on the leadership has been a cause or effect of this changing profile.

Reinvigorated opposition

A third theme has been pushback to the various pathologies of the Zuma regime from three sources. The formal opposition, those parties that compete in elections and try to hold the government accountable in parliament, has seen its numbers and variety of forms increase and Zuma, backed by loyalist MPs and the Speaker of parliament, was forced into ever more blatant manoeuvres to avoid being held accountable in a reinvigorated parliament. Zuma's domination of the large ANC majority meant that the generous resources of South Africa's justiciable constitution were more important than increases in voting percentages for the opposition in narrowing the political space available to Zuma. Civil society organizations, organized on varying bases including defence of the Constitution, anti-corruption and accountability of public expenditure, were also important and (somewhat belatedly) organized business began to assert itself from early 2016 onwards. The most important factor in facilitating this pushback was the independence of the courts and isolated but effective instances of statutory bodies which Zuma failed to control, notably the office of Public Protector under the leadership of Thuli Madonsela, during her non-renewable seven-year term (2009–16). A marked feature of the Zuma years was that the asymmetrical democracy, which was the preferred mode for many politically aware South Africans, came to flourish.

Economic stagnation

During Zuma's second administration a sense of economic crisis developed, composed of stagnating growth, continuing high levels of unemployment (the main contributor to high levels of poverty), policy uncertainty and persistently low levels of confidence by business and markets. This sense of crisis made itself felt in regular warnings from international financial organizations (IFIs), investors and rating agencies – in the case of the last, a series of downgrades of South Africa's sovereign debt rating in 2016–17.

By late 2017, Zuma's leadership was confronted by challenges thrown up by the linked themes of compromised governance and state capture, a fragmenting Alliance, the demands of a remodelled and more narrowly focused support base, increased threat from both inside and outside the ANC and a gathering economic crisis. In response, he relied on the patronage politics that were partly responsible for fomenting the challenges in the first place and added a flirtation with economic populism under the vague rubric of 'radical economic transformation'. As befits its populist provenance, this was not a structured programme, nor was it based on comprehensive and evidence-based analysis of South Africa's political economy. Instead, it relied on scapegoating with a pronounced racial flavour, summed up in the phrase, 'white monopoly capitalism', whose 'overthrow' would solve South Africa's economic problems, and on a revived iteration of the ANC's long-standing global conspiracy theories, in which Western intelligence agencies in alliance with rating agencies, multinational companies and IFIs seek 'regime change'. Insofar as radical economic transformation had content by late 2017, it was confined to a vague commitment by Zuma to land expropriation without compensation and to greatly ramped-up BEE requirements, exemplified by the 2017 revision of the Mining Charter, which late in that year was the subject of a court standoff between the government and the minister of mineral resources, Mosebenzi Zwane. By that time Zwane had already been named in various reports on state capture by investigative journalists and academics as a key link between the Gupta family and Zuma. The obvious suspicion, shared in the second half of Zuma's second administration by virtually everyone who was not a Zuma loyalist, was that radical economic transformation was a populist smokescreen to conceal continued crony rent-seeking at the expense of state resources.

From Polokwane to Mangaung
(December 2007–December 2012)

The five years between the ANC conferences that gave Zuma his two terms as ANC president also saw him negotiate the 'recall' of Mbeki in September 2008, the eight-month interregnum of the Motlanthe presidency and his first general election as ANC leader. The result was a comfortable victory, with the ANC winning 65.9 per cent of votes cast, representing 38.8 per cent of the voting-age population, compared to 69.89 per cent and 39 per cent, respectively, under Mbeki's leadership in the 2004 general election. The seeds of later trouble, however, were planted early. Work on his private residence in his ancestral home of Nkandla in Zululand, financed by public money, began in August 2009. By December, investigative journalists were reporting on the extent of the work and the likelihood that Zuma was benefitting unduly from the expanding budget. By December 2011, complaints to this effect had been laid with the Public Protector and her investigations had begun. The opposition Democratic Alliance (DA) began what would turn out to be a protracted but in the end successful court battle (2009–14), for the release of the 'spy tapes' on which the then National Director of Public Prosecutions' (NDPP's) decision to drop Zuma's corruption charges was based. Scrutiny of the tapes allowed a further court challenge, which determined in 2016 that the grounds for the decision were flawed and the charges could be reinstated. In addition, the support of the left-wing components of the coalition that swept him to power unravelled with breathtaking speed. As late as June 2008, by which time Zuma was comfortably installed as ANC president but still faced corruption charges, Cosatu leader Zwelinzima Vavi was saying,

> Because Jacob Zuma is one of us and he is one of our leaders, for him we are prepared to lay down our lives and shoot to kill.[4]

By late 2009 at a South African Communist Party (SACP) special congress, he was admitting that support for Zuma was a miscalculation and that 'I never thought I would face this moment so soon'. By August 2010 he was describing 'political hyenas in a feeding frenzy', singling out a controversial transaction that enriched friends and family of Zuma, concluding, 'We are heading for a predator state where a powerful, corrupt and demagogic elite of political hyenas are increasingly using the state to get rich.'[5] Such U-turns did little to enhance Vavi's credibility; in any case, other Cosatu leaders, although critical, were more circumspect, focusing on their disappointment with economic policy and failure to deliver on promises they believe had been agreed at Polokwane rather than direct criticism of Zuma as an individual or the allegations and dire predictions made by Vavi.[6] As a result, Cosatu was divided into pro- and anti-Zuma unions, the unions themselves were internally divided and Cosatu's influence in the ANC was compromised.

Further evidence of the speedy disintegration of Zuma's initial power base came with the challenge presented by Julius Malema, president of the ANCYL (2008–12). Malema's fiery and violent rhetoric was an essential element in Zuma's rise to power in 2005–7. As late as October 2009, Zuma was praising him as a leader of the future, saying,

> Some of us are no longer young and when we go across the mountain in terms of age, we are happy that when we go on, the organisation will remain in the real hands of those who will think of the people.[7]

However, after he became head of the ANCYL, Malema's militant populism became too erratic and volatile to accommodate in the ANC and within six months of Zuma's endorsement, he was facing 'hate speech' charges, ANC disciplinary processes and, later, charges of tax evasion and racketeering. His expulsion from the ANC was a protracted process, finally concluded in April 2012.

The ANC and Alliance were, as befits their enduring character, preoccupied with looking inwards at shifting allegiances and other organizational dynamics in the run-up to the Mangaung elective conference in December 2012. However, four months before this there was a violent reminder that a chaotic world was developing outside the Alliance. On 16 August 2012, thirty-four wildcat striking miners were shot dead by police at Marikana in North West province. Four days of anarchic violence between striking miners and National Union of Mineworker (NUM) officials, as well as police and mine security personnel, cost ten lives in the days preceding the police shootings. These events were a warning signal of how far things had unravelled from the stable labour relations regime envisaged by the legislation of the Mandela years and the assumption that incorporation of Cosatu in the ruling Alliance would channel worker militancy. The chaos surrounding the strike and the police overreaction spelled out the lesson that neither the government nor the Alliance any longer had the resources to manage events without extraordinary measures.

After Mangaung: The gathering storm

Remarkably, despite the shock of Marikana, opposition from Cosatu, some provinces and the ANCYL (like Cosatu divided in its allegiances), Zuma comfortably won a second term as ANC president at the Mangaung conference in December 2012. The main reasons for this were the divisions of the opposition, the lack of a challenger with the stature and appetite for taking on the incumbent and the Zuma camp's domination of delegations from the provinces, especially KZN, where ANC membership had expanded the most. Not only was the outcome of the conference a personal triumph for Zuma, the elections consolidated his hold on the ANC, notably through the National Executive Committee (NEC). The choice of Cyril Ramaphosa as ANC vice president and of Gwede Mantashe, a senior SACP figure and former head of the NUM, as secretary general masked this dominance to some extent by erecting a façade of balance and unity and, until he overreached himself in 2016, Zuma was able to rule largely unchecked.

Zuma's apparent dominance of the ANC was mirrored by the ANC's continued electoral hegemony. In the 2014 elections, the ANC's share declined by 3.75 per cent but still stood at 62.15 per cent (249 seats); the DA raised its share by 5.75–22.3 per cent (89 seats) and the new opposition party the EFF, founded by Malema in July 2013, less than a year before the election, took 6.5 per cent (25 seats). Various minor parties took 37 seats, which left the ANC (and Zuma, provided his party kept behind him) with a comfortable absolute majority of 249 over 151.

However, this reflected a false image and in the aftermath of the 2014 election it became clear that in some respects a new era had begun for South African politics. In addition to being invigorated by its increased parliamentary representation, the DA had emerged, for the foreseeable future at least, as the natural party of government in the Western Cape by greatly increasing the absolute majority it had won there in 2009 (it had also won an absolute majority in the City of Cape Town in the municipal elections of 2011). The EFF may only have won twenty-five seats in parliament, but the youthfulness of its members and its shock tactics, both inside and outside the chamber, helped it punch considerably above its weight. Above all, its relentless and scornful targeting of Zuma personally signalled complete rejection of the hitherto customary deference towards the liberation generation of the ANC. This symbolism marked a significant sea change: respect was no longer a matter of historic entitlement and would have to be earned.

Material for reinvigorated opposition had begun to accumulate even before the election. In April 2013, the privileged and politically connected position of the Gupta family was highlighted when an aircraft transporting over two hundred guests from India to South Africa for the wedding of the Gupta brothers' niece was irregularly given special status to land in South Africa. Although the ANC and government shrugged off 'Guptagate', the affair helped fuel suspicions about and investigations of the Gupta's closeness to Zuma and other politicians. In 2017, when a large number of emails to and from Gupta companies were leaked, it transpired that the wedding had been paid for by laundered funds originating from the Free State government.

In March 2014, two months before the election, the Public Protector's report on Zuma's Nkandla residence concluded that he had unreasonably benefited from expenditure of government funds. Thanks to the support of the ANC majority in parliament, marshalled sympathetically by the Speaker, Baleka Mbete, who, in a brazen conflict of interest, was also national chairperson of the ANC until December 2017, Zuma declined to accept the Protector's ruling that he should pay back a portion of the undue benefit. However, in March 2016, the constitutional court unanimously ruled that the Protector's rule was binding and that Zuma had failed in his duty to respect its constitutional force.

The momentum of opposition and civil society efforts to hold Zuma to account continued with the eventual ruling of the Supreme Court of Appeal in August 2014 that the DA could have access to the so-called spy tapes. This in turn led the DA to request a court review of the NPA's decision to drop charges against Zuma in 2009. In November 2016, the North Gauteng (Pretoria) High Court ruled that the decision had been 'irrational' and that the charges could be reinstated. The NPA's appeal against this finding was turned down by the Supreme Court of Appeal in October 2017.

From the turn of 2015–16, concerns about Zuma began to focus on misgovernment in state-owned enterprises (SOEs) and the effects of their poor performance and increasingly institutionalized need for treasury bailouts on the wider economy and the government's fiscal integrity. Cronyism had taken root from the beginning of Zuma's first term in 2009, during Malusi Gigaba's term of office as minister of public enterprises (2009–14). It was only when Zuma's drive to take control of the Treasury became blatant with the firing of Nhlanhla Nene as minister of finance in December 2015 that the issue moved up the agenda of public debate, stimulated significant pushback and attracted extensive and systematic scrutiny. Such were the adverse reactions of markets and of some senior ANC people that within three days Zuma reinstated Pravin Gordhan, whom he had moved from the post in 2014 because he too was an obstacle to large-scale, unaffordable projects and cronyism. Almost immediately, Gordhan was subjected to a campaign of harassment and intimidation by law enforcement agencies (principally the Hawks, the Scorpions' replacement).

No charges were brought, and Gordhan became a symbol of rectitude against cronyism and corruption both before and after he was fired in March 2017. So did Mcebisi Jonas, Gordhan's deputy minister, who was fired alongside him. In the aftermath of the firing, Jonas went public with the allegation that one of the Gupta brothers offered him the post of finance minister in October 2015 (shortly before Nene was fired), along with a bribe of R600 million, claiming that 'We control Zuma' and threatening to have Jonas murdered if he revealed the offer and the threat (the Guptas deny the allegations).[8]

The Gordhan/Jonas firing was a turning point, which brought the narrative of state capture out of the shadows and turned Zuma's leadership from being an exclusively opposition preoccupation into the heart of the ANC itself. The shock to markets was profound and helped edge South African business towards a more activist stance. The momentum of court decisions and investigative revelations increased to the point where Zuma's position became untenable, though it took Ramaphosa's narrow (and pyrrhic) victory in December 2017 to pave the way for his ousting.

Zuma as a representative individual

How a political leader's persona is composed is perennially difficult to assess. To what extent is it a matter of 'natural' traits? To what extent is it consciously assembled and shaped? And to what extent is the hard work done not by political marketing but, in the eye of the beholder, a matter of projection and seeing what the audience wants to see?

In Western democracies, it is increasingly believed that political public relations are the paramount element in the creation of leaders' images as representative individuals and this is one of the main sources of disillusionment with political classes, with elites and with 'spin'. In the case of Zuma, however, it is tempting to speculate that projection – in the sense of overestimating the extent to which a representative individual actually shares our beliefs and values – was unusually important in creating him as a leader and that this did not require an enormous amount of encouragement from public relations. This could partly be because the sense of crisis that Mbeki's leadership failings brought to the ANC encouraged a mood among many that anyone who was so opposed to Mbeki must be on the side of the angels and the possessor of all sorts of desirable traits. This interpretation is reinforced by the speed and the vehemence with which some of Zuma's principal sponsors subsequently turned on him, Cosatu's Zwelinzima Vavi and the ANCYL's Julius Malema being only the best-known examples. Their quick about-turn bore all the hallmarks of the fury of the self-deceived.

Whatever the respective contributions were of artifice and the gullibility of key constituencies, an aura of authenticity was the key to Zuma's claim to be a representative individual. This in turn had several sources. These were a set of presumed individual character traits; struggle credentials; a personal history whose narrative arc went from sacrifice in the struggle to triumph with his generation of ANC peers and on to betrayal and victimization by the very power structure he helped to create; representation of authentic African tradition in his person, his conservative social values and his championing of rural social and political structures; and finally the promise that in him the ANC would revert to a leader who, unlike his predecessor, would not set himself up as the architect of new institutional beginnings and underhand ideological revisions but would remain its humble servant and return to the mythical, old ways of leadership.

Virtually all these elements of personal mythology relied heavily for their meaning, in the eyes of Zuma's supporters at least, on Mbeki as a Dark Other who was intrinsically different and sinister. Indeed, there is a strong case for saying that without Mbeki, Zuma's leadership pretensions made little sense. However, it is worth noting before discussing them, something Mbeki and Zuma had in common and which set them both off against Mandela.

The exile experience

It would be going too far to say that Mandela had a normal life prior to his immersions in the underground, his trial and jail sentence. A life constrained by pass laws and other repressive legislation of racial classification and discrimination made a mockery of 'normal' for all Africans, especially those who were politically aware and who involved themselves initially in opposition and then in resistance. Nevertheless, there was a clear difference between Mandela's early adult years and those of Mbeki and Zuma, both of whom were of a younger generation. Mandela had gone to a university that could still claim (just) to be 'open' and was not yet subject to the more rigid segregation that came later. Mandela may have been the only African in his class and experienced racism there, but he also lived and studied in a diverse, multiracial South African context. Indeed, the University of the Witwatersrand could claim to be more open than many universities in the Southern States of America in the years (1943–8) that Mandela was enrolled there. He practised law on behalf of urban Africans, was able to enjoy the ANC's years of open, political mobilization and the last years of the cultural flowering of the Sophiatown Renaissance. Even if we date the end of relative normality for Mandela at 1956, when he was arrested and subsequently charged with high treason (to be acquitted in 1962), rather than at the banning of the ANC in 1960, he still had around thirteen years of above-ground existence where he could participate in a rapidly changing South Africa.

All of this may have been darkened by increasing repression and progressively taken up by a life of resistance, but it was a more recognizable grounding in normal life than that afforded to Mbeki and Zuma. Mandela was forty-one years old when the ANC was banned in 1960, while both Mbeki and Zuma were seventeen. Exile and underground existence began for Mbeki when he was twenty, and Zuma was twenty-one when he was jailed, thirty-one when he was released and thirty-three when he went into exile.

It would not be true to say that Zuma completely lacked grounding in normal life, but it was not in the urban, industrializing and rapidly changing South African life that Mandela knew. Insofar as he was rooted, it was in a desperately poor, but in its way prelapsarian, African peasant life of tending animals and warlike boys' games. A romanticized version of this hard life was an undeniable part of his attraction, but it was greatly overlaid by the culture of exile. In any case, it was a heritage of only limited transferability to the rapidly modernizing, diverse and, above all, infinitely freer South Africa in which he had to operate as a leader. The regularity with which his conception of grounded normality ran up against the new South Africa of constitutionalism and citizens' rights and, more pertinently, the values that underlay them bore witness to this, beginning with his rape trial.

Part of what the first two post-Mandela presidents had in common, then, was the culture of the exiled ANC: that conspiracy was the natural order of things, that you had to be perpetually on the lookout for plots against you and you had to be prepared to plot against others in your own defence. Whatever else divided the two men, and, given the sheer force and pervasiveness of the ANC's political culture, this was less than the supporters of each would have the world believe, they were at one with the exile's world of anxiety and fear, at times to the point of irrationality and they lacked the grounding in normality that Mandela had. This was to have an important influence on their presidencies and not least on the struggle between them.

Zuma's personal qualities

There is no shortage of testimony to Zuma's attractive personal qualities. Virtually all journalists, political opponents, historians and biographers who have published their impressions of him record that he is down-to-earth, affable, unpretentious, approachable and exuberantly expressive in song and dance, as well as informal discourse, though less so in formal presentations. He is calm, a good listener, treats other people's opinions with respect and, for all his pride in ethno-tribalist display, is comfortable with ethnic and racial difference, with an especially soft spot for Afrikaners, whom he regards in a rather clichéd way (which accords comfortably with Afrikaans speakers' own self-estimation) as true Africans, unlike Anglophone white South Africans. As one (English) observer put it on the eve of Zuma's first administration, 'If South Africa is lucky, Zuma will be its Ronald Reagan.' With his folksy charm, he would reassure South Africans and '(He will) make the country feel good about itself after the awkward questions that Mbeki asked of it, and leave the business of government to the technocrats.'[9]

There is no reason to doubt the quality of these testimonies – the sheer weight and variety of witness accounts ensures that – but the context has to be taken into account. None of the assessments was unqualified; all that are cited here come from (or recall) a period when his leadership was anticipated but untried (2007–9), and that was a period in which the sense of relief that Mbeki was on his way out (or actually gone) was palpable right across the range of political players and the commentariat. Nevertheless, it is still striking how much space was given to the enumeration of Zuma's positive, human qualities in ushering in his period as leader. This, in turn, raises a number of questions about the general nature of political leadership and the specifics of leadership in South Africa.

These are especially prompted by the benefit of hindsight, which has made plain how unsatisfactory the leadership outcomes of Zuma's tenure have been (except of course for those who benefited from patronage and cronyism under his regime). Do South Africans or observers of South Africa pay too much attention to the character attributes of leaders as markers of their fitness for leadership, as distinct, say, from their political judgement, democratic values and technocratic capabilities? If so, is this something to do with the self-image of most South Africans, white as well as black? This includes a diffuse spiritualism and celebration of human warmth and authenticity, which they like to contrast with what they see as the greyness, reserve, individualism and impersonality of the Western world. Perhaps the legacy of Mandela's emotional intelligence prompts South Africans to overinvest in looking for human qualities in their leaders. The implication may be, among all these imponderables, that South Africans will get bad leaders until they start to look for the right qualities in the right places and calibrate their expectations better.

There is another, simpler possibility, applicable to both Mbeki and Zuma, that given the awfulness of its history and the fragility of its future, (nearly) everyone, at home and abroad, wants to give the country and its leaders the benefit of the doubt until it is no longer possible to do so.

Zuma and the struggle

Up to and including Zuma, strong struggle credentials were a very important part of ANC leadership profiles for anyone wishing to establish a commanding image within the organization. How important this is to the wider electorate is an open question, as is the extent to which such measures of credibility will remain essential in the future when generational change works itself out. Before the 2014 general election, 25 per cent of registered voters were under the age of thirty and 50 per cent under forty.[10] In Zimbabwe, the durability of struggle credentials is very marked, but this can be partly accounted for the prominence of classic rural guerrilla warfare in Zimbabwe's liberation struggle and, consequently, the central role the armed forces play in Zimbabwean politics as well as the strong element of gerontocracy in ZanuPF's leadership. In South Africa, the influence of the armed forces is negligible and constitutional term limits enforce greater leadership turnover than in its neighbour.

Zuma was very well placed to capitalize on struggle credentials. He was active in three out of four of the main theatres of resistance (there were five if the diplomatic sphere – Mbeki's forte – is included). Zuma's contributions were in prison, exile and the underground resistance in South Africa, the latter two being bound together by Zuma's participation in Umkhonto We Sizwe (MK) and the armed struggle. While he couldn't simultaneously be prominent in the above-ground resistance of the United Democratic Front (UDF), his involvement in the internal underground brought him closer to that sphere than did the experience many exiles.

This clandestine military involvement did much, we may surmise, to complement and toughen up the image of an affable singer and dancer. The precise nature of the involvement – counter-intelligence – would have done even more, adding a sinister and mysterious element and marking him as a man to be feared as well as liked. The American playwright Arthur Miller provides a clue to how this combination worked to Zuma's advantage, in his treatise, *On Politics and the Art of Acting*. Miller generalizes,

> The perfect model of both star and political leader is that smiling and implicitly dangerous man or woman who likes you.[11]

This is arguably one of the best summaries of the attraction of Zuma's representative profile.

From 1975, when he went into exile and after four months training in the USSR, Zuma worked for the ANC's National Department of Security and Intelligence, known by its isiZulu nickname, Mbokodo, 'the grindstone'. Gevisser describes Mbokodo as having 'a fearsome reputation' and 'supralegal status' within the exiled ANC and that it 'fuelled movement-wide paranoia about agents and spies'.[12] Zuma served there until the ANC was unbanned in 1990 and was head of counter-intelligence from 1987. Not much is known of this period and his sympathetic biographer refers to a 'missing 15 years'.[13]

Given that it is universally recognized that the ANC was riddled with informers, especially in the climactic years of the struggle, as head of counter-intelligence, Zuma was privy to investigations that would have yielded much tradable information in a later political career. This is especially so since the ANC, fearing the effects on morale of publicly moving against informers, was more inclined to 'turn' them again against the apartheid forces or 'reform' them. This leverage has its limitations, however. If his intelligence background has indeed been useful to Zuma, it is likely to have been more in private than public. The potential for allegations of apartheid spying to backfire when they are made publicly in an open democracy was dramatically demonstrated when Mac Maharaj, key ANC strategist in the military struggle, as well as an early and staunch supporter of Zuma against Mbeki, attempted by this means to discredit Bulelani Ngcuka as NDPP. Mbeki called his bluff and set-up a judicial commission to review the allegations (the 'Hefer Commission') in late 2003. The results demonstrated the collateral damage that accusations and counter-accusations of traitorous behaviours could cause. Maharaj was personally humiliated and his political career was ended (although he did go on to be Zuma's sorely tried spokesman). Ngcuka was vindicated but left shaken and he resigned shortly afterwards. Mbeki was strengthened in his developing struggle with Zuma, but the outcome of the commission may have led him to underestimate the durability of the threat that he faced. However, although Mbeki and Ngcuka's triumph was only short-lived, it was a long-term warning about using dirty tricks in the open, without a cast-iron case to back them up.[14]

Two other things are worthy of note concerning struggle credentials in leadership profiles. The first is that senior commanders on both sides of counter-insurgency wars are often responsible for, or at least accused of, deeds that are reprehensible, even by the standards of wartime; but the truth is usually very difficult to establish even in conditions of peacetime openness. Zuma is no exception; the question of whether he was directly involved in the death of a senior MK commander has never been resolved, nor is it likely ever to be beyond reasonable doubt.

'Thami Zulu' (an operational alias) was accused of being a spy, detained by the ANC under atrocious conditions for fourteen months and murdered by poison a handful of days after being released in Lusaka in 1987, when Zuma was head of Mbokodo there. The ANC's official version is that apartheid security forces murdered him, but there are other versions that raise suspicions about Zuma on circumstantial grounds at least.[15] A cloud of suspicion such as this probably counts for little in wider public estimation – relatively few people outside of political elites will have even heard of the Thami Zulu. Even within them, allegations of this sort can be dismissed if a leader is in a relatively strong position, but they can chip away at the credibility of an increasingly beleaguered one.

A final noteworthy point is that bonds forged under wartime conditions do not necessarily last. One of Zuma's key operatives in the internal underground was Pravin Gordhan, who, as finance minister, became the most substantial obstacle to Zuma's project of state capture and whose dismissal did more than anything else to crystallize the opposition to Zuma and hasten his end. Another close associate, first from the underground and later in mobilizing Zuma's campaign against Mbeki, was Mo Shaik, brother of Schabir, Zuma's corrupt, financial backer. Mo was involved in orchestrating the 'spy' allegations against Ngcuka, which led to the Hefer Commission and, like Maharaj, was humiliated under cross-examination. Zuma appointed Mo Shaik as head of the South African Secret Service (SASS: foreign intelligence), but Shaik, along with the heads of two other security bodies, balked at being used for undercover operations against ANC cabinet ministers in a cynical rerun of the 'plot' gambits of Mbeki's presidency and he (on his later testimony, which is impossible to verify) wished to investigate the Gupta family's links to government. All three were dismissed.[16]

Zuma's struggle experience was important in his career not only for the enhancement of his representative profile. As Stephen Ellis points out,

> For the remainder of his political career, this experience in charge of intelligence was to be Zuma's key institutional base.[17]

Zuma as victim

Victimhood and martyrdom can be potent elements in the profiles of leaders of nationalist parties or movements. Many examples can be drawn from instances such as Irish and Polish struggles for freedom. However, the part played by victimhood in post-apartheid South African politics is more complex and subtle than in the days of simply mobilizing against the oppressor.

Apartheid created two classes of black victims. In the first place, all black people were victims, since all were subject to the uniform humiliations that went with classification, statutory discrimination and the practice of casual racist denigration that was common to most white people in one form or another, though not universal. Those black people who resisted were victimized in other ways, through torture, imprisonment and murder; for those who escaped these things, the fear of them meant the loss even of whatever 'normal' life could be lived under apartheid's cruel distortions.

Victimhood at the hands of the oppressor became history in 1994 and was difficult to fit into post-apartheid politics. White guilt, white privilege and the status for all whites as beneficiaries of apartheid, irrespective of how much they contributed directly and personally to the system, are built into post-apartheid politics; they serve many functions and will remain functional for as far as the eye can see into the future. But this is structural victimhood of all black people. There may be some mileage for individual, representative victimhood in leader profiles, but not much. This is partly because victimhood clashes with the narratives of ANC triumph and of nation-building, partly because Zuma's leadership predecessors were seen, respectively, as transcending victimhood (Mandela) and outwitting the oppressor (Mbeki). These restraints displaced victimhood from the place it might reasonably have been expected to take in post-apartheid politics, given the inhumanity and injustice of the country's history.

If there was indeed a reservoir of displaced victimhood and if there was a constituency open, by virtue of its own past humiliations, to identification with a martyred leader, then Zuma either instinctively understood it or simply stumbled on it and exploited it to the full. However, his martyrdom came with a twist; it was not victimization at the hands of the (former) oppressor. This was priced into his life, as it was for all black people. It came instead, in his version, as a gross betrayal of the ANC's victory, at the hands of one of his closest associates and through the perversion of the state institutions that he had risked and sacrificed so much to bring into being. The mythology of betrayal is so deeply etched into South Africa's history and political culture that it is a narrative accessible to all and at all times. For instance, betrayal, victimhood and martyrdom were key elements in Afrikaner nationalism. The narrative of victimization that Zuma and his supporters built around him wove together some key elements of his history, which contributed to his authenticity.

In this narrative, he was despised by elites because he subscribed to traditional ways such as polygamy, which he has always defended (as polygamists always do) as being more honest and responsible than multiple, clandestine affairs; he was uneducated by comparison with many in the ANC elite, but his years of sacrifice in prison – where he learned to read and write – were years of dedication to self-improvement; still, he was looked down upon. In this way, Zuma's victimization narrative was a prototype for the kind of populist revolts against out-of-touch and snobbish elites of experts and remote political classes that have become commonplace in other democracies. However, a victim myth is too passive to drive a movement alone. Another side of Zuma's narrative was that he is a warrior and that to despise him is to underestimate him. Zuma's second name, given to him by his father, is Gedleyihlekisa; it is subject to quite varied translations usually involving combinations of cunning ability to see through people and ability to do harm to others while laughing.[18] Whatever the linguistic variations, it is a name of someone you should not underestimate.

It is the need for Zuma's warrior/victim persona to evolve that makes it distinctive. It began by being remarkable for its incoherence. It remains incoherent, but it is perpetually a work in progress, needing to broaden the sources of victimization and to find new perpetrators as the old ones are vanquished.

The incoherence of Zuma's narrative of victimization during his rise to power is shown in the way that the instruments of persecution – the courts are the obvious example – could turn in a moment into his saviours. In the eyes of his supporters, the elements of the Constitution are personalized: good if the right decisions come out or, if as later happened, Zuma controls them; bad if the wrong decisions are delivered or the wrong people are in charge. With Mbeki, everything was viewed in systemic and structural terms – imperialism, capitalism, racial oppression – and individuals and their works (especially white individuals) were irrelevant, except when he needed an occasional convenient whipping boy or pantomime villain to spice up the abstractions about racial oppression. With Zuma it was an exciting free-for-all in which heroes and villains were known by their works more than by their colour.

With Mbeki vanquished and the power structures associated with him dissolved like the Scorpions, which were disbanded at the ANC's insistence in 2008, or passing under his own control, Zuma still had need of the victim narrative. Up to a point this is not surprising because, as evidence of his misuse of power began to mount, especially in his second term, opposition parties and civil-society bodies increasingly had recourse to the courts, seeing that the criminal justice system had been captured by Zuma. Without becoming any more coherent, Zuma's sense of injustice and victimization took on dimensions of religiosity, laced with comparisons to Jesus, as well as broadening to take in 'clevers' – blacks who get above themselves – and taking on a more structural aspect.

At times, he appeared to be at odds with the very notion of impersonal, legal process, which he increasingly associated with 'Western' ideas and institutions, incompatible with the 'African way'. In November 2012, he addressed the National House of Traditional Leaders at a time when the kings and chiefs who are its members were threatening to take the government to court over their grievances. It was also at a time when adverse court judgements were beginning to pile up against him. In trying to persuade the traditional leaders not to go to court, he had this to say:

> I think we can resolve these matters in an African way, not through the law. You can't stand in court and defend yourselves. You need a lawyer. The law goes to the other side. The judges convict you, even if you tell the truth. Let us solve African problems the African way, not the white man's way. Let us not be influenced by other cultures and try to think the lawyers are going to help. They will tell you they are dealing with cold facts. They will never tell you that these cold facts have warm bodies, they are dealing with warm bodies, that is the contradiction. The law looks at one side only; they do not look at any other thing.[19]

Zuma's spin doctors (including Maharaj) argued that his words should not be taken out of their immediate context, which was that of negotiation between the government and traditional leaders. However, it is also possible to see them in a broader view, as expressing extempore frustration at being victimized by the impersonal force of laws that lack human understanding and perhaps by the very force of alien modernity itself.

Zuma and tradition

The insurgency that brought Zuma to leadership of the ANC and of the country filled a vacuum in ANC identity. The content that he represented was not universally shared and approved within the movement, but enough people responded to its linguistic, cultural and value cues to add substantially to his leadership claims and to have a profound effect on the ANC. This, according to taste and political orientation within the community of believers, could be deplored as an irrevocable deviation from the values and traditions that constituted the soul of the movement and gave it its unique moral authority, or it could be celebrated for wrenching it back from queasy cosmopolitanism to authentic Africanism. From outside, it could be (and frequently was) viewed as merely predictable conformity to African nationalist type.

The ANC had always cultivated African nationalism in a generalized way but was hesitant about specific, demotic content. Early, post-1990 rallies were much more at home with the comfortable choreography of Third-World internationalism, including generalized anti-imperialism, which heavily featured Cuba and (Gaddafi's) Libya, wordy solidarity with Palestine, the Polisario Front (an especial favourite) and a long list of such anti-colonial, micro-struggles as could be identified in the 1990s. All this was understandable for a movement that believed it owed so much to internationalism, but it left the ANC very short of colloquial content closer to home. There were of course good reasons for carefully rationing such content. It could be associated with the African chauvinism that caused the Pan Africanist Congress (PAC) split and which might compromise non-racialism, a quality deemed to be implanted in the ANC's DNA and essential to its well-being but notoriously difficult to define in operational terms. Equally, it could threaten to open the Pandora's box of tribalism as well as strike discordant notes with the ANC's overall commitment to modernization and its globalized, secular agenda of human rights and social democratic ideology.

Mbeki's solution was an Africanism that combined the syncretism and self-assertion of 'I am an African' with the far, continental horizons of the African Renaissance and New Partnership for African Development (NEPAD). 'I am an African' was a fastidious inoculation against the cruder excesses of identity politics, but while it may have excited African intellectuals and was greeted with puzzled relief by non-Africans, it did not have much to offer the street. The African Renaissance and NEPAD at least had a sound economic and geopolitical logic; South Africa needed Africa to prosper and be democratic in order to safeguard its own (comparative) prosperity and democracy. However, Africa was a distant concept for most South Africans outside elite circles. To judge by the xenophobic riots and killings (May 2008) that disfigured Mbeki's last year in office and clearly left him uncomprehending and bereft of leadership qualities, it was an uncongenial, as well as an unfamiliar, marker of identity for many of them. Whatever the case, it seems clear that Mbeki exaggerated the attractiveness of continental sentiments and deluded himself about their reach.

It was into this identity vacuum that Zuma swept in 2006–9. The most widely noted of Zuma's personal attributes at that time were those of being natural, at ease with himself and authentic in his outlook and sentiments. These are referred to approvingly in numerous interviews and profiles, including (indeed especially) those that went on to express doubts about his potential as a leader. This easy-going, even ingenuous aspect of his personality sealed the authenticity of his mixture of conservative social values, cultural fluency and linguistic rootedness in South Africa's rural past and present for those who valued and saw themselves in these things and, initially at least, assuaged the unease of some of those who manifestly did not. The conventional view of Zuma's ascent is that it was powered by a popular rejection in the ANC rank and file of Mbeki, his person and his leadership style. There is undoubtedly much truth in this view, but it is likely that the populist revolt was much broader-based than that. It is difficult to exaggerate the degree of disconnect between the elite-driven, progressive views enshrined in the Constitution, which express the most progressive positions on individual rights to choice on social issues, as well as the right to be free from discrimination on very wide range of grounds, and a citizen body that, in response to social surveys, expresses strong religiosity and highly conservative social attitudes.[20] It is true that there is no significant move to curb the generosity of constitutional rights; the only political party that specifically advocates this, the African Christian Democratic Party, polls infinitesimal numbers. However, it may be safely assumed that the appearance of a leader who was blithely unconcerned about what has come to be known as political correctness and prepared to offer robust views on gender relations, sexual orientation and crime and punishment, cheerfully ignoring rather than criticizing or flouting the Constitution, offered for many people a form of release from the cognitive dissonance between elite and official South Africa's views and their own.[21] Of course, this kind of cultural disconnection and such disaffection with political correctness are increasingly familiar in many democratic countries. However, what set off Zuma's alternative to political correctness from other similar forms of populism was that he could clothe himself in the authority of traditional culture and, for good measure, claim to be the agent of reclamation after centuries of cultural suppression by missionaries, colonial administrators and heartless capitalists.

No doubt the authenticity claims of some of this are debatable if not downright spurious. What constitutes authenticity in culture and tradition is always hard to establish, especially in a society such as South Africa. Apartheid actively encouraged African people to value approved versions of traditional life, while structural features such as industrialization, urbanization under apartheid rules and the migrant labour system encouraged people to mix modernity and tradition in their working and political lives. Today, this does not matter much politically. Western-educated cultural anthropologists can agonize all they like about authenticity and syncretism, but what matters is that Zuma as an aspirant leader spoke literally and figuratively in their own language to people who felt themselves to be culturally and economically marginalized.

Zuma's image as a representative champion of African tradition was a crucial element in his successful bid for leadership, but it should be seen in perspective. He was too experienced a political operator to be unaware that tradition could only be one strand in his make-up. As a result, despite his emphatically Zulu roots, his appeal was pitched at a sufficiently inclusive level for rural African people from other provinces and language groups to be comfortable with it. It was also modulated by insistent deference to the ANC as an organizational centre and repository of value as well as, when he was challenged, by lip service to the Constitution. In this sense, tradition was part of a balancing act, but far more was at stake than Zuma's personal identification with his cultural roots. It was greatly to Zuma's advantage that this was a balancing act with which the whole of the ANC had been grappling ever since 1990.

Zuma as party manager

The young lady from Riga (2): The Left and the real 'devil's pact'

As with Mbeki before him alliance relationships were an important part of party management. And for Zuma, the fundamentals were the same as they were for Mbeki.

It used to be, and for diehards still is, a staple of left-wing rhetoric in South Africa that under Mbeki (and Mandela before him) the ANC concluded a 'devil's pact' with capitalism, globalization and neo-liberalism. There is an alternative case, however, for labelling the Left's affair with African nationalism as the real devil's pact. This fatal embrace has been enervating and disarming to the Left's independence and ability to cultivate its own individual leaders with a substantial profile in wider society and has obfuscated the institutional purposes of the Left's component organizations.

In a scathing critique from a left-wing perspective, Hein Marais summarizes the fate of the Left's flirtation with Zuma. Having helped propel him into the leadership of the ANC, Cosatu and the SACP worked hard to present the new leader and the ANC with a decisive victory in the 2009 election, in the process helping to see off the challenge of the ANC breakaway party COPE. Then,

> (They) found themselves flummoxed by a question they had chosen to ignore as they trekked across the land stumping for Zuma: why exactly should the transition from Thabo Mbeki to Jacob Zuma have opened vistas for radical change? In what way did the 'new conjuncture' favour breakthroughs that were not on the cards in the 1990s?

They had acted as if they were confronting the apartheid state (although more in unconscious parody than in tribute to the liberation struggle), in doing so contributing to the 'factional destabilisation' of the democratic state and they

> wilfully chose the route of theatrical campaigning around a half-baked messianic figure over the painstaking slog of building a genuinely democratic left movement that could challenge for hegemony. Entryism and trying to lever influence by proxy is no substitute.[22]

Marais' account attributes the Left's failure to make significant gains from attaching itself to Zuma to its lack of institutional leverage inside the ANC and to an unfavourable domestic and international balance of forces. It is certainly true that the post-1990 period was very difficult for left-wing movements of the traditional kind all over the world. South African unions and the SACP were (and remain) doggedly traditional, wedded to militant class-war rhetoric and statist policies that take for granted a national economy built around heavy extractive and manufacturing industries as their frame of reference, while being deeply suspicious of South African business's global adaptability. It is equally true that the Left lacked institutional leverage within the ANC, but acknowledging this only opens the question of why they chose the strategy of entryism and influence by proxy. The answer probably is that they overestimated themselves and underestimated Zuma and the forces other than themselves that had brought him to power.

It is possible, then, that the Left mistook an anti-elitist coup that had strong overtones of ethnic populism and racial nationalism for a popular movement against austerity and neo-liberalism. Or it is possible that at least some of the Left's more astute leaders saw the Zuma phenomenon for what it was, an essentially directionless populism driven by a variety of resentments and Zuma's warrior/victim charisma, and they calculated that in the upheaval of Mbeki's overthrow such anti-elitist populism could be disciplined and directed by the organizationally more sophisticated and ideologically better informed cadres of the unions and the SACP. This is implied in an article written by SACP deputy general secretary Jeremy Cronin as Zuma's challenge to Mbeki gathered force:

> The challenge is now to move beyond personalities and to address the systemic issues that are prompting the turmoil. The question is not who should be president, but what kind of presidency our emerging democracy deserves.[23]

Cronin is correct to point to the danger of investing too much in the personal qualities of any given leader – something that South Africans of all political persuasions are prone to. However, there is another side to this coin; if you want to 'address the systemic issues that are prompting the turmoil' then it matters very much who is leader. What you need is either a credible leader who shares your orientation to the systemic issues, which the Left has never been able to provide from its own ranks nor find in the wider ranks of African nationalism, or you find one who is malleable enough to be persuaded to address the systemic issues in your way, either because he is a political lightweight or because you have sufficient political leverage over him. Neither of these things turned out to be true of Jacob Zuma.

Zuma's supporters on the Left regarded Mbeki and Zuma as polar opposites for the duration of the struggle between them, but once he was in office, he handled the Left in ways that were uncannily similar to his predecessor. He was much more politically astute than Mbeki and did not resort to the latter's scourging and teasing with lofty exegesis of the Left's own sacred texts to prove that he understood them much better than any collection of Marxist trade unionists and communists (in fairness, Zuma would not in any case be capable of this). Nonetheless, couched in much more down-to-earth terms, the same classic Mbeki-era motifs were there, for instance in Zuma's speech to the SACP's congress in December 2009: the ANC is at the centre of the Alliance and gives it unity and focus; each component of the Alliance guards its autonomy and that goes especially for the ANC; the Alliance thrives on robust debate but there should be a clear line between constructive criticism and opposition that gives comfort to the Alliance's enemies; even constructive criticism must be kept inside Alliance structures and not be part of wider debate.[24] This was not the new wave that the Left hoped for but an Mbeki tribute act.

On other occasions, Zuma like Mbeki would underline such friendly warnings with reminders to the Left that it is cold outside the ANC. His tactics as well as his rhetoric were similar. Zuma used co-option even more extensively than Mbeki by appointing large numbers of communists and trade unionists to the government, multiplying posts and even ministries with an abandon that would have shocked his more frugal predecessor. This was not only straightforward patronage but also created an illusion of policy influence that was greater than the actuality and helped divide the SACP and to a greater extent Cosatu into pro- and anti-Zuma factions. These management ploys came against a policy background that angered the Left: the Left's bogey man Trevor Manuel may have been moved from the Treasury, but he was given the task of working on the country's long-term development plan, the National Development Plan (NDP, 2011) and he was in any case replaced at the Treasury by Pravin Gordhan, the former head of the South African Revenue Service (SARS) another exponent of fiscal rectitude (without, however, being as zealous as Manuel himself). To make matters worse, Zuma regularly uttered platitudes designed to placate investors and held out the occasional policy sweetener to them, such as tentative proposals for a more flexible labour market. The Left was forced into defensive and firefighting postures on such issues, just as it had been in the Mbeki years.

All of this came as a rude shock to the Left, although it should not have. The history of the ANC's relations with its left allies has been played out around two crude polarities: whether the ANC is there to provide a nationalist veneer for an essentially socialist project or the Left's role is to organize workers on behalf of the ANC for a project of racial nationalism. Neither side has been able to impose an extreme version of these possibilities nor would probably want to; both would prefer polite platitudes about unity of purpose. However, each side suspects and fears the other's motives. In the event, the balance of real power in the disputed territory between the extremes has always been heavily in favour of nationalists, even at the moment of the Left's triumph in discarding Mbeki.

Zuma's task of management was probably made easier by poor leadership on the left. This was exemplified in the arrogant approach taken by Zwelinzima Vavi at the beginning of Zuma's first term. Immediately after being elected ANC president at Polokwane in 2007, Zuma was quoted as saying that he would only serve one term.[25] A month after he was inaugurated as state president in May 2009, Vavi – not Zuma – announced to the media that the new president would now serve two terms, having been 'persuaded' by Cosatu. For good measure, he added that while some people were complaining that Zuma would be the 'stooge of Luthuli House' (ANC headquarters), that is what Cosatu wanted:

> We are the policy makers: the government must implement. No minister must be allowed to develop policy. The policy is developed by the Alliance and the ANC and the appropriate minister must implement it.[26]

Conflating the Alliance and the ANC in this way was a serious error of interpretation and an indication of extreme political naivety. It totally missed the possibility that Zuma would be comfortable with the ANC determining policy, provided that he (and not the Alliance Left) dominated the ANC, which was always the more likely outcome. What is more, such examples of gratuitously provocative public overreach as Vavi's press conference were likely to have strengthened Zuma's resolve to be his own man and to construct an alternative support base to the one that had contributed so much to putting him in power.

Malema and the ANC Youth League: Expelling unruly pupils

Zuma was also assisted in asserting his control over the ANC and Alliance by similar displays of overreach on the part of the other main component of his support coalition, the ANCYL led by Julius Malema. Having successfully thrown his own and the ANCYL's energies into Zuma's campaign to oust Mbeki, Malema might have been expected to enjoy the status and influence that came with leading a key constituency in the ANC and to take the predictable route up the movement's hierarchy to the NEC and government jobs. There were precedents for this in the career profiles of two contrasting, but essentially similar, former ANCYL leaders, Fikile Mbalula and Malusi Gigaba. Mbalula was the more aggressive and less polished of the two, lacking Gigaba's higher education and his (arguably spurious) air of technocratic capability. However, both projected organizational loyalty as well as willing familiarity with the rules of the ANC generation game and were rewarded early with places on the NEC and ministerial posts. When Zuma anointed Malema as a future leader, he presumably counted on Malema following this conventional pattern by trading loyalty to Zuma himself and to the ANC for advancement.

However, Malema was nobody's protégé. Instead of understanding how succession was supposed to work in the ANC, he embarked on a path of apparently random destabilization that seemed perversely self-destructive. Not content with causing policy and ideological mayhem by aggressively espousing nationalization and land expropriation, both to be without compensation, he threatened to destabilize South Africa's foreign relations by ardently supporting Mugabe at a time when Zuma was trying to salvage something from the wreckage of Mbeki's quiet diplomacy towards Zimbabwe, also by labelling Botswana a 'puppet state' and calling for regime change there. In short order, between early 2010 and late 2012, he acquired court rulings against him for 'hate speech' (for singing the struggle song 'Shoot the Boer'), warnings and suspensions from the ANC for bringing the organization into disrepute and causing disunity. These were followed by final expulsion and, for good measure, charges in his personal capacity (later dropped) for fraud and money laundering related to tender corruption in his home province of Limpopo.

It is difficult to place Malema's erratic conduct during this period within any conventional framework for understanding political motivation and ambition and this added to Zuma's and the ANC's difficulties in dealing with him. Perhaps he was simply unsuited by temperament and profile to taking the conventional path to political leadership and he sought shortcuts through shock tactics. Perhaps he drew inspiration from the ANC's history, in which the youth league has a much-mythologized role as a ginger group, at intervals jolting a sluggish older generation into life; this was after all a key element in the Mandela myth and legacy and in the broader history of the liberation struggle. It was the youth of Soweto who in 1976 put their elders to shame by their resistance and sacrifice and breathed new life into the struggle. If so, he misapplied history to a very different set of circumstances, although he was far from alone in trying to force politics in democratic South Africa into the templates of the anti-apartheid struggle. Indeed, he might reasonably point out that the ANC's official documents, by insisting on the seamless continuity of anti-apartheid and post-apartheid struggles, invite just such an injection of pace and intensity as he claimed (and continues to claim) that he and the younger generation represent.

Malema himself offers few clues as to his motivations in this period and where he does he is notably agile and creative with them. His most recent comment on the fall out with Zuma maintains that the cause was Zuma reneging on the alleged promise to seek only one term.[27] This allegation, viewed along with Vavi's claim (quoted above) that it was Cosatu who talked Zuma into a second term, and Zuma's own assertion that he never made a formal 'one-term' pledge in the first place, helps create a picture of the contradictions and chaos surrounding Zuma's leadership.

Perhaps the most economical explanation of the chaotic disintegration of the 'coalition of the disenchanted' was that Vavi and Malema were simply out of their depth in believing that, on Vavi's part, the mass mobilization that eroded Mbeki's position could be sustained and transferred to pressurize his successor as a permanent feature of politics, and on Malema's part, that a form of youth punk politics could ride on the mythology of past icons such as the youth league of Mandela's day to propel him upwards in today's ANC. What these jejune failures of leadership did was to give Zuma political time, space and capital to remake the ANC to his purposes, completing as he did so the erasure of Mbeki's and Mandela's legacies. Zuma's latitude was increased by the SACP's post-Polokwane choice of embedding itself snugly but ineffectively, silent and neutered, within the Zuma ANC.

Patronage and identity: A juggler not an architect

There is no doubt that Zuma has left his mark on the ANC, but 'remake' may be the wrong word since it implies a degree of purposive planning that is absent. Mbeki aspired to be an architect, but Zuma is more like a juggler and, thanks in part to the charges he has been fending off since 2005–6 but which have never gone away, his career has been a long-term exercise in crisis management. The crisis deepened after 2016 and went from nagging at his heels to throttling him. As a result, there has been an element of opportunism and improvisation in his repertoire of management and control. This does not mean that his leadership was haphazard. He may not have had grand visions on the scale of his predecessor, but he has had a strong grip on some basic principles that Mbeki seemed incapable of grasping. These were not abstractions but working rules firmly located in current South African realities and, in the nature of what the ANC was becoming at the time Zuma took it over, not what it had been in history or mythology. The most significant of them are the importance of local centres of power, the advantage to a leader of having a strong geopolitical base and the relative value of networks over hierarchies. These are contextual and not universal principles (although they may fit many contexts) and they will not necessarily apply to South Africa in the long run; however, they have fitted Zuma's time and situation and the use he has made of them will make it difficult for those who follow to dispense with or even downplay them.

It is Zuma's grasp and application of these principles that help explain an apparent puzzle; why, when the coalition that brought him to power so

swiftly dissolved, was he able to win a sweeping victory at the Mangaung
conference of the ANC in 2012? It is true that there were no serious rivals.
Mbeki had conveniently knocked out all other plausible possibilities from
his own era or, in the case of Ramaphosa, at least knocked him back and
apparently shrunk his appetite for competing for power, which seemed in
any case far from ravenous. This was one of several ways in which Mbeki
was an obliging, if unwitting, facilitator for Zuma. It was too early for a
generational change; although the ranks of struggle veterans were thinning,
to be one was still a non-negotiable qualification. The exile grandees were
no longer the decisive force they had been when they anointed Mbeki, and
Zuma had broken the power of the ANCYL, which had been pretender to the
role of kingmaker. The Left's leaders were individuals who were lightweights
in ANC terms (perhaps in anyone's terms); Vavi's spectacular U-turn from
being willing to 'die for Zuma' to denouncing the 'hyena predators' of his
regime was suicidal in terms of his own credibility as a kingmaker; in any
case, perhaps to his credit, he had never really looked as if he belonged in
the ANC.

Provinces redux

However, this vacuum of leadership contenders alone is not enough to explain
Zuma's successful achievement of a second term. His recipe for success
was to turn the ANC around from being, at least in Mbeki's aspirations, a
metropolitan-dominated and hierarchical organization to an association
of provincially based networks, reflecting its strength in rural numbers
and simultaneously condoning and exploiting its organizational weakness
there. South Africa's quasi-federal system and uneven socio-economic
development, especially between the metropolitan centres of previously white
South Africa and the former Bantustans, have between them posed difficult
problems for the ANC. The ANC's history was one of predominantly urban
and exile development (the two sometimes at loggerheads after 1990) and the
far provincial and rural areas were hard to integrate.

To make matters worse, South Africa's severest poverty and most
intractable development policy challenges are sited there; grandiose plans for
rural development have come to nothing under both Mbeki and Zuma and
land reform has been stymied by confusions of purpose, changing directions
and sheer bureaucratic incapacity. Under such circumstances, the stakes of
rent-seeking opportunities are relatively much higher away from the centre;
legitimate opportunities for occupational advancement or accumulation are
virtually non-existent there and fantasies of a land reform revolution that

will give birth to a self-sufficient peasantry collide with all manner of brute realities in South Africa's climatic, physical, political and economic landscape.

In this simultaneously unpromising and inviting context, Zuma, rather than following Mbeki in attempting to control provincial barons in an organizational hierarchy of order givers and order takers, capitalized on their ability to organize branches through patronage (or fraud) and allowed them wide autonomy, as long as their delegates supported him at national conferences. This required little in the way of organizational penetration or even shared vision and purpose, never mind ideological uniformity and sophistication. These are the goals Mbeki and his close circle of ideologues and bureaucrats sought, to create a highly ordered, interlocking model of state, government and party that would reach to every corner of the land and be run by revolutionary 'new cadres'. Zuma was content with a network of networks.[28] These relationships are routinely characterized by commentators and critics as 'feudal', trading local autonomy for support, while some have detected an echo of the colonial practice of indirect rule through chiefs:

> In the post-apartheid period nobody has done more than President Zuma to re-establish the hated system of 'indirect rule', a centrepiece of British colonialism, whereby people were ruled through conquered or compliant chiefs on government payroll. And he has resurrected apartheid's Bantustan borders to strip rights and turn citizens into subjects.[29]

It is hard to draw clear-cut cause-and-effect conclusions on the relationship between Zuma's ascendancy and the changing balance between rural and urban interests, influence and orientations in the ANC. Did he consciously mould the party to reflect a greater weight for the rural areas in order to develop a new support base, as the incompatibility between him and the one that had brought him to power became apparent? Or did he astutely take advantage of a tide of influence and events that was running strongly anyway? The answer, prosaically enough, is that there was probably a synergy between his interests and some currents that had their own momentum and impact on the organization he led.

The growing African middle class is a largely urban phenomenon. Far from homogeneous and subject to elastic and clashing definitions on the part of marketers and sociologists, it ranges from people precariously escaped from poverty to well-established professional and managerial classes. However, among this diverse constituency there are many that were sceptical of Zuma's demotic profile: his lack of education; the warrior symbolism; the polygamy and the erratic cultural pronouncements that contradict the values of the Constitution. The coarseness of his followers' behaviour during the struggle with Mbeki (notably the violent misogyny displayed by some of them during the rape trial) offended and frightened the respectable. Not all Mbeki sympathizers defected to COPE and those that remained were angered by his recall. This did not mean that the middle classes deserted the ANC; the ANC vote held up well in Gauteng, the most urbanized province with the largest concentrations of African working-class people, at least until the municipal elections in 2016. However, Gauteng was the earliest and strongest centre of opposition to Zuma within the party. The implosion of organized labour as a political force as it grappled with its own contradictions brought on by the growing distance between the middle-class lifestyles of officials and those of the worker members, breakaway unions and involvement in ANC factionalism, combined with middle-class scepticism and outright hostility to Zuma, also helped to make the major urban areas an unpromising support base.

By contrast, Zuma's grass-roots appeal and his loose understanding with provincial power brokers, be they traditional leaders, provincial politicians, tenderpreneurs or individuals who combined some or all of these localist features, were enough to sustain him in power. This alliance was greatly facilitated by the collapse of Mbeki's centralizing and modernizing project and failure to understand the local roots of political power in a country as dispersed and unevenly developed as South Africa. This left a vacuum that Zuma did not have to work too hard to fill. The new coincidence of interests between centre and periphery served Zuma well across the provinces where African demographic majorities are greatest, ANC percentages of the vote the highest, poverty and unemployment the greatest and where there are long histories of unscrupulous dealings stretching back to Bantustans and involving corrupt white officials in the late apartheid years. These include Free State, Mpumalanga, North West and Limpopo. The strongmen who dominate ANC politics in the first three constituted an informal lobby grouping during peak and late Zuma years, which acquired the sobriquet 'the Premier League' and which is widely believed to have had the influence to determine ANC elections.[30]

The KwaZulu-Natal cockpit

Although these patterns and dynamics are important, their full effects on organizational politics depended on Zuma's ability to have a more specific personal base. Zuma's home province of KwaZulu-Natal (KZN) showed how important it was for him to be geographically and culturally grounded and demonstrated that the sources of provincial political leverage were not reducible to material factors.

From having had the largest share of South Africa's population in the 1996 and 2001 censuses (21 per cent), KZN has been overtaken by Gauteng (19.85 to Gauteng's 23.7 per cent in 2011).[31] KZN is also second in contribution to national GDP, but its share (16 per cent) is less than half of Gauteng's 33.8 per cent. Despite its second place, its large population means that it is ranked only seventh in GDP per capita.[32] KZN's population was 86.8 per cent black African in 2011 against 79.2 per cent for the whole country, giving it the fourth highest concentration of black Africans among the nine provinces.[33] It also has a low urbanization rate: in the 2001 census, this was measured at 45 per cent as against a national average of 56 per cent and 96 per cent for Gauteng.[34] In 2016, an economic review of the provinces noted that this had not changed: 'Half the population lives in impoverished former homeland regions compared to the national average of 30 per cent.'[35] However it would be wrong to interpret KZN's importance to the ANC and in particular to Zuma purely in terms of rural impoverishment. Unlike the other centres of support for Zuma that are cited above, and despite its low urbanization rate, KZN has a major urban centre of national economic importance. eThekwini (Durban) metropolitan municipality is the third largest economic centre in the country and contributes 10 per cent to national GDP. What is more, Zuma's ANC defended its share of the vote in eThekwini much better in the municipal elections of 2016 than it did in other urban centres, where the party lost control of three of the biggest metropolitan areas. For instance, in the City of Johannesburg, the ANC's share of the vote declined by 13.64 per cent from the 2011 municipal election to the 2016 poll (from 58.6 per cent to 44.92 per cent). In eThekwini, the corresponding loss was only 5.06 per cent (from 61.07 per cent to 56.01 per cent).

Arguably, in its contrasting mixtures of urban and rural populations, relative economic dynamism and underdevelopment, as well as the relatively low proportion of minorities in its population, KZN is the province that is most representative of South Africa's overall profile, something that tends to be overlooked by commentators based in Johannesburg, Cape Town and overseas. This leaves open the possibility that the high level of support for Zuma there places him in the mainstream and marks those provinces where opposition to him is concentrated as outliers. Certainly, KZN has been very important to the reproduction of his support. The province sent 393 delegates to the ANC national conference in 2002, 608 in 2007, 974 in 2012 and 870 in 2017. By contrast, although Gauteng – the centre of opposition to Zuma – is the most populous and economically important province, it sent 280 to the 2007 conference, 500 in 2012 and 508 in 2017.[36]

However, while there is a case for KZN's typicality, there is also one for attributing the province's importance to the ANC in general and Zuma's leadership in particular to its distinctive character. The roots of this distinctiveness lie in the domination of African popular politics there in the late apartheid, transition and early democratic years, by Mangosuthu Buthelezi and the Inkatha Freedom Party. Buthelezi and the IFP relied heavily on the cultivation of Zulu ethnic identity, expressed through cultural and linguistic tradition, the monarchy and the associated phenomenon of traditional leadership based on chiefs and headmen. In the first democratic years, KZN was the only province in which the ANC faced significant competition for African votes; the IFP took 48.59 per cent of the vote there in 1994 to the ANC's 31.61 per cent. If the ANC was to compete effectively with the IFP, then it faced choices concerning how to view the various cultural and political manifestations of 'tradition'.

Traditional leadership and the culture associated with it could be viewed as a challenge to the values and practices of the ANC, with its recently formulated, globalized agenda of citizen rights and social democracy, and in any case, this leadership was an institution that had been corrupted by colonial and white minority rule and politicized by the IFP's partisan self-identification with it. Alternatively, it could be viewed as a distinctly African phenomenon that has a genuine place in the loyalties of many (mainly) rural African people and a genuine claim to a continued place in the social and political life of the country. No party with the word 'African' in its name (and one short of distinctively African markers) could afford to ignore its importance.

These alternative ways of looking at tradition shaped the strategic options facing the ANC: dismiss and sweep aside traditional leadership and ethnic identity in a wholesale process of modernization and democratization; sensitively but firmly reform the institutions of traditional leadership so that they would find a legitimate place in the new order that would respect both their historic provenance and the values of the Constitution; cynically use the institutions of traditional leadership to outflank the IFP by becoming *plus royaliste que le roi* while bribing and flattering the Zulu king and tribal chiefs to detach themselves from the IFP. In practice, the ANC pursued a combination of the second and third of these options.

The politico-diplomatic offensive began even before the 1994 elections. In October 1993, the Natal regions of the ANC held a huge rally in Durban to celebrate African traditional culture. Its theme was inclusiveness, its name was 'Sonke' (isiZulu for 'all of us') and its slogan was 'many cultures, one people'.[37] However, the choice to hold the event in KZN and the crisis in ANC/IFP relations together amounted to a clear signal that the ANC was comfortable with 'Zuluness'. Many monarchs and traditional leaders from around Southern Africa were invited, but none of the other invitations had the political resonance of the one extended to Zulu King Goodwill Zwelithini. It hardly mattered though, since King Goodwill did not accept. From this point on, KZN became the only part of South Africa in which the ANC consciously and explicitly cultivated and exploited ethnic culture and identity for political purposes. It was the only place where such things really mattered and they could, the ANC calculated, be invoked in a quarantined way for a limited purpose – to overtake and defeat the IFP – and for a limited time.

Election results from 1999 to 2014 (see Table 1) point to the rapid decline of the IFP and the equally swift advance of the ANC.

Within five years of the IFP's comfortable victory in 1994, the two rivals were neck and neck and had formed a provincial coalition government after the 1999 election. At the next election in 2004, the ANC could form a government on its own and in 2009, with Zuma at the helm and KZN showing the largest ANC membership, the ANC's share had almost doubled from the 1994 result and was only a little less than the party's national share of the vote (65.9 per cent). By 2014, the IFP had split and was a negligible electoral force, even in what used to be its heartland.

The virtual destruction of the ANC's only serious rival for the African popular vote was a very important, symbolic achievement. It gave some substance (for true believers at least) to the ANC's claim to be the embodiment of an undivided, African nation, which, from an Africanist perspective, stands behind the minimum and somewhat bloodless citizen nation, giving it meaning and substance. More prosaically, the spectacular increase of nearly 16 per cent of the ANC's share of the vote in populous KZN in 2009 over 2004 masked stagnant or even falling shares elsewhere and kept the ruling party within hailing distance of a two-thirds majority.

Table 1 Election results (provincial ballot[a]) in KwaZulu-Natal 1999–2014

	1999 (%)	2004 (%)	2009 (%)	2014 (%)
ANC	39.38	46.98	62.95	64.52
IFP	41.9	36.82	22.40	10.86

Source: Independent Electoral Commission results page: http://www.elections.org.za/content/Elections/Election-results/.
[a]The results differ slightly between the provincial ballot and the national ballot in any given province. It is the provincial ballot that decides the composition of the provincial parliament.

How much of this was due to Zuma's leadership and, more particularly, to the politics of ethno-tribal identification that some believe he represents? Inevitably, it is difficult to assign weight to what, equally inevitably, are multiple causes. The IFP was never more than a regional party and it was so beset with its own contradictions (between ethno-nationalism and neo-liberal economics for instance) that it contributed much to its own demise. The ANC government's national policies of infrastructural development, expansion of social grants and service delivery to grossly underdeveloped, rural areas outshone the IFP's provincial government and were, unsurprisingly, popular with voters. Having said that, Zuma's largesse with appointments for people from KZN (or as those who are wedded to ethnic explanations would have it, 'Zulus') in national government and quasi-government bodies may have had a stiffening effect on his support there.

On the other hand, the latitude extended to local elites to enjoy patronage networks through tenders and other provincial rent-seeking opportunities seems no different from similar situations in provinces such as Mpumalanga, Limpopo, Free State and North West. Far from reserving such things for his own people, or even insisting in classic, pork barrel politics fashion that disproportionate resources be diverted to them, every province had its place at the trough. Perhaps this is the material reality that underlay Zuma's gift of exuding a kind of pan-tribal Africanism, that may have been based in the language and rural roots of his background in Zululand, but did not exclude other Africans or provoke a resentful backlash. In the end, perhaps ethnic identity is only one of the many ingredients he managed to keep in his improvised leadership recipe.

Zuma as government head

Considering the prevalence of 'betrayal' as a recurring idea in post-apartheid politics, it comes as no surprise that this motif is prominent in both commentary on and systematic analysis of Zuma's presidency. The most comprehensive anatomy of state capture to be produced so far invokes betrayal of the promise of Nelson Mandela's inaugural speech in its title and reminds readers of Mandela's promissory words:

> To liberate all our people from the continuing bondage of poverty, deprivation, suffering, gender and other discrimination ... [to] build [a] society in which all South Africans, both black and white, will be able to walk tall, without any fear in their hearts, assured of their inalienable

right to human dignity – a rainbow nation at peace with itself and the world.[38]

This 'founding promise' of the new South Africa serves as a statement of what has been stolen in addition to the sum of state resources diverted to private use. Concerns about corruption have been endemic in South Africa at least since the Arms Deal and it is common for treatments of the subject to trace the origins of the problem back to the late apartheid years, to sanctions busting and endgame looting, much of it centred on the Bantustans, on the part of apartheid regime functionaries (including their black Bantustan acolytes) and to unorthodox fund raising (drug smuggling, stolen cars and bank robberies) as well as 'struggle accounting' on the part of the ANC in exile and at home.[39] However, from approximately the beginning of Zuma's second term these concerns crystallized into a perception that something much more systematic than uncoordinated personal enrichment through abuse of state power was going on. This perception solidified in the term 'state capture', a landmark in the phrase's widening currency being the publication of the then Public Protector's report, 'State of Capture' in November 2016. This was followed by copious, ongoing coverage by investigative journalists and anti-corruption NGOs. In *Betrayal of the Promise*, a much fuller single account draws together much of the investigative work, especially the detective skills of the AmaBhungane Centre for Investigative Journalism.[40] Each of these sources brings something to the accumulating body of evidence about state capture – and the flow of information into the public domain shows no sign of diminishing – but *Betrayal of the Promise* is the most systematic and analytically ambitious of them.[41]

The essential elements of *Betrayal of the Promise*'s conceptual framework are a 'constitutional state' and a 'shadow state' as well as a 'silent coup' aimed at shrinking the constitutional state and subordinating it to the expanding shadow state. The motivation was a political project to 'repurpose state institutions to suit a constellation of rent-seeking networks that have been constructed and now span the symbiotic relationship between the constitutional and shadow state'.[42] As well as being silent, this was a creeping coup, beginning with strategic infiltration of the boards of SOEs and the capture of most elements of the criminal justice system, especially the NPA and its head the NDPP, the Directorate for Priority Crime Investigation (DPCI: 'The Hawks'), which replaced the Scorpions, the Crime Intelligence Division of the police and the National Intelligence Agency (NIA). Central to the whole process and taking much longer to achieve was the only partly successful project of obtaining control of the Treasury and with it, of the following state bodies that report to the Ministry of Finance: the Financial

Intelligence Centre, which detects unlawful transactions and the flow of illicit funds; the Office of the Chief Procurement Officer, which combats corruption in government tenders and the Public Investment Corporation, which makes investments on behalf of public-sector pension funds. Zuma worked for years to destabilize the Treasury, suffering a reverse in December 2015 when, having fired Nhlanhla Nene and replaced him with a pliable substitute, he was forced to retract and reappoint Pravin Gordhan. Zuma in turn fired Gordhan in March 2017, replacing him with Malusi Gigaba, who had been minister of public enterprises during Zuma's first government (2010–14), the period when the first crony appointments to SOE boards were made. The purpose of capturing the Treasury was to centralize the management and concentrate the direction of rents to a few, favoured individuals and companies connected to the Gupta and Zuma family networks, and to remove financial controls that take the public interest and fiscal sustainability as their criteria. The Treasury was never captured to the extent that Zuma wanted and the most important coup for the shadow state in the field of economic management was the appointment of Tom Moyane to be head of the South African Revenue Service (SARS) in September 2014.[43]

Betrayal of the Promise summarizes the strategic coordination of the shadow state in the following way:

> Well-placed individuals located in the most significant centres of state power (in government, SOEs and the bureaucracy) make decisions about what happens within the constitutional state. Those, like [Mcebisi] Jonas, Vytjie Mentor, Pravin Gordhan and Themba Maseko who resist this agenda in one way or another are systematically removed, redeployed to other lucrative positions to silence them, placed under tremendous pressure, or hounded out by trumped up internal and/or external charges and dubious intelligence reports. This is a world where deniability is valued, culpability is distributed (though indispensability is not taken for granted) and where trust is maintained through mutually binding fear. Unsurprisingly, therefore, the shadow state is not only the space for extra-legal action facilitated by criminal networks, but also where key security and intelligence actions are coordinated.[44]

Cover for this nefarious system was provided in three ways. First, democratic cover was available, if precariously. The constitutional state was undermined, circumvented and rerouted rather than overthrown or even legally suspended or curtailed. Journalists were not imprisoned, freedom of expression were not formally curbed, states of emergency were not declared and there were not arrests on blatantly political grounds. This does not mean that there was no atmosphere of menace and intimidation: surveillance by the many intelligence agencies was taken for granted by anyone who might be a danger or even an irritant to the shadow state (whistle-blowers, opposition leaders, editors, investigative journalists, civil society oppositionists, public servants who take public service seriously and such cautiously dissident voices as there have been in the ANC); there were unexplained burglaries of judges' rooms and the homes and offices of those senior civil servants viewed as obstructive; assassinations of ANC contenders for minor office (especially in KZN municipalities) have became common; but in a high-crime society such as South Africa it is very difficult to conclusively label any given criminal act as politically motivated on purely circumstantial grounds and the assassinations are probably the result of parochial fights over patronage scraps rather than part of anything like shadow state subversion. However, despite these things and the rising anger at mounting revelations of blatant misconduct, enough remained of the constitutional state to provide cover for Zuma, especially to constituencies of true believers in the ANC. Ironically enough the constitutional state has had its uses even to those that wish to undermine it: Zuma himself enjoyed extensive legal rights (including taxpayer-funded defence) to delay the progress of charges against him.

Second, Zuma had political cover provided by the networks of provincial political bosses that he cultivated and which gave him a strong enough position in his own party to dominate the NEC and the parliamentary party.

The third source of cover was ideological: 'At the epicentre of the political project mounted by the Zuma-centred power elite is a rhetorical commitment to radical economic transformation.'[45] At this point the political dynamics of the Zuma years (and indeed of the post-Zuma years too) become increasingly difficult to follow because, with the possible exception of the opposition DA, everybody (including, it should be noted, the authors of *Betrayal of the Promise*) is in favour of 'radical economic transformation' in one form or another and it has become an all-purpose, all-occasions phrase of impressive flexibility.[46] Zuma's version, which was and still is shared for various motives and to various degrees by interest and ideological groupings across the ANC ecosystem, proposed to use the procurement spending of the SOEs to promote a class of black industrialists, sponsoring them to scale the commanding heights of the economy, wrest its control from 'white monopoly capitalism' and hugely tilt the balance of 'ownership' in the economy away from whites and towards black people. However, the problem is that radical economic transformation has been turned into an 'ideological football, kicked around by factional political players within the ANC and the Alliance in general who use the term to mean very different things'.[47]

To make matters worse there is a deep underlying division between those elements in the ANC who believe that radical economic transformation can be achieved within constitutional guidelines and (in the interests of sustainability) within the bounds of fiscal orthodoxy and those who are prepared to take the political risks of jettisoning the constitutional settlement as well as the economic risks of loosening restraints on public expenditure in what is already a situation of dangerously stagnant growth. To make matters even worse, fearing open disunity and a possible split in the ANC, neither side has had the political courage to organize openly and canvass support on either side of this divide. This kind of short-term denialism may well have the effect of strengthening the possibility of terminal fragmentation of the Alliance and the ANC in the medium or long term.

Under these confused circumstances, to carry on the *Betrayal of Promise*'s soccer metaphor, Zuma and the Guptas picked up the political football and ran off with it to play on their own pitch and to their own rules, using the cover of radical economic transformation to camouflage wholesale looting.[48]

Appointment chaos

An instrument of Zuma's leadership that is frequently cited by commentators and academics to explain this state of affairs is his use of appointments, exploiting the wide latitude granted to the president by the Constitution. There are four aspects to this: the 'ballooning' of high-level appointments in government and the public service; the strategic placement of trusted allies (or incompetent pawns) at key points in the security apparatus; high turnover or 'churn' in cabinet ministers and directors general (DGs: the civil service heads of government departments); and the assignment of ministers and top-level officials and board members in SOEs from obscure backgrounds, who had no experience or aptitude for the job and often were downright incompetent.

On taking office in 2009, Zuma appointed thirty-four cabinet ministers, an increase of six over Mbeki's last cabinet. With the addition of twenty-eight junior ministers as well as himself as president and Kgalema Motlanthe as deputy president, that made a national executive of sixty-four (thanks to further junior appointments during the course of his first administration, it peaked at sixty-eight). Although Zuma was criticized for increasing the size of the executive, it is striking what little portent there was at the time of how his government would develop. He was reported to have consulted widely (unlike Mbeki) on the executive's composition, which was quite well received; it was said to be balanced, broader-based than Mbeki's and what was initially and naively seen to be the introduction of much-needed new blood; Mbeki rarely shuffled his cabinet, did not fire non-performing ministers and his government was regarded as thoroughly stale by the end of his tenure.

'Balance' was unavoidable given Zuma's debts to his (then) core constituencies of the SACP and Cosatu, along with his repeated public assurances of continuity of responsible macroeconomic policies and the need to accommodate Mbeki supporters. Four members of the SACP's central committee, including two senior office bearers, were given government posts, though without any heavyweight ministries. The main dividend for Cosatu was the appointment of Ebrahim Patel, the general secretary of the South African Clothing and Textile Workers' Union (SACTU), as minister in a new department, the Department of Economic Growth, which the Left erroneously believed would be the focal point of a new departure in economic policy.

Superficially there was a substantial degree of continuity with Mbeki's last cabinet, although the status of some of its members was clearly diminished: eleven of Mbeki's full ministers survived into Zuma's cabinet, but only two kept their previous portfolios; four were moved to equally or more important posts and the others were demoted. On the other hand, two Mbeki-era deputy ministers were elevated to cabinet rank; of them, Rob Davies (a senior SACP cadre), at the Department of Trade and Industry, was one of the very few who served throughout Zuma's two terms.

The main sources of recruitment for ministerial appointments were provincial government and the national parliament. Four former provincial premiers became cabinet ministers and one was appointed as a deputy minister. Six full ministers and several deputy ministers had been provincial ministers (members of the executive councils (MECs)). The ten cabinet ministers who were promoted from the provinces came from six provinces: only Limpopo, the home province of three of them, had more than two representatives in this new crop of ministers, giving rise to approving comments about how broad-based the new government appeared to be and how astutely Zuma had appeared to redress Mbeki's neglect of the provinces. However, two crucial posts went to ministers from Zuma's home province of KZN: Siyabonga Cwele, minister of state security (renamed from the Ministry of Intelligence), and minister of police, Nathi Mthethwa. Although both were first appointed by Kgalema Motlanthe to replace two Mbeki loyalists when the latter was 'recalled' in September 2008, doubtless Zuma had a deciding hand in choosing them and he reappointed them when he became president in 2009. This was beginning of the popular perception of a 'praetorian guard' of loyalists from KZN in key security-sector appointments.

Overall, however, apart from questions of political balance, which all democratic political leaders have to deal with, Zuma's first administration could be viewed, whether critically or sympathetically, as being well within a rational political/bureaucratic framework for restructuring government. If he had increased the size of the government, then that is what the logic of his party, to which he had promised to restore the policymaking initiative, had demanded of the leadership in its resolutions at Polokwane and the policy direction of Mbeki's last few years in government had in any case been towards a more interventionist state (the 'developmental state'): departmental remits had been changed and reassigned; new departments had been created and major new planning, coordination, oversight and monitoring arrangements were introduced via two distinct ministries located within the presidency, again something that had been on Mbeki's agenda. What is more, the lead role in the planning initiative was given to Trevor Manuel, the executor of GEAR, whose long tenure as minister of finance was the bedrock of Mbeki's government and his successor there was Pravin Gordhan, who, as its head (commissioner) under Manuel and Mbeki, had turned the SARS into a highly effective tax-collection agency and a reliable source of increased government revenue. By such signs and signals orthodoxy seemed to be confirmed. Order seemed to have been restored after the populist spasm that brought Zuma to power, offending and frightening the respectable. The resources of continuity and accepted wisdom, if not exactly of 'deep state' magnitude, seemed to have wielded substantial influence on the new leader.

In appointing his second cabinet, five years later after the 2014 election, far from rationalizing and cutting the size of government, Zuma increased the size by one minister to thirty-five and created a fourth economic ministry, ignoring criticisms that in such a bloated (and expensive) administration, there were already signs of drift, gridlock and policy uncertainty. While these criticisms were perfectly valid, it later became apparent that critics were for the most part looking in the wrong place. It was only with escalating concern at the influence of the Guptas, beginning with the special diplomatic privileges granted to them for their family wedding in 2013 and continuing with Zuma's increasingly brazen (and ham-handed) efforts to capture the Treasury that the narrative of state capture in pursuit of rent-seeking on a massive scale began to take a hold.

With the benefit of hindsight *Betrayal of the Promise* marks the beginning in earnest of the project to suborn the boards of SOEs with the appointment of Malusi Gigaba, who later became Gordhan's replacement as minister of finance in 2017, as minister of public enterprises in November 2010.[49] Gigaba's predecessor, Barbara Hogan, had served only since the appointment of Zuma's first cabinet in May 2009 and it is widely believed that she was fired so soon into the life of the administration for being insufficiently flexible on matters of SOE governance. Unsurprisingly, she became one of Zuma's fiercest critics inside the ANC, using the ANC veterans grouping as a base.

Weakening the governance and operational structures of the SOEs by appointing morally compromised, incompetent or pliant individuals to their boards and top management constitutes one of the main axes of central control that define state capture. Others include capture of the Treasury ('control over the country's fiscal sovereignty'), 'weakening key technical institutions' in order to control strategic procurement, ensuring loyalist appointments to the security and intelligence services as well as the criminal justice system, and creating 'parallel government and decision-making structures that undermine the executive'. The last of these strategies hollows out the state by undermining statutory bodies – principally the cabinet – that are responsible (however imperfectly) to parliament, then replacing them with a variety of kitchen cabinets, camouflaged as 'inter-ministerial committees'. In all, *Betrayal of the Promise* lists seven broad areas over which Zuma's power elite centralized control, of which these are the most important.[50]

Perhaps the most striking feature of Zuma's appointments over the whole period of his presidency is how labile the executive was. This feature applied not only to ministers and deputy ministers but also to DGs. The instability of executive appointments has been charted in great detail, showing that during Zuma's two administrations: only seven ministers out of the 34 appointed in 2009 remained in post in 2017; the average relationship between a minister and a director general (crucial for policy and governance) lasted fourteen months; the average DG served twenty-two months before he/she was suspended, fired, redeployed or eased out with a severance payment; over the eight years covered by the study, the communications ministry had six ministers and ten DGs; while extreme, this example was not untypical.[51] The result has been summarized by the most comprehensive study of Zuma's appointments as, 'a perfect storm of organised chaos and a compromised administration on all fronts',[52] working to Zuma's advantage because:

> If no one is secure in their position, then not only are they likely to be deferential, but the broader pool – the ANC parliamentary caucus – will be all the more loyal in turn; for their potential turn at the top is always just one reshuffle away.[53]

This assessment may indeed be the case, but it should not create the impression that the way to a cabinet post was long and patient service as an ANC member of the National Assembly. The 'broader pool' was a lot broader than the National Assembly. The typical profile for a place in a Zuma reshuffle was undistinguished service in obscurity in the provinces and a relatively short period in the National Assembly before elevation. In some key instances, prior service in the National Assembly was not necessary at all. Mosebenzi Zwane, who became minister of mineral resources in September 2015, had previously been MEC for agriculture in the Free State government: his place at fifteenth in the ANC provincial election list for Free State in 2009 (there are thirty seats in the legislature of which the ANC won twenty-two, and ten government posts) does not suggest that he was regarded as an ANC heavyweight even in his home province. However, subsequent leaks of Gupta emails revealed close Gupta connections and involvement in dubious transactions favouring the family during his tenure as agriculture MEC. This pattern expanded and accelerated on his assumption of the mining portfolio in national government.

It was always very hard to see any rational organizational or political pattern in Zuma's appointments that conforms to classic concerns of political leadership: succession planning? Rewarding some asset other than ability to do the job, such as personal following or electoral appeal? The need to reward some faction or another in the ANC or Alliance? The observer looks in vain for evidence of these. Zuma himself was never willing to give a straightforward account of his reshuffles. His responses to questions about them varied from determined evasiveness to outrageous mendacity[54] and in the final phase the changes were accompanied by lofty silence. This refusal to be accountable compounded the suspicions and conspiratorial interpretations that inevitably accumulate when crucial appointments are made without apparent regard for qualifications, experience or seniority in the party. However, it was only when hard evidence of the existence of networks of relationships involved in dubious or outright illegal transactions was provided by the leaked Gupta emails and other sources, that the extent of state capture and the dynamics of its various processes were laid bare.

'Smoking gun' evidence of the sort provided by the Gupta emails is less readily available in the case of the NPA, but the accumulation of circumstantial evidence pointing to chaos and incompetence at best, and at worst institutional capture, is impressive enough. The NPA had five permanent heads between 1998 and the end of the Zuma era, but any impression of stable three-four-year terms and smooth institutional succession would be false. One national director (Ngcuka, 1998–2004), resigned under pressure from the ANC. His successor (Vusi Pikoli, 2005–7) was suspended by Mbeki and dismissed by Kgalema Motlanthe. Pikoli was followed by Menzi Simelane (2009–12) whose entire period in office was overshadowed by suspension and legal challenges to his fitness for office, which were upheld by a ruling of the constitutional court confirming the invalidity of his appointment. Zuma took two years from Simelane's suspension and one year from the annulment of his appointment to replace him with Mxolisi Nxasana in October 2013; nine months later, Zuma announced an enquiry into Nxasana's fitness to hold office, prompting suggestions, including from Nxasana himself, that the real reason for the investigation was that he had shown more independence of judgement than Zuma was comfortable with. Nearly a year, later the enquiry was terminated without finding against Nxasana, but he resigned his post and was paid out in full for his ten-year contract, of which he had served less than two years, most of it under suspension. The summary of this stormy history is that the NPA had acting heads for more than one quarter of its entire existence and every one of its 'permanent' heads left under a cloud. In 2015 Zuma appointed Shaun Abrahams, who was widely believed to be Zuma's pawn and whose appointment was found by the constitutional court to be invalid and unconstitutional on 13 August 2018. Abrahams retired shortly afterwards.

The state of the NPA was central to misgivings about the integrity of the criminal justice system and the rule of law in South Africa throughout the Zuma period, concerns that extend to the police, notably the special units, the Hawks and crime intelligence.[55] Against this background it is remarkable that the judiciary was able to play an independent role. This was supportive of the Constitution and a thorn in Zuma's side in his efforts to escape accountability, as well as a source of judgements that put pressure on some of his acolytes. In effect, executive misuse of power and dereliction of the legislature's responsibility for oversight, thanks to executive dominance and slavish party loyalty on the part of the ANC, amounted to political failure, which has led opposition parties and civil society groups to turn to the courts.[56]

There were numerous instances of this, perhaps the most important being the constitutional court's ruling on the responses of Zuma, the minister of police and parliament to the Public Protector's report on Nkandla.

Taking on the shadow state: The Public Protector and the judges

The Public Protector's report on Nkandla found that Zuma had unlawfully profited from the misuse of public funds in upgrading his residence at Nkandla and that he should pay back a reasonable proportion of the money thus expended. Zuma and the National Assembly mandated the minister of police to rule on whether or not the upgrades were justified on security grounds (they included a visitor centre, a swimming pool, a chicken run and a cattle kraal). The minister affirmed that they were justified, and the National Assembly, on this basis and on the deliberations of two ad hoc committees, both dominated by the ANC, passed a resolution absolving Zuma from the remedial action in the Public Protector's report. The ANC at the time held 249 seats in the 400-seat assembly. The EFF, supported by the DA, took the matter to the constitutional court. The court's ruling held that

> the National Assembly's resolution, based on the Minister's findings exonerating the President from liability, was inconsistent with the Constitution and unlawful. The Court also held that, by failing to comply with the Public Protector's order, the President failed to 'uphold, defend and respect' the Constitution because a duty to repay the money was specifically imposed on him through the Public Protector's constitutional power.[57]

The ability of the courts to hold Zuma as head of government accountable under the Constitution on this and on numerous other occasions stands in sharp contrast to the apparent ease with which he dominated his own party in and out of parliament and manipulated state and quasi-state bodies by his powers of appointment to construct a shadow state. The president has considerable, though not unfettered, power to appoint judges.[58] He puts forward a nominee for the post of chief justice and makes the appointment 'after consultation' with the leaders of the parties represented in the National Assembly and the Judicial Services Commission (JSC), a body composed of representatives of political parties and the legal profession. Presidential powers are diminished in appointments below the highest level; the JSC puts forward nominees for positions on the constitutional court from which the president chooses, and for lower courts the president merely confirms the JSC's choices.

The fraught coexistence of one-party dominance with a justiciable constitution that is the supreme law inevitably leads to ongoing concern with the independence of the South African judiciary. Such concerns identify three sources of pressure on judges' independence. The first comes from 'official' ANC expressions of concern and displeasure at what is usually termed 'judicial overreach'. They are official in the sense that senior ANC leaders acting in their official capacities express them and they are couched in terms of simple, democratic majoritarianism. The second also comes from ANC leaders, this time in the form of accusations that judges are part of a 'counter-revolutionary conspiracy' to destroy the ANC. In 2008, the constitutional court lodged a complaint with the JSC alleging that the judge president of the Western Cape, John Hlope, had improperly tried to influence two of its judges to deal favourably with Zuma in cases involving him.[59] ANC secretary general, Gwede Mantashe, called this a counter-revolutionary conspiracy on the part of the court and 'psychological preparation of society for judges "pouncing on" Zuma', adding,

> You hit the head, you kill the snake. Where there is that attack on him it is a concerted attack on the head of the ANC.[60]

The third source of pressure is populist in origin, exemplified by the unofficial street theatre orchestrated by Zuma supporters in the ANC and Alliance during his court appearances between 2006 and 2009.

In the light of these pressures and as suspicions about Zuma's manipulation of other appointments began to mount, it is not surprising that he and the ANC have been suspected of wanting to appoint more pliant judges. The ANC 'more often than not' can command a majority on the JSC[61] and some appointments made during the Zuma years were controversial. In particular, the elevation of Mogoeng Mogoeng, first to the constitutional court in 2009 and then to the Office of Chief Justice in 2011, caused a storm of dissent from across the political and legal worlds on the various grounds of his lack of experience, intellectual depth and alleged failure to grasp properly the values of the Constitution, especially in matters of gender and sexual orientation.

Calland's (2013) verdict was particularly scathing first on the constitutional court appointment:

> But the president did appoint Mogoeng: the process of neutering the Constitutional Court was under way. Zuma's revenge, anti-intellectualism, dumbing down, call it what you like: the last frontier was being breached.[62]

And then on the promotion to chief justice:

> And so it came to pass: a president who doesn't read appoints a chief justice who doesn't write: it makes perfect sense.[63]

As it turned out, however, Mogoeng Mogoeng has emerged as a staunch bulwark of the Constitution – he wrote the Nkandla judgement and the judgement enabling a secret ballot for a parliamentary vote of no confidence in Zuma[64] – rather than a lap dog of the executive. There are several reasons why the courts, and in particular the constitutional court, were better able to resist the influence of the president and of the shadow state he has constructed through powers of appointment and dominance of the ruling party, than other, nominally independent, statutory institutions.

In the first place it is very difficult to remove a judge from office. This can only be done if the JSC finds that a judge suffers from an incapacity, is grossly incompetent or is guilty of gross misconduct; such a finding has to be confirmed by a resolution of the National Assembly, supported by two thirds of its members.[65] Only then can (indeed must) a president dismiss a judge. A spurious 'intelligence report', an allegation of misconduct concocted by captured bodies such as the NPA or the Hawks, or the president's whim, all of which sufficed in other appointments and dismissals, would not be enough in the case of judges. In addition, the courts, especially the constitutional court, are collegial in nature and judges can support each other (and keep an eye on each other), while their professional lives – unlike those for instance of the boards of SOEs – are insulated from the kind of contacts and transactions through which illicit influence peddling can thrive. Not only do these conditions support independence, but also perhaps allow the kind of personal and professional development that Mogoeng Mogoeng seems to have experienced, despite the initial misgivings of the legal establishment (on which Calland based his criticisms of Mogoeng's elevation), to the extent that he is now popularly lauded as an alternative leader figure.

The office of Public Protector also highlights the importance of appointments in the politics of the Zuma era, as well as their unpredictability. As with the appointment of judges, the Constitution gives significant power to parliament in appointing and removing holders of this office. The president appoints a Public Protector for a seven-year, non-renewable term after she or he is nominated by a committee of parliament composed in proportion to party strengths and the choice confirmed by a vote of at least 60 per cent of members of the house. It is possible for the president to reject the nomination but unlikely, given the weight of parliamentary approval. Removal is by the president but not at his/her initiative. The grounds are 'misbehaviour, incapacity or incompetence' as assessed by a committee of the house or a resolution of at least two-thirds of members.[66] Since 1995 four Public Protectors have been appointed and served under this system, leaving strikingly different public impressions.[67] The first two, Selby Baqwa (1995–2002) and Lawrence Mushwana (2002–9), were both former ANC MPs and were criticized for being too embedded in the movement and too lenient on ANC figures against whom complaints were made (Mushwana more than his predecessor).

Thuli Madonsela (2009–16) had been an ordinary member of the ANC but declined political office after 1994, preferring public service. Her reports on Nkandla and state capture (cited above) gave her the status of rallying point for anti-corruption activists and, in the eyes of constitution-supporting South Africans, whether in the opposition, civil society or the ANC itself, she became national heroine. The synergy between her influence and that of the Mogoeng-led constitutional court was clear: the court's Nkandla judgement called her, 'The embodiment of the biblical David' and 'One of the most invaluable gifts to our nation and one of the true crusaders and champions of anti-corruption and clean governance.'[68] The ANC was quick to sense the danger she posed to its leader and to the party's grip on power, so its full weight was deployed against her: cabinet ministers, MPs, associated organizations such as the youth and women's leagues, and in particular, the secretary general Gwede Mantashe, queued up to vilify her. The deputy minister of defence accused her of working for the Central Intelligence Agency (CIA). Legal battles continued after both the reports were published over the status of her recommendations, that is, in the case of Nkandla that Zuma should pay back some of the money spent on his residence and in the case of state capture that he should set up a commission of enquiry under a judge appointed by Chief Justice Mogoeng. Although the Constitution gave Zuma the right to carry on his war of attrition against accountability, Madonsela greatly invigorated and empowered opposition to him by the way she went about her duties.

The limits of accountability: A new Public Protector

It is highly unlikely that the same will be said about Madonsela's successor Busisiwe Mkhwebane and those who thought that Madonsela's appointment and tenure marked an enduring shift in the balance of power between the Constitution and the shadow state were swiftly disabused. The influence of some of Zuma-era appointments may be felt long after he is gone.

Only the DA opposed Mkhwebane during parliament's nomination process. It did so on the alleged grounds that she had been a state security operative for considerably longer than the brief period as an 'analyst' acknowledged on her curriculum vitae.[69]

However, the DA had only unattributable private information to back the allegation and Mkhwebane's appointment was generally welcomed. Nine months into her tenure, in June 2017, Mkhwebane issued a report that included, as a requirement for remedial action, an instruction to the chairman of the justice parliamentary portfolio committee (with responsibility for constitutional matters) to take certain steps to amend the constitutional mandate of the South African Reserve Bank (SARB) from 'the protection of the value of the currency in the interest of balanced and sustainable economic growth to the promotion of balanced and sustainable economic growth, "while ensuring that the socio-economic well-being of the citizens are protected [*sic*]." '[70]

The independence of the SARB is one of the primary concerns of investors and rating agencies and, after the Treasury, the SARB is a principal target of populist proponents of radical economic transformation and Zuma's state-capture networks, who have survived his fall from power. When the Protector's report was made public the Rand fell immediately by over 2 per cent and overseas investors sold South African bonds to the value of R1.3 billion. This was, in the words of the SARB governor, 'gross overreach' on the part of the Protector. In the most charitable interpretation possible (that of gross incompetence amounting to unfitness for office), she simply did not understand the Constitution with respect to her own role and powers, the status of the SARB and the role of parliament in amending the Constitution. The SARB challenged the 'remedial action' in the High Court and although the Protector, having been advised she had no legal grounds for defence, did not contest the SARB's application, the court nevertheless heard the matter. The judgement (15 August 2017) was scathing:

> In view of the various grounds upon which the remedial action can and must be set aside, there is no need to pronounce conclusively on the validity of all of the Governor's many criticisms. Suffice it to say, the Public Protector's explanation and begrudging concession of unconstitutionality offer no defence to the charges of illegality, irrationality and procedural unfairness. It is disconcerting that she seems impervious to the criticism, or otherwise disinclined to address it.
>
> She risks the charge of hypocrisy and incompetence if she does not hold herself to an equal or higher standard than that to which she holds those subject to her writ. A dismissive and procedurally unfair approach by the Public Protector to important matters placed before her by prominent role players in the affairs of state will tarnish her reputation and damage the legitimacy of the office. She would do well to reflect more deeply on her conduct of this investigation and the criticism of her by the Governor of the Reserve Bank and the Speaker of Parliament.[71]

Such was the scope of Mkhwebane's breathtaking incompetence that understandably other explanations were sought for her actions, which even diehard ANC (and Zuma) loyalists in parliament rejected. Even the Speaker, Baleka Mbete, perhaps anticipating the curtain falling on the Zuma era, joined the SARB governor in taking the matter to court. An obvious candidate as an alternative explanation is furtherance of state capture at the behest of

Zuma and his surviving networks in order to compromise the independence of the SARB and loosen the fiscal discipline which the Bank practised in tandem with the Treasury.[72] Once again a 'smoking gun' – in the form of hard evidence that Mkhwebane's appointment was secured for the ends of state capture – is unlikely to emerge. It is possible that Zuma used his control of the ANC caucus to secure the deployment of a former state security operative to the post as revenge for reverses he suffered at the hands of Madonsela, made more bitter by her elevation in the eyes of (respectable) popular opinion to the status of 'a true leader' of the country. It is equally possible that Mkhwebane was appointed because, like Madonsela, she is a youngish (forty-six on appointment) African woman, presentable (by all accounts she interviewed very well before the parliamentary committee) who epitomized the emerging talent that should be empowered and trusted. When she turned out to be ignorant of the founding document that sets out her own powers and duties, as well as those of other arms and organs of governance, Zuma and those close to him were quick to seize their opportunity to extend the attack on fiscal responsibility from the Treasury to the last frontier, the SARB.

Given what has already emerged about the Zuma years and, in a longer perspective the history of appointments in post-apartheid South Africa, either explanation for Mkhwebane's appointment and subsequent actions could be plausible. What does seem sure, however, is that it is hard to think of a third possible explanation outside these parameters. The relevance of these competing explanations for understanding Zuma's leadership is the whether he was a chess master playing a long game, or a juggler and improviser?

Mbeki and Zuma

Between 2005 and 2007, at a crucial point in South Africa's short democratic trajectory, the fulcrum on which the country's democratic future turned was a contest between two leaders, both of whom had form where conspiracies and paranoia (metaphorical if not clinical) were concerned. Whether this was a matter of genuine psychopathology or merely a handy instrument to be used in the world of their primary political socialization – where both in fairness had real enemies – hardly matters. What does matter is whether this leadership reflex has been transplanted into South Africa's wider body politic and is immune to rejection or whether it is an endowment of the exile and underground world whose currency will expire with the passing of that generation. This will be one of the major questions of Ramaphosa's tenure of the ANC and state presidencies.

This was not the only thing Mbeki and Zuma had in common. Each in his own fashion was a destroyer and both, specifically, were destroyers of their predecessors' legacies. Mbeki destroyed the careers of rivals and did his best to destroy the spirit of the Constitution by fusing party and state. A generous assessment might be that he did these things to allow himself enough space to build a new party and a new state that would serve higher purposes than the compromises of the settlement. That would be a very generous assessment. In any case, motives aside, both were disastrous miscalculations, which opened the way for Zuma. When he felt more secure, Mbeki broke with Mandela's legacy to be more honest with whites and the Left. But honesty in political leadership requires empathy, not destructive coldness, disdain and open contempt, which he seemed to relish dispensing on all sides. It may have been the right message (another generous assessment) but Mbeki was the wrong messenger.

It did not take long to work out that Zuma was all messenger and no message. One way in which he was a destroyer was as a bringer of entropy – that is through negligence, lack of vision and interest in policy and possibly an inability to tell right from wrong, he ushered in a period that lacked order and predictability and threatened decline into disorder. In these things he could hardly have been more different from Mbeki whom he made to look in retrospect like a hyperactive micromanager. In at least one respect however his destructive agency was consciously directed and the target was Mbeki's legacy. To Mbeki's credit he built capacity in at least a few parts of the state, those charged with financial management. Zuma targeted these and worked hard to dismantle their capabilities. His greatest success was with the revenues service SARS. By mid-2018 evidence presented to the early hearings of the Zondo commission outlined the disastrous effects on tax collection capabilities of the Zuma-sponsored takeover of SARS.[73] The melancholy lesson of the Mbeki-Zuma years appears to be that insofar as there is a leadership pattern, it is of discontinuity and destruction. This is remarkable, given the degree to which the ANC has practised ancestor worship and demands continuity with pieties, rituals and founding documents. It is simply not feasible to believe that cognitive dissonance of this magnitude has been purely a function of the individual characters of Mandela's first two successors. It is more likely that the explanation is to be found in features of the context in which they operated and, arguably, the failure of a whole leadership generation, a possibility to which we will return in the final chapter of this book.

Part Four

Leadership in the altered future

8

Endgame: From Zuma to Ramaphosa

The ANC national conference

In the lead up to the ANC national conference (15–18 December 2017), pressure on Zuma escalated from three sources. First, his situation was structured by the disjuncture between the terms of office of ANC president and the state president. This was exacerbated by the ANC's lack of appetite for 'two centres of power' especially where the ANC president and the state president were not in harmony, as was the case between Zuma and Mbeki. By late 2017, Zuma was held in low esteem outside the ANC and even to a growing extent within it and the Alliance. As a result, the party was suffering such reputational damage that it was clear that only an ANC president that was beholden to Zuma would be able to cohabit with him for the remaining fifteen months of his second term. However, if this came about there was a very real danger of a split, which would be a much more serious rupture than the splinter breakaways that led to the formation of the opposition parties Congress of the People (COPE) and Economic Freedom Fighters (EFF) and which would truly lead South African politics into uncharted territory as the 2019 general election approached. This situation left little room for manoeuvre and imposed a ruthless time frame.

A second source of pressure came from the relentless and apparently inexhaustible flow of evidence about state capture. The 'Gupta emails' and *The Betrayal of the Promise* (both cited above) came out in the first half of the year and at the end of October they were joined by *The President's Keepers: Those Keeping Zuma in Power and out of Prison* by veteran investigative journalist Jacques Pauw.[1] This work presented more evidence of the creation of a shadow, 'mafia' state. It focused, in particular, on the capture of the South African Revenue Services (SARS) under the guise of 'restructuring' under Zuma's appointee Tom Moyane. This in turn enabled quashing investigations into gangsters and corrupt individuals. It also presented further and updated documentation of the manipulation of criminal investigation, prosecution and security services. While the book tended to confirm, emphasize and extend what was already in the public domain with further evidence, rather than break entirely new ground, it became a publishing sensation. This was partly due to the credibility of its author – who is one of the most experienced and respected of South Africa's investigative journalists, with a pedigree reaching back to the exposures of apartheid death squads – but more to the heavy-handed response of Zuma's security establishment and of SARS, with attempts to interdict publication and threats to Pauw himself. The only result was to ignite sales (a first run of 20,000 sold out within hours) and trigger the canny decision to make 'pirated' copies free on the Internet, thus securing even wider circulation.

The exposure of the role played by British public relations firm Bell Pottinger in crafting messages aimed at defending the Guptas and discrediting their and Zuma's critics also caused reputational damage. These messages relied on populist themes of what was widely perceived to be a racially divisive nature ('white monopoly capital') distributed among other routes by fake social media accounts. The blowback from this ill-judged venture was enough to put Bell Pottinger out of business and further discredit the Guptas. Apparent ethical lapses by other high-profile accountancy and management consultancy firms in their dealings with state bodies and Gupta firms added fuel to the flames that were now illuminating the shadow state.[2]

The third source of pressure came from the maturation of ongoing court proceedings, which Zuma had been fending off with his representatives' 'Stalingrad tactics'. In mid-October, the Supreme Court of Appeal (SCA) dismissed Zuma's and the National Prosecuting Authority's (NPA's) appeal against the 2016 verdict of the North Gauteng High Court (NGHC) that the NPA's 2009 decision to drop the charges against Zuma was 'irrational'. It did not help Zuma's case that the director who dropped the charges, Mokotedi Mpshe, admitted in an affidavit to the SCA that he had been 'untruthful' in previous proceedings. Unsurprisingly, the court was of the opinion that this undermined Mpshe's credibility and the validity of his decision to discontinue the case against Zuma. Neither did it help that Zuma himself, in arguments before the SCA, conceded that the decision was indeed irrational, but that he now wanted a chance to make fresh representations to the NPA so that a rational decision could be made.[3]

This verdict threw into sharp relief the position of National Director of Public Prosecutions (NDPP) Sean Abrahams, given that his was widely believed to be a 'captured' appointment and that he could not be relied on to discharge his duties irrespective of fear or favour where Zuma was concerned. On 8 December 2017, the NGHC handed down the judgement that Abrahams's predecessor had been effectively bribed to leave office (the inference drawn outside the court was that he had shown signs of being independent and Zuma had to get rid of him), that Abrahams' appointment was invalid and set aside and, because he was 'conflicted' as a potential target of NPA charges, Zuma could not appoint a successor. The duty of appointing a new NDPP devolved upon Ramaphosa as deputy state president.[4] Predictably enough, Zuma filed papers in the constitutional court on 19 January 2018 challenging this verdict on the grounds that it was not constitutionally permissible to have 'two presidents' both exercising powers simultaneously. At the same time and equally predictably, Abrahams challenged the NGHC verdict, also in the constitutional court, on the grounds that it interfered with the independence of the NPA (under the circumstances an impudent submission) and made unjustifiable assumptions about his appointment.[5]

The unfavourable verdicts continued throughout December. On the 13th, the NGHC dismissed Zuma's attempt to review former Public Protector Thuli Madonsela's remedial action in her report on state capture. This had required Zuma to appoint a judicial commission on the subject with the stipulation that it should be headed by a judge appointed by the chief justice, Mogoeng Mogoeng, and not by Zuma. The judgement, like the Abrahams judgement, labelled Zuma as 'personally conflicted', saw no merit whatever in his arguments, stated that he had been ill-advised and reckless in his attempt at review and that his conduct had fallen short of the standards demanded by his constitutional responsibilities. With unconcealed impatience, the court described the attempted review as a 'delaying tactic' and that it was time for courts to consider making high officials personally responsible for costs under such circumstances. Zuma was given thirty days to appoint the commission and although he stated that he had 'legal reservations' about the judgement he complied by 9 January, with Mogoeng Mogoeng appointing Deputy Chief Justice Raymond Zondo to head the commission.[6]

Finally, to end 2017, on 29 December the constitutional court ruled that the National Assembly must devise clear criteria for impeachment of a president. The court had been asked by opposition parties to consider and pronounce on their complaints that parliament had failed in its constitutional obligation to hold the president to account. The Constitution allows for removal of a president from office[7] but is vague on the grounds that might trigger the process.[8] Zuma had survived several attempts to remove him from office by both constitutional routes, those of impeachment and vote of no confidence.[9] Six votes of no confidence were brought between April 2015 and August 2017: four were voted on, one amended by the ANC to become a vote of confidence *in* the president and one was withdrawn.[10]

The most significant of these was the vote of no confidence of 8 August 2017. This was because in June the constitutional court had ruled that the Speaker of the House was in error when she maintained that she had no power to allow a secret ballot for a vote of no confidence. The court would not order her to provide a secret ballot, for that would be a violation of the separation of powers, but the judgement made it clear that she was empowered to do so. This Baleka Mbete duly did, to the surprise of many observers, since she had previously expended considerable energy and ingenuity in protecting Zuma, sailing close to the constitutional wind in doing so.[11] The 8 August 2017 motion attracted 177 votes with 198 votes against. The most votes any previous motion of no confidence had attracted were 126, in November 2016.[12] Deepening disillusion with Zuma and the security of the secret ballot presumably emboldened ANC members to vote against him. It is difficult to calculate how many, since the effects of abstentions and the voting choices of some of the micro parties in the House – which are officially aligned neither to the ANC nor the opposition in any consistent way – cloud the issue. However, a range of between thirty-one and forty ANC defectors (12.4–16 per cent of the parliamentary party) was suggested.[13] Small as the numbers might seem, given the mythology of ANC unity and the need not to break ranks in the face of the 'enemy', defection on this scale still represented unprecedented defiance.

In the face of this assault from the opposition, the courts, civil society and the media, Zuma had a number of options. The first was to continue with the Stalingrad strategy of challenging every adverse court ruling and using to the full all avenues of appeal, even when appeal courts would find his questioning of the lower courts to be a mere delaying tactic, reckless and without substance. Increasingly, as the adverse judgements mounted, he would vary this strategy with tactical withdrawals.

A second option would be to run for a third term as ANC president, to which, as we have seen, there is no impediment in the party's rules. He seems to have ruled this option out at an early stage, given the ANC's antipathy towards having two centres of power, which would inevitably be the case after his second term as state president expired. It would in any case have been difficult for him to brazen out a bid for a third term and for the ANC to swallow this, when one of the principal grievances of the coalition that brought him to power was the similar bid on Mbeki's part.

A more extreme option would be to escape the tightening noose of constitutional and democratic processes by overthrowing them. Throughout 2017 there was some media speculation on the possibility that Zuma, either by exploiting or even contriving a crisis, could call a state of emergency on the pretext of dealing with public disorder but in fact with the aim of suspending the Constitution or at least parts of it (media freedom for one) that were inconvenient for him. Two potential crises were student unrest over fees and, more importantly, a real prospect that, in March–April 2017, social welfare payments, which go to over 17 million South Africans, would not be paid because the constitutional court had ruled that a contract with the distributor was invalid. The minister responsible (a key Zuma supporter and head of the ANC Women's League) had through rank incompetence, or possibly a corrupt relationship with the existing holder of the contract, failed to deal with the fallout.[14]

Given the ANC's culture of paranoia, the routine use of spurious 'intelligence' reports in leadership battles, the capture of state security agencies and the endemic violence of both social and industrial protest in South Africa, the threat of such a constitutional coup could appear to be a real one. However, this would be a desperate option given the run-down state of the South African military, the general inefficiency of the police, the factionalized condition of state agencies and of the ANC itself, as well as the likelihood of vigorous citizen resistance along the lines of the UDF in the anti-apartheid struggle, in the event of anything that resembled a coup. It could indeed easily seal Zuma's fate rather than keep him safe and rule out a dignified exit with his assets intact.

Effectively, by the second half of 2017, Zuma was in a similar position to that of Mbeki ten years earlier in 2007. He was saddled with a vice president he did not trust, was becoming increasingly unpopular in his own party and the leadership elective conference was looming. Two things exacerbated his situation compared to his predecessor's. First, his position in the ANC was greatly undermined by the growing belief that he had become an electoral liability; this was not true of Mbeki who right to the end could point to unbroken electoral success. In any case, by 2017 electoral dynamics had changed and the party could no longer rely on the easy reproduction of its support base, irrespective of who was leader. Second, compared to Mbeki the personal stakes were much higher for Zuma. Mbeki's misgivings about Zuma concerned his all too prescient fears about what two terms of his putative successor would do to the country and the ANC. Mbeki would have many regrets about the dissipation of what he saw as the legacy of his leadership, but he had nothing to fear personally. By contrast, Zuma's liberty and the fortunes, present and future, of himself, his family and associates were at stake.

Under these circumstances, it is not surprising that he chose the tactical alternative of controlling the succession to the presidency of the ANC, and thus effectively that of the state presidency, in the hope that he could negotiate an acceptable exit or even stay in power to the end of his term. By winning the 2007 succession battle himself, he made sure he stayed out of jail and by securing it for a chosen successor he could do the same in 2017. So while he continued the stalling tactics to fend off court proceedings, he made it known that his preferred candidate for the ANC presidency was his ex-wife

Nkosasana Dlamini-Zuma. At one point, no fewer than seven candidates had declared themselves – a scarcely believable reversal of previous ANC succession practice – but there were only ever two serious contenders, vice president Cyril Ramaphosa and Dlamini-Zuma.

From the start, outside her own camp (and probably inside it too), Dlamini-Zuma was recognized only as a stalking horse for Zuma. On the face of it, this was a little unfair. She had had a substantial political career in her own right, having served in every cabinet between 1994 and 2012 and as chair of the African Union Commission between 2012 and 2017. She had been minister of health (she is a qualified doctor) from 1994 to 1999, minister of foreign affairs (1999–2009) and minister of home affairs (2009–12). However, arguably there was less to this career than meets the eye: she was embroiled in a cronyism scandal at the Ministry of Health where she also energetically sponsored a quack cure for HIV/AIDS (a toxic industrial solvent named Virodene); at foreign affairs, she was very much in the shadow of Mbeki who took the lead on all major (and some minor) issues; at home affairs, she received credit for a turnaround of this notoriously corrupt and incompetent department, credit that largely belonged to predecessors, officials and consultants.

Whatever her merits or lack of them as a minister, however, it swiftly became clear when her bid got underway that she had no gift whatever for retail politics. She came across as charmless, lacklustre, without a distinctive political vision of her own, content with passionless parroting of the populist clichés of the late Zuma era. She was terminally unpersuasive to anyone outside of Zuma's camp. She did have the gender card to play but it was her ex-husband rather than the candidate herself who made something of this. The ANC has placed great emphasis on increasing female participation and representation in politics and across the board. That is as it should be, but there are times when it has appeared that expedience takes its place alongside principle and that gender parity has been used as a ploy to appoint individuals who are mediocre at best, thoroughly incompetent at worst and at all times politically pliable. There have of course been plenty of incompetent and pliable male appointees in both the Mbeki and Zuma administrations; the gender card is merely another useful one to play. The cry, 'it is time for South Africa to have a woman president!' with which Zuma launched his ex-wife's candidacy, does have some genuine leverage, but this was somewhat undercut by Zuma's own traditional views on gender and the deep vein of patriarchal chauvinism among ANC supporters, which was exposed by his rise to power, especially during his trial for rape.[15] It was also undercut by the fact that the president of the ANC Women's League, Bathabile Dlamini, minister of social development and key organizer of Dlamini-Zuma's campaign, was one of Zuma's most incompetent ministerial appointments (she was responsible for the social grants fiasco) and one of his most diehard supporters. With Dlamini's support so prominent, it could not have been clearer that a vote for Dlamini-Zuma was a vote for Jacob Zuma.

In a somewhat counterintuitive way, despite the blessing of the sitting president and her own ministerial pedigree, Dlamini-Zuma could appear to be the insurgent candidate by comparison with her rival and her campaign, such as it was, relied heavily on playing this card. Ramaphosa was clearly the choice of the broader establishment: the media, the markets, the respectable of all colours and persuasions, the urban and constitutional ANC that could appeal to the legacy of Mandela, the SACP and Cosatu; all were behind him. On top of that he was in a sense the expected choice, by virtue of his occupation of the deputy (state) presidency. The 'crown prince' syndrome was weakening in the ANC leadership stakes, but it still had some influence. However, Dlamini-Zuma's association with her ex-husband diluted any putative anti-establishment, anti-elite credentials. Ramaphosa's supporters and the political mainstream constantly played upon the assumption that she would protect him, perhaps allow him to leave the presidency early but gracefully through the medium of an amnesty deal and at the same time allow space for the continuation of the project of state capture.

Why she would do this was never spelled out. She was married to him from 1982 until she divorced him in 1998 and had four daughters with him (though none of them are among the Zuma progeny most implicated with the Guptas). Whether this would be enough for her to subordinate herself to him in the way her opponents assumed was never justified with hard arguments. However, she never backed up her somewhat mechanical repetitions that she would be 'her own person' with any strong projection of individual philosophy, values or policy vision and she was clearly unable or unwilling to distance herself from her husband's indiscretions or even mount a vigorous defence of them. It was these absences and self-damning reticences that allowed critics to draw the assumption, rightly or wrongly, that she would inevitably be her ex-husband's cat's paw.

However, the ANC presidency is not determined by the opinions of the urban South African establishment and the preferences of global markets. When the ANC provinces reported on the composition of their delegations and electoral choices in early December 2017, it was clear that the race was going to be close.[16] Ramaphosa was ahead at that point by 1,860 votes to 1,333 but many imponderables could affect the final vote.[17] Factional strife erupted in violence at the Eastern Cape's provincial elective conference and court cases arising out of factional struggles for control challenged the legitimacy of provincial executive councils in the Free State, KwaZulu-Natal and the Eastern Cape. The final number of delegates would not be known until the last moment. At the final tally on 17 December, Ramaphosa won by a mere 179 votes in a total of 4,701 (rather fewer than the 5,300 odd that had been expected in November). The division of posts in the so-called 'top six' leadership group also muddied the verdict. The consensus verdict was that they were split down the middle: three pro-Ramaphosa and three pro-Zuma. The same kind of measuring stick was applied to the National Executive Committee (NEC) and the National Working Committee (NWC), the two top decision-making and managing bodies. In each case, a slim majority was judged to have gone to Ramaphosa.

The long(ish) goodbye

Following the drama of the conference, the next few weeks had their own tensions but owned a different theatrical quality. The ANC as keen students of Marx presumably knows that history repeats itself, first as tragedy then as farce. Fond of believing itself to be history's agent, the ANC duly cut short Jacob Zuma's tenure of the state presidency as it had done to Mbeki ten years previously. This time, however, history skipped tragedy and went straight to farce.

Zuma had long since completely lost all legitimacy and authority with a multiracial urban elite both inside and outside the ANC. All were heartily sick of his publicly funded Stalingrad tactics, which exploited the Constitution that he had subverted for so long.[18] The coalition of the disaffected that had brought Mbeki down had torn up the protocols of deference based on liberation movement history and African culture, by which the ANC fondly imagined society should treat its leaders. Now it was Zuma's turn. However the decision where it mattered, with the ANC branches, went against him only by a whisker, emboldening him to fight on.

Everything appeared to be on the table: resignation, recall, impeachment, a vote of no confidence in Zuma by the House of Assembly, more rulings by the higher courts, amnesty or prosecution. Despite the best efforts of the media to float the possibility that Zuma would resort to dirty tricks – fire Ramaphosa as deputy president on the basis of a spurious 'intelligence' report or declare a state of emergency – there was no fear, only derision and exasperation, which soon transferred itself to the ANC's NEC and even Ramaphosa as they struggled to manage what came, inevitably, to be known as 'Zexit'. With such an extensive menu of possibilities on the table, perhaps it is not surprising that it took from late December to mid-February to prise Zuma from office. However the public mood – as reflected in both mainstream and social media – was not as understanding.

South Africa's pre-eminent political cartoonist, Zapiro, caught this mood by depicting a classic Western movie shoot-out between gunslingers Ramaphosa and Zuma. Above the dusty street a banner proclaimed, 'High Noon High Noonish Middling Noon Low Noon Whenever.'[19]

Zuma's defiant refusal to resign even in the face of the 'recall' mechanism that did for Mbeki lasted until 14 February, by which time the NEC (after a marathon thirteen-hour meeting) announced that ANC MPs would support an opposition motion of no confidence in the parliament. Zuma continued his defiance in a rambling, confused and angry broadcast of nearly an hour on the SABC[20] shortly after the NEC announcement, but late that evening he made another broadcast to announce his resignation. As Ramaphosa took office, all right-thinking people cheered and the Rand rallied. It remained to be seen whether what was immediately dubbed 'Ramaphoria' would be a new dawn or a poisoned chalice.

9

Ramaphosa

Cometh the hour? The return of Ramaphosa

The election by a narrow margin of Cyril Ramaphosa as president of the ANC on 18 December 2017 was not strictly speaking a 'return' to politics. After all, at the time of his election to the party leadership he had been its deputy president since December 2012 and deputy state president since June 2014. However, after his glory days as lead negotiator for the ANC in the transitional and constitutional negotiations (1991–4), midwife of the Constitution as chairman of the Constitutional Assembly (1994–6) and secretary general of the ANC (1991–7), there had been a ten-year hiatus (1997–2007) during which he held no party or state post and he seemed to be one of the lost leaders of the post-apartheid era.

During this break he went into business, taking advantage of Black Economic Empowerment (BEE) opportunities, which, after a shaky start, he exploited to become a very wealthy investor in a wide range of business sectors including mining, the source of much of South Africa's historic wealth, not to mention a fair share of the genesis of the country's class and racial tensions. He also served as chairman of the BEE Commission, which laid the groundwork for the BEE policy under Mbeki in the late 1990s.

This break was ended in 2007 when he was elected as an ordinary member (although not an office holder) of the National Executive Committee (NEC), but it was not until he became deputy state president in 2014 that he put aside his business career and declared and divested his wealth in order to resume his political career proper. If we add the five years between his election to the NEC and assumption of the deputy presidency of the ANC, he was out of top-flight and front-line politics for fifteen years, a substantial slice of any political lifetime.

His political career path, which was built on the foundation of his involvement in the liberation struggle through the trade union movement, is unique in the top leadership of the post-apartheid ANC and gives him a profile that is very different from his predecessors. This career path can be viewed on the one hand as patchy and lacking in long-term political commitment or multifaceted, varied and governed by strategic shrewdness. The choice depends on whether the observer is looking for strengths or weaknesses in his claims to leadership. As competing perspectives within which to see Ramaphosa's career as preparation to leading the ANC, we can either designate him an individual who, past and present, has had much broader experience of actually existing South Africa than Mandela, Mbeki and Zuma, and is thus much better equipped than them for the role of leading in wider society, in the economy and in an increasingly competitive electoral system, or we can see him as fatally flawed by being in the ANC but not truly of it, and as a result lacking in the core leadership credentials for party management, which is the essential basis for all other leadership competencies to flourish.

Although Ramaphosa's victory was greeted with broadly expressed relief across civil society, the media and markets as well as on the part of his supporters in the ANC, plenty of cautionary voices were raised.[1] The principal point of concern was the slim margin of victory, in Ramaphosa's accession to the presidency, compounded by divisions in the top six posts, which included on past form at least, three identifiable supporters of Zuma, as well as in the NEC. These things seemed to point to tight constraints on Ramaphosa's exercise of power and ambivalence about the mandate for change he had been given.

In particular, Ramaphosa depended on the votes of delegates from Mpumalanga, which had the second largest number of ANC branches after KwaZulu-Natal. Mpumalanga's provincial ANC chief, David Mabuza, had long been a Zuma supporter, was a prominent member of the 'premier league' of provincial barons and had emerged as a key power broker in the run-up to the ANC conference.[2] However, by whatever means – a unilateral calculation of self-interest or a backstairs deal with Ramaphosa – Mabuza swung the vote behind Ramaphosa and earned himself the ANC vice presidency, which put him in pole position for further elevation to the state vice presidency and ultimately the top job. However, even if Mabuza and Ace Magashule, the Free State provincial leader who was elected to the post of secretary general, were to abandon their previous allegiance to Zuma, both are associated with corruption and state capture and neither has ever given any evidence of being committed to the kind of reformist agenda espoused by Ramaphosa for the ANC and the country. They, particularly Magashule who was already under investigation by the Hawks for his Gupta links as early as January 2018, remain vulnerable to any extensive investigation of state capture. As of mid-2019, both are still there, still threatened by the clean-up of the state apparatus but still clearly capable of rearguard self-defence and of being a significant obstruction to Ramaphosa's freedom of action.

Other concerns included the most pressing of the challenges faced by Ramaphosa: the management of the transition from Zuma's occupancy of the state presidency to his successor's appointment. At best, there might be a swift transition to Ramaphosa himself; but how would this be managed and to what timetable? Would it involve resignation or 'recall'? A vote of no confidence or impeachment? Immunity or amnesty? Or the full force of forensic investigation, trials and punishment? At worst, there could be a protracted power struggle for part or all of the period until the expiry of Zuma's constitutional mandate, a stalemate dictated by the disjuncture between the ANC's and the Constitution's electoral cycles, the source of so much political dysfunction. No one could tell in the immediate aftermath of Ramaphosa's election how long Zuma and Ramaphosa might theoretically coexist as dual presidents, the former in union buildings, the seat of government, and the latter in Luthuli House, the headquarters of the ANC. The longer this standoff lasted, the greater the chance that Zuma might pull off a last gasp twist to the narrative and deny Ramaphosa the succession to the state presidency, perhaps by firing him from the state vice presidency or even by means of a fabricated state of emergency and suspension of the Constitution. Unlikely as these outcomes might seem in retrospect, they were very much part of public discussion in what was a very jittery time of transition.[3]

Questions of authority, legitimacy and unity in the ANC provided an uncertain background to the question of transition. Significantly, the partners in the ANC Alliance were scarcely mentioned in the various comments and analyses of the post-conference situation, a telling indication of their decline in influence under Zuma and a marked difference from the corresponding transition from Mbeki to Zuma, in which the unions and the South African Communist Party (SACP) had been the major players. Speculation about the calculations of the opposition also lurked beneath the surface, a further indication of the febrile atmosphere. How far-fetched would it be for them to drag their feet in cooperating to remove Zuma, since his occupancy of the presidency was their greatest electoral asset and an ANC transformed by Ramaphosa would be the greatest threat to their ambitions in the 2019 national poll? The precedent of a secret ballot for the last vote of no confidence before the ANC conference added another twist to this Machiavellian possibility since no one would know who voted to keep Zuma in office.

If the most pressing concerns facing Ramaphosa centred on 'Zexit', there was also a formidable array of challenges waiting for a post-Zuma administration, if one could be brought into being. With the national budget set for 21 February 2019, the shadows of sluggish growth, ballooning deficit and potential for further downgrades of South Africa's sovereign debt lay long over the economy. The restoration of public and market confidence in governance, through the return of rationality and integrity to policy and administration (particularly in the SOEs and criminal justice system), would require more than the removal of Zuma. How far and how deep the pursuit of the corrupt could go without destroying what remained of unity in the ANC would be a pressing issue. Policy matters also required urgent attention. In the late Zuma period, the policy drift that characterized his early years in office had been partly replaced by erratic populism in brazen denial of fiscal strains.

As a result, escalating uncertainty had attached itself to policies for land, mining and the funding of higher education, all of which destroyed confidence in macroeconomic policy and the prospects for growth, especially against the background of corruption and state capture. Specific poison pills were Zuma's unilateral announcement of free (means tested) tertiary education shortly before the ANC conference and the ANC's adoption of the policy goal of expropriation without compensation in pursuit of land reform.

Building the image

In the weeks of uncertainty between Ramaphosa's election and his assumption of the state presidency, the question of what he could bring to the resolution of those issues that could be resolved and the management of those that could not (in the short term at least) also had to be faced. What, in short, were his leadership credentials? In keeping with his fractured career, the sources were patchy.[4] Anthony Butler's is the only substantial biography. It was written without the cooperation of its subject, who combines intense political ambition with an equally fierce desire for privacy, a self-indulgent balancing act that will not be possible to sustain as state president. Despite Butler's lack of access, the biography is a largely sympathetic treatment – one reviewer called it a 'campaign biography for a candidate that refused to run' (in 2007, against Zuma).[5] It ends at a time when Ramaphosa was out of the fray and receding from the public eye, though not quite on the sidelines; however, an online interview with its author in late December 2017 provides some updated interpretations. Further updating is provided by Ray Hartley's account of Ramaphosa in the late Zuma years.

In addition to these full-length biographical works, the following sources are available: specialized academic studies of the early years of the National Union of Mineworkers (NUM) which focus on Ramaphosa's leadership;[6] standard accounts of the negotiation and constitution-making period, 1991–6;[7] general accounts of the post-apartheid period;[8] and a rash of journalistic profiles and commentary on Ramaphosa's leadership qualities which appeared with increasing regularity during the endgame of Zuma's presidency and the transition to the new administration.[9]

The composite picture that emerges from these relatively sparse sources is remarkably consistent. This may simply and forgivably be a case of having to make the best of scanty material or, given Ramaphosa's parsimony with self-revelation, the difficulty of making bricks without straw. On the other hand, it might also betray a tendency for members of the South African commentariat (with very few exceptions) to feed on each other and slide towards a middle ground that verges on groupthink.

The key components of this picture are of a leader who has been long in the making, who is ambitious but cautious and a player of 'the long game'. In doing so he is a pragmatist, a great negotiator, charming when necessary and ruthless at other times. He is an enigma, who tends to give little away about himself, who values privacy and prefers to conceal rather than communicate on any matters other than high-level political generalities.

The picture emerges of a personality shaped by a strong family base in a lower-middle-class urban setting (his father was a Soweto policeman) in which traditional and ethno-tribal affiliations were worn lightly or not at all. Early-life Christianity and Black Consciousness philosophies – which themselves had strong roots in churches and student Christian organizations – helped shape early political leanings in the setting of the Bantustan University of the North. Ramaphosa's subsequent contributions to the anti-apartheid struggle were very strong, although they are in some respects quite far out of the ANC mainstream. He served seventeen months in detention without trial but, perhaps significantly, in solitary confinement rather than in the kind of prison conditions that shaped the group ethos, loyalties and networks of ANC elites that emerged from imprisonment on Robben Island and were so influential thereafter. Having qualified as a lawyer, his contribution to the development of the NUM came from the angle of legal adviser and organizer rather than underground or shop floor operative. As a result, he was always deferential to the worker ethos, insistent on the importance of empowering the worker members rather than emphasizing his own personal leadership contribution, which nonetheless was enormous.

Part of the union

One treatment of the evolution of the NUM focuses closely on Ramaphosa's leadership style.[10] Following Foucault, Dunbar Moodie invokes 'pastoral' leadership in which the leader does not dominate but creates consent, limiting himself to 'beneficent guiding' towards a 'complex mutual relationship of responsibility' in which he is 'not a judge but a healer'. In this paradigm, wielding power is a duty requiring endless application, 'a burden rather than an honour' and 'offering care to others but denying it to oneself'. In short, 'Ramaphosa never lost sight of the moral and redemptive pastoral imperative that had driven him at the outset.' This characterisation certainly chimes with some elements of Ramaphosa's observable history, character and work ethic, though it might amount in the end to a conjectural bridge too far. In any case, however, it is difficult to see this leadership template being appropriate on a wider scale – to a whole country – and under very different historical circumstances. It must, of course, be stressed that Moodie did not make such claims, confining himself to the historical period of the NUM's rise and contribution to the wider struggle. A potentially more interesting critical take on Moodie's interpretation would be that such a leadership style would in any case be self-limiting. Ramaphosa's priority of empowering the workers to lead their own union defines his goal as creating subjects who would no longer require the kind of 'pastoral' leadership he deployed to encourage their emerging empowerment.

Despite his crucial role in making the NUM and Cosatu a powerful force in the anti-apartheid struggle, there is more doubt about the effectiveness of his leadership in advancing workers' material interests. The question mark arises over the great 1987 mineworkers' strike (1–30 August).[11] At the time, this was South Africa's biggest strike in terms of numbers of workers involved and days lost. Under Ramaphosa's leadership, the NUM demanded a 30 per cent increase, raising it to variable increases from 40 per cent to 55 per cent. The employers responded with 12.5 per cent raised later to variable 15–23 per cent. When no progress was made, Ramaphosa called a strike ballot. A total of 210,000 out of an estimated 344,000 membership voted, 95 per cent for the strike and on this basis, the strike was declared.

The strike was less a bargaining strategy with wages and conditions the objective – though of course these were the ostensible reasons for it – more a power struggle with each side intent on determining the future framework of industrial relations. The turning point came on 21 August when the mining companies began mass sackings: by 30 August, when the strike was called off, 50,000 had been dismissed with obvious consequences for the miners themselves and for the NUM's membership numbers. The union accepted the employer's offer without any improvement but saved a little face by securing agreement that sacked workers would be reinstated.

To a large extent, despite the apparent rashness of the decision to strike and the humiliation of the outcome, there is a tendency to spin the narrative into an endorsement of Ramaphosa's leadership. Typical sympathetic comments were that the union showed new strength and 'unprecedented power' for holding out for a month and that Ramaphosa's achievement was to satisfy the militants among his members without destroying the union.[12] According to Cosatu's sympathetic historian,

> NUM did not achieve the wage increases it intended. However, the union was not destroyed, nor did it lose its capacity to organise. It took over two years to rebuild membership levels to those existing before the strike. But the strike also built a tougher and more experienced union.[13]

This kind of 'glass half full' verdict was not surprising considering the context of the strike, a popular anti-apartheid uprising met by brutal state repression under a state of emergency. On the industrial front, 1.3 million days had been lost to strike action in 1986, and in that year, according to NUM figures, mineworkers participated in 113 strikes involving 'well over 250 000 workers'.[14]

It was bad enough that industrial relations in the mining industry were so closely intertwined with national resistance to a racist and repressive regime, which amounted to insurrection, but they were also affected by escalating, multifaceted violence. According to one treatment of the period from the 1970s to the 1990s,[15] violence on the mines transformed from 'the character of rural games of masculinity' to overlapping categories of ethnic, criminal and political clashes including ethno-tribal 'faction fighting', struggle for illegal rackets in compounds and violence and counter-violence between striking and non-striking miners. This violence cost the lives of at least 490 miners between 1974 and 1994.[16] Under these circumstances, mines and miners were extremely difficult to manage, not only for mining companies but for the union too. Rival forms of leadership, described by Moodie as millenarian, charismatic and insurrectionist,[17] challenged the representative legitimacy of the NUM and its leaders, until the individual who exemplified them – he was widely believed to possess magical powers – was killed in Lesotho under unexplained circumstances in 1985. However, the threat of ungovernability that he represented survived him. Under these circumstances, it is possible that Ramaphosa felt he needed a dramatic gamble to make a militant statement in order to consolidate the union's authority and the strike – which after all was sanctioned by an overwhelming majority of miners – should be seen in this light.

Whatever the facts of the case, the strike has been woven, for the most part, into Ramaphosa's favourable personal mythology. Two key ideas figure in this. The first is Ramaphosa as a negotiator and the second sees him as a player of 'the long game', an ever-present feature in profiles and commentaries[18] and a convenient formula for dissolving doubts about his leadership stemming from short-term setbacks or even failures.

The great negotiator

Important as the NUM years are in compiling his composite image, they come second to the years of negotiation and constitution making in establishing Cyril Ramaphosa's leadership credentials. Ramaphosa is clearly the star of a somewhat star-struck literature of this period. He stands out as a persuader and driver of bargains, a charmer who is also a hard man with the ability to spot weaknesses and go for the jugular; but having established dominance (as he always does), he refrains from humiliating his adversary. The metaphors of poker and chess are routinely invoked for his abilities in contests of will, skill and endurance. According to taste and in keeping with prevalent ambiguous attitudes to the settlement as a whole, he is either the man who outwitted the Boers and put them collectively and individually in their place or the symbol of a cooperative transition from authoritarian to democratic rule: the 'rainbow miracle' made flesh. Within this picture, he is known for two things in particular: the calculated bonding with his (junior) partner, Roelf Meyer the National Party (NP) negotiator, and the hard-nosed formula of 'sufficient consensus', the operating principle designed to move things along in the face of minor party intransigence, by which if the ANC and NP agreed, everybody else could (reportedly in Ramaphosa's own words) 'get stuffed'.[19] This bulldozer approach, which Ramaphosa is credited with devising, stands in sharp contrast to the somewhat feline repertoire of constructive ambiguity with which Mbeki led first the Afrikaner Right and then Buthelezi's Zulus up the garden path, before picking their pockets. In the end, however, the two approaches rested on the same base, a balance of power that greatly favoured the ANC. Both also gave fertile grounds for feelings of resentment and betrayal and contributed to the generalized lack of trust that is such a feature of post-apartheid politics. Despite this, Ramaphosa's image makers have promoted him as an astute negotiator and charming hard man, equally capable of facing down troublemakers on his own side as he is of seeing off well-resourced opponents on the other side of the table.

Turning points

A turning point of sorts is reached in the Ramaphosa narrative with Mandela's choice of Mbeki as deputy president in 1994, the latter's election as ANC president in 1997 and Ramaphosa's subsequent defection to a business career. This sequence of events has suggested to some that Ramaphosa does not have the appetite for contests that he cannot win, an impression strengthened by his decision not to run for the presidency of the ANC in 2007. For others, it is merely further proof that Ramaphosa is adept at playing the long game. One aspect of the period that has neither been interrogated nor even explored is why he chose a business career. Speculation that he had been deployed by the ANC as a Trojan Horse of African nationalism in the commanding heights of Capital is as unconvincing as its mirror image, that he was lured by Capital into being their man in the high counsels of the ANC.

What is more interesting is his abandonment of the Left. As a union leader and in his fledgling ANC career, he was strongly identified with the left of the movement and the Alliance. He described himself as a committed socialist and his 1980s rhetoric conformed to the 'smash capitalism' template. He was a close associate of Chris Hani and Joe Slovo and his appointment as ANC chief negotiator, sidelining Mbeki in the process, was a left-wing coup. His election as ANC secretary general in 1991, beating exile veteran Alfred Nzo, was also sponsored by the Left and by the United Democratic Front (UDF), a short-lived high point from which the exiles, orchestrated by Mbeki, wrested back control. Despite this leftist pedigree, when his accession to the top level of government was thwarted, he did not choose to build a credible, mass-based, truly independent left-wing force in or attached to the ANC but to become a businessman. It is hard to believe that the woeful performance of the Left during the Mbeki presidency and especially under Zuma would not have been greatly improved if the leadership talents that Ramaphosa showed in the 1980s had been at the helm of a genuine mass movement, rather than a coalition of ideological hangers on to the ANC with a labour aristocracy increasingly led by the corporate interests of public service unions. Perhaps after the collapse of actually existing communism and the deaths of Hani and Slovo, he could see this scenario emerging and simply felt the odds were too great.

Another aspect of this period that has received little critical attention is Ramaphosa's performance as ANC secretary general (1991–7). It is clear from the reports of his successor Kgalema Motlanthe that the decline of the party organization was a long-term phenomenon that did not start on Motlanthe's watch. This raises the question of whether Ramaphosa was too distracted by his onerous duties as chairperson of the Constitutional Assembly (1994–6) to do the job properly, whether he had little appetite for the chores and the diplomacy of party management anyway or indeed whether the problems of managing the ANC into some kind of rational organizational form in which local and regional leaders conduct themselves with integrity rather than the motivations of factionalism and patronage are beyond the capacities of any mere mortal leader to solve. Some sort of epiphany of this latter sort may have hastened his departure from politics.

Man of wealth

The wealth that Ramaphosa accumulated in his business career can be read in various ways, as either an asset or a liability to the prospects of his second coming as a political leader. South Africa is a society in which both black and white people value material success and many of them, other than diehard opponents of BEE, will see Ramaphosa's success as vindication and celebration of all the black talents that were previously suppressed by racism as can the post-apartheid success of black people in any sphere. No taint of corruption or indeed any kind of irregularity has yet attached itself to how he made his wealth and such riches have a useful by-product as insulation against temptations to corruption in office, although it is doubtful if Ramaphosa will wish to remind people that this claim to wealth-based incorruptibility was one of Donald Trump's main calling cards in his rise to the US presidency. Insofar as Ramaphosa's consumption is conspicuous, it is not vulgar and it is leavened by well-chosen charitable initiatives, including the sponsorship of many young black people in their studies.

None of this means that Ramaphosa has escaped populist disapprobation on the grounds of his wealth. In 2012, he felt constrained to make a public apology for bidding R18 million (some sources say R19.5 million) in an unsuccessful auction attempt to buy a buffalo mother and calf (the successful bid was R20 million). Since his main accuser – of insensitivity to poverty and inequality – was Julius Malema, the affair should be seen in perspective. A short time before, Ramaphosa had been the ANC's chosen disciplinary instrument to orchestrate the expulsion of the former youth league president from the party. Nonetheless, Ramaphosa appears to have learnt from the experience how to spin a more favourable interpretation of his 'great obsession'[20] with livestock, notably the Ankole cattle he discovered in Uganda and imported to South Africa, using ingenious though perfectly legal means to comply with strict importation regulations. Ramaphosa's published account of the breed and of his herd is a narrative and pictorial record, which artfully combines heritage and good works to legitimize his possessions.[21] That is, he loans the animals to emerging black farmers to improve the bloodlines of their stock and explains his love of the cattle in terms of reconnecting with the land and African heritage through explicit reference to his father, the township policeman who never had a chance to acquire his own herd. This is a far cry from Zuma's earthy and rumbustious evocations of 'tradition', but it is clearly aimed at filling a gap in Ramaphosa's profile as an African leader.

Marikana

Potentially more significant and dangerous than blanket denunciations of wealth in the midst of poverty are accusations that he is a sellout and tool of big capital. Such accusations centre on his alleged role in pushing the police towards a violent approach to the Marikana strikers in August 2012. On 17 August 2012, thirty-four miners participating in a wildcat strike, unprotected by labour legislation, at a mine owned by Lonmin on South Africa's North West platinum belt, were shot dead by police, the deaths being evenly divided between two locations. Cyril Ramaphosa was a board member of Lonmin by virtue of his company Shanduka's shareholding in the company. In a three-day period prior to the police shootings (12–14 August), ten people (miners – striking and non-striking – police and mining company security personnel) were killed, seven of them by strikers.[22]

Unsurprisingly, Malema and other members of the Economic Freedom Fighters (EFF) were quick to denounce Ramaphosa as a sellout and cat's paw of ('white') international capital. This time they were joined by more respectable commentators, including Gevisser, who, not without whiff of nostalgia for the 'old' Ramaphosa of the struggle years, as well as a spot of virtue signalling, opined that Ramaphosa's 'unseemly role at Marikana had become an indicator of the extent that he had lost his soul'.[23] At issue was an email sent by Ramaphosa to Lonmin's chief commercial officer on 16 August, the eve of the shootings, and produced at the inquiry. This described the clashes of 12–14 August in the following terms:

> The terrible events that have unfolded cannot be described as a labour dispute. They are plainly dastardly criminal and must be viewed as such … There needs to be concomitant action to address the situation.[24]

However, the commission of inquiry 'rejected the allegation that Mr Ramaphosa had played a role in authorising the massacre'.[25] It did not exonerate him completely, finding him 'not completely innocent in relation to the course of events'. This was on the hypothetical grounds that the situation 'could have been defused' and the strikers would 'likely' have agreed to surrender their weapons, 'had Lonmin not refused to negotiate with them'.[26] This was partly because

> Mr Ramaphosa was one of those who used his influence to discourage the resolution of the dispute through negotiation.[27]

This is a somewhat ironic finding on the behaviour of one whose claim to leadership credentials rests in large part on being the 'great negotiator'. Leaving to one side the confidence with which the commission was prepared to proclaim on counterfactuals ('could have been defused'), why would Ramaphosa take the view expressed in the quoted email? The 'cat's paw' theory is lazy populist pamphleteering and the 'loss of soul' version comes from an equally lazy, superficial and romantic view of crisis – indeed life and death – situations. There is another possible interpretation of Ramaphosa's characterization of the events leading up to his email, one that is much closer to and better grounded in what we know of his character and history up to that point.

The Marikana strike was a wildcat enterprise independent of any union but set against a background of hostility between the NUM and the Association of Mineworkers and Construction Union (AMCU), its upstart rival on the platinum belt for membership, bargaining rights, prestige and commercial opportunities. The NUM was in large measure Ramaphosa's creation and so was the institutional framework of industrial relations and worker rights that the NUM and the wider labour movement had sacrificed much to achieve. In their violent clashes with NUM officials, in particular, the Marikana strikers represented the atavistic ungovernability that Ramaphosa had to manage as he was building the NUM and it was all the more unacceptable now because it was being unleashed in what amounted to a rejection of the labour relations framework and wider democratic dispensation to which Ramaphosa had contributed so much. Ramaphosa may have had to manage and tolerate – and on occasions even exploit – such phenomena as the murder of non-striking miners in a wider struggle against violent racist repression. It would not be surprising if he completely rejected them as 'criminal' under the greatly altered political circumstances of 2012 and with the limited second- and third-hand information he had at his disposal when he sent the email using this designation.

It is also worth recalling that Ramaphosa had several times been the chosen instrument of the respectable ANC establishment in disciplining or rebuking such badly behaved populist outliers as Winnie Madikizela Mandela, Peter Mokaba and Julius Malema. The respectable and rule-bound side of Ramaphosa is apparent throughout his career and can easily be linked to family and religious influences in his early years. It is not hard to believe that the Marikana strikers would outrage this part of him and contribute to the characterization of them that he later regretted.

Marikana, like all chaotic sequences of events that erupt in violence and loss of life, thereby acquiring tragic symbolism, will continue to be a reservoir of division and blame. This quality, as well as the perennial elusiveness of truth about confused events, is illustrated by David Bruce's exhaustive micro hypothesizing around who on the strikers' side did what, to whom and when in the violent events of 12–14 August described as 'criminal' by Ramaphosa.[28] While protesting on several occasions that he does not intend, 'to underestimate the seriousness of the violence that some of the strikers engaged in after 11 August',[29] he finds, unsurprisingly, that things may have been a bit more complicated than Ramaphosa thought in real time or the investigating commission concluded later. That is as may be, since uncertainty can always be found in confusion. However, a scattering of question marks, their own motivation and evidential bases open to challenge, is not the same as an indictment and although Marikana will always be available for exploitation by determined opponents of Ramaphosa, it is a reasonable wager that there is a numerous constituency of the respectable among the wider electorate and in the ranks of the ANC who quietly share his views on strikers who arm themselves with deadly weapons for the purpose of intimidation and are unimpressed with ex post facto claims that they were armed primarily for self-defence.

Interrogating the image

Thus, we have Ramaphosa at the point of his assumption of the presidency: the enigmatic negotiator who pragmatically plays the long game; the wealthy man who understands both business and labour from first hand and is insulated from the temptations of corruption by his riches; and, it might be added, the unambiguous modernizer, midwife and defender of the Constitution, truly rooted in urban South Africa and unimpressed by the atavisms of tribe, tradition and ethnicity by virtue, among other things, of 'membership'[30] of a language group – the Venda people – that constitutes only 2.2 per cent of the South African population. Of these components, the ones that invite further interrogation are the enigma, the pragmatist, the negotiator and the player of the long game.

The enigma and the pragmatist

There may be more than one reason for labelling a political leader as an enigma. It might be a half-conscious complicity on the part of the commentator or chronicler in contributing to the mystique of the leader. Something of the sort was likely going on during and immediately after Mbeki's ascent to the presidency when the ANC as a whole was untried, unknown and even to a large extent unformed. It might also be part of South Africans' undue cultural restraint when it comes to pushing leaders hard, according them too much safe space and too much respect for their privacy and thus drying up the material for more penetrating insight than 'enigma'. South Africa's relatively free press, despite recent newsroom attrition typical of all Western democracies, rates highly for investigative journalism, quite highly for analytical comment, but very low when it comes to the ability to interrogate leaders directly. The 'enigma' phenomenon might simply be a tacit admission of failure to pin a leader down in the face of insufficient evidence and a lack of cooperation from the individual concerned.

In the case of Ramaphosa, his insistence on privacy and non-cooperation has been an essential part of his personal myth. He seems to enjoy the idea of being enigmatic, perhaps even to relish using it as a boyish provocation.[31] As a result, his evasiveness leaves its imprint on his chroniclers, leaving them to rely on pithy but elusive characterizations such as 'visionary pragmatist'[32] or to resort to playing hopefully with paradox. For example, according to his most recent biographer, Ramaphosa is

> charming and reserved. He defers to authority and yet he projects authority. He is driven to navigate the country's destiny and yet at times appears helplessly afloat on the tide.[33]

What to make of this is anyone's guess, but it is still possible to feel sympathy for the biographer who is driven to such expedients by the thin materials on offer and his subject's tightfistedness with them.

However, there are real problems with the 'enigma' label. Elusiveness can easily make the subtle shift to evasiveness; as a result, being an enigma is not a solid basis for leadership. It may be a legitimate part of a distancing mystique to give a leader a little breathing space, but only a small dose is tolerable in an open democracy. It is harder to hold an enigma accountable. Mbeki could get away with it, partly for the reasons suggested above and partly because, during his rise to power and for the first part of his exercise of it, the real politics of the ANC took place behind closed doors and the rest of the country didn't matter. But even Mbeki could only sustain the mystique for a relatively short time. The political culture of the ANC has been in transition from Leninist secrecy to celebrity chasing throughout the Mbeki and Zuma years, and it currently displays some of the pathologies of each. One of the challenges Ramaphosa faces is to establish a stable base for his own and his party's engagement with the media and wider society that avoids these excesses.

Another component of Ramaphosa's personal myth might also nudge in the direction of evasiveness; several of those who have sought to pin him down lay great emphasis on the quality of 'pragmatism'. For instance, for Butler he is a 'visionary pragmatist' and for Sparks he is a 'tough pragmatist'. Of course, it is not a bad thing for a leader to be a pragmatist, providing that is not all he or she is, in a country that needs unifying inspiration. That Ramaphosa could make the seamless transition from committed socialist to empowerment billionaire without in any way nailing his ideological colours to the mast suggests that under his reserved pragmatism there may be a flexibility that could prove useful in communicating with South Africa's increasingly diverse interests and classes. So far so good; but in the country's seething political culture, a sense of betrayal is one of the most readily available reflexes and such flexibility can easily come to be seen as downright shifty and proof of potential for betrayal.

The great negotiator

It is important to remember that most of the material drawn on by commentators for their assessments of Ramaphosa on his accession to governing power – especially in relation to his reputation as a negotiator – dates from more than thirty years ago in the case of his leadership of the NUM and more than twenty years ago in the case of the transitional and constitutional negotiations. In both cases, the conditions under which he acted in leadership roles are very different now. In both, he enjoyed the advantages of asymmetrical power including the moral high ground and the popular backing of a rightless but numerically overwhelming majority against state power wielded by a minority whose own support base was fragmenting and which was the object of pressures that were global as well as local.

Today, he is no longer the remorseless gadfly who tormented Tertius Delport (the NP's chief negotiator until ill health forced him to withdraw) and was able to use his moral advantage to put Roelf Meyer who succeeded Delport in his place. Now he is the statesman at whose desk the buck stops and he has gadflies of his own (Julius Malema for one) to deal with. Today, Ramaphosa may temporarily hold the moral high ground but from these heights he is looking down on his own party, not on a discredited party of racial nationalists, which was en route to the dustbin of history. Today, it is his own party that is discredited and without moral advantage. It remains to be seen whether or not his skills are transferable to these different historical circumstances. Furthermore, in the case of the transitional negotiations, he was performing a highly specific and specialized task, which is part though not the whole of leadership. While he took the lead role at that time, he was not even strictly speaking a leader, or at least not *the* leader, but under the leadership and in the giant, benign shadow of Mandela, while at the same time being part of a collective leadership of much more substantial figures than the ANC (and the country) can call on today.

It is hardly surprising that South Africans typically elevate negotiating skills above all other arts of political leadership; after all, the founding myth of the country is based on negotiation and this is one of the few things that nearly all South Africans can agree on as a source of national pride. An alleged national talent for negotiation is the essential ingredient in South Africa's regional and global projection of soft power and of the country's self-image. In the first few post-apartheid years, Ramaphosa and Meyer were invited as a celebrity double act to other conflict-ridden countries to share their experience and expertise. However, it is worth noting that negotiation is only one of a large range of leadership competencies; after all, both Mbeki (in and out of power) and Zuma based their claims to leadership in large measure on their skills as negotiators. This is not unreasonable since both had considerable success in negotiations in their own country, albeit in this respect, like Ramaphosa they held strong hands. They were also frequently in demand for negotiations in and between other countries, though their track record is patchy and Zimbabwe is a terrible blot on Mbeki's record. The key point is, however, that both so signally lacked other important leadership competencies that they serve as a warning not to overprivilege negotiating skills in any assessment of leadership.

The long game

Eleven years ago, shortly before the ANC national conference that first elected Zuma as president of the movement, Ramaphosa's biographer wrote,

> Ramaphosa is a natural politician who gravitates towards and embraces power. It would not be a surprise to find out that at last his time has come.[34]

It was not to be in 2007 and it took more than another decade for his time to arrive, albeit by a whisker. The well-worn saying, 'A week is a long time in politics' (commonly attributed to British prime minister of the 1960s, Harold

Wilson) may be a bit overdone, in more than one sense. But there is no doubt that ten years is a *very* long time in politics, even for one who is credited as a player of the long game. We have already noted, in the context of the 1987 mining strike, that a reputation as a patient strategist can be a useful asset in compensating for major frustrations, setbacks and even failures. To a degree, the 'long game' image played that comforting role right across the anti-apartheid struggle because it could always be argued that the struggle was on the right side of history no matter how long it took. Contemporary conditions are less forgiving. Events are remorseless: the long game isn't much use in dealing with, say, a global financial crisis (though in fairness it can be useful in averting or preparing for one); demands on governments and leaders are clamorous, immediate and often contradictory; there isn't a single moral imperative such as resistance to apartheid to concentrate and focus the long-term goal, nor is there an obvious obstacle such as the apartheid state's intransigence and military power to justify any delays and setbacks.

The long game motif served the Ramaphosa myth well in the aftermath of the 1987 strike and when Mandela passed him over for the deputy state presidency in 1994, when he declined to contest the ANC deputy presidency in 1997 and again in 2007. It is true that there were murmurings that he had no appetite for contests in which he was not guaranteed success, but these were largely drowned out by the long game orthodoxy, in the mainstream media at least (misgivings may have had more resonance inside the ANC itself). This orthodoxy was set to promote him again in 2012 when he did come forward to stand for the ANC deputy presidency and was successful, leading to the curious case of the vanishing prime minister.

The vanishing prime minister

Some influential commentators interpreted Ramaphosa's candidacy in 2012 as part of a long-term, strategic master plan, including but not confined to the candidate himself. In this interpretation, certain senior ANC figures acknowledged that a second Zuma administration was impossible to prevent but believed that it was possible to contain him and limit the damage his presidency would do. As one such commentator wrote before the conference and election, it would be better for the ANC

> to stick with the ineffectual devil the ANC knows and surround him with handlers, policy wonks and fiscal conservatives. Given his age and hands-off style, Zuma might even be persuaded to perform an increasingly ceremonial role from his attractive new residence in Nkandla.[35]

This, it might be noticed, was before Zuma's image had evolved from that of hands-off and ineffectual entertainer to evil genius. Central to the alleged strategy of containment was Ramaphosa's elevation to the deputy presidencies of the ANC and the state. Some weeks later, when he was duly elected to the first of these offices, the plan appeared to be confirmed. On the day of the ANC poll, two of South Africa's best informed and respected political reporters published a piece, carrying copious direct quotes from ANC secretary general Gwede Mantashe, stating that that Ramaphosa would be South Africa's 'de facto prime minister', a presumably conscious reference to the way in which Mbeki's role as deputy state president to Mandela (1994–9) was habitually labelled. He would be an 'assertive' leader of government business, 'charged with keeping watch over cabinet ministers' accountability to parliament' and with supervising their work.[36] However, on the same day, Mantashe, who was a general secretary of the NUM (1998–2006), and believed by some to be an ally and even former protégé of Ramaphosa,[37] was quoted in another paper as flatly denying any such role for Ramaphosa.[38] Kgalema Motlanthe remained deputy state president until the 2014 general election.

It is possible that the whole idea of a plan to contain Zuma involving Ramaphosa was a figment of journalists' wishful thinking, undeserving of resurrection now from the obscurity into which it has sunk. However, the degree of confidence with which well-respected journalists directly quoted Mantashe and the hasty brevity with which he brushed aside the 'prime minister' idea suggest otherwise. The other possibility is that there was such a plan and it badly misfired to the extent that Ramaphosa was left playing a long game to Zuma's rules. Strictly speaking, they were Mbeki's rules, for it was he who stripped the vice president's office of many of its functions and resources in order to deny Zuma a power base. It would not be surprising if Zuma, who had to endure years of frustrating underemployment on the margins as vice president, would know how to turn the tables on any putative strategy to keep him in check. Indeed, Zuma is likely to have indulged in his trademark chuckles at the irony. Whatever the case, if anyone was kept in check it was Ramaphosa and it was after 2012 that Zuma's construction of the shadow state accelerated and diversified, leaving Ramaphosa impotent or in the dark.

After the 2014 general election, Ramaphosa became deputy state president. Once again the long game motif was dusted off, though it was wearing thin, even for Ramaphosa's admirers, as doubts grew about the 'insider game'[39] he was playing under Zuma:

> How could he keep singing the praises of his venal boss? Was he still playing the long game, or had he succumbed? Was he so intent on

attaining power at any cost that he would not take a stand against the naked abuse of power that was happening under his watch? He was the deputy president, after all.[40]

Such questions can be addressed from an institutional and circumstantial perspective rather than one that relies solely on speculative insights into the psychology of motivation. Looked at in this way, the long game can be justified on the grounds that Ramaphosa had to wait for a critical mass of sources of influence in the ANC – for instance, MPs, functionaries and local power brokers – to be ready to break ranks with Zuma, before he could switch from a war of position to a war of manoeuvre, that is from hidden to open conflict for influence and power. However, this may tip the balance between functionalist and intentionalist explanations of leadership choices too far towards the former. Understanding leadership involves understanding how given individuals engage with structural and contextual conditions. Key questions in this instance include, what *kind* of long game was Ramaphosa playing? A passive waiting game until the tide turned and the political weather changed of its own accord? Or was it a long march through the ANC labyrinth engaging in a day-to-day struggle to change hearts and minds by persuasion and example? That Ramaphosa was vulnerable to being fired as state vice president by Zuma, and thus losing his prestigious inside track, may explain his apparent passivity. Moreover, the ANC's collective obsession with unity would make long-game mobilization difficult. The verdict on Ramaphosa's 'insider game' by his most recent biographer is as follows:

> He has spent many years playing the game of accommodation and refusing to define his politics to the public other than at the broad symbolic level of anti-apartheid, pro-transformation.[41]

This suggests that caution in the face of the ANC's sheer inertial weight and of its sprawling tangle of interests, networks and loyalties might answer the various questions about Ramaphosa's long game, which are posed above by Gevisser.

Assessing the image

Any assessment of the portfolio of qualities Ramaphosa brought to the presidency has to take into account the fact that there is no other executive position quite like it, and track records gained in other leadership roles are only of temporary relevance until a presidential one can be established. As a result any evaluation, especially one that is written in the first year of his incumbency, should err on the side of caution. However, a workable interim verdict might be that these qualities have made a good combination to propel him to the presidency and conceivably to keep him there. Nevertheless, there are enough qualifications and uncertainties to ask legitimately whether they are sufficient for him to do anything more with it than keep things on an even keel, given the formidable challenges he faces both in his own party and wider society.

A new dawn?

It is a new dawn that is inspired by our collective memory of Nelson Mandela and the changes that are unfolding.[42]
—Cyril Ramaphosa, *State of the Nation Speech*, February 2018

Whatever the provenance and validity of the information we possess about a debutant president, what we know or think we know about the individual is only part of the story because all political leadership takes place in engagement with its context. It is hardly surprising that Cyril Ramaphosa should have declared a new dawn in his maiden state-of-the-nation speech, but more important than his predictable resort to cliché is whether or not the dawn, which after all rises every day, is rising on an altered landscape. It is always tempting to believe, after the kind of upheavals that despatched first Mbeki and Zuma, that it has.

Indeed, we have been here before. It is worth revisiting the words of Tony Leon on Mbeki's departure from office, which we have already noted above. Leon confidently predicted that a new order had dawned:

With Mbeki gone, the ANC cadres and MPs are unlikely to go back to their meek ways. The media and judiciary have also flexed their muscles after a fairly lengthy slumber during the Mbeki presidency. This is likely to continue and our democracy will be the better for it.[43]

He went on to say that politics had changed, that the arrogant assumptions of the past had been challenged and that the uncertainty of the moment would usher in a far less predictable future. Politics did indeed change but not in the way Leon predicted; or at least it did not until eight years of crony depredations, irrational policymaking and flirtation with economic ruin woke a bare majority of 'ANC cadres and MPs' to the danger. It is not that the ANC's generals and foot soldiers were 'meek' during the Zuma years; on the contrary, a good majority of them were impassioned in their defence of Zuma until close to the end. The only ones who were not were his *previously* impassioned supporters, the outcast rebels Malema and Vavi, who had performed the fastest handbrake turn in South African political history. This would be worth the label 'ironic' if South African politics did not exist in a dimension beyond irony. Other than the noises off provided by Malema and Vavi, we have to take it on trust that there were silent players of the long game for whom some things at least were changed.

That someone like Leon, who was well informed as well as hardened by the daily experience of confronting an arrogant and triumphalist ANC in parliament and the public sphere,[44] could misread the situation so badly is testimony not only to the forgivable difficulties of reading South African political dynamics but also to the cultural disposition of many South Africans to hope for the best and welcome new beginnings whatever the evidence. However, such misconceptions do not justify the belief that nothing changed at all through the Mbeki and Zuma years. On the contrary, much has changed and in assessing the landscape that Ramaphosa has inherited as his theatre of leadership it is necessary to restate and revisit some of this book's earlier treatment of the changing context of South African politics.

Economic and social change

Change has occurred through the attrition of time and the passing of generations. This has combined with social and economic movement, some of it engineered by the effects, both intended and unintended, of policy and some of it arising, it may reasonably be surmised, out of less tangible sources such as the greater self-confidence and assertiveness, as well as expanding and diversifying expectations and interests, that for black people are among the dividends of the end of apartheid.

Affirmative action, BEE and the bargaining power of organized labour (especially in the public sector) have affected the size and shape of the black middle class. It has shown impressive growth (though this is eternally disputed between optimists and pessimists), but its existential basis remains precarious for reasons such as indebtedness, high family dependence ratios and job insecurity, which affect many of its members. In addition, the undeniable growth of the black middle class is confronted not only by the persistence of high levels of interracial inequality but also by rapidly rising levels of inequality among black people. Unsurprisingly, the ANC chooses to foreground racial inequality, but the latter development – given that African people account for 80.9 per cent of the population – is too important to be as downplayed as it has been.

Destabilizing economic forces have operated in the background of these developments. These include urbanization, deindustrialization, declining employment in primary industries such as mining and agriculture, the rise of the service sector and the underdevelopment of South Africa's informal sector by comparison with many developing countries. The expansion of tertiary education has greatly expanded the possibilities of social mobility for relatively small numbers of black people and the failures of basic education have set narrow limits to the advancement of the majority of them.

These changes can be encapsulated with reference to a cleavage between 'insiders' and 'outsiders', which is evident particularly but not exclusively in the condition of young people. Insiders are characterized by education and social capital, whether gained through legacy effects favouring whites or from political and new middle-class networks reflecting post-apartheid black advancement. Outsiders, virtually exclusively black, are marked by poor education, high unemployment rates (particularly among young people), exclusion from the formal economy, dependence on state benefits and family support, poverty and vulnerability to illness, HIV/AIDS in particular, and interpersonal violence (again especially the young).

One general effect of this has been the increasing practical irrelevance of traditional overarching definitions of class and even to some extent of race and ethnicity. Despite this, the traditional vocabulary continues to supply labels and rallying cries, especially on the Left. In practical terms, a diffuse anti-elitism, which confusingly combines class, race, generation and a rural–urban divide, better expresses the tensions in society and the spirit of the day than classic rhetoric of race and class. But while this new discourse bubbles below the surface, animating new identities, demands and expressions of interest, too much is invested in the old vocabulary for a new language of politics to take over. The political effects that are woven together with these economic and social changes in complex relationships of cause and effect have been profound but are hard to express cogently in practical politics.

Political change

By the end of the Zuma years, the ANC could no longer believe it was the self-assured, self-enclosed, self-correcting, self-sustaining system that enjoyed hegemonic legitimacy, automatic deference and entitlement to electoral majorities at or near to two-thirds of votes cast. Inside it, the exile generation that had dominated the movement and branded it with its conspiratorial, often paranoid tone as well as its vanguardist pretensions and its one-partyism, had devoured itself in the conflict between Mbeki and Zuma and was exhausted, dying both literally and figuratively. The exile (and prisoner) generation was in any case self-limiting: these experiences could not be replicated in a democracy and new generations could not be socialized into it. In retrospect, exile dominance was a dead end, dying from the beginning. Yet for two decades – in common with liberation movements throughout Southern Africa – its exponents and beneficiaries behaved as if it would live and rule forever. It is true that an ad hoc group of ANC veterans, many of them former exiles and prisoners, was belatedly active in opposing Zuma but it is hard to believe its influence was decisive. In fact, the veterans looked like a group of bewildered elderly people contemplating the ruin of the moral universe that had sustained them but whose foundations they had never taken the trouble to interrogate or had the political courage to defend until there was a chance that Zuma's days were numbered. That many of them were rightly celebrated for fighting apartheid with great physical courage and sacrifice was neither here nor there: it takes a special kind of political courage to confront your own side rather than a universally loathed external and racially defined other, and for the most part they simply did not have the appetite for such moral leadership until it was too late to locate the ANC's missing soul.

The foundation myths of the ANC were dying along with the generation that fostered them. The lazy assumption that the ANC would always be the unified revolutionary vanguard of a homogeneous, allegiant and deferential African people still drifts like ritual incense above conferences and other devotional exercises (especially and appropriately funerals), but it has drifted far from a contemporary political reality in which it has to accommodate the different interests of insiders and outsiders, old and young, educated and less educated, traditional and modern, metropolitan and provincial, urban and rural. It is important to remember, however, that all these identities and interests are fluid rather than fixed, which complicates all political readings of their significance: the young are divided between insiders and outsiders; the cities are home to many poor people; circular migration between rural and urban areas blurs lines of identity and traditional values can coexist in complex ways with modern aspirations.

As the ANC has declined into incoherence, the props on which it relied to bolster its legitimacy have become increasingly unsteady.

The founding myth of the inclusive citizen nation has scarcely survived Mbeki's single-minded and spiteful attack on 'rainbowism', although arguably it would have had a limited shelf life even without him. No settled articulation has been found for an Africanist narrative nor yet an answer for the perennial question of whether the African nation is subsumed in the citizen nation or stands above and superior to it. This is not surprising since the question is unanswerable. For all its poetry and continental architecture, Mbeki's Africanism was largely irrelevant (and even incomprehensible) at grass-roots level. Zuma's Africanism was a loose, at times seemingly random, collection of cultural tropes and glosses on folk wisdom, shading as time went on into essentialist generalizations about what 'races' believed, that were borderline racist themselves.

For the ANC, the state was the focal point for achieving growth and transformation and thereby progressive realization of the Constitution's promises. Instead, it was enfeebled by the disastrous intent to fuse party and state under Mbeki. As if that were not enough, it was brought close to ruin by Zuma's capture of the criminal justice system and his assault, cheered on until the last moment by the majority of his party, on the only parts of the state apparatus – principally the Treasury, the Reserve Bank and the South African Revenue Service – that had managed to combine racial transformation of its personnel with capability, merit, corporate integrity and commitment to the national interest.

If the state was at the apex of the ANC's grand plan, it was to be supported by corporatist interests and institutions. Central to these was organized labour, by now a much-diminished political force, at least as measured by the old rules of politics. Cosatu has been debauched by its subordinate association with Zuma's ANC. It is riven by defections and bitter conflicts in the mining industry (formerly, its key area of organization) with upstart competitors. These conflicts have been fuelled by Cosatu's role as a conveyer belt of its leaders to government and quasi-governmental posts and the growth of its own comfortable managerial class, both of which have had their own debilitating effects. Much the same can be said of the SACP, yet in spite or because of these weaknesses, both principal components of the Left remain hesitant to take independent leadership of a left alternative, despite tactical feints in this direction in the late Zuma years. The fear of an adverse, even humiliating verdict from the electorate remains too great. The Left has not been helped by the difficulties of constructing a compelling narrative of class in an economy with between 30 and 40 per cent unemployment by the expanded definition and where the black middle class defies easy definition of its contours and analysis of how its members see their interests.

The various corporatist institutions that have made up the government-labour-business Golden Triangle have not worn well. Whether viewed from a left or a centre-right perspective, statutory bodies such as Nedlac and informal practices meant to support them, such as job summits, have done much to delay and dilute reform, forcing policy into the lowest common denominator of what business and labour will accept and undervaluing the needs and interests of society's and the economy's outsiders. This has contributed to a growing tendency to portray the state of South Africa today as the product of elite pacting and to discredit this model of politics, which saw the country through the crisis of the early 1990s but has proved inadequate since. The prevailing atmosphere of anti-elitism owes much to this aura of discredit.

The campaign against Zuma breathed fresh life into opposition political parties but strategic and tactical dilemmas that were obscured by what in effect became a crusade to save democracy have re-emerged in the aftermath of Ramaphosa's assumption of the leadership of the ANC and the presidency. Because the ANC for all its faults so closely represents the broad aspirations of so many African people, opposition parties are forced into the roles of shadowing and outflanking it. The EFF with its populist and raucous street theatre (literally) performs this double act of shadowing and outflanking from the standpoint of a more radical and openly racial nationalism. The DA promises a cleaner, more efficient, economically sustainable and constitutionally proper version of what the ANC itself offers, growth and shared prosperity. Critics of the DA (some of them internal) deride this as 'ANC-lite'. This pithy characterization may be a little unfair, but there is no doubt that to some extent at least the imperative of attracting a larger share of the African electorate pushes the DA towards the implicit position that the main problem is not so much the ANC's policies but that the wrong people are applying them. Shadowing and outflanking may have been the most rational responses to a period of ANC electoral hegemony, but they leave both parties vulnerable to changes in leadership and direction in their principal antagonist and uncertainty over whether that hegemony has gone forever or such changes can restore it.

The anti-Zuma movement also energized civil society, enabling it to emerge strengthened from the contempt which Mbeki's ANC poured on it and from his efforts to co-opt, discredit and disarm it. Suspicion of civil society still runs deep in the ANC for reasons of crude majoritarianism and race-based suspicion of conspiracies, but the utility of a vigorous civil society and independent media was sufficiently clear during Zuma's tenure for them to have gained respect, in parts of the ANC at least.

However, the organizations that make up civil society are divided between those that prioritize the realization of the Constitution's promises of social rights, in fields such as education, health and housing, and those whose priorities include property rights, non-discrimination (in contexts such as affirmative action and BEE), combating the abuse of executive power and the integrity of the rule of law. Of course, independence and diversity are good things in themselves for democracy, and in any case the two approaches are not necessarily antagonistic; they can be broadly in alignment, as in the peak and late Zuma years. However, neither individually nor collectively, can they offer a compelling and overarching narrative, given their sometimes diverging points of departure. For both of them, recourse to the courts has been an essential weapon and the integrity of the judiciary has stood up very well. But this is only a supplementary weapon to restore democratic government, not a sustainable basis for its permanent exercise. At its simplest, civil society cannot provide answers to the crucial questions of economic management and development on which the future of democracy and the Constitution rest.

As a result of these changes, South African politics takes place in a populous and clamorous landscape composed of the following: ANC fiefdoms and factions, supplemented by a much attenuated Alliance and other associates such as traditional leaders; opposition parties that thanks to Zuma have been able to 'punch above' their electoral weight; well-organized single issue and constitutional defence organizations; a spontaneous protest culture aimed at failures of government service delivery; an assertive youth-driven populism motivated first by 'colonial' issues in higher education ('Rhodes must fall'), developing into the campaign for 'free' higher education ('fees must fall'); and an ill-defined populist racial nationalism centred on the land issue, which overlaps party boundaries between the EFF and ANC and is used as a lever in intra-ANC struggles.

Fixed categories of class, ethnicity and even race retain leverage in popular mobilization but as flexible labels of convenience rather than stable analysis. They are increasingly challenged by a persuasive but elusive anti-elitism, which has no particular political home but stokes resentments across the board. It is difficult to tell which of these manifestations of interest, sentiment and identity will have staying power and evolve organizationally. It is clear, however, what is missing. The first thing is an unquestioned narrative such as the ANC fostered to its profit from the final years of the struggle until the dawn of peak Zuma. It is possible still to believe with the late Martin Luther King that 'the arc of the moral universe is long but it bends towards justice' in South Africa, but after Zuma it is harder to believe in the ANC as the chosen and only possible agency to tilt the direction of human affairs in that direction. The declining purchase of teleology goes with the increasing encroachment of retail or transactional politics onto the territory of heroic politics. That is, it is increasingly difficult to justify programmes and platforms in global terms of social justice such as 'transformation' and 'empowerment' or especially 'national democratic revolution', when voters in an increasingly diverse electorate begin to think in terms of costs and benefits for themselves and performance criteria for the government. The politics of taxation under conditions of threatened fiscal crisis is an obvious case in point.

What have also been missing from South African party and electoral politics are the informal norms, the unspoken rules and conventions that support a formal constitution and hold a democracy together. The erosion of such norms, or in the case of South Africa their failure to develop, is labelled in a recent study as 'the greatest threat to contemporary democracy'.[45] The threat comes from rulers who 'pay lip service to the constitution while behaving as though it did not exist'.[46] They:

> deride their opponents as criminals, show contempt for their critics in the media, stoke conspiracy theories about opposition movements and question the legitimacy of any vote that goes against them.[47]

This characterization of global trends is all too familiar in a South African setting. In their own different ways, Mbeki and Zuma led the ANC in this way, with the added twist that they were as, if not more, likely to treat their own internal critics and competitors in this way as to do so to their opposition and civil society antagonists. The overall effect was to contribute to the lack of coherence and consistency of political processes.

An ordering moment?

The upshot of all this is that South African politics is much more diverse and much less predictable than it was in the Mbeki and early Zuma years. It is understandable that some people find this development exciting and empowering because a wider range of voices and interests have made space for themselves. It is equally understandable that others find the loss of coherence bewildering and even threatening. The important question, however, is whether or not the present conjuncture amounts to 'an ordering moment', what its implications are for leadership in South African politics generally and for Cyril Ramaphosa in particular.

'Ordering moment' is a coinage borrowed from international relations theory:

> Such a moment may be defined as a crucial but limited time period when previous authorities, identities, norms, and structures lose their dominance and multiple new paths to the future become feasible.[48]

A case can be made for viewing the sum of changes to South Africa's society and political system, culminating in the rise and fall of Zuma and Zuma-ism, as an ordering moment. However, at this stage it is at best a description of an opportunity, not of an event, raising questions as to who sees matters in these terms, who has the motivation and capacity to act on them and whether there is enough resilience in the old political power structures, forms of organization and cultural assumptions to adapt to, stall or stave off new possibilities.

It is not difficult to identify changes to the culture of governance that could constructively capitalize on the post-Zuma conjuncture and help bring coherence to political processes. A good start would be an end to the culture of impunity that is associated with his years in office. This would mean building accountability into government so that it does not have to be extorted by the courts after exhausting struggles. This in turn means not only a principled leadership that takes the Constitution seriously and a more vigorous oversight role for parliament but also acceptance of the kind of engagement with critical media that has been completely lacking. It would also help to treat opposition, whether from rival parties, media or civil society, as legitimate democratic expressions rather than conspiracies in league with foreign powers. Acceptance that transactional politics is here to stay before it is forced on government might also be salutary. That is, increasing numbers of voters will calculate whether or not they will be better off as the result of a given policy rather than feel they are part of a heroic struggle to inch forward the National Democratic Revolution. Engagement on these terms with the whole country in order to articulate, explain and defend policies, especially those that demand some kind of trade-off by imposing costs in the national interest on some or even all of the electorate and the interests into which it is grouped, would be a lot more honest than trading in myths about the ANC's soul and revolutionary mission, around which the ever-present spectre of betrayal hovers, ready to descend at any time on individual and corporate leadership. Rebuilding the state will require more than a purge of Zuma's worst placemen and women, also perhaps revisiting presidential powers of appointment and certainly an end to cadre deployment, which has been the essential camouflage for patronage, cronyism, factionalism and executive abuse of power. The realization has been very slow to dawn that cadre deployment has not only corrupted the state but has also been one of the principal agencies of corruption, decay and dissolution in the ANC itself.

These changes are all desirable – some would say essential – but although they are to some extent interdependent, they are effectively discrete and amount to essential running repairs rather than a paradigm shift. What stands in the way of a substantial reordering of the drifting elements of South

Africa's political landscape is the waning but still potent assumption of the necessity for ANC monopolism. This in turn rests on two myths. The first is that the identification between the ANC and the whole African people is so close and so enduring that there is no viable political home for African people outside it. The second and somewhat contradictory premise is that South Africa's social fabric is so fragile and riven by real and threatened divisions – racial, class, regional, tribal – that only in a single political home can they be safely managed. As we have already noted, this latter belief extends beyond the obviously self-interested ambit of the ANC to analysts and observers that have no obvious connection to the party. What it amounts to is a lack of faith in democracy under the shadow of South Africa's history and distorted social conditions to produce good outcomes without modulated one-partyism, managing through corporatism, elite pacting and alliance politics. There is also the fear, prevalent especially on the Left, that the electorate simply cannot be trusted to deliver a good verdict.

This has meant corralling as many significant interests as possible within the ANC's orbit and managing them as satellites while demonizing all those that resist incorporation or are deemed inassimilable. Even if these terms of engagement are accepted as valid, a political framework of this sort bears costs. It means that the only hope of coherence is hegemony; so far this has been secured either by authoritarian party management (Mbeki) or slavish support of a dubious leader in the interests of party 'unity' (Zuma). The ANC has tested both models of leadership to destruction. It also means that putatively significant political forces – organized labour and the SACP foremost among them – have not been forced to identify what they stand for clearly enough and have their actual strength measured. Instead, they have chosen the shortcut of behind-the-scenes influence peddling at the expense of having to perform undignified contortions of alignment with policies and leaders that they find hard to defend. This is not good for democratic openness and accountability; neither does it enhance the credibility of those involved in such 'partnerships'. Last, because the ANC occupies so much political space, possibilities for constructive and rational cooperation are closed off. It is ludicrous that insofar as political coalitions exist in South Africa, the significant players are the EFF and the DA, who are farcically incompatible bedfellows, when each has clearer affinities with parts of the ANC labyrinth. All of these things have contributed to disillusionment with and alienation from political classes and political processes generally.

Under the leadership of Mbeki and Zuma, the weaknesses of political relationships in the ANC and across the political system have been exposed. However, it is one thing to point this out and quite another to prescribe how these relationships might be recalibrated. Much ink has been spilled and much air heated by speculation about political realignment over the last decade or so. This has been at best premature, at worst blue-sky, wishful thinking and in general a waste of time. The truth is that universally this sort of realignment is one of the most difficult things to do in politics. It rarely, if ever, succeeds by strategic choice and force of will, although it might be imposed by circumstances. South Africa is no exception to this general rule of politics and it is naive to expect any political organization like the ANC to dissolve itself or indulge in self-inflicted asset stripping. Too much has accumulated in the way of careerism, patronage, expectations of entitlement and shared mythology for anything but clinging to the wreckage of the status quo, no matter how irrational an option.

None of this will be much help to Ramaphosa as he faces the daunting challenges of the long march to cleanse and restore his party, give it organizational and ideological coherence, rebuild the state and make a bid for himself and his party to give leadership to the whole country. These tasks will be much more difficult if he has to address them from a base that has to house and express every identity, interest and shade of opinion found in the African majority of the population, while professing a special relationship with every one of them and at the same time claiming to be ruling in the interests of all South Africans. Handicapped in this way, he could face continued draining of support for the ANC, exacerbated by escalating, popular anti-elitism and alienation from political classes as well as an attritional struggle with legacy and new patronage networks. These in turn will be vulnerable to ongoing exposure by energized, investigative journalism and emboldened whistle-blowers who can capitalize on the shrinking possibilities of concealment in a digital world.

Into the future looking backwards

If the past is another country, as it is often said, then it is one in which many South Africans feel more at home than in the present, never mind the future. As a result, in South African politics there is a tendency to confuse the rays of yesterday's sunset with the glow of a new dawn. Both the moral certainties of the anti-apartheid struggle and the spirit of compromise that delivered the Constitution are oversimplifications, but they bring relief and comfort from the complexities and contradictions that have emerged since 1994 and which have been summarized above. Cyril Ramaphosa is of all people other than Mandela himself the figure who symbolizes the transition away from apartheid and for the first time ever he brings to the highest level of leadership the democratic spirit of the 'inzile' struggle. Not only is he the most substantial survivor of this golden age (though still relatively young in political leadership terms at sixty-five), but he is also untainted by the Mbeki years and by Zuma's first administration as well as being credited with playing the long game during his second.

For these reasons, he represents, in some eyes at least, hopes of a return to an era of optimism and the values that underpinned it: national rather than sectarian leadership; negotiation; pacting; reconciliation; modernization; and urban, cosmopolitan values that are shared across shades of political difference. How much of this can be taken on trust about a man who, as we have seen, shuns self-revelation and enjoys being an enigma is an uncertainty worth noting. However, viewed objectively, his career suggests that such hopes are not wholly misplaced. On the other hand, the problem may not be the man but the changed context and, for that matter, which version of the past is on offer.

One signpost to the past points in the direction of a revived culture of negotiation. A recurrent complaint about the transition period and the years that followed is that there has been no 'economic Codesa' to reorder the economy in the way that the polity was grounded in the constitutional negotiations. Over the last decade or more, such a return to the culture of negotiation has been commended by a wide range of voices as the way to deal with intractable problems of poverty, inequality and unemployment, all in the context of apartheid's legacy.[49] Indeed, outside the major political parties it has been the most frequently cited prescription for South Africa's economic woes. This, of course, is the problem. Proponents of an economic Codesa tend to misunderstand or forget the provenance of the culture of negotiation. The constitutional negotiations took place in the absence of representative government and in the face of an existential crisis for the whole country. Negotiation was not a supplement to, far less a replacement for, representative government; it was a crisis expedient for its absence. Unsurprisingly, the ANC and the DA are not so keen on the Codesa idea: it would mean giving up their claims to policy leadership and acknowledging the failure of the system of government that gives their existence meaning. For the DA in particular, it would threaten incorporation into a carefully stage-managed and ANC-led process and eventual policy package. Other potential participants may also have their doubts: Cosatu has expressed interest from time to time but would prefer to wield influence through alliance structures; business would fear being outnumbered in a societal context that is very hostile to private enterprise and despite the public pronouncements of organized business, businesspeople grumble vociferously in private about the futility of the job summits and other corporatist negotiating initiatives that dotted the early Mbeki years.

However, the accession of the great negotiator and builder of consensus to the presidency may appear to have strengthened the case for negotiations of this sort. Viewed from one perspective, it could give him an opening for a stunning coup that would broaden his credibility and support across the entire country as the custodian of the national interest. Viewed from another, it would, right at the outset, merely dilute the powers he played such a long and patient game to acquire and force him to manage every bit player and fringe interest in South African politics at a time when he has not even stamped his authority on his own party.

The question of management raises another aspect of the constitutional negotiations that tends to be overlooked in the general South African fondness for negotiated solutions. Ramaphosa did not orchestrate the negotiations alone, although his was the decisive contribution. He and the ANC had an adversary partner in the NP government. Without the combination of the NP's state power and the ANC's popular mobilization, agreement would not have been possible. It may be a good thing if all South Africa's diverse voices and economic interests could be brought to one table, but without the steamroller of sufficient consensus, where will agreement come from? The only source is the ANC and who will want to submit to that steamroller? Ramaphosa is no longer in the position of his younger, brasher self who could be blithely quoted as saying that in the face of NP/ANC agreement, everyone else can get stuffed'.

Another possible signpost to the past lies in the direction of renovating ANC monopolism and trying to make it fit for purpose in altered circumstances by shedding at least some of its arrogance, cleaving to constitutional rectitude, respecting alternative voices, but still claiming to be the only credible force for managing the country's diversity – albeit under new and more ethical leadership. A hint of this came in Ramaphosa's speech, annually given by the president of the ANC on the anniversary of the movement's founding, three weeks after he was elected to the post. He was quoted as saying,

Our organisation belongs to you, the people of South Africa ... *it is the parliament of the people of South Africa*. It is the duty of members of the ANC to safeguard the heritage we were given by our forebears.'[50] (Emphasis added)

This may have been a permissible rhetorical flourish delivered to the faithful on a sacred day. Even so, it was remarkable that he – of all people, the orchestrator of the Constitution – chose his first speech after replacing the man who regularly elevated the ANC above the Constitution to give the impression that the ANC and not the constitutionally mandated National

Assembly is 'the parliament of the people'. It was at best an error of judgement or a Freudian slip and at worst a breathtaking restatement of all the old arrogant reflexes of the Mbeki and Zuma years, a depressing indication that the ANC is incapable of learning anything, even from a catastrophe like Zuma. While the speech also acknowledged the need 'to reach out to civil society in all its forms to regain trust', it will be a matter of concern which version of the ANC's past will mark Ramaphosa's tenure.

Perhaps the most compelling continuity with the past will come if Ramaphosa takes on the role of Mbeki Ver. 2, providing an upgrade with the psychological bugs eliminated. The principal leadership theme of the Mbeki years was how to modulate grass-roots ANC populism; Mbeki did it by refracting it and filtering it, stress testing its policy wishlist with evidence-based exposure to economic 'realities' and making it fit for purpose in the real world. It was a challenge Mbeki clearly relished, allowing him to take on the role of responsible adult. Relief at Ramaphosa's takeover – especially in markets – clearly has a quality of 'the grown ups are back' and carries expectations to match. Such hopes are clearly that Ramaphosa can rebuild the institutional framework – notably of course a strong National Treasury – that armed Mbeki to match grass-roots aspirations to the exigencies of global and local economic structures. The clearest signals so far that this scenario may develop are in what Ramaphosa has had to say about the land issue. Having been handed a hospital pass by the ANC conference that elected him, in the form of a commitment to expropriation of land without compensation, Ramaphosa has boldly adopted the policy despite its immediately evoking echoes of Zimbabwe's land seizures. However, he has also made promises that such expropriation will not damage economic growth or food security – indeed, it will enhance the latter by bringing more land under cultivation – and will take place under a clear legal framework that will rule out land occupation and seizures.[51]

There is a certain inevitability about this scenario, given that any rational ANC leader is likely to find him or herself caught between populist aspirations and economic constraints. Ramaphosa himself seemed to recognize this as a young union leader as far back as 1985 when he said,

> Organising workers in the mining industry is the art of the impossible … because [we are] trying to make a revolution with moderate tools that were invented to prevent a revolution.[52]

Of all the evidence from his career, perhaps these words are the best guide to how this latest phase of it will unfold. It is encouraging that he was so prescient about the dilemmas of leadership in South Africa so long ago.

This, however, might not be enough. It has to be remembered that Mbeki failed in being the intermediary between populism and pragmatism. And even if Ramaphosa is a better leader by criteria of inspiration, communication and the human qualities of people management, conditions in which to repeat Mbeki's approach are less favourable than they were for his predecessor. Mbeki enjoyed benign global conditions, which supported South Africa's growth. There is now, after the global crash of 2008, greater and broader-based scepticism over whether the economic 'realities' to which Mbeki deferred are really realities or self-interested elite assumptions; the populist genie is out of the bottle in South Africa and in many other electoral democracies. Mbeki's policies increased inequality and left endemic poverty and unemployment, so while Ramaphosa may copy Mbeki's approach, he will need new policies to improve on the latter's record. Lastly, he will have to succeed at the challenge that brought Mbeki down – the need to cultivate a permanent base of political support, a critical mass and a centre of gravity, and in doing this he cannot afford too many compromises, such as the one which installed David Mabuza as his vice president, which may prove to be hostages to fortune. If anything, the ANC that Ramaphosa leads presents a stiffer challenge on this front than the one in which Mbeki failed.

Finally, what will doubtless come to be labelled 'the Ramaphosa years' will clarify whether or not South Africans can afford to continue confronting their future with their eyes fixed so firmly on the past.

10

Conclusions

According to a recent compendium of theory in the field, political leadership can be viewed in two ways. First as a cause and a shaping force:

> Leadership is commonly portrayed as source of dynamism in the polity, breathing life into parties and institutions as they struggle with major changes. In this view, leadership is about injecting ideas and ambitions into the public arena. It is about grasping existing realities and recognising that they can effect transformations. Leadership produces collective meaning and harnesses collective energy for a common cause.[1]

The second main point of departure is leadership as a consequence, as a dependent variable in which diversity of leadership styles and outcomes can be explained by other variables that influence who becomes a leader and what he or she does in and with the role.[2] In this way, leadership studies are about the factors governing the getting, using, keeping and losing power. We ought to ask who becomes a leader? How do they consolidate their hold on office? When, how and by whom are they removed?

It should be clear from the foregoing pages that it is the second approach that has shaped this book. The three post-Mandela South African presidents who are at the heart of its subject have all led – and in Ramaphosa's case is leading – in an enclosed space with little room for manoeuvre. They were produced by the political culture of the ANC, which has sprawled across and dominated South Africa's general political culture, forced all other stakeholders and political players to define themselves in engagement with it and challenged the Constitution itself for primacy in the political culture. This picture is complicated by the ANC's own lack of organizational, ideological and policy coherence, which in turn makes its political culture labile, its forms and expressions depending greatly on which constituency is being addressed by which part of the ANC (and Alliance) at any given time. This instability has, however, offered the best hope to leaders of some freedom of action, allowing them if they wish to attempt divide-and-rule tactics, and to be all things to all the constituencies that subscribe to various versions of the ANC's political culture.

Mandela's period in office was short enough, and the combination of his own extraordinary qualities and the extended euphoria of the settlement and liberation period was potent enough for him to carry off this balancing act. What is more, these assets enabled him to extend the effect beyond the ANC itself to the rest of the country. Mbeki and Zuma had to look to the longer term, and each had his own way of trying to create wider freedom for himself. For Mbeki, the choice was trying to impose his version of coherence on the ANC, while Zuma chose to manipulate and exploit its incoherence. A comparative summary of the ways in which Mbeki and Zuma achieved power, consolidated it, used it and lost it, accounts for this essential difference and in doing so brings into focus the engagement between leaders and context. This in turn will suggest that despite their different characters, individual traits and purposes there has been substantial continuity between them. One commonality is that both approaches had significant costs, and each in the end destroyed its protagonist.

Entrances, projects and exits

Mbeki rose to power without having to test his leadership mettle in any context wider than the inner councils of the ANC, which at the time were heavily influenced by the exile and prisoner experiences and the networks (especially the SACP) that had shared them. This does not mean, of course, that he had an entirely smooth ascent: the scepticism of the Left about his leadership predated his exercise of presidential powers in government and in the wider ANC that scepticism later provoked the rebellion against him. However this prequel of scepticism, which centred on Joe Slovo and, until his death, Chris Hani, was in itself a subset of exile politicking, details of which may have been leaked to a wider audience via the progressive newspaper the *Weekly Mail* but remained to all intents and purposes of political outcomes, backstairs intrigue.

Once in power, the true focus of Mbeki's leadership was the ANC. Armed with the blunt instruments of his party's electoral majority and self-righteous vanguardism, he was happy to abandon all semblance of the kind of presidential presence and role for the whole country that Mandela triumphantly carried off. Indeed he gave the impression, which was shared with most of his party, that the ANC *was* the whole country and any person, group or organization that voluntarily placed itself outside, never mind in opposition to the movement, was by definition alien and hostile.

His principal focus in the exercise of power was to impose coherence on the ANC partly by stealth and partly by overbearing argument. However, his principal instrument was the state. In making this choice, Mbeki was practising a highly complex and audacious politics of reverse takeover. He wanted to make the ANC utterly dominant in perpetuity in electoral politics and to use this base to legitimate the fusion of state with party through cadre deployment. However, having done this, he wanted to reverse engineer his way to dominance of the ANC and the Alliance by the state through the same cadres, ministers and technocrats. In this way, the various spectres that for him haunted the ANC and Alliance – populism, ultra-leftism, tribalism, factionalism and patronage – could be disciplined. He was liberated in his pursuit of this delusive hybrid of one-partyism and constitutionalism by the intoxicating possibilities presented by the size of the ANC's majorities, which in fairness would have turned the heads of many political leaders, even those whose psyches were better grounded than Mbeki's.

He was also driven on by his own commandist conception of politics, which owed much to engineering and military metaphor; among the suggestive images most frequently used by Mbeki and his acolytes being 'the levers of power' and 'the commanding heights of the economy'. He owed much less to emotional intelligence, which, irrespective of whether it is genuine or calculated and manipulative, is an essential part of the repertoire of successful leaders in a democracy. What his strategies and projects lacked, however, was a secure base of personal following and the personal qualities and traits that equip a leader to assemble or manufacture one – not least the appetite for taking on the task.

Mbeki's exit from power was inextricably bound up with Zuma's ascent, and it is best summarized from this latter angle of approach. It is worth noting to begin with that his departure, which involved a strong element of popular mobilization both on the streets and in ANC branches, contrasts sharply with the inside manoeuvres that elevated him. This alone served notice of how the ANC's culture of leaders and leadership was changing. Another hint of the future came with the role played by the first stirrings of reawakened civil society, in the form of the groups (notably, the AIDS Law Project), which successfully challenged government policy on the pandemic and did much to undermine Mbeki's legitimacy and credibility as a leader.

Zuma achieved power thanks to a perfect storm of enabling conditions, which not only propelled him upwards but also set the terms of his presidential tenure. Mbeki figures strongly as an enabler in this ascent. In the first place, he chose Zuma as a vice president then apparently had second thoughts and wished to thwart his succession, which gave Zuma a grievance and a cause. At the same time, Mbeki showed himself willing to entertain investigations of the arms deal, having ruthlessly squashed the previous pursuit of irregularities and denounced with outrage and contempt any previous allegations of corruption that prompted investigation. The reason for Mbeki's spectacular U-turn seemed clear, rightly or wrongly, to Zuma and the growing band of anti-Mbeki dissidents; it was because this time Zuma was the target of the investigations. This set of contingent circumstances meant that Zuma's presidential ambitions had a motivation that was singular, if not unique. That is, as tensions developed between him and Mbeki, there was a real prospect that if he did not wrest control from Mbeki and find ways to influence or even control the criminal justice system, at the very least his career would be ruined and in addition there was a strong possibility that he might go to jail. In this sense, contingency played a very large role in leadership selection.

Mbeki also played the part of enabler by making sure that Zuma could rise in what was a near vacuum of selection. As we have seen, Mbeki destroyed the careers of others rather than build them so that when he faced in Zuma a candidate with genuine popular following, he was reduced to the transparently opportunistic strategy of declaring that it was 'time for a woman president'.[3] His choice to replace Jacob Zuma as deputy state president was Phumzile Mlambo-Ngcuka who had held two ministerial posts (one of them a deputy) but was better known for two other things. The first was having said while addressing a group of black businesspeople in 1997 that 'Blacks should not be ashamed to be filthy rich'. In a society that valued individualism and capital accumulation highly, this would have been a crass but unremarkable sentiment to be expressed by a government minister. It was harder to defend in the face of an anti-elitist revolt in a movement that subscribes (no matter how often in the breach) to a mythology of communalism and self-sacrifice. Second and more important was the fact that she was the spouse of Bulelani Ngcuka, who as head of the NPA was Zuma's would-be nemesis. When Mbeki replaced Zuma as vice president with Mlambo Ngcuka, it is hard to think of a more provocative and inept choice.

It is possible, of course, that Mbeki had the last laugh as he watched history repeating itself; forced into a corner in 2017, Zuma resorted to the same 'woman president' ploy and tried to promote Nkosazana Dlamini-Zuma as his successor, as if his gender sensitivities and her gender qualifications were more important in his choice than the fact that she was his ex-wife.

Mbeki also played an enabling role for Zuma by normalizing the idea of a shadow state staffed with party partisans and promoting it with a zeal that bordered on the fanatical as an essential part of the ANC's ethos and operating principles. The fact that Mbeki did this not for personal gain but for lofty (albeit dangerously crazy) ideological reasons that were already part of the movement's stock of ideas is neither here nor there. Mbeki had set up the apparatus and Zuma was able to convert the shadow state model to his own individual purposes with the flick of a switch.

Mbeki was not the only enabler. The opportunism of the alliance Left, which thought Zuma could be controlled in order to give a leftward direction to the ANC and government, and thus achieve a different kind of ideological and policy coherence for the whole Alliance movement to that sought by Mbeki, was the crucial factor in his rise. This catastrophic miscalculation was based on a number of misunderstandings. These stemmed from the Left believing the ANC's rhetoric to the effect that in the relationship between state and party, the latter was the dominant player. In this way, it grossly underestimated the powers – appointment, patronage, public profile – of a leader in government to resist control from the movement and party that put him there. Getting rid of one leader and installing another by means of an insurgent spasm is one thing; converting this into day-to-day and issue-by-issue and appointment-by-appointment control of the new incumbent is quite another. Under South African conditions, when a leader is an aspirant, his backers have much influence; once he is in office, this is instantly and greatly reduced and the balance of power accordingly greatly altered. The miscalculation was also based on misunderstanding the role of numbers. In the 2004 election, one year before the firing of Zuma, under Mbeki's leadership the ANC polled more than 10.8 million votes; at that time, Cosatu had a membership of perhaps 1.7 million and the SACP 30,000.[4] The Left took the somewhat smug attitude that quality of numbers trumped quantity. This was based on their belief that left cadres had a higher political consciousness, on the ideological dominance of the SACP in the exile ANC and on Cosatu's efficiency in getting out the ANC vote. Zuma was happy to disabuse them of their pretensions to entitlement and instruct them in the value of raw numbers and alternative tools of political mobilization and management – including patronage, ethno-tribalism and cultural atavism.

The catalyst that converted contingency and enablers into change was the ANC's culture of leadership. In any leadership culture that valued initiative, vision, conviction politics and transformative energy, Zuma's bid would have been a non-starter. Fortunately for him, the reverse was true (and to a large extent still is). The ANC is set up to produce consensus leaders who lead from behind, not in front of the party. This owes something to a powerful though poorly articulated notion of a purer and more direct form of democracy than 'Western' representative versions, which are seen as putting too much power in the hands of leaders and elites. This is combined with the equally powerful notion of African exceptionalism, which demands expression in a prelapsarian form of bond between leaders and people that suits African conditions and people and is essential for the recovery of African self-respect after the humiliations of colonialism and apartheid.

Under such influences, vision and programmes are seen as the preserve of the party and virtue resides in the collective; the mandate of crowds prevails because all wisdom rises from the bottom. In addition the informal ban on individuals putting themselves forward and lobbying competitively for leadership roles meant that there was no formal process through which leaders could emerge. This had two main effects: it helped empower Mbeki to create an atmosphere so hostile to emerging leaders that, as we have seen, it left the field open to Zuma; second, the myth that leaders would be selected by some collective alchemy in which the contenders remained entirely passive was so absurdly out of tune with the needs of government and the reality of political freedom and careers open to the talents of ambitious black people in a diversifying society, that it invited the kind of defiant upheaval that would (and did) unseat the incumbent leaders and split the party while at the same time making the movement's archaic informal rules a laughing stock.

The final way in which the ANC's leadership culture and procedures enabled Zuma's takeover lay in the disjuncture between its election timetable and the Constitution's fixed-term parliaments, which in turn exacerbates the 'two centres of power' problem when the ANC president and the state president are not the same person. Unease with this situation provided the ideal cause to despatch Mbeki. Happenstance provided the occasion; Judge Nicholson's opinion that Mbeki interfered with the prosecution of Zuma – a view which the Supreme Court of Appeal thought so misguided – served two purposes: to legitimize dropping charges against the president-in-waiting and to send Mbeki on his way with a message to his supporters that he would cease to have any influence whatsoever. Zuma was already nearly there, but Nicholson's judgement was the final enabler. It anointed his succession and gave it momentum; it was the bottle of champagne broken on the vessel of his leadership as it slid triumphantly into the water.

Making sense of Zuma

In marked contrast to Mbeki and Ramaphosa, nobody called Zuma 'an enigma' during his rise to the presidency and in the early years of his tenure. Perhaps, this is a symptom of how he was patronized and underestimated, to South Africa's great cost. There is, however, a good case for attaching the enigma label to him now. An increasing amount is known about what happened during his almost nine years as president, thanks to the investigative and analytical revelations about state capture and the shadow state. However, much less is known about *how* and *why* it happened. Was Zuma the evil genius who pulled all the strings? Or was he the hapless pawn of the Guptas and other cronies? Much will doubtless emerge from the commission of enquiry into state capture led by deputy chief justice Raymond Zondo, as well as from future court cases prosecuting individuals involved in corruption, to clarify which of these polarities (or more likely what combination of them) will better explain the years of Zuma's leadership. Until then, the choices remain open.

At the height of his power, some saw him as a chess master who engineered a stunning coup that overturned all sorts of ANC orthodoxies, outwitting not only his antagonists but also later his backers, on the way to building an imperial presidency dedicated to his own and his cronies' interests. Others saw him as a juggler who stumbled into power as the beneficiary of an anti-elite revolt, an early exemplar of the kind of insurgency that in more recent years has lain waste to traditional patterns of democratic politics in the West and which temporarily coincided with his own need to stay out of jail. Thereafter, he had to improvise as best he could, like a serial debtor maxing out one credit card after another to stave off the inevitable, which in this case is his day in court.

What he represents is also the stuff of enigma and projection of the observer's own preoccupations and perhaps prejudices. He can be seen in the lineage of African neo-patrimonial leaders but marooned in a constitutional state; or as a small-time strongman manqué, without the strength of purpose or the resources to be a Putin or an Erdogan and as a result, like Shakespeare's Macbeth, 'letting I dare not wait upon I would'. His open reintroduction of ethno-tribalism into South African politics can also be interpreted in different guises, in which he appears as an unreconstructed traditionalist or a canny operator who could see the limitations of both modernization and tradition in South Africa today and was light-footed enough to exploit them both simultaneously. He can be seen from various political angles as either the logical and predictable outcome of African nationalism's development from liberation moment to patrimonial Big Man[5] or as a tragic denouement stemming from the failure to sweep aside the legacy of colonialism and apartheid in a truly revolutionary transformation.[6]

Leadership and anti-leadership

None of this uncertainty means that there is nothing useful to be said about Zuma's leadership at this stage. Arguably, the key insight about post-Mandela leadership in the ANC (which for the most part, given the party's electoral dominance, has meant political leadership of South Africa) is that leaders are greatly constrained by ANC conventions and have to find their own ways to create political space for themselves and their purposes. Mbeki tried to do this by remaking the party, the state and the relationship between the two for it to be fit for his purposes as a would-be philosopher king. Zuma's approach was radically different from this misguided leadership overreach. His version amounts to a kind of anti-leadership, that is, leading by abdicating responsibility for rational leadership.

He appeared to base this approach on several crucial insights (or perhaps they were instincts). The first insight is that the ANC is easy to capture but impossible to lead by following the conventional wisdom of political leadership, which is set out in the quotation that opens this chapter. Three other principles follow from this this basic assumption: local networks are more important than central hierarchies in coping with the ANC's basic ungovernability; chaos is a better strategy for managing the ANC in government and in the country than getting your hands on 'the levers of power'; and finally, the leader functions not as a rational centre of vision and direction but the living embodiment of the people who elevated him to the position, inseparable from the movement, irrespective of his qualities.

The point is not that these are 'better' principles of leadership than Mbeki's, or that they are 'true' even for the context in which Zuma found himself; they were in fact disastrous for the ANC, for the country and in the end for Zuma himself; but they suited better who he was and what his purpose was – personal rule and freedom to exploit the resources of the state.

Zuma's embrace of the provinces had more than a hint of feudalism about it. ANC barons were left free to exploit the various roles of provincial government in disbursing central government funds for patronage purposes. In turn, they backed Zuma and kept him secure, a massive counterweight to stirrings of ANC discontent in the urban centres. It is significant that the first specific post-Zuma anti-corruption investigations were triggered by a Gupta-related project in Free State involving provincial politicians. It is also significant that the swing factor in Ramaphosa's election to the ANC presidency in December 2017 was not his attractiveness to urban ANC branches, which could be taken for granted, but the defection of Mpumalanga leader David Mabuza from the Zuma camp, securing his election as vice president of the ANC and appointment to the state vice presidency thereafter. This neatly reveals how important Zuma's provincial strategy had been to gaining, exercising and losing power, as well delivering a powerful reminder of how temporary all ANC allegiances of the Zuma era were, but how enduring the provincial power nexus threatens to be.

The chaos theory of Zuma's leadership rests principally on observation of the churn of government and quasi-government appointments so ably documented by Gareth van Onselen and discussed above. Zuma's appointments also mark the point where chaos dovetails with his focus on the provinces and his use of patronage to replace the support base he lost so quickly after his accession. Zuma may have been of the prisoner/exile struggle aristocracy but he promoted people in and around government without these old ANC connections. That is, he elevated men and, despite (or because of) his patriarchal leanings many women, the overwhelming majority from provincial obscurity, whose struggle records were undistinguished and whose talents were unremarkable or absent altogether. If this was an initiative to bring forward a new elite, it was one that largely ignored the new generation of upwardly mobile Africans who had gone to formerly white or private schools, attended elite universities and had trained in and for the professions and business. This may have been a conscious choice to broaden the base of the leadership cadre and give it a less elite cast, by giving a chance to and easing the way for those without obvious conventional advantages. More likely, it was because the urban 'clevers' that he disdained so much were inauthentic in his eyes, made him uncomfortable and might be more loyal to a conception of the ANC he was deviating from – or even to the Constitution – rather than to himself. This was generational change but not how it might have been envisaged when the career open to the talents, education and social mobility became available to Africans in the 1990s. Time will tell whether Ramaphosa's new dawn will bring forward the kind of people Zuma ignored or whether they will continue to find more congenial opportunities in the private sector (or emigration).

The evidence of chaos is clear but its provenance less so. It may have been deliberately willed as a strategy to make party and government so unpredictable that there was no firm ground on which countermovements to his construction of the shadow state could grow. The alternative is that it was the by-product of an endless series of improvisations conjured to deal with events, threats and the need to buy off support as well as to promote ad hoc initiatives in the interests of cronyism and self-/family enrichment. The shadow state was on such a scale as to incline interpretation towards the strategic. However, Zuma's apparent lack of vision and grasp of detail, as well as his scattergun and inconsistent pronouncements on policy, culture, the ANC and the Constitution, among many other things, suggests otherwise.

The belief in the inseparability of leader and movement meant that Zuma was neither the servant nor the master of the entity he 'led'. Instead, he used the ANC's culture as a shield and shelter for his personal rule. In this he was vociferously abetted, virtually to the end, by the ANC, especially by

Baleka Mbete as Speaker of Parliament (she was also national chairperson of the ANC throughout the Zuma years) and by Secretary General Gwede Mantashe (who is now a staunch Ramaphosa supporter). They used their prestige and the authority of their offices to repeat the strident message that an 'attack' on Zuma was an attack on the movement itself, where 'attack' meant any attempt by the opposition, civil society, the head of a constitutional body, such as Thuli Madonsela, or the courts, to hold him accountable under the Constitution by constitutionally sanctioned means. Indeed, Mantashe's defence of Zuma included direct attacks on judges and on Madonsela.

Signposts in the literature

Identifying these three working principles as central to Zuma's leadership opens up the possibility of placing South Africa's post-Mandela leaders within the general framework of political leadership studies. The search for fixed points in the academic literature around which to build generalizations about political leadership often focuses on opposed pairs of leadership qualities as basic points of reference: strong as opposed to consensual/collegiate; transactional as opposed to transformative; functionalist as opposed to intentionalist. These rough and ready polarizations simplify and dramatize leadership qualities, creating templates that allow comparison across political cultures. However, like all simplifiers, they can slide into caricature. This is partly because in democracies, political leaders are forced to adopt expected and approved roles – especially in terms of strong/consensual qualities – whether or not they conform to their own inclinations and abilities. Perhaps, more importantly, it should be recognized that successful leaders ought to be able to combine opposed qualities such as transformative and transactional, rather than simply be one or other kind of leader.

Both Mbeki and Zuma were would-be strong leaders who struggled to escape from structural constraints and find political space to exercise what they, in their different ways, saw as the prerogatives of leadership. They felt the constraints both of the Constitution and the party that they led, notably in the ANC's wholly unrealistic expectations of collegiality, to which its leaders have to pay extravagant homage, even as they struggle to escape them. Civil society groups used the Constitution and the courts to discredit Mbeki's maverick AIDS policy within the ANC and in the country and by extension to undermine his leadership in general. Zuma lost his long drawn-out war of attrition with the opposition, civil society, the Public Protector and the courts over his constitutional violations. Mbeki was brought down by his failure to develop consensual ways to manage party and Alliance organization and relations. Zuma's diminishing credibility in the face of escalating revelations and multiplying defeats finally sparked his party's opposition to him.

The most notable feature that the two situations shared was that the post-Mandela ANC apparently has only two bases for relationships with its leaders. These are, on the one hand, extreme acquiescence, solidarity and obedience, and on the other, open revolt. That this should be the case for a movement that devotes so much time and energy to cultivating and broadcasting a harmonious self-image of grass-roots initiative, direct democracy and humanist, African consensual leadership verges on the bizarre and is one of many sources of the cognitive dissonance that characterizes the ANC.

While the classification of political leaders as strong or consensual is useful in polarizing types and styles of leadership, in contexts such as South Africa, where political structure and culture weigh so heavily on leadership agency, such categories are at best simplifiers of what are highly complex relationships.

The same may be said for the classification transformative/transactional. What Mbeki in particular seemed to illustrate is not the polarization but the interdependence of these qualities. The quality of transformative leadership itself seems to be a compound. One element is conviction in the service of changing the political weather – the sense of what is possible in a given context. The other, in Rotberg's terms discussed above in Chapter 1, is to do with motivating the party and the general populace by challenging expectations and driving the nation forward by instilling both pride and higher levels of national and governmental performance. Transactional leaders, on the other hand, are incrementalists, with only a limited repertoire, focusing on the mechanics of statecraft and on perpetuating themselves and their party in office.

What this useful polarization misses is that transformational leaders either need themselves to have the abilities of the transactionalist in order to follow through and deliver the transformations or to have support from colleagues with these qualities and who are sufficiently senior to do the job for the leader. Mbeki clearly saw himself as a transformative leader in the first sense used above – running against his party on macroeconomic policy in the service of large visionary goals. However, in human terms, he was a destroyer rather than a builder and motivator and he simply did not have the transactional skills to build a critical mass of support in his party. Also for these reasons, he relied on *apparatchiki* as his closest colleagues rather than political heavyweights who could support his transformational purposes because they had substantial political constituencies in their own right. The most important deviation from this pattern was Mbeki's close working relationship with Trevor Manuel as his finance minister. However, Manuel was a polarizing figure, like Mbeki himself, and despite his undoubted authority in office, his influence in the movement did not long survive Mbeki's exit.

There were other obstacles to Mbeki's hopes of being a transformational leader. Other transformational leaders had the whip of failure with which to scourge unbelievers within and outside their parties: Reagan and Thatcher had their countries' turmoil of the 1970s; Blair had Labour's serial electoral failure; Gorbachev and De Klerk had the stagnation crises of communism's and apartheid's endgames. Conversely and more positively, Mandela had the momentum, euphoria and South African exceptionalism of the transition to negotiated democracy. Mbeki had none of these things. South Africa had become an ordinary country with high expectations and low capacities. He was also hampered by his own lack of grasp of how to manage the transactions that would deliver his transformations. Used to being comfortable with small-scale and face-to-face persuasions (albeit with very large implications) behind closed doors in an atmosphere of crisis, he did not know how to carry off large-scale democratic persuasions, especially those that required him to be polarizing and divisive (as his – and Mandela's – macroeconomic policy did).

Superficially, Zuma presents no uncertainties of classification on the transformative/functionalist scale. He has always projected an image of being cheerfully without convictions or to be at least flexible on that score. With no apparent commitment in public to anything but stock ANC ideological clichés, and in private wedded alone to his own material interests, he did have a strong grasp of the necessities for staying in power. In this way, he appears as the arch functionalist exploiter of networks and improvised bargains. Yet it was in the early Zuma years (in 2011) that the ANC government committed itself to the ambitious and comprehensive National Development Plan (NDP: subtitled 'Vision 2030'). This was the product, not of the ANC grass roots but of broad-based technocratic research, bolstered by a (somewhat cosmetic) public consultative process. Not only was the planning broad-based, but its recommendations were also sufficiently innovative and inclusive (at least by the standards of the ANC's governing record) to qualify as potentially transformative. Quite how to ascribe its leadership provenance is not easy. It was somewhat in the spirit of Mbeki-ism, although it was much clearer, less pretentious and ideologically hidebound than Mbeki's own visionary statements. Trevor Manuel headed the planning secretariat that drove it, one of the reasons that the Alliance Left hated it. Zuma paid lip service to its alleged centrality to government policy and handed it over to Ramaphosa when the latter became vice president. The plan subsequently went nowhere, doubtless partly because its transformative potential threatened to disrupt ANC ideological pieties and interests (especially of trade unions).

Resurrecting a more focused version (the original weighed in at more than four hundred pages), which nonetheless retains the transformative potential of the original, is one of Ramaphosa's leadership options. Why the NDP should have surfaced under Zuma remains a puzzle for the moment, but the question serves to reinforce further the leadership complexities that are inadequately caught by neat classifications.

Another broad-brush categorization that works better on the theorist's page than in the confused specifics of South Africa's evolving political context is functionalist/intentionalist. The former leads by single steps in response to events while the latter is inspired by comprehensive visions, which unfold in grand plans. It is easy to portray Zuma as the archetypal functionalist in everything from the Stalingrad tactics of his legal defenders to the churn of his ministerial and other high state appointments. Mbeki is harder to accommodate in this classificatory scheme, partly because it is hard to ascribe 'intentionalist' qualities in any pure form to any democratic leader, and it is perhaps the most suspect of the theoretical labels to be used in a democracy. In any case, insofar as any post-apartheid South African president dealt in grand plans and visions, he did so at the behest of the ANC, in its conference resolutions and laboriously reworked ideological documents. These tended to be constraining rather than enabling, especially as the various interest groups and factions, ideological and otherwise, saw themselves free to interpret the ideological templates as they wished. So while Mbeki may have superficially appeared in the guise of an intentionalist leader, particularly in his grandiose visions for the African continent, and chose this guise as his self-image, his leadership was characterized more by technocratic concerns about unintended consequences of domestic policymaking in a context shaped by fiscal limits and global constraints. No matter how much he may have fumed about them and railed against the unequal and unjust legacies of imperialism that he saw as bequeathing the constraints on him, he saw them as real and equally fumed about those who could not similarly recognize them and who believed that the politics of revolutionary will and populist initiative could overcome them.

Ramaphosa's challenges

These reflections on Mbeki and Zuma invite speculation on what sort of leader Ramaphosa might be, using the same conventional criteria. The direction such speculations will take as he grows into the presidency, especially now that he has led the ANC to a general election victory with a reduced but still respectable vote share of 57.5 per cent, will depend less on himself, more on the context. The overbearing influence of structure and political culture on leadership in South Africa has been the main theme of this book. A central truth that Ramaphosa faces is that South Africa does not allow the conditions for strong, or transformative or intentionalist leadership in the senses that the literature of leadership understands them. If Ramaphosa aspires to these qualities – and it will hard for him to be a leader in any meaningful sense if he does not – then he will have to practise considerable subterfuge in deploying them. The ironic truth is that a substantial portion of South Africa's politically aware population, certainly outside the ANC but also within it, hankers for what they see as strong and transformative political leadership. In this way, both the general and the ANC political culture invests much in leaders and the idea of leadership, and has high expectations of them, while simultaneously denying the conditions in which leadership might flourish. This is one reason why, where its leaders are concerned, the ANC swings like a pendulum from euphoria to betrayal.

Much of this can be ascribed to the vagaries of followership in South Africa. Among the influences here are the tenacious hold of poorly digested ideals about direct democracy, with their undermining of trust in distancing features of representative democracy such as institutions, parties and leaders; the equally durable grip of the mythology of African leadership; the prevalence of betrayal as a political reflex, which is the sharpest expression of a general climate of lack of trust; and the failure of a whole leadership generation, which has meant that presidents have been without adequate collegial support, or critical peer checks, or even simply competition.

Since these cultural features are likely to change in the short term, Ramaphosa faces formidable challenges. He has to find his own leadership agency while still professing continuity, unity and in the end subordination to the collective will of the ANC. He has to create his own personal support base without alienating other interests and factions in the ramshackle edifice of the ANC's broad church. He has to present himself as a leader beyond partisanship, whose role includes representing the whole country but do so in such a way that he is not brought down for pandering to whites or capitulating to markets. Last, but arguably most important, he has to choose how to deal with the populist genie which escaped from the bottle in both the Mbeki and the Zuma end times. In its latest manifestation populism owes much to Malema's exploitation of disaffection with Zuma, much to Zuma's own vengeful opportunism but more to the failure of the last twenty years to deal credibly with poverty and inequality, which has fuelled a wave of anti-elitism and racial resentment.

Since these challenges contain all manner of contradictions and dilemmas, Ramaphosa may well continue to embrace the risky persona of an enigma for a while longer.

Changing the rules of the game

It remains only to ask how the context can change to allow for better leadership outcomes. The need to do so seems clear.

With Mbeki and Zuma, the ANC has tested to destruction some of its ideas and practices of leadership, both explicit and implicit. Twice the ANC has been caught believing its own publicity about collective leadership and got more than it bargained for from these two individuals. It remains to be seen whether or not the organization will learn from the experience.

What sort of things might the organization and its aspirant leaders learn from the past? The following list is worthy of consideration: don't overinvest in leaders in the hope of manipulating them on behalf of one or another faction of ideology or interest, as the Left did with Zuma; strong institutions are more important than leaders and this goes as much to protect the ANC from its own bad leaders as it does to protect civil society from overweening presidential power; a much broader talent pool for leadership is needed not only for succession planning but also as a corporate check on current leaders; leaders need time and space and a collegial atmosphere to grow before making the step to the highest leadership; be wary of cultural ('African') concepts of leadership, which are susceptible to manipulation, as in the 'respect for elders' cover for suppressing criticism of ANC leaders; suspect the wisdom of crowds and beware the tyranny of policymaking from below; be prepared to build support for unpopular policies and/or counsel against economically rash ones instead of making policy by coup (like GEAR) or taking on board populist policies and subjecting them to endless delays (like the National Health Insurance scheme) or proceeding with hopelessly inadequate resources and institutional capacity (like land reform); devise better processes for selection and deal with the two centres of power issue, perhaps by giving parliamentarians a share in choosing the party leader (while raising the standard of the election list) and downgrading the ANC presidency altogether while strengthening the office of ANC secretary general as arbiter and manager of party structures and guarantor of organizational integrity.

In order to do even some of these things, the ANC will have to confront the task of reconciling two worlds openly and honestly. These are the worlds in which ANC leaders are perforce condemned to operate. The first is the world of the national liberation movement, which is a world without limits in which 'victory is certain!' and the people's will, the party, the state, the nation and the force of history are all rolled into one unstoppable movement. The other world is the world of uncertainty and limits in which leaders have to grapple with irreconcilables and diverse managerial crises within the politics of limits; the global economy; the Constitution; electoral and fiscal arithmetic; the hand that history has dealt. It is not that ANC leaders have been oblivious to these contradictions – Mbeki was certainly aware of them – just that they haven't dealt with them honestly and insofar as they have been dealt with at all, it has been by stealth and temporizing.

If the ANC learns from its leadership history, it can move towards a more balanced leadership model. Such a model would be collegial, consultative and accountable but not collective. It would be individual in the sense of driven by a strong personality, capable of communicating not only with the ANC faithful but (as long as the ANC is in power) also of leading the whole country. Such a leader would be respectful of grass roots but be prepared to challenge the dogma that all wisdom comes from below.

If the ANC cannot or will not confront these leadership issues, it will be condemned in perpetuity (if it survives at all in its present form) to lurch from leadership euphoria to bitter feelings of betrayal and then to regicide, before even two presidential terms of office have been served.

Notes

Preface

1   Alec Russell, *After Mandela: The Battle for the Soul of South Africa* (London, 2009), p. 2.

Introduction

1   For instance: *Towards a Ten Year Review: A Synthesis Report on Implementation of Government Programmes* (Pretoria, 2004) and *Twenty Year Review: South Africa 1994–2014* (Pretoria, 2014). Both were compiled from reports commissioned by the presidency from academics and consultants.

2   Richard Calland, *The Zuma Years: South Africa's Changing Face of Power* (Cape Town, 2013), p. 412.

3   Kgalema Motlanthe was elected president by the ANC majority in the National Assembly on Mbeki's forced departure from office but he served only from 25 September 2008 until 9 May 2009 when Jacob Zuma was elected president by the new ANC majority in the National Assembly in the aftermath of the 2009 general election. Motlanthe served as Zuma's deputy president until the general election of 2014. Under the Constitution, article 87(2), such a period of acting office is not considered to be a term and an acting president could later serve two full elected terms.

4   Rita Barnard (ed.), *The Cambridge Companion to Nelson Mandela* (Cambridge, 2014), p. 3. See the contribution to this volume by Deborah Posel, ' "Madiba Magic": Politics as enchantment' (2014), pp. 70–92, for an extended discussion of Mandela, 'the metaphysics of daily life during the transition' and the 'miracle' of the transition.

5   John Carlin, *Playing the Enemy: Nelson Mandela and the Game That Made a Nation* (New York, 2008), pp. 252–3.

6   Stanley Greenberg, *Despatches from the War Room: In the Trenches with Five Extraordinary Leaders* (New York, 2009).

7   Hermann Giliomee, *The Afrikaners: Biography of a People* (London, 2003), p. 648.

8   'Is Thabo Mbeki Fit to Rule?', *Mail and Guardian*, 17 May 1996, https://mg.co.za/article/1996-05-17-is-thabo-mbeki-fit-to-rule.

9   Adekeye Adebajo, *Thabo Mbeki: Africa's Philosopher King* (Johannesburg, 2016).

1 The rediscovery of political leadership

1 Robert Rotberg, 'The need for strengthened political leadership', in Robert Rotberg (ed.), Strengthening Governance in South Africa: Building on Mandela's Legacy, *Annals of the American Academy of Political and Social Science*, Vol. 652, March 2014, pp. 238–56 at p. 247. See also Robert Rotberg, *Transformative Political Leadership: Making a Difference in the Developing World* (Chicago, 2012).

2 Edmund Burke, 'Speech to the electors of Bristol, 3 November 1774', *The Founders Constitution*, Vol. 1, Chapter 13, Document 7 (Chicago, 1987).

3 It remains to be seen whether or not this piece of wisdom will survive the current wave of populism in Western democracies.

4 First published in *Avenues of History*, Hamish Hamilton (1952), published again in *Vanished Supremacies*, Hamish Hamilton (1958) and Penguin Books (1962).

5 *Guilty Men* was published under the pseudonym 'Cato' by the left-wing publisher Victor Gollancz. It was jointly authored by three journalists, one liberal, one labour and one conservative. One of them, Michael Foot, later became leader of the Labour Party (1980–3).

6 Beginning with A. J. P. Taylor, *Origins of the Second World War* (London, 1961).

7 Archie Brown, *The Myth of the Strong Leader* (New York, 2014).

8 It has retained its classic status to the extent, reportedly, of being a favoured text of former Trump appointee, Chief White House Strategist Steve Bannon: Marc Tracy, 'Steve Bannon's book club', *New York Times* 2 April 2017.

9 To date, Woodward has written about nine US presidents, the latest being Donald Trump in *Fear: Trump in the White House* (New York, 2018).

10 Robert A. Caro, *The Years of Lyndon Johnson*, Vols. 1–4 (New York, 1982–2012). The four volumes take Johnson's life to the point where, in 1964, he had been president for only a year. The fifth will be devoted to the bulk of his presidential years.

11 See Irving L. Janis, *Victims of Groupthink: A Psychological Study of Foreign Policy Decisions and Fiascoes* (Oxford, 1972).

12 Woodward, in particular, has come in for criticism on both these scores. See, for instance, Joan Didion, 'The deferential spirit', *New York Review of Books*, Vol. 43 (14), 19 September 1996.

13 The term is named for Joseph P. Overton. It postulates a restrictive range of ideas and policies that are acceptable to a wide enough public for a leader and party to espouse them and still hope to be elected.

14 Simon Jenkins, *Thatcher and Sons*, revised edition (London, 2007).

15 For an account by one of New Labour's architects, see Philip Gould, *Unfinished Revolution* (London, 1998). Of course, the fact that New Labour was a group project carried with it the seeds of its destruction in the leadership rivalry between Gordon Brown and Tony Blair.

16 A landmark was Jean Blondel, *Political Leadership: Towards a General Analysis* (Beverly Hills, 1987).
17 Gillian Peele, 'Leadership and politics: A case for a closer relationship?', *Leadership*, Vol. 1 (2), June 2005.
18 S. P. Huntington, *The Third Wave: Democratization in the Late 20th Century* (Norman, 1999).
19 'New model for Africa: Good leaders above all', *New York Times*, 25 March 1998.
20 For a discussion, see Pauline H. Baker and Princeton Lyman, 'South Africa: From beacon of hope to rogue democracy?', with a discussion by Khehla Shubane, *Stanley Foundation Working Paper*, December 2008. Baker is a former member of the US Foreign Relations Committee; Lyman is a former US ambassador to South Africa.
21 See for instance Gideon Rachman, 'Donald Trump is more than a blip in history', *Financial Times*, 9 October 2017, https://www.ft.com/content/ecfcbf32-acca-11e7-aab9-abaa44b1e130.
22 Jean Blondel's seminal text, though not the first in the new wave of leadership studies, provides an approximate date (1987): *Political Leadership*.
23 Barbara Kellerman (ed.), *Political Leadership: A Source Book* (Pittsburgh, 1986), p. xiii.
24 Howard Elcock, *Political Leadership* (Cheltenham, 2001).
25 R. A. W. Rhodes and Paul t'Hart (eds), *The Oxford Handbook of Political Leadership* (Oxford, 2014).
26 Ibid., p. 1.
27 Keith Grint, *The Arts of Leadership* (New York, 2000).
28 Ibid., p. 6.
29 Rotberg, 'Strengthened Political Leadership'.
30 Ibid.
31 Barbara Kellerman, *Followership: How Followers Are Creating Change and Changing Leaders* (Boston, MA, 2008).
32 James MacGregor Burns, *Leadership* (New York, 1978), p. 452.
33 Alexander Johnston, *Inventing the Nation: South Africa* (London, 2014), p. 266.
34 Brown, *Myth of the Strong Leader*.
35 Ibid., p. 2.
36 Ibid.

2 The South African context of political leadership

1 The ANC's preferred nomenclature has always been 'ANC-led' government. This used to recognize the participation of other parties in government, in very small numbers and in minor posts. Since the model for this was co-option, ANC-led has always been a wholly unconvincing attempt to give

the impression of an element of power sharing. In any case, there has always been an element of ambiguity in the term. It can also signal the participation in government of members of one or other component of the ANC Alliance (usually members of the communist party or trade unionists). This is now the predominant meaning of 'ANC-led'. Since such participation is by individuals who are also ANC members, any intended impression of shared power in a coalition sense would also be misleading. 'Single-party rule' is more accurate.

2 John Dunn (ed.), *The Economic Limits to Modern Politics* (New York, 1992), p. 24.

3 Ibid., p. 19.

4 Ibid., p. 37.

5 Alexander Johnston, *Inventing the Nation: South Africa* (London, 2014). Chapter 3: 'Improvising the nation 1990–96', pp. 99–134.

6 Chapter Nine institutions are named for the part of the Constitution in which their functions and powers are set out. They include the Public Protector, the Auditor General, the Independent Electoral Commission and the South African Human Rights Commission.

7 Dikgang Moseneke, 'Reflections on South African constitutional democracy – transition and transformation'. Keynote address, conference: *20 Years of South African Democracy: So Where to Now?* University of South Africa, 12 November 2014. Moseneke, a former political prisoner and Pan Africanist Congress activist, was twice passed over for the post of chief justice, despite being considered by many legal authorities to be by far the best-qualified candidate, at least on the second occasion. It is widely believed that his disposition to be critical of the ANC was influential in denying him the chief justice post. See Richard Calland, *The Zuma Years: South Africa's Changing Face of Power* (Cape Town, 2013), pp. 269–95, for an insider-observer account of legal appointments, including Moseneke's passing over for the chief justice post.

8 Moseneke, 'Reflections', p. 16, note 54.

9 Ibid.

10 Ibid.

11 *Constitution of the Republic of South Africa*, pp. 83–90.

12 *Constitution of the Republic of South Africa*, Chapter 5: The president and national executive.

13 Tip O'Neill, the Speaker of the US House of Representatives (1977–87), made the phrase popular. It is commonly associated with him, although he was not the first to use it and its coinage long preceded his tenure as Speaker.

14 Lucian Pye, 'Political culture', in Seymour Martin Lipset (ed.), *Encyclopedia of Democracy* (London, 1995), p. 965.

15 On the ambiguities of the ANC's non-racialism historically and today, see David Everatt, 'Nationalism, class and non-racialism in the 1950s and

beyond' (conference paper, 2009), available at www.sahistory.org and *The Origins of Non-Racialism: White opposition to apartheid in the 1950s* (Johannesburg, 2009). On concerns that the ANC fails to live up to non-racialism today, see Ahmed Kathrada Foundation, *Still a Home for All?* (Johannesburg, 2012). The late Ahmed Kathrada was a close comrade of Nelson Mandela before, during and after their prison sentences.

16 Statistics South Africa (StatsSA), *Mid-Year Population Estimate*, August 2017.

17 The government is trying to force mining companies to conclude a new empowerment deal every time a black empowerment partner sells out its stake; mining companies argue for a principle of 'once empowered, always empowered'. In April 2018, the High Court gave a declaratory ruling favouring the companies; the minister of mines stated that the government would challenge this on appeal, then changed his mind. There the matter rests at the time of writing, though it is likely to be only a matter of time before controversy reignites.

18 For discussion see Darryl Glaser, *Politics and Society in South Africa* (London, 2001), pp. 132–60. See also Johnston, *Inventing the Nation*, pp. 38–46 and 93–6.

19 Anthony Butler, 'Mbeki partly responsible for "demon of tribalism"', *Business Day*, 24 January 2014.

20 Department of Cooperative Governance and Traditional Affairs, *Annual Report*, 2012. The significance of the institution of traditional leadership and of its contemporary corps of kings, chiefs and headmen is disputed between those who see them as an authentic expression of African communalism and a repository of African cultural and spiritual values, and those for whom they represent a corrupted tool of indirect rule, first by British colonialism, then by settler governments culminating in high apartheid. See J. M. Williams, *Chieftaincy, the State and Democracy in Post-Apartheid South Africa* (Bloomington, 2010).

21 The DP became the Democratic Alliance (DA) in 2000. All further mentions of the party in this work will use the title DP before 2000 and DA after.

22 Hermann Giliomee and Charles Simkins, *The Awkward Embrace: One Party Domination in Industrialised Societies* (Cape Town, 1999). See also Roger Southall, 'The "Dominant Party Debate" in South Africa', *Africa Spectrum*, Vol. 40 (1), 2005, pp. 61–82.

23 In the sixth election (May 2019), the ANC's share of the vote dropped to its lowest yet, 57.5 per cent, a decline of nearly 5 per cent. However, it is too early to say with confidence that the era of one party dominance is drawing to a close.

24 Karen Ferree, *Framing the Race in South Africa: The Political Origins of Racial Census Elections* (Cambridge, 2010).

25 Anthony Butler, 'South Africa's political futures', *Government and Opposition*, Vol. 38 (1) January 2003, pp. 93–112.

26 The classic conceptualization was in Andrew Mack's 1975 article, 'Why big nations lose small wars', *World Politics*, Vol. 27 (2), January 1975, pp. 175–200. Post-Cold War interventions by the United States in the Middle East and the 'blowback' of resistance and retaliation to them have led to greatly increased interest in and further development of Mack's original thesis.

27 This summary is taken from a speech delivered in May 1987 on behalf of UDF leader Murphy Morobe (who was detained by apartheid security forces at the time) and published in the *Review of African Political Economy*, Vol. 40, December 1987, pp. 81–7.

28 For a discussion see Johnston, *Inventing the Nation*, pp. 206–11.

29 See Karl Von Holdt et al., *The Smoke That Calls: Insurgent Citizenship, Collective Violence and the Struggle for a Place in the New South Africa* (Johannesburg, 2011).

30 For a summary see Johnston, *Inventing the Nation*, pp. 237–44.

31 Tom Lodge, 'Neo-patrimonial politics in the ANC', *African Affairs*, Vol. 113 (450), 2014, p. 17.

32 Laura Phillips, Ariana Lissoni and Ivor Chipkin, 'Bantustans are dead – long live Bantustans', *Mail and Guardian*, 11 July 2014. See also Ivor Chipkin, 'In Jacob Zuma, South Africa has found its Gorbachev', *Daily Maverick*, 31 July 2016; Jason Robinson, 'Fragments of the past: Homeland politics and the South African transition, 1990–2014', *Journal of Southern African Studies*, Vol. 41 (5), 2015, pp. 953–67.

33 See Sindiso Mnisi Weeks, 'South Africa's traditional courts bill 2.0: Improved but still flawed', *Conversation*, 4 April 2017, https://theconversation.com/.

34 *Report of the Presidential Review Commission on the Reform and Transformation of the Public Service in South Africa*, Government Printer, 1999, Conclusions and Recommendations.

35 National Planning Commission, *National Development Plan*, 2011, p. 364.

36 The Presidency: Department of Performance Monitoring and Evaluation, *Twenty Year Report: South Africa 1994–2014*: Background Paper: Changing Public Service, p. 22.

37 Quoted in Centre for Development and Enterprise (CDE), *Reforming Health Care: What Role for the Private Sector* (Johannesburg, 2011). For a discussion of the issue see this source at pp. 32–4. See also Mike Dent, et al., *The Routledge Companion to Professions and Professionalism* (London, 2016), p. 259.

38 The Presidency: Background Report: Changing Public Service, p. 21.

39 Ibid., pp. 25–6.

40 ANC 53rd National Conference, December 2012, Organisational Report by the Secretary-General, Gwede Mantashe, p. 3.

41 ANC Fifth National Policy Conference, Secretary-general's Discussion Document: 'Organisational Renewal and Organisational Design', p. 15.

42 Ibid., p. 28.

43 The strict definition counts as unemployed only those who are actively and unsuccessfully seeking work, while the expanded definition counts discouraged work seekers as unemployed.

44 National Planning Commission, *National Development Plan 2030*, p. 39.

45 Calculated from World Bank figures at www.data.worldbank.org.

46 www.worldbank.org/en/country/southafrica/overview/.

47 Averages since 2000 from www.data.worldbank.org: figures for Q4 2016: media release, Quarterly Labour Force Survey (QLFS), Statistics South Africa (StatsSA) www.statssa.gov.za/?p=9561. University of KwaZulu/Natal study, 'The unemployed in South Africa: Why are so many not counted?', www.econ3x3.org/article/unemployed-south-africa-why-are-so-many-not-counted.

48 Statistics South Africa (StatsSA) Quarterly Labour Force Survey Q1 2019, www.statssa.gov.za.

49 Centre for Development and Enterprise (CDE), *The Growth Agenda*, 'Insights and Key Recommendations' (Johannesburg, April 2016), pp. 5 and 7, www.cde.org.za. Figures from StatsSA, QLFS, Q4 2015.

3 Possession and betrayal: Mandela's ambiguous legacy in South African politics

1 Tom Lodge, *Mandela: A Critical Life* (Oxford, 2007).

2 Tom Lodge, 'Assessing the icon', *Open Democracy*, 17 July 2009.

3 Ibid.

4 David Smith, *Young Mandela* (London, 2010).

5 Daniel Roux, 'Mandela writing/writing Mandela', in *The Cambridge Companion to Nelson Mandela* (2014), p. 209.

6 https://www.youtube.com/watch?v=7ov_jfKaxa4 and https://www.youtube.com/watch?v=OuocHCwGi88.

7 Ranjeni Munsamy, 'Scrum over Mandela's legacy exposes hollow heart of SA politics', *Daily Maverick*, 27 July 2016, www.dailymaverick.co.za.

8 Ibid. The Royal Family is not a stranger to cashing in on Madiba's name. Among its offerings are a range of royal wines, apparel and precious metal coins and medallions, the latter including a range of 'Mandela Prison Life' gift sets (www.houseofmandela.com).

9 Gareth van Onselen, 'The ANC and the DA battle for the past', *Business Day*, 27 July 2016.

10 Munsamy, 'Scrum over Mandela's legacy'.

11 Alexander Johnston, *Inventing the Nation: South Africa* (2014), p. 150.

12 The author writes from the perspective of one (among many) who was frequently commissioned to produce such assessments.

13 Winnie Madikizela-Mandela, 'Oliver Tambo created Nelson Mandela', *New African*, Vol. 468, December 2007.

14 See Tim Cohen, 'Point of order: Zuma's state of conflict', *Business Day*, 12 September 2016. Zuma's quoted words are taken from this source.

15 Cf. Howard Wimberley and Joel Savishinsky, 'Ancestral Memorialism', in W. H. Newell and Walter de Gruyter (eds), *Ancestors* (Oxford, 1979), pp. 241–61.

16 Colin Bundy, *Nelson Mandela* (Johannesburg, 2015), p. 110.

17 Zakes Mda, 'Nelson Mandela, neither sell-out nor saint', *Guardian*, 6 December 2013.

18 Zakes Mda, 'The contradictions of Mandela', *New York Times*, 6 December 2013.

19 Colin Bundy, 'Mandela was no superhero and his legacy has its critics', *Business Day*, 17 July 2015.

20 Statistics South Africa (StatsSA), *Census In Brief, 2011* (Pretoria, 2012), p. 34.

21 Centre for Development and Enterprise, *No Country for Young People: The Crisis of Youth Unemployment and What to Do about It* (Johannesburg, 2017), p. 5.

22 For a contemporary critique of the 'moral panic' about young people, see Jeremy Seekings, 'The "Lost Generation": South Africa's "Youth Problem" in the early 1990s', *Transformation*, 1996, pp. 103–25. See also, Colin Bundy, 'At war with the future? Black South African youth in the 1990s', *Southern African Report*, Vol. 8 (1), 1992, p. 18.

23 The Fallist movement has its origins in protest against colonial symbols on campuses, especially a statue of Cecil John Rhodes at the University of Cape Town (UCT). The statue was removed in 2015, but the protest broadened to other student issues, notably the demand that 'fees must fall' in campaigns that included destruction of property, notably the burning of some of UCT's art collection and violent intimidation of staff and students. Some Fallists also reject 'Western' science on the grounds that it is racist. See Doreh Taghavi, *Exploring Fallism: Student Protests and the Decolonization of Education in South Africa*, Masters thesis, University of Cologne, December 2017. See also Mohammed Jameel Abdulla, 'In defence of fallism', *Mail and Guardian*, 1 March 2017.

24 South African History Online, *Nelson Mandela's Address to Rally in Durban 25 February 1990*, https://www.sahistory.org.za/archive/nelson-mandelas-address-rally-durban-25-february-1990.

25 In addition to the Mda and Bundy references already cited, see Raymond Suttner (former political prisoner, activist and ANC MP), 'Did Mandela "sell out" the struggle for freedom?' *Daily Maverick*, 8 March 2016; David Everatt, 'The Mandela Foundation's verdict on the Mandela era: It failed …', *Conversation*, 30 September 2016, https://theconversation.com/the-mandela-foundations-verdict-on-the-mandela-era-it-failed-65257.

26 Ranjeni Munsamy, 'Julius Malema and the move towards #MandelaMust Fall', *Daily Maverick*, 12 April 2015.

27 Ibid.

28 Useful summaries and discussions of this extensive literature can be found in Naomi Klein, 'Democracy born in chains: South Africa's constricted freedom', in Naomi Klein (ed.), *The Shock Doctrine: The Rise of Disaster Capitalism* (Toronto, 2007), pp. 233–61; John Saul and Patrick Bond, 'The apartheid endgame 1990–1994', in John Saul (ed.), *South Africa: The Present as History* (Martlesham, Suffolk, 2014).

29 A comprehensive but still economical list of 'Mandela's' compromises, which fall under the 'Faustian' rubric, can be found in Patrick Bond, 'Why South Africa should undo Mandela's economic deals', *Conversation*, 12 January 2016, https://theconversation.com/why-south-africa-should-undo-mandelas-economic-deals-52767.

30 Ronnie Kasrils, 'How the ANC's Faustian pact sold out South Africa's poorest', *Guardian*, 24 June 2013. The article is an edited version of the introduction to the fourth edition of Kasrils' autobiographical account of his part in the liberation struggle, *Armed and Dangerous* (Johannesburg, 2013).

31 Ibid.

32 Ibid. South African exceptionalism has worked across the board. If there is one thing the anti-apartheid left and apartheid regime governments had in common, it is that the world (or the West) 'cannot do without' some or another South African asset.

33 In a speech to trade union South African Clothing and Textile Workers' Union (SACTWU), 8 August 2013, and quoted in Saul and Bond, 'Apartheid's endgame', p. 128. Bond adds 'took our eye off the ball' for nineteen years.

34 For discussion, see the references in note 24.

35 Saul and Bond, 'Apartheid's endgame', p. 128.

36 Bond, 'Mandela's economic deals'.

37 On seduction as a tactic in the negotiations, see M. Gevisser, *Thabo Mbeki*, 2007; Allister Sparks, *Tomorrow Is Another Country* (Johannesburg, 1994) on Ramaphosa; and Patti Waldmeir, *Anatomy of a Miracle* (London, 1997) on Mandela.

38 Hermann Giliomee, *The Last Afrikaner Leaders* (Cape Town, 2012), pp. 420–1.

39 Ibid.

40 R. W. Johnson, *South Africa's Brave New World* (London, 2010), p. 92.

41 ANC 50th National Conference: Report by the President of the ANC 16 December 1997, https://www.sahistory.org.za/archive/report-president-anc-nelson-mandela-50th-national-conference-african-national-congress-mafik.
For a critical exegesis see Johnson, *South Africa's Brave New World*, pp. 132–6.

42 Johnson, *South Africa's Brave New World*, pp. 132–6.

43 See, for instance, an interview with Anthony Sampson published in the *Observer*, 18 February 1990, one week after his release: 'He insists on subjecting himself to the collective decision-making of his party. He

defers to the national executive committee in Lusaka and the ANC's ailing president, Oliver Tambo, who is in a Swedish clinic recovering from a stroke.'

44 James Myburgh, 'Who is the real ANC?', *Politicsweb*, 22 December 2016, http://www.politicsweb.co.za/opinion/who-is-the-real-anc. This article is based on a paper presented at the annual conference of the African Studies Association, Washington, DC, 13 December 2016.

45 Stephen Ellis, *External Mission: The ANC in Exile 1960–1990* (Johannesburg, 2012); Irina Filatova and Apollon Davidson, *The Hidden Thread: Russia and South Africa in the Soviet Era* (Johannesburg, 2013). The phrase 'bodyguard of lies' is Myburgh's in 'Who is the real ANC'.

46 Myburgh, 'Who is the real ANC?'

47 Ibid.

48 Ibid.

49 Jeff Guy, 'A chief rules by people power', *Mail and Guardian*, 14 June 2012. The late Jeff Guy was professor of history at the University of KwaZulu-Natal.

50 Luli Callinicoss, *Oliver Tambo: Beyond the Engeli Mountains* (Cape Town, 2004), pp. 34–5.

51 Ibid., pp. 449–50.

52 *Lekgotla* (Sesotho) means traditional community meeting or law court involving a chief and his council. The word is much used in South Africa across languages (especially in government) to mean a strategy meeting. A similar word in isiZulu and isiXhosa is *indaba*.

53 Callinicoss, *Oliver Tambo*, p. 624.

54 The Thembu, like the Amapondo, are one of several groups of isiXhosa-speaking peoples in the Eastern Cape.

55 Philip Bonner, 'The antimonies of Nelson Mandela', in Rita Barnard (ed.), *The Cambridge Companion to Nelson Mandela* (Cambridge, 2014), pp. 29–49 at p. 32.

56 Elleke Boehmer, *Nelson Mandela* (New York, 2010), p. 26.

57 Bonner, 'Antimonies of Nelson Mandela', p. 30.

58 Ibid., p. 32.

59 Boehmer, *Nelson Mandela*, p. 26.

60 ANC National Working Committee, 'Through the eye of a needle? Choosing the best cadres to lead transformation', *Umrabulo*, Vol. 11, June–July 2001, http://ramaphosa.org.za/downloads/Eye-of-the-needle.pdf. At the time of download (mid-October 2018), the ANC website, which houses the original, was suspended due to 'non-payment to the service provider'.

61 ANC Constitution, Rule 3: The Character of the ANC (3.1).

62 Robert Michels (1876–1936), *Political Parties* (New York, 1968 edition), p. 365.

63 W. G. Runciman goes so far as to ask 'is it more than a truism?' *Social Science and Political Theory* (Cambridge, 1969), p. 67.

64 Maurice Duverger, *Political Parties* (London, 1954), p. 425.

65 ANC Constitution, Rule 3: The Character of the Organisation (3.2), www.anc.org.za.

66 ANC, *Organisational Democracy and Discipline in the Movement*, 1 July 1997, www.anc.org.za.

67 ANC Constitution, 16.1: The President.

68 On SACP influence through 'caucus tactics', and on Tambo's temperament, see Stephen Ellis and Tsepo Sechaba, *Comrades against Apartheid* (Melton, Woodbridge, 1992), p. 60.

69 Anthony Butler, *The Idea of the ANC* (Athens, Ohio, 2012), p. 90.

70 Ibid.

71 James Myburgh, 'The African National Congress and the evolution of South Africa's one party dominant system', *European Consortium for Political Research*, conference paper, April 2005, https://ecpr.eu/Filestore/PaperProposal/56f77ccc-91f9-40e5-8fc8-d139087ca431.pdf.

72 ANC, *Organisational Democracy and Discipline*.

73 Ibid.

74 Ibid.

75 Zamani Saul, 'The anatomy of a faction: A negative tendency', *ANC Today*, 18–24 September 2016, http://www.anc.org.za/content/anc-today-volume-15-no-30-0. The author was, at the time of writing, provincial secretary of the ANC in the Northern Cape. He was elected provincial leader (chairman) in May 2017 as a supporter of Cyril Ramaphosa for succession to Zuma as ANC president.

76 Callinicoss, *Oliver Tambo*, p. 17.

77 Ibid., p. 626.

78 Tokyo Sexwale, 'The death that mobilised a nation', *Sunday Times*, 13 April 2008.

79 An exposition and assessment of this theory can be found in Johnson, *South Africa's Brave New World*, pp. 25–51.

80 Ibid., p. 48.

81 Ibid.

82 This effect among whites sometimes overlaps with the 'lost leader' syndrome. The author remembers being on the fringes of a group of middle-aged white bankers at some *lekgotla* or another in the late 1990s, all of them clamouring to buy a beer for Van Zyl Slabbert (the leader of the liberal opposition Progressive Federal Party, 1979–86, and the keynote speaker at the *lekgotla*). 'Ag come back Van, we need a leader like you!' they enthused. 'If that's the fucking case' retorted Van, revisiting the frustration with 'white politics' of the apartheid era that induced him to go the extra-parliamentary route, 'Why didn't you fucking vote for me in the 1980s?'

4 Mandela's successors: A framework for analysis

1 Events that are hard to predict, very rare and sometimes in hindsight inappropriately explained and rationalized.

2 It should in fairness be noted that during Mbeki's tenure as Mandela's deputy president, he wielded much more power than any deputy would normally. However, wielded as it was in the shadow of Mandela, these powers, substantial as they were, did not make it a presidential or even a quasi-presidential term.

3 There are of course unusual exceptions to this democratic norm, Australia being the most striking. It has become the norm in recent years for prime ministers there to be removed from office by palace coups, which brazenly trade on party disunity and personal animus. Kevin Rudd and Julia Gillard (Labor) and Tony Abbot and Malcolm Turnbull have all been victims of such insurgency in recent years, with the result that to mid-2018 Australia has had six prime ministers in a decade.

4 Statistics South Africa (StasSA), *Mid-Year Population Estimate*, 12 July 2018, Statistical Release P0302, http://www.statssa.gov.za.

5 Mbeki

1 For instance M. Gevisser, *Thabo Mbeki* (Johannesburg, 2007); R. W. Johnson, *South Africa's Brave New World* (London, 2010); W. M. Gumede, *Thabo Mbeki and the Battle for the Soul of the ANC* (London, 2008).

2 'Spear of the Nation'.

3 Gevisser, *Thabo Mbeki*, p. 632.

4 Gumede, *Thabo Mbeki and the Battle*, p. 44.

5 There were an estimated 14,000 deaths in political violence in South Africa between 1990 and 1994. See David Bruce, 'Political killings in South Africa', *Policy Brief*, Vol. 64, 2014, p. 1.

6 Thabo Mbeki, 'Unmandated Reflections: DP's discussion document on the tasks of the ANC in the new epoch of democratic transformation (August 9 1994)', *Politicsweb*, 17 April 2015, http://www.politicsweb.co.za/documents/unmandated-reflections--thabo-mbeki.

7 Gumede, *Thabo Mbeki and the Battle*, p. 49.

8 'Do not look where you fell but where you slipped', *Mail and Guardian*, 25 October 2006, https://mg.co.za/article/2006-10-25-do-not-look-where-you-fell-but-slipped.

9 Gevisser, *Thabo Mbeki*, p. 642.

10 Johnson, *South Africa's Brave New World*, p. 59.

11 Gevisser, *Thabo Mbeki*, p. 650.

12 'Mandela hands the baton to Mbeki', *BBC News*, 20 December 1997, http://news.bbc.co.uk/1/hi/41252.stm.

13 Statistics South Africa (StatsSA), *Mid-Year Population Estimate 2018*, http://www.statssa.gov.za/publications/P0302/P03022018.pdf.

14 Ivor Chipkin, *Do South Africans Exist? Nationalism, Democracy and the Identity of 'the People'* (Johannesburg, 2007). Alexander Johnston, *Inventing the Nation: South Africa* (London, 2014), pp. 319–26. See this source (parts 1 and 4) for an appraisal of the extent to which the life patterns of black African and minority South Africans do or do not overlap.

15 Gevisser, *Thabo Mbeki*, p. 223.

16 Ibid.

17 The chief cultivator of the 'Englishness' trope was Anthony Sampson. See (on the occasion of Mbeki's state visit to the UK), 'President select', *The Observer*, 10 June 2001. However, there were many other practitioners.

18 Jonathan Powell, *Great Hatred, Little Room* (London, 2010), p. 108.

19 'I am an African': Statement of Deputy President T. M. Mbeki, on behalf of the African National Congress, on the occasion of the adoption by the Constitutional Assembly of *The Republic of South Africa Constitution Bill 1996*, Cape Town, 8 May 1996. 'Two Nations': statement of Deputy President Thabo Mbeki at the opening of the debate in the National Assembly, on *Reconciliation and Nation Building*, Cape Town, 29 May 1988.

20 Mbeki, 'I am an African speech'.

21 Ibid.

22 Johnston, *Inventing the Nation*, p. 181.

23 Gevisser, *Thabo Mbeki*, p. 326.

24 Alistair Horne, *A Savage War of Peace* (London, 1987), p. 303. Horne discusses the speech in depth, pp. 301–3. Newsreel captures the electric reaction of the crowd to de Gaulle's words: https://www.youtube.com/watch?v=vzm0APfrflk.

25 It is hard to know what to make of Mbeki's habitual use of plural rather than singular personal pronouns, which was one of the most pronounced features of his discourse. The usage had probably something to do with conformity to the ANC's obsessive collectivism and the intention was probably to strike a note of humbleness. This may, or again may not, have worked for ANC activists. For anyone else, it risked contrary effects of alienation rather than inclusiveness ('we, the elect') and arrogance, most educated anglophones being familiar with the implications of 'the royal we'.

26 Mbeki, 'Two Nations speech'.

27 Nicoli Nattrass and Jeremy Seekings, '"Two nations?" Race and economic inequality in South Africa today', *Daedalus*, Vol. 130 (1), 2001, pp. 45–70 at p. 66.

28 Gumede, *Thabo Mbeki and the Battle*, p. 49.

29 For numbers (quoting the estimates, among others, of *Africa* Confidential), see Gevisser, *Thabo Mbeki*, p. 465.

30 See Ibid., pp. 465–73 for Mbeki's membership.

31 Padraig O'Malley, *Nelson Mandela Centre of Memory*, General Information, The Tripartite Alliance, 1993, https://www.nelsonmandela.org/omalley/index.php/site/q/03lv02424.htm.

32 Simon Adams, 'What's left? The South African Communist Party after apartheid', *Review of African Political Economy*, Vol. 72, 1997, pp. 237–48. Another estimate put the membership as low as 14,000 in June 1998: Sechaba ka'Nkosi, 'SACP split over who will lead', *Mail and Guardian*, 19 June 1998.

33 See, 'Mandela slams SACP and Cosatu over Gear criticism', *Mercury* (South African Press Association: SAPA), 2 July 1998; 'Moment of truth for SACP', *Mail and Guardian*, 3 July–9 July 1998; 'SACP licks its wounds', *Independent on Sunday*, 4 July 1998.

34 'Mandela slams SACP and Cosatu'.

35 'Moment of truth for SACP'.

36 Mandela's words of admonishment do not appear in the archive version of the speech, which contains among the fraternal sentiments only the mild cautionary reminder that all concerned should bear in mind the differences in character between the member organizations of the Alliance. http://db.nelsonmandela.org/speeches/pub_view.asp?pg=item&ItemID=NMS598&txtstr=South%20African%20Communist%20Party.

37 An edited extract appeared in Thabo Mbeki, 'ANC's allies must set their sights on the real enemies', *Sunday Times*, 5 July 1998.

38 The slogan originated with the African Party for the Independence of Guinea and the Cape Verde Islands (PAIGC) and is generally attributed to its leader Amilcar Cabral. Cabral was something of an icon in the SACP as this tribute shows, http://www.sacp.org.za/docs/history/dadoo-19.html. This would give Mbeki's use of his words a particular resonance.

39 See, for instance, one week after the congress, Jeremy Cronin, 'Why the SACP rejects GEAR', *Mail and Guardian*, 10–16 July 1998.

40 'Moment of truth for the SACP'.

41 Roger Southall, *Opposition and Democracy in South Africa* (London, 2014), p. 200.

42 For names and posts of co-opted communists and unionists, see Southall, *Opposition and Democracy*, p. 199.

43 See, for instance, Sechaba ka'Nkosi, 'SACP split over who will lead', *Mail and Guardian*, 19 June 1998.

44 For detailed treatment of this subject, see Geoffrey Hawker, 'Political leadership in the ANC: The South African provinces 1994–1999', *Journal of Modern African Studies*, Vol. 38 (4), 2000, pp. 631–58.

45 Ibid., p. 642.

46 Ibid., p. 639.

47 For examples of corruption at provincial level stretching back to the mid-1990s, see 'Soul for sale: The ANC and business', *Financial Mail*, 19 January 2007.

48 For a list, see Hawker, 'Political leadership', p. 638.
49 See, for instance, 'Line-up of ANC's would-be kingmakers', *Sunday Independent*, 28 October 2007. This article profiles all eighteen ANC provincial secretaries and chairmen/women at the time of the succession struggle between Mbeki and Zuma in 2006–7.
50 For a summary of the disruptions and a somewhat hagiographical profile of Magashule, see Moipone Malefane, 'The "people's choice" just keeps bouncing back', *Sunday Times*, 12 August 2007.
51 *The Constitution of the Republic of South Africa* (Act 108 of 1996), Chapter 9, State Institutions Supporting Democracy, 181 (2).
52 The ANC, *State, Property Relations and Social Transformation* (1998).
53 See Farouk Chothia and Sean Jacobs, 'Re-making the Presidency: The tension between co-ordination and centralisation', in Sean Jacobs and Richard Calland (eds), *Thabo Mbeki's World* (Pietermaritzburg, 2002), pp. 145–62.
54 On the RDP, see Alan Hirsch, *Season of Hope: Economic Reform under Mandela and Mbeki* (Pietermaritzburg, 2005), pp. 29–108. For a contemporary view, see Jesmond Blumenfeld, 'RDP RIP?', *International Update*, South African Institute of International Affairs, October 1996.
55 See Chothia and Jacobs, 'Remaking the presidency', pp. 156–7. Andrew Feinstein, an ANC MP who fell foul of Pahad when he challenged the government over the issue of corruption in the arms deal and resigned over the matter in 2001, has described Pahad as 'an uncouth enforcer of limited principle'. Andrew Feinstein, *After the Party: A Personal and Political Journey Inside the ANC* (Johannesburg, 2007), p. 116.
56 See, for instance, Jeremy Cronin, 'What kind of presidency?', *Mail and Guardian*, 27 May 2006.
57 Joel Pearson, Sarita Pillay and Ivor Chipkin, *State-Building in South Africa after Apartheid: The History of the National Treasury* (Johannesburg, 2016), p. 2.
58 Gill Marcus, et al., 'Public Management Reform: A Case Study of South Africa, 1994–2004', Genesis Analytics for the Commonwealth Secretariat (July 2005), pp. 13–14.
59 Pearson, Pillay and Chipkin, *State-Building in South Africa*, p. 12.
60 For detailed evaluation and assessment, see Pearson, Pillay and Chipkin, *State-Building in South Africa*.
61 Ibid., p. 1.
62 James Myburgh, 'The African National Congress and the evolution of South Africa's one party dominant system', *European Consortium for Political Research*, conference paper, April 2005, p. 10.
63 See Andrew Feinstein, 'A story that had to be told', in *After the Party*, pp. 154–208.
64 Mbeki admitted authorship in a newspaper interview in February 2006; Feinstein, *After the Party*, p. 189, note 35.

65 Ibid., p. 185.
66 Johnson, *South Africa's Brave New World*, p. 250.
67 Ibid., pp. 249–54. Also, Gevisser, *Thabo Mbeki*, pp. 646–50.
68 Gevisser, *Thabo Mbeki*, p. 648.
69 Sam Sole, 'Of justice or king-making', *Mail and Guardian*, 24 December 2004.
70 The names of the NIA and SASS were changed in 2005 to the Domestic and the International Branch, respectively, of the State Security Agency. It is commonplace, however, for the original acronyms to be used.
71 Johnson, *South Africa's Brave New World*, pp. 544–9.
72 See the *Mail and Guardian*'s compendium of coverage, https://mg.co.za/tag/special-browse-mole-report.
73 Ivor Powell, 'Smoke and mirrors', *Mail and Guardian*, 5 January 2009, https://mg.co.za/article/2009-05-01-smoke-and-mirrors.
74 The full text of Browse Mole is available at https://cdn.mg.co.za/uploads/2009/04/30/special-browse-mole-report.pdf.
75 Ibid.
76 Ibid.
77 'The spy who saved Zuma', *Mail and Guardian*, 9 April 2009.
78 These events will be dealt with in the next chapter.

6 From Mbeki to Zuma

1 Andrew Rawnsley, 'How long will Theresa May survive? She is the very last person to ask', *The Observer*, 3 September 2017, https://www.theguardian.com/commentisfree/2017/sep/02/how-long-will-mrs-may-survive-last-person-to-ask-lead-conservatives-election.
2 An authoritative source is Nicoli Nattrass, 'AIDS and the scientific governance of medicine in post-apartheid South Africa', *African Affairs*, Vol. 107 (427), 2008, pp. 157–76. See also M. Gevisser, *Thabo Mbeki* (Johannesburg, 2007).
3 Gevisser, *Thabo Mbeki*, p. 736.
4 *Castro Hlongwane, Caravans, Cats, Geese, Foot and Mouth and Statistics: HIV/AIDS and the Struggle for the Humanisation of the African* (2002). http://ccs.ukzn.ac.za/files/Mbeki%27s%20document.pdf.
5 Gevisser, *Thabo Mbeki*, p. 736.
6 Vaclav Havel, *Disturbing the Peace: A Conversation with Karel Hvizdala* (New York, 1991), p. 167.
7 Illustrating the truism that a week is a long time in politics, many mainstream commentators at the beginning of Mbeki's second term reflected the view that he 'is unassailable in the party going forward ... so powerful now in the ANC that not only will he be able to command the

loyalty and obedience of key officials up to the last moment, he may also decisively be able to influence his succession'. Peter Bruce, 'Mbeki's second term', *Business Day*, 26 April 2004. The article reflected the views of the editors of South Africa's two most influential newspapers.

8 Average calculated from World Bank figures: http://www.worldbank.org/en/country/southafrica.

9 This optimistic picture is based on a government document, *Accelerated and Shared Growth Initiative for South Africa (Asgisa)*, hosted on the O'Malley archive: https://www.nelsonmandela.org/omalley/index.php/site/q/03lv02409/04lv02410/05lv02415/06lv02416.htm.

10 Ricardo Hausmann, *Final Recommendations of the International Panel on the Accelerated and Shared Growth Initiative for South Africa (Asgisa)*, Harvard Kennedy School, June 2008, https://papers.ssrn.com/sol3/papers.cfm?abstract_id=1124292.

11 Zuma's acquittal smoothed his path to the leadership but for the long-term effects of the case on his reputation see Shireen Hassim, 'Why, a decade on a new book on Zuma's rape trial has finally hit home', *Conversation*, 5 October 2017, https://theconversation.com/why-a-decade-on-a-new-book-on-zumas-rape-trial-has-finally-hit-home-85262. The book in question is Redi Thlabi, *Kwhezi* (Cape Town, 2017). 'Khwezi' is the pseudonym of Zuma's (now deceased) accuser.

12 'Zuma case struck from the roll', *Mail and Guardian*, 20 September 2006, https://mg.co.za/article/2006-09-20-zuma-case-struck-from-the-roll.

13 The Nicholson judgement: In the High Court of South Africa, Natal Provincial Division: case number 8652/08: *In the matter between Jacob Gedleyihlekisa Zuma and the National Director of Public Prosecutions*, http://www.politicsweb.co.za/politicsweb/action/media/downloadFile?media_fileid=1077.

14 Supreme Court of Appeal: Judgement: *National Director of Public Prosecutions v. Zuma* Case No: 573/08, 12 January 2009, http://www.justice.gov.za/sca/judgments%5Csca_2009/sca09-001.pdf. A full bench heard the case and the judgement, which Judge Louis Harms wrote, was unanimous. Quotations are from paragraphs 44 to 52 and paragraph 81.

15 A diehard African racial nationalist could point out that irrespective of when they were appointed, the judges of the full bench in this case consisted of two whites, two Indians and only one African.

16 For a breakdown of the provincial branch nominations, see 'Decisions, Decisions', *Sunday Times*, 25 November 2007.

17 For instance, 'The presidency of Jacob Zuma looms', *The Economist*, 18 September 2008, http://www.economist.com/node/12263140.

18 Anthony Butler, 'Challenges for Mbeki's successor', *Business Day*, 28 June 2006.

19 Ibid.

20 Information in the rest of this paragraph is based on, Jonathan Faull, 'Reading the ANC's National Membership Audit', *ePoliticsSA*, Vol. 4, 2007, Institute for a Democratic South Africa.

21 Exact numbers vary in different reports: 3,834 is one calculation, 3,675 is another. Some delegates were credentialed at the conference and others disqualified, which may account for the discrepancies.

22 See Steven Friedman, 'The person may change but the policy lingers on', *Thought Leader (Mail and Guardian)*, 11 December 2007, http://thoughtleader.co.za/stevenfriedman/2007/12/11/ changing-the-person-not-the-policy/.

23 Gevisser, *Thabo Mbeki*, p. 792.

24 R. W. Johnson, *How Long Will South Africa Survive? The Looming Crisis* (Johannesburg, 2015), p. 66.

25 Tony Leon, 'On the end of Mbeki and Mbeki-ism', Speech at the University of Cape Town, 25 September 2008, http://politicsweb.co.za/politics/ tony-leon-on-the-end-of-mbeki-and-mbekiism.

7 Zuma from 2009 to 2017: A narrative of decay

1 *Mail and Guardian*, 'The good, the bad and the ugly: The 2000 report card', 22 December 2000, http://allafrica.com/stories/200012220171.html.

2 *Mail and Guardian* (n.d.), 'Cabinet report card 2016', Jacob Zuma: http:// cabinet.mg.co.za/2016/jacob-zuma.

3 See for instance, Joel Hellman, Geraint Jones and Daniel Kaufmann, 'Seize the state, seize the day: An empirical analysis of state capture and corruption in transition', *World Bank*, 2000.

4 'Motsoko Pheko, ' "Insulted" by Malema, Vavi comments', *Mail and Guardian*, 22 June 2008, https://mg.co.za/ article/2008-06-22-motsoko-pheko-insulted-by-malema-vavi-comments.

5 'Political hyenas in feeding frenzy –Vavi', *News24.com*, 26 August 2010, http://www.news24.com/SouthAfrica/Politics/ Political-hyenas-in-feeding-frenzy-20100826.

6 See 'Zuma and Cosatu: The end of the affair', *Mail and Guardian*, 19 February 2010.

7 'Zuma calls Malema "leader in the making" ', *Pretoria News*, 26 October 2009, https://www.iol.co.za/news/politics/ zuma-calls-malema-leader-in-the-making-462670.

8 'Ajay Gupta threatened to kill me', *Sunday Times*, 24 August 2018, previews the evidence Jonas was to give to the Zondo commission of inquiry into state capture. https://www.timeslive.co.za/politics/2018-08-24-ajay-gupta-threatened-to-kill-me-mcebisi-jonass-shocking-revelations/.

9 Alec Russell, *After Mandela: The Battle for the Soul of South Africa* (London, 2009), p. 238.

10 Independent Electoral Commission (IEC) press release 14 March 2014, http://www.politicsweb.co.za/party/808-of-eligible-voters-registered--iec.

11 Arthur Miller, *On Politics and the Art of Acting* (New York, 2001), p. 74.

12 Mark Gevisser, *Thabo Mbeki* (Johannesburg, 2007), p. 393.

13 Jeremy Gordin, *Zuma: A Biography* (Johannesburg, 2008), p. 25.

14 For the archive of the *Mail and Guardian*'s coverage of the Hefer Commission, see https://mg.co.za/tag/hefer-commission. For the O'Malley archive's coverage see https://www.nelsonmandela.org/omalley/index.php/site/q/03lv03445/04lv04015/05lv04120.htm.

15 For discussions see: Steven Ellis, *External Mission: The ANC in Exile 1960–1990* (Johannesburg, 2012); Paul Trewhela, 'Jacob Zuma, Mbokodo and the death of Thami Zulu', *Politicsweb*, 12 February 2009, http://www.politicsweb.co.za/news-and-analysis/jacob-zuma-mbokodo-and-the-death-of-thami-zulu and Kenneth Good, 'How the killing of Thami Zulu contradicts Zuma's claims', *Politicsweb*, 13 May 2013.

16 'Minister versus top spooks', *amaBhungane Centre for Investigative Journalism*, 16 September 2011 ('amaBhungane' is isiZulu for 'the dung beetles'), http://amabhungane.co.za/article/2011-09-16-minister-vs-top-spooks; 'Ex-Spy bosses to spill beans on Guptas', *Mail and Guardian*, 24 March 2016, https://mg.co.za/article/2016-03-23-ex-spy-bosses-to-spill-beans-on-guptas. In September 2018, the *Sunday Times* ran an article claiming that the three intelligence heads concluded (after a CIA tip off) that the Guptas were 'a threat to national security' and were fired when they confronted Zuma with this assessment. 'National security threat: CIA alerted SA to the Gupta's "dodgy deals" in 2009', *Sunday Times*, 2 September 2018.

17 Ellis, *External Mission*, p. 240.

18 On the meaning of Gedleyihlekisa see Jeremy Gordin, *Zuma: A Biography* (Johannesburg, 2008), p. 1, http://www.sahistory.org.za/people/jacob-gedleyihlekisa-zuma. The name appears as 'he who laughs while he is hurting you' in Adriaan Basson, 'Gedleyihlekisa is laughing at you', *News24*, 15 February 2016, http://www.news24.com/Columnists/GuestColumn/Gedleyihlekisa-is-laughing-at-you-20150215. See also Tinyiko Maluleke, 'Why Zuma's chuckles are no laughing matter', *Independent Online*, https://www.iol.co.za/news/opinion/why-zumas-chuckles-are-no-laughing-matter-8051328.

19 The Presidency, *Annual Address by President Zuma to the National House of Traditional Leaders*, Cape Town, 1 November 2012.

20 For a discussion of the gulf between the Constitution and popularly held values see Alexander Johnston, *Inventing the Nation: South Africa* (London, 2014), pp. 237–9.

21 A compilation of Zuma's quoted views (many of them off the cuff) gives the flavour of his populist insouciance in these matters: See Gareth van Onselen,

Clever Blacks, Jesus and Nkandla: The Real Jacob Zuma in His Own Words (Johannesburg, 2014).

22 Hein Marais, *South Africa Pushed to the Limit: The Political Economy of Change* (London, 2011), pp. 442–3.

23 Jeremy Cronin, 'What kind of presidency?', *Mail and Guardian*, 27 May 2006.

24 'ANC: Zuma: Speech by the ANC president to the SACP congress 12 December 2009', *Polity*, 12 December 2009.

25 'JZ will serve only one term as president', *Sowetan*, 14 December 2007, http://www.sowetanlive.co.za/sowetan/archive/2007/12/14/jz-will-serve-only-one-term-as-president.

26 'Zuma now willing to serve two terms', *Business Day*, 5 June 2009.

27 'Absence of the best led to Zuma election: Malema', *News24*, 6 November 2015, http://www.news24.com/SouthAfrica/News/Absence-of-the-best-led-to-Zuma-election-Malema-20150611.

28 Niall Ferguson's depiction of the contest between hierarchies and networks as a way of understanding history is suggestive of the differences between Mbeki's and Zuma's approach to managing the ANC. See *The Square and the Tower: Hierarchies and the Struggle for Global Power* (2017).

29 Tshepo Motsepe, 'Five reasons why Zuma is unfit to govern', *Business Report*, 18 December 2015, https://www.iol.co.za/business-report/opinion/five-reasons-why-zuma-is-unfit-to-govern-1961637.

30 Ranjeni Munsamy, 'ANC's leadership race: The rise of the "Premier League"', *Daily Maverick*, 7 September 2015, https://www.dailymaverick.co.za/article/2015-09-07-ancs-leadership-race-the-rise-of-the-premier-league/#.WeSx-0x7HeQ.

31 Statistics South Africa (StatsSA), *Census 2011*, Table 3.1, p. 14: Total Population by Province: 1996, 2001, 2011.

32 South African Institute of Race Relations (SAIRR), *Mirror, Mirror on the Wall: Provinces Compared*, Fast Facts 12, December 2014.

33 StatsSA, *Census 2011*, Percentage Distribution of Population by Population Group and Province, Table 3.3, p. 17. KZN has the highest percentage of Indians in its population (7.3 per cent) and 4.2 per cent are white, compared to 18.4 per cent whites for the Western Cape and 15.6 per cent for Gauteng.

34 StatsSA, *Migration and Urbanisation in South Africa*, Report 03-04-02 (2006), p. 22.

35 Trade and Industrial Policy Strategies (TIPS), *The Real Economy Bulletin: Provincial Review 2016*, https://www.tips.org.za/images/The_REB_Provincial_Review_2016_KwaZulu-Natal.pdf.

36 See Tim Cohen, 'Trench warfare is all in the numbers', *Weekender*, 24 May 2007 and Carien du Plessis, 'ANC leadership race: Allocation of branch delegates to each province', *Daily Maverick*, 9 October 2017, https://www.dailymaverick.co.za/article/2017-10-06-anc-leadership-race-allocation-of-branch-delegates-to-each-province-reveals-mpumalangas-strength/.

37 For a discussion of the significance of this event, see Alexander Johnston, 'South Africa: The election and the transition process – five contradictions in search of a resolution', *Third World Quarterly*, Vol. 15 (2), 1994, pp. 187–204.

38 Quoted in, State Capacity Research Project, *Betrayal of the Promise: How South Africa Is Being Stolen* (2017), p. 4, http://pari.org.za/wp-content/uploads/2017/05/Betrayal-of-the-Promise-25052017.pdf. This report credits eight academic authors who are members of an 'interdisciplinary and inter-university research partnership that aims to contribute to public debate about "state capture" in South Africa'.

39 On the ANC in exile, see Ellis, *External Mission*. See also R. W. Johnson, 'Godfathers and assassins', in *South Africa's Brave New World*, 2010, pp. 13–51. On corruption under apartheid, see Jonathan Hyslop, 'Political corruption: Before and after apartheid', *Journal of Southern African Studies*, Vol. 31 (4), 2005, pp. 773–89.

40 Public Protector South Africa, *State of Capture*, 2016, http://cdn.24.co.za/files/Cms/General/d/4666/3f63a8b78d2b495d88f10ed060997f76.pdf. See also the South African Council of Churches *Unburdening Panel* report; this publication is the product of a project to provide a 'safe space' for individuals who had been approached to or had been coerced into unethical acts connected to state capture to tell their stories. South African newspapers, particularly *Business Day*, the *Mail and Guardian* and the *Daily Maverick* have covered state capture intensively. *AmaBhungane* (http://amabhungane.co.za) is perhaps the most important single source, along with the leaked emails to and from Gupta companies. *Business Day* hosts a dedicated page for stories on the emails, https://www.businesslive.co.za/group/bd/Gupta_Emails_Revealed/. The originals can be viewed through several newspapers, including *News24.com* and *Timeslive.co.za*. On the Guptas, see Peter-Louis Myburgh, *The Republic of Gupta* (Johannesburg, 2017).

41 See also: Roger Southall, 'Family and favour at the court of Jacob Zuma', *Review of African Political Economy*, Vol. 38 (130), 2011, pp. 617–26; Tom Lodge, 'Neo-patrimonial politics in the ANC', *African Affairs*, Vol. 113 (450), 2014, pp. 1–23; Alexander Beresford, 'Power, patronage and gatekeeper politics in South Africa', *African Affairs*, Vol. 114 (455), 2015, pp. 226–48.

42 *Betrayal of the Promise*, p. 2.

43 The investigation of Moyane's restructuring of SARS was an early centrepiece of investigations of state capture by the Ramaphosa administration.

44 *Betrayal of the Promise*, p. 23. Mcebisi Jonas was deputy minister of finance from 2014 until he was fired along with Pravin Gordhan. His allegation, that the Guptas offered him R600 million and the post of minister of finance if he supported their agenda, formed part of the Public Protector's grounds for investigation. Vytjie Mentor was an ANC MP who has also alleged she was

offered a cabinet post (minister of public enterprises) by the Guptas under similar circumstances. Themba Maseko testified to the Public Protector that he had been threatened and pressurized by the Guptas to arrange for government advertising to be placed with their newspaper *New Age* in 2010 when he was head of the government information service. His verbatim testimony can be read here: *Eyewitness News*, 3 November 2016, http://ewn. co.za/2016/11/03/gupta-brother-to-themba-maseko-you-will-be-sorted-out.

45 *Betrayal of the Promise*, p. 3.

46 For instance, at a two-day 'funeral indaba' in Durban in September 2017, presidential contender Nkosasana Dlamini-Zuma told undertakers that their industry would benefit from radical economic transformation since 'it responds to the land question, which is an important part of the funeral sector'. 'Dlamini-Zuma urges undertakers to back radical economic transformation', *Eyewitness News*, 19 September 2017, http:// ewn.co.za/2017/09/20/dlamini-zuma-urges-undertakers-to-back-radical-economic-transformation.

47 *Betrayal of the Promise*, p. 3.

48 In addition to the three sources of cover for state capture emphasized by *Betrayal of the Promise*, there is a fourth: the enabling role played by entities from outside politics and sometimes outside South Africa. These included consultants, accountants and auditors, greedy for lucrative government work. Among them were Bain (SARS restructuring), KPMG (a report discrediting an anti-corruption task force in SARS), McKinsey (Gupta deals with Eskom) and UK public relations firm Bell Pottinger who worked to intimidate and discredit critics of Zuma and to develop the 'white monopoly capital' slogan. All suffered serious reputational damage and Bell Pottinger was forced out of business.

49 *Betrayal of the Promise*, p. 16.

50 Ibid.

51 Gareth van Onselen, *Political Musical Chairs: Turnover in the National Executive and Administration since 2009*, South African Institute of Race Relations Occasional Report, August 2017. For a summary see: 'How Zuma's lethal cabinet churn has caused chaos and instability', *Business Day*, 7 August 2017, https://www.businesslive.co.za/bd/opinion/editorials/2017-08-07-editorial-how-zumas-lethal-cabinet-churn-has-caused-chaos-and-instability/.

52 van Onselen, *Political Musical Chairs*, p. 13.

53 Ibid., p. 12.

54 When he removed the respected Nhlanhla Nene from the post of minister of finance in December 2015, he claimed that Nene was going to take up a 'senior post' at the new BRICS Development Bank. This turned out to be news to Nene and in fact proved to be complete fiction.

55 The best available account of the decay of the South African justice system is by a former insider: Glynnis Breytenbach (with Nehama

Brodie), *Rule of Law: A Memoir* (Johannesburg, 2017). Breytenbach is a former senior prosecutor in the NPA and regional head of its specialized commercial crime unit. In 2013, she was acquitted of fifteen disciplinary charges designed, she claims, to silence and remove her because she had continued to pursue charges against (among others) the head of police crime intelligence Richard Mdluli. The presiding officer at her hearing said she had been 'victimized'. She is now a DA MP and shadow minister of justice. See Pierre de Vos, 'Breytenbach: Too little fear, favour and prejudice', *Daily Maverick*, 28 May 2013, https://www.dailymaverick.co.za/opinionista/2013-05-28-breytenbach-too-little-fear-favour-and-prejudice/#.WetirUyQ3eQ. De Vos is a professor of law at the University of Cape Town.

56 See Richard Calland, 'In the secret ballot case the issue is political failure, not judicial overreach', *Huffington Post*, 17 May 2017, http://www.huffingtonpost.co.za/richard-calland/in-the-secret-ballot-case-the-issue-is-political-failure-not-j_a_22094848/.

57 Constitutional Court of South Africa, *Cases CCT 143/15 and CCT 171/15* (decided 31 March 2016), http://www.news24.com/SouthAfrica/News/full-text-constitutional-court-rules-on-nkandla-public-protector-20160331. The wording quoted here comes from the court's summary for the media.

58 *Constitution of the Republic of South Africa*, Section 174. For a discussion of the judicial appointment process and of appointments made during Zuma's presidency to 2013, see the participant-observer account in Richard Calland, *The Zuma Years: South Africa's Changing Face of Power* (Cape Town, 2013), pp. 269–95.

59 After 11 years of court deliberations on procedural and jurisdictional matters, requiring many postponements, the complaint remained unresolved in mid-2019.

60 *Mail and Guardian*, 'ANC boss accuses judges of conspiracy against Zuma', 4 July 2008, https://mg.co.za/article/2008-07-04-anc-boss-accuses-judges-of-conspiracy-against-zuma.

61 Calland, *The Zuma Years*, p. 285.

62 Ibid., p. 281.

63 Ibid., p. 294. 'Does not write' is a reference to the fact that Mogoeng had not written many judgements when he was elevated.

64 Constitutional Court of the Republic of South Africa, *Case CCT 89/17* (decided 22 June 2017).

65 Constitution of the Republic of South Africa, Section 177.

66 Ibid., Section 193.

67 See: *City Press*, 'The highlights and lowlights of being Public Protector', 14 April 2016, http://city-press.news24.com/News/the-highlights-and-lowlights-of-being-public-protector-20160414. *Independent Online*, 'Public protector: Watchdog or lapdog?', 26 July 2004, https://www.iol.co.za/news/politics/public-protector-watchdog-or-lapdog-217323 and

Mail and Guardian, 'Watchdog or lapdog', 28 May 2004, https://mg.co.za/article/2004-05-28-watchdog-or-lapdog.

68 Constitutional Court of South Africa, *Cases CCT 143/15 and CCT 171/15* (decided 31 March 2016), Section 52.

69 'Public protector nominee Mkhwebane on state security payroll DA claims', *News24*, 6 September 2016, http://www.news24.com/SouthAfrica/News/public-protector-nominee-mkhwebane-on-state-security-payroll-da-claims-20160906.

70 High Court of South Africa North Gauteng (Pretoria) Division, *South African Reserve Bank v Public Protector and Others*, Case no: 43769/17, Sections 4 and 5. http://www.saflii.org/za/cases/ZAGPPHC/2017/443.pdf (Southern African Legal Information Institute).

71 Ibid., Section 59.

72 See for instance, Marianne Thamm, 'Zuma, state security and Public Protector behind attack on SA Reserve Bank court papers reveal', *Daily Maverick*, 12 September 2017, https://www.dailymaverick.co.za/article/2017-09-12-zuma-state-security-and-public-protector-behind-attack-on-sa-reserve-bank-court-papers-reveal/#.WfBcrEyQ3eQ and Dawie Roodt, 'The medium term budget, the SARB, and the Public Protector: A mystery solved', *Business Day*, 24 October 2017, https://www.businesslive.co.za/bd/opinion/2017-10-24-the-medium-term-budget-the-sarb-and-the-public-protector-a-mystery-solved/.

73 'SARS emerges as most devastating example of state capture', *Business Day*, 24 August 2018, https://www.businesslive.co.za/bd/opinion/columnists/2018-08-24-natasha-marrian-sars-staff-paint-sad-picture-of-devastation/. Transcripts of the evidence to the Zondo Commission are posted on the commission's website: www.sastatecapture.org.za.

8 Endgame: From Zuma to Ramaphosa

1 Jacques Pauw, *The President's Keepers: Those Keeping Zuma in Power and out of Prison* (Cape Town, 2017).

2 These included Bain, KPMG and McKinsey. See Chapter 7.

3 'Supreme Court of Appeal dismisses Zuma NPA bid on corruption charges', *Business Day*, 13 October 2017, https://www.businesslive.co.za/bd/national/2017-10-13-supreme-court-of-appeal-dismisses-zuma-npa-bid-on-corruption-charges/.

4 'Court sets aside #Shaun Abrahams' appointment as NDPP', *IOL Online*, 8 December 2017, https://www.iol.co.za/news/south-africa/gauteng/court-sets-aside-shaunabrahams-appointment-as-ndpp-12315116. The North Gauteng High Court's full judgement can be found on the website of the Southern African Legal Information Institute (SAFLII), http://www.saflii.org/za/cases/ZAGPPHC/2017/743.pdf.

5 'Cyril's bid to nail Zuma in ConCourt', *IOL online*, 20 January 2018, https://www.iol.co.za/news/south-africa/gauteng/cyrils-bid-to-nail-zuma-in-concourt-12819456.

6 'Deputy Chief Justice to head state capture commission of inquiry', *Mail and Guardian*, 9 January 2018, https://mg.co.za/article/2018-01-09-deputy-chief-justice-raymond-zondo-to-head-state-capture-commission-of-inquiry.

7 Section 89 of the Constitution allows for the removal of the president by a two-thirds majority of the House of Assembly on the grounds of 'serious violation of the Constitution; serious misconduct; and inability to perform the functions of the office'. It does not, however, use the word 'impeachment'.

8 Pierre de Vos 'A few tips for parliamentarians on developing rules for impeachment of a sitting president', *Daily Maverick*, 12 January 2018, https://www.dailymaverick.co.za/opinionista/2018-01-12-a-few-tips-for-parliamentarians-on-developing-rules-for-impeachment-of-a-sitting-president/#.WmB4syOZPMI. The full judgement of the constitutional court in the matter of impeachment criteria can be found on the SAFLII website, http://www.saflii.org/za/cases/ZACC/2017/47.html.

9 Removal by vote of no confidence is provided for by Section 102 of the Constitution, which requires a simple majority of the (four hundred member) House of Assembly. In that event, the whole cabinet and deputy ministers must resign along with the president.

10 A summary of the attempts to remove Zuma under Sections 89 and 102 of the Constitution can be found in 'Factsheet: The 2 ways SA's parliament can boot a president from office', Africa Check, 28 June 2017 (updated 5 January 2018), https://africacheck.org/factsheets/factsheet-many-motions-no-confidence-sa-president-zuma-faced/. Africa Check is an independent non-partisan NGO based in Johannesburg, which evaluates claims made in the public sphere.

11 For the text of the judgement, see SAFLII: http://www.saflii.org/za/cases/ZACC/2017/21.html#_ftnref52. For a discussion, see 'South African constitutional court allows secret ballot for motion of no confidence in the president', *Oxford Human Rights Hub*, 23 June 2017, http://ohrh.law.ox.ac.uk/south-african-constitutional-court-allows-secret-ballot-for-motion-of-no-confidence-in-president/.

12 *Africa Check*, 'The two ways SA's parliament can boot a president from office', 5 January 2018.

13 'Zuma vote: How many ANC MPs broke ranks?', *News24.com*, 9 August 2017, https://www.news24.com/SouthAfrica/News/zuma-vote-how-many-anc-mps-broke-ranks-20170808.

14 The most fully developed warnings that Zuma might resort to a constitutional coup are to be found in anonymous articles under the pseudonym 'Lily Gosam'. These long articles combine academic-style research (one of them for instance has over six hundred footnotes), investigative journalism and intelligence analysis. They have much in

common with other treatments of the shadow state and state capture and use many of the same sources. They heavily emphasize Zuma's alleged links with Vladimir Putin and Russian state agencies aimed at promoting an unaffordable nuclear power deal with the purpose of allegedly enriching Zuma, his family and cronies. The articles were published in *Business Day* among other places and can be accessed via this link, https://www.businesslive.co.za/authors/lily-gosam/. The 'coup scenarios' outlined in the articles did not come to pass, but the articles still add much to the documentation of state capture. The theory that the crisis over social security payments could be a trigger for a state of emergency figures largely in one of them.

15 'ANC Women's league believes men used Nkosazana Dlamini-Zuma', *Mail and Guardian*, 19 December 2017, https://mg.co.za/article/2017-12-19-anc-womens-league-believes-men-used-nkosazana-dlamini-zuma.

16 For an overview of the pre-conference manoeuvring, see 'A fight to the photo finish', *Africa Confidential*, Vol. 58 (25), 15 December 2017, https://www.africa-confidential.com/article/id/12192/A_fight_to_the_photo-finish. On the process issues affecting branch nominations, see Susan Booysen, 'The ANC leadership race will go down to the wire: Here's why', *Timeslive*, 6 December 2017, https://www.timeslive.co.za/sunday-times/opinion-and-analysis/2017-12-06-the-anc-leadership-race-will-go-down-to-the-wire-heres-why/. Susan Booysen is a professor in the school of governance at the University of the Witwatersrand, Johannesburg.

17 Booysen, 'The ANC leadership race'.

18 In September 2018, Ramaphosa disclosed to parliament that Zuma's legal fees, incurred in delaying criminal proceedings against him, had cost the taxpayer R16.8 million since 2006. *Business Day*, 'Jacob Zuma's legal fees have cost us a bit more than we thought', http://www.businesslive.co.za/bd/national/2018-09-07-jacob-zumas-legal-fees-have-cost-us-a-bit-more-than-we-thought/.

19 Zapiro, 'High Noon', *Daily Maverick*, 6 February 2018, https://www.zapiro.com/180206dm.

20 Jacob Zuma's address on the ANC NEC's recall: https://www.news24.com/Video/SouthAfrica/News/watch-live-president-zuma-addresses-nation-on-anc-recall-20180214.

9 Ramaphosa

1 See for instance: Mzukisi Qobo, 'The dangers of false optimism in a Ramaphosa presidency', *Daily Maverick*, 16 January 2018, https://www.dailymaverick.co.za/opinionista/2018-01-16-the-dangers-of-false-optimism-in-a-ramaphosa-presidency/#.Wnl1eyOZPMI.
Claire Bisseker, 'SA cannot wait long for "Cyril dividend"', *Business Day*, 6

February 2018, https://www.businesslive.co.za/bd/opinion/columnists/2018-02-06-claire-bisseker-sa-cannot-wait-long-for-cyril-dividend/; Roger Southall, 'The ANC has a new leader but South Africa remains on a political precipice', *Conversation*, 18 December 2017, https://theconversation.com/the-anc-has-a-new-leader-but-south-africa-remains-on-a-political-precipice-89248. A more bullish version was provided by Ramaphosa's biographer: Anthony Butler, 'Ramaphosa's ruthlessness prevailed against faction with huge resources', *Business Day*, 20 December 2017, https://www.businesslive.co.za/bd/opinion/columnists/2017-12-20-anthony-butler-ramaphosas-ruthlessness-prevailed-against-faction-with-huge-resources/.

2 Under Mabuza's leadership, Mpumalanga registered spectacular growth in number of delegates between the ANC's 2012 and 2017 national conferences. See Carien du Plessis, 'ANC leadership race: Allocation of branch delegates to each province', *Daily Maverick*, 9 October 2017, https://www.dailymaverick.co.za/article/2017-10-06-anc-leadership-race-allocation-of-branch-delegates-to-each-province-reveals-mpumalangas-strength/.

3 See for instance Southall, 'South Africa has a new leader'. See also 'Security bosses reveal how Cyril dodged a coup: Security bosses reveal all', *City Press*, 22 July 2018, https://www.news24.com/SouthAfrica/News/security-bosses-reveal-how-cyril-dodged-a-coup-20180722-2.

4 Anthony Butler, *Cyril Ramaphosa* (Johannesburg, 2007). A new, revised and extended edition was published in 2019, after this book had gone into production. Anthony Butler, 'Who is presidential contender Cyril Ramaphosa?', *All Africa.com*, 4 December 2017, http://allafrica.com/stories/201712040357.html ; Ray Hartley, *Ramaphosa: The Man Who Would Be King* (Johannesburg, 2017). This recent addition generously acknowledges its debt to Butler's earlier work while adding an account of Ramaphosa in the late Zuma period.

5 R. W. Johnson, 'End of the Road', *London Review of Books*, Vol. 30, 22 November 2008.

6 Jonathan Crush, 'Migrancy and militance: The case of the National Union of Mineworkers of South Africa', *African Affairs*, 88 (350), 1989, pp. 5–23; T. Dunbar Moodie, 'Becoming a social movement union: Cyril Ramaphosa and the National Union of Mineworkers', *Transformation*, 72 (73), 2010, pp. 152–80.

7 These include works by Patti Waldmeir and Alasdair Sparks, which are referred to in footnotes earlier in this work and cited in the bibliography.

8 These include works by R. W. Johnson and Richard Calland as well as Mark Gevisser's biography of Mbeki, all of which are referred to in footnotes in earlier chapters and cited in the bibliography of this work.

9 See for instance: Mashupye Herbert Maserumule, 'To lead South Africa, Ramaphosa must balance populism and pragmatism', *Conversation*, 4 January 2018, https://theconversation.com/to-lead-south-africa-ramaphosa-must-balance-populism-and-pragmatism-89660; David Everatt, 'South

Africans are trying to decode Ramaphosa – and getting it wrong', *Business Day*, 10 January 2018, https://www.businesslive.co.za/rdm/politics/2018-01-10-south-africans-are-trying-to-decode-ramaphosa-and-getting-it-wrong/; Tim Cohen, 'Ramaphosa, tactician of the long game', *Business Day*, 18 December 2017, https://www.businesslive.co.za/bd/opinion/columnists/2017-12-18-tim-cohen-ramaphosa-tactician-of-the-long-game/#; Jakkie Cilliers 'South Africa's future hinges on Ramaphosa's strategic skills', *Conversation*, 7 February 2018, https://theconversation.com/south-africas-future-hinges-on-ramaphosas-strategic-skills-90955; Mark Gevisser, 'South Africa's cattle king president', *New York Review of Books*, 22 December 2017, http://www.nybooks.com/daily/2017/12/22/south-africas-cattle-king-president/.

10 Moodie, 'Becoming a social movement union', pp. 171–2.

11 See Jeremy Baskin, *Striking Back: A History of COSATU* (Johannesburg, 1991).

12 Contemporary comments quoted in: John Battersby, 'Miners end strike in South Africa with no wage gain', *New York Times*, 31 August 1987, http://www.nytimes.com/1987/08/31/world/miners-end-strike-in-south-africa-with-no-wage-gain.html.

13 Jeremy Baskin, *Striking Back: A History of COSATU* (Johannesburg, 1991), p. 239.

14 Ibid., p. 224.

15 Donald L. Donham, *Violence in a Time of Liberation: Murder and Ethnicity in a South African Gold Mine* (Durham, NC, 2011), p. 22.

16 Ibid.

17 Moodie, 'Becoming a social movement union', pp. 155–60.

18 An example of the enduring mythology of the strike as 'the long game' is Cohen's profile/reminiscence 'Ramaphosa, tactician of the long game', published on the day of Ramaphosa's election as ANC president (see note 7). At the time, Cohen was editor of *Business Day*. See also T. Dunbar Moodie, 'Managing the 1987 mineworkers' strike', *Journal of Southern African Studies*, 35 (1), 2009, pp. 45–64.

19 P. Waldmeir, *Anatomy of a Miracle* (London, 1997), p. 226.

20 Gevisser, 'South Africa's cattle king president'.

21 Ibid for a discussion.

22 See David Bruce, *Summary and Analysis of the Report of the Marikana Commission of Inquiry*, Document prepared for the Council for the Advancement of the South African Constitution (CASAC), https://www.casac.org.za/wp-content/uploads/2015/02/Summary-and-Analysis-of-the-Report-of-the-Marikana-Commission-of-Inquiry.pdf. The press coverage of Marikana is extensively documented in footnotes to the CASAC summary and analysis. The full Marikana Commission Inquiry Report is available on the website of the South African Human Rights Commission, https://www.sahrc.org.za/home/21/files/marikana-report-1.pdf.

23 Gevisser, 'South Africa's cattle king president'.
24 Graeme Hosken, 'Marikana inquiry shown Ramaphosa e mails', *Sowetan Live*, 24 October 2012, https://www.sowetanlive.co.za/ news/2012-10-24-marikana-inquiry-shown-ramaphosa-emails/.
25 Bruce, *Summary and Analysis*, paragraph 93(b).
26 Ibid., paragraph 94.
27 Ibid.
28 Ibid., paragraphs 29–88.
29 Ibid., paragraph 48.
30 Though not apparently identification with in any strong or public sense.
31 See for instance Butler, *Cyril Ramaphosa*, pp. ix–xii.
32 Ibid.
33 Hartley, *Ramaphosa*, p. 5.
34 Butler, *Cyril Ramaphosa*, p. 396 (the book was published in January 2008).
35 Anthony Butler, 'Much hangs on Ramaphosa's next step', *Mail and Guardian*, 2 November 2012, https://mg.co.za/ article/2012-11-02-00-much-hangs-on-ramaphosas-next-step.
36 Sam Mkokeli and Carol Paton, 'Ramaphosa SA's "prime minister" – Mantashe', *Business Day*, 20 December 2012, https://www.pressreader.com/ south-africa/business-day/20121220/281479273739269.
37 Butler, 'Ramaphosa's next step'.
38 'We haven't anointed Cyril prime minister yet – Mantashe', *City Press*, 20 December 2012, https://www.news24.com/Archives/City-Press/ We-havent-anointed-Cyril-prime-minister-Mantashe-20150429.
39 Hartley, *Ramaphosa*, p. 358.
40 Gevisser, 'South Africa's cattle king president'.
41 Hartley, *Ramaphosa*, p. 360.
42 '"A new dawn" – President Cyril Ramaphosa's maiden SONA in full', *Mail and Guardian*, 16 February 2018, https://mg.co.za/ article/2018-02-16-a-new-dawn-president-cyril-ramaphosas-maiden-sona.
43 'Tony Leon on the end of Mbeki and Mbeki-ism: Quo vadis South Africa?', *Politicsweb*, 25 September 2008, http://www.politicsweb.co.za/ news-and-analysis/tony-leon-on-the-end-of-mbeki-and-mbekiism.
44 Tony Leon, *On the Contrary: Leading the Opposition in Democratic South Africa* (Johannesburg, 2008).
45 Steven Levistsky and Daniel Ziblatt, *How Democracies Die: What History Reveals about Our Future* (New York, 2017).
46 David Runciman, 'Review of *How Democracies Die*', *Guardian*, 27 January 2018.
47 Ibid.
48 Marie Elise Sarotte, *The Renewal of the Russian Challenge in European Security: History as a Guide to Policy*, Transatlantic Academy 2017 Paper series No. 9, p. 2. This author credits international relations theorist John Ikenberry with the coinage 'ordering moment'.

49 An internet search for 'economic CODESA' brings up examples too
numerous to cite including such widely diverging sources as F. W. de Klerk,
Nkosasana Dlamini-Zuma, the radical black lobby Black Management
Forum, the legacy white right party the Freedom Front Plus, archbishops
and a wide swathe of South Africa's commentariat.

50 The speech is known as the 'January 8th speech' from the date of
the ANC's founding, although Ramaphosa delivered it on 13th.
See 'Winds of change in SA blowing strong', *Daily Maverick*, 15
January 2018, https://www.dailymaverick.co.za/article/2018-01-15-
analysis-winds-of-anc-change-blowing-strong/#.WnrdQCOZPMI.
Also: 'Ramaphosa: ANC is the parliament of the people of South
Africa', *Eyewitness News*, 13 January 2018, http://ewn.co.za/2018/01/13/
ramaphosa-anc-is-the-parliament-of-the-people-of-south-africa.

51 See for instance: 'Food security the target of land expropriation without
compensation says Ramaphosa', *Business Day*, 16 February 2018, https://
www.businesslive.co.za/bd/national/2018-02-16-food-security-the-target-
of-land-expropriation-without-compensation-says-ramaphosa/; 'SA's
Ramaphosa assures Moody's on land reform', *Reuters* (Cape Town), 8 March
2018, https://af.reuters.com/article/africaTech/idAFKCN1GK0TY-OZATP;
'South Africa's Ramaphosa warns against land invasions', *Reuters* (UK), 11
March 2018, https://uk.reuters.com/article/uk-safrica-politics/south-africas-
ramaphosa-warns-against-land-invasions-idUKKCN1GN0K4?il=0.

52 Ramaphosa in May 1985, quoted in Jonathan Crush, 'Migrancy and
militance: The case of the National Union of Mineworkers of South Africa'.

10 Conclusions

1 R. Rhodes and P. t'Hart, 'Puzzles of political leadership', in P. Rhodes and
P. t'Hart (eds) *Oxford Handbook of Political Leadership* (Oxford, 2014), p. 8.

2 Ibid., p. 9.

3 On Mbeki's call for a woman president, see Carol Paton and Prakash
Naidoo, 'Who will take on Zuma?', *Financial Mail*, 2 June 2006. Nkosazana
Dlamini-Zuma had been tipped in the media for years as a potential
successor to Mbeki. It is a measure of the depth of the ANC's commitment
to equal gender representation that she has twice been designated as a
possible ANC leader and state president, but in both cases as a stalking
horse and surrogate for a wounded male president whose term limits
were up.

4 W. M. Gumede, *Thabo Mbeki and the Battle for the Soul of the ANC*
(London, 2008), p. 345.

5 For instance, for R. W. Johnson the ANC's evolution into a 'federation of
warlords' was attributable to 'the "natural" evolution of forces within African
society'. Had Mandela or Mbeki stayed in power long enough, 'the party

would have evolved in the same direction, whatever attempts they have made to hinder it'. R. W. Johnson, *How Long Will South Africa Survive? The Looming Crisis* (Johannesburg, 2015), pp. 70, 50–1.

6 A recent version of this view comes from Oxford political scientist Jonny Steinberg. According to him, the ANC's failure to uproot wholesale what it inherited left the 'marginal people' who supported Zuma frustrated and: 'If you can't move the obdurate structures built by Verwoerd you can loot them.' Jonny Steinberg, 'Ransacking the house apartheid built', *Business Day*, 2 February 2018.

Bibliography

Books and authored articles

Abdulla, M. J. 'In defence of fallism', *Mail and Guardian*, 1 March 2017.

Adams, S. 'What's left? The South African Communist Party after apartheid', *Review of African Political Economy*, Vol. 72, 1997, pp. 237–48.

Adebajo, A. *Thabo Mbeki: Africa's Philosopher King*, Johannesburg, 2016.

African National Congress, *Constitution*, www.anc.org.za.

African National Congress, *Organisational Democracy and Discipline in the Movement*, 1 July 1997, www.anc.org.za.

African National Congress, 'Speech by the ANC president to the SACP congress', *Polity*, 12 December 2009, http://www.polity.org.za/article/anc-zuma-speech-by-the-anc-president-to-the-sacpcongress-polokwane-12122009-2009-12-12.

African National Congress, *State, Property Relations and Social Transformation*, 1998.

African National Congress. 53rd National Conference, December 2012, *Organisational Report by the Secretary General*.

African National Congress, 50th National Conference: Report by the President of the ANC, 16 December 1997, http://anc.org.za/content/50th-national-conference-report-president-anc-nelson-mandela.

Ahmed Kathrada Foundation, *Still a Home for All?* Johannesburg, 2012.

ANC Fifth National Policy Conference, 2017. Secretary-General's Discussion Document, *Organisational Renewal and Organisational Design*.

Baker, P. H. and Lyman, P. (with Kehla Shubane). 'South Africa: From beacon of hope to rogue democracy?' *Stanley Foundation Working Paper*, December 2008.

Barnard, R. (ed.). *The Cambridge Companion to Nelson Mandela*, Cambridge, 2014.

Basson, A. 'Gedleyihlekisa is laughing at you', *News24*, 15 February 2016, http://www.news24.com/Columnists/GuestColumn/Gedleyihlekisa-is-laughing-at-you-20150215.

Battersby, J. 'Miners end strike in South Africa with no wage gain', *New York Times*, 31 August 1987, http://www.nytimes.com/1987/08/31/world/miners-end-strike-in-south-africa-with-no-wage-gain.html.

Beresford, A. 'Power, patronage and gatekeeper politics in South Africa', *African Affairs*, Vol. 114 (455), 2015, pp. 226–48.

Bisseker, C. 'SA cannot wait long for "Cyril dividend"', *Business Day*, 6 February 2018, https://www.businesslive.co.za/bd/opinion/columnists/2018-02-06-claire-bisseker-sa-cannot-wait-long-for-cyril-dividend/.

Blondel, J. *Political Leadership: Towards a General Analysis*, Beverly Hills, 1987.

Blumenfeld, J. 'RDP RIP?' *International Update*, South African Institute of International Affairs, October 1996.

Boehmer, E. *Nelson Mandela*, New York, 2010.

Bond, P. 'Why South Africa should undo Mandela's economic deals', *The Conversation*, 12 January 2016, https://theconversation.com/ why-south-africa-should-undo-mandelas-economic-deals-52767.

Bonner, P. 'The antimonies of Nelson Mandela', in Rita Barnard (ed.), *The Cambridge Companion to Nelson Mandela*, 2014, pp. 29–49.

Booysen, S. 'The ANC leadership race will go down to the wire: Here's why', *Sunday Times*, 6 December 2017, https://www.timeslive.co.za/sunday-times/ opinion-and-analysis/2017-12-06-the-anc-leadership-race-will-go-down-to-the-wire-heres-why/.

Breytenbach, G. (with Nehama Brodie). *Rule of Law: A Memoir*, Johannesburg, 2017.

Brown, A. *The Myth of the Strong Leader*, New York, 2014.

Bruce, P. 'Mbeki's second term', *Business Day*, 26 April 2004.

Bundy, C. 'At war with the future? Black South African youth in the 1990s', *Southern African Report*, Vol. 8 (1), 1992, p. 18.

Bundy, C. 'Mandela was no superhero and his legacy has its critics', *Business Day*, 17 July 2015.

Bundy, C. *Nelson Mandela*, Johannesburg, 2015.

Burke, Edmund, 'Speech to the Electors of Bristol, 3 November 1774', *The Founders Constitution*, Vol. 1, Chapter 13, Document 7, 1987.

Burns, J. MacGregor. *Leadership*, New York, 1978.

Butler, A. 'Challenges for Mbeki's successor', *Business Day*, 28 June 2006.

Butler, A. *Cyril Ramaphosa*, Johannesburg, 2007.

Butler, A. *The Idea of the ANC*, Athens, Ohio, 2012.

Butler, A. 'Mbeki partly responsible for "demon of tribalism"', *Business Day*, 24 January 2014.

Butler, A. 'Much hangs on Ramaphosa's next step', *Mail and Guardian*, 2 November 2012, https://mg.co.za/article/2012-11-02-00-much-hangs-on-ramaphosas-next-step.

Butler, A. 'Ramaphosa's ruthlessness prevailed against faction with huge resources', *Business Day*, 20 December 2017, https://www.businesslive. co.za/bd/opinion/columnists/2017-12-20-anthony-butler-ramaphosas-ruthlessness-prevailed-against-faction-with-huge-resources/.

Butler, A. 'South Africa's political futures', *Government and Opposition*, Vol. 38 (1), January 2003, pp. 93–112.

Butler, A. 'Who is presidential contender Cyril Ramaphosa?' *All Africa.com*, 4 December 2017.

Calland, R. 'In the secret ballot case the issue is political failure, not judicial overreach', *Huffington Post*, 17 May

2017, http://www.huffingtonpost.co.za/richard-calland/
in-the-secret-ballot-case-the-issue-is-political-failure-not-j_a_22094848/.

Calland, R. *The Zuma Years: South Africa's Changing Face of Power*, Cape Town, 2013.

Callinicoss, L. *Oliver Tambo: Beyond the Engeli Mountains*, Cape Town, 2004.

Carlin, J. *Playing the Enemy: Nelson Mandela and the Game That Made a Nation*, New York, 2008.

Caro, R. A. *The Years of Lyndon Johnson*, Vols. 1–4, New York, 1982–2012.

'Cato' (pseudonym). *Guilty Men*, London, 1940.

Centre for Development and Enterprise (CDE). *The Growth Agenda*, 'Insights and Key Recommendations', Johannesburg, April 2016, www.cde.org.za.

Centre for Development and Enterprise. *No Country for Young People: The Crisis of Youth Unemployment and What to Do about It*, Johannesburg, 2017.

Centre for Development and Enterprise (CDE). *Reforming Health Care: What Role for the Private Sector*, Johannesburg, 2011.

Chipkin, I. *Do South Africans Exist? Nationalism, Democracy and the Identity of 'the People'*, Johannesburg, 2007.

Chipkin, I. 'In Jacob Zuma, South Africa has found its Gorbachev', *Daily Maverick*, 31 July 2016.

Chothia, F. and S. Jacobs. 'Re-making the Presidency: The tension between co-ordination and centralisation', in S. Jacobs and R. Calland (eds), *Thabo Mbeki's World*, 2002, pp. 145–62.

Chris Hani Institute, *Remember Our Heroes*, Ekurhuleni Municipality, 2007.

Cilliers, J. 'South Africa's future hinges on Ramaphosa's strategic skills', *The Conversation*, 7 February 2018, https://theconversation.com/
south-africas-future-hinges-on-ramaphosas-strategic-skills-90955.

Cohen, T. 'Point of order: Zuma's state of conflict', *Business Day*, 12 September 2016.

Cohen, T. 'Ramaphosa, tactician of the long game', *Business Day*, 18 December 2017, https://www.businesslive.co.za/bd/opinion/
columnists/2017-12-18-tim-cohen-ramaphosa-tactician-of-the-long-game/#.

Cohen, T. 'Trench warfare is all in the numbers', *Weekender*, 24 May 2007.

Cronin, J. 'Why the SACP rejects GEAR', *Mail and Guardian*, 10–16 July 1998.

Cronin, J. 'What kind of presidency?' *Mail and Guardian*, 27 May 2006.

Crush, J. 'Migrancy and militance: The case of the National Union of Mineworkers of South Africa', *African Affairs*, Vol. 88 (350), 1989, pp. 5–23.

Dent, M., et al. (eds). *The Routledge Companion to Professions and Professionalism*, London, 2016.

De Vos, P. 'Breytenbach: Too little fear, favour and prejudice', *Daily Maverick*, 28 May 2013, https://www.dailymaverick.co.za/opinionista/2013-05-28-
breytenbach-too-little-fear-favour-and-prejudice/#.WetirUyQ3eQ.

De Vos, P. 'A few tips for parliamentarians on developing rules for impeachment of a sitting president', *Daily Maverick*, 12 January 2018, https://www.dailymaverick.co.za/

opinionista/2018-01-12-a-few-tips-for-parliamentarians-on-developing-rules-for-impeachment-of-a-sitting-president/#.WmB4syOZPMI.

Didion, J. 'The Deferential Spirit', *New York Review of Books*, Vol. 43 (14), 19 September 1996.

Donham, D. L. *Violence in a Time of Liberation: Murder and Ethnicity in a South African Gold Mine*, Durham, NC, 2011, p. 22.

Dunn, J. (Ed.). *The Economic Limits to Modern Politics*, Cambridge, 1992.

Du Plessis, C. 'ANC leadership race: Allocation of branch delegates to each province', *Daily Maverick*, 9 October 2017, https://www.dailymaverick.co.za/article/2017-10-06-anc-leadership-race-allocation-of-branch-delegates-to-each-province-reveals-mpumalangas-strength/.

Duverger, M. *Political Parties*, London, 1954.

Elcock, H. *Political Leadership*, Cheltenham, 2001.

Ellis, S. *External Mission: The ANC in Exile 1960–1990*, Johannesburg, 2012.

Ellis, S. and T. Sechaba. *Comrades against Apartheid*, Melton, Woodbridge, 1992.

Everatt, D. 'The Mandela Foundation's verdict on the Mandela era: It failed …', *The Conversation*, 30 September 2016, https://theconversation.com/the-mandela-foundations-verdict-on-the-mandela-era-it-failed-65257.

Everatt, D. 'Nationalism, class and non-racialism in the 1950s and beyond' (conference paper), 2009, available at www.sahistory.org.

Everatt, D. *The Origins of Non-Racialism: White Opposition to Apartheid in the 1950s*, Johannesburg, 2009.

Everatt, D. 'South Africans are trying to decode Ramaphosa – and getting it wrong', *Business Day*, 10 January 2018, https://www.businesslive.co.za/rdm/politics/2018-01-10-south-africans-are-trying-to-decode-ramaphosa-and-getting-it-wrong/.

Faull, J. 'Reading the ANC's National Membership Audit', *ePoliticsSA*, Vol. 4, 2007, Institute for a Democratic South Africa.

Feinstein, A. *After the Party*, Johannesburg, 2007.

Ferguson, N. *The Square and the Tower: Hierarchies and the Struggle for Global Power*, London, 2017.

Ferree, K. *Framing the Race in South Africa: The Political Origins of Racial Census Elections*, Cambridge, 2010.

Filatova, I. and A. Davidson. *The Hidden Thread: Russia and South Africa in the Soviet Era*, Johannesburg, 2013.

Friedman, S. 'The person may change but the policy lingers on', *Mail and Guardian*, 11 December 2007, http://thoughtleader.co.za/stevenfriedman/2007/12/11/changing-the-person-not-the-policy/.

Gevisser, M. 'South Africa's cattle king president', *New York Review of Books*, 22 December 2017, http://www.nybooks.com/daily/2017/12/22/south-africas-cattle-king-president/.

Gevisser, M. *Thabo Mbeki*, Johannesburg, 2007.

Giliomee, H. *The Afrikaners: Biography of a People*, London, 2003.

Giliomee, H. *The Last Afrikaner Leaders*, Cape Town, 2012.

Giliomee, H. and C. Simkins. *The Awkward Embrace: One Party Domination in Industrialised Societies*, Cape Town, 1999.

Glaser, G. *Politics and Society in South Africa*, London, 2001.

Good, K. 'How the killing of Thami Zulu contradicts Zuma's claims', *Politicsweb*, 13 May 2013, http://www.politicsweb.co.za/news-and-analysis/how-the-killing-of-thami-zulu-contradicts-zumas-claims.

Gordin, J. *Zuma: A Biography*, Johannesburg, 2008.

Gould, P. *Unfinished Revolution*, London, 1998.

Greenberg, S. *Despatches from the War Room: In the Trenches with Five Extraordinary Leaders*, New York, 2009.

Grint, K. *The Arts of Leadership*, New York, 2000.

Guy, J. 'A chief rules by people power', *Mail and Guardian*, 14 June 2012.

Gumede, W. M. *Thabo Mbeki and the Battle for the Soul of the ANC*, London, 2008.

Hartley, R. *Ramaphosa: The Man Who Would Be King*, Johannesburg, 2017.

Hassim, S. 'Why, a decade on a new book on Zuma's rape trial has finally hit home', *The Conversation*, 5 October 2017, https://theconversation.com/why-a-decade-on-a-new-book-on-zumas-rape-trial-has-finally-hit-home-85262.

Haussmann, R. *Final Recommendations of the International Panel on the Accelerated and Shared Growth Initiative for South Africa (Asgisa)*, Harvard Kennedy School, June 2008, https://papers.ssrn.com/sol3/papers.cfm?abstract_id=1124292.

Havel, V. *Disturbing the Peace: A Conversation with Karel Hvizdala*, New York, 1991.

Hawker, G. 'Political leadership in the ANC: The South African provinces 1994–1999', *Journal of Modern African Studies*, Vol. 38 (4), 2000, pp. 631–58.

Hellman, J., G. Jones and D. Kaufmann. 'Seize the state, seize the day: An empirical analysis of state capture and corruption in transition', *World Bank*, 2000, http://siteresources.worldbank.org/INTABCDEWASHINGTON2000/Resources/hellman.pdf.

Hirsch, A. *Season of Hope: Economic Reform under Mandela and Mbeki*, Pietermaritzburg, 2005.

Horne, A. *A Savage War of Peace*, London, 1987.

Huntington, S. P. *The Third Wave: Democratization in the Late 20th Century*, Norman, OK, 1999.

Hyslop, J. 'Political corruption: Before and after apartheid', *Journal of Southern African Studies*, Vol. 31 (4), 2005, pp. 773–89.

Jacobs, S. and R. Calland. *Thabo Mbeki's World*, Pietermaritzburg, 2002.

Janis, I. L. *Victims of Groupthink: A Psychological Study of Foreign Policy Decisions and Fiascoes*, Oxford, 1972.

Jenkins, S. *Thatcher and Sons: A Revolution in Three Acts*, London, 2007.

Johnson, R. W. 'End of the Road', *London Review of Books*, Vol. 30, 22 November 2008.

Johnson, R. W. *How Long Will South Africa Survive? The Looming Crisis*, Johannesburg, 2015.

Johnson, R. W. *South Africa's Brave New World*, London, 2010, p. 92.

Johnston, A. *Inventing the Nation: South Africa*, London, 2014.

Johnston, A. 'South Africa: The election and the transition process – five contradictions in search of a resolution', *Third World Quarterly*, Vol. 15 (2), 1994, pp. 187–204.

Jordan, Z. P. *Oliver Tambo Remembered*, Johannesburg, 2007.

Kasrils, R. *Armed and Dangerous*, Johannesburg, 2013.

Kasrils, R. 'How the ANC's Faustian pact sold out South Africa's poorest', *Guardian*, 24 June 2013.

Kellerman, B. *Followership: How Followers Are Creating Change and Changing Leaders*, Boston, MA, 2008.

Kellerman, B. (ed.). *Political Leadership: A Source Book*, Pittsburgh, 1986.

Klein, N. *The Shock Doctrine: The Rise of Disaster Capitalism*, Toronto, 2007.

Leon, T. *On the Contrary: Leading the Opposition in Democratic South Africa*, Johannesburg, 2008.

Leon, T. 'On the end of Mbeki and Mbeki-ism', Speech at the University of Cape Town, 25 September 2008, http://politicsweb.co.za/politics/tony-leon-on-the-end-of-mbeki-and-mbekiism.

Levistsky, S. and D. Ziblatt. *How Democracies Die: What History Reveals about Our Future*, New York, 2017.

Lodge, T. 'Assessing the icon', *Open Democracy*, 17 July 2009.

Lodge, T. *Mandela: A Critical Life*, Oxford, 2007.

Lodge, T. 'Neo-patrimonial politics in the ANC', *African Affairs*, Vol. 113 (450), 2014, pp. 1–23.

Mack, A. 'Why big nations lose small wars', *World Politics*, Vol. 27 (2), January 1975, pp. 175–200.

Macmillan, H. *Chris Hani*, Johannesburg, 2014.

Madikizela-Mandela, W. 'Oliver Tambo created Nelson Mandela', *New African*, Vol. 468, December 2007.

Malefane, M. 'The "people's choice" just keeps bouncing back', *Sunday Times*, 12 August 2007.

Maluleke, T. 'Why Zuma's chuckles are no laughing matter', *Independent Online*, 5 March 2017, https://www.iol.co.za/news/opinion/why-zumas-chuckles-are-no-laughing-matter-8051328.

Marais, H. *South Africa Pushed to the Limit: The Political Economy of Change*, London, 2011.

Marcus, G., et al. 'Public Management Reform: A Case Study of South Africa, 1994–2004', Genesis Analytics for the Commonwealth Secretariat, July 2005.

Marrian, N. 'SARS emerges as most devastating example of state capture', *Business Day*, 24 August 2018, https://www.businesslive.co.za/bd/opinion/columnists/2018-08-24-natasha-marrian-sars-staff-paint-sad-picture-of-devastation/.

Maseko, T. 'Verbatim testimony to Zondo Commission', *Eyewitness News*, 3 November 2016, http://ewn.co.za/2016/11/03/gupta-brother-to-themba-maseko-you-will-be-sorted-out.

Maserumule, H. M. 'To lead South Africa, Ramaphosa must balance populism and pragmatism', *The Conversation*, 4 January 2018, https://theconversation.com/to-lead-south-africa-ramaphosa-must-balance-populism-and-pragmatism-89660.

Mbeki, T. 'ANC's allies must set their sights on the real enemies', *Sunday Times*, 5 July 1998.

Mbeki, T. (attributed). *Castro Hlongwane, Caravans, Cats, Geese, Foot and Mouth and Statistics: HIV/AIDS and the Struggle for the Humanisation of the African*, http://ccs.ukzn.ac.za/files/Mbeki%27s%20document.pdf.

Mbeki, T. *I am an African* Statement of Deputy President T. M. Mbeki, on behalf of the African National Congress, on the occasion of the adoption by the Constitutional Assembly of the Republic of South Africa Constitution Bill 1996, Cape Town, 8 May 1996.

Mbeki, T. 'Two Nations': Statement of deputy president Thabo Mbeki at the opening of the debate in the National Assembly, on *Reconciliation and Nation Building*, Cape Town, 29 May 1998.

Mbeki, T. 'Unmandated Reflections: DP's discussion document on the tasks of the ANC in the new epoch of democratic transformation (August 9 1994)', *Politicsweb*, 17 April 2015, http://www.politicsweb.co.za/documents/unmandated-reflections--thabo-mbeki.

Mda, Z. 'The contradictions of Mandela', *The New York Times*, 6 December 2013.

Mda, Z. 'Nelson Mandela, neither sell-out nor saint', *The Guardian*, 6 December 2013.

Michels, R. (1876–1936). *Political Parties*, New York, 1968.

Miller, A. *On Politics and the Art of Acting*, New York, 2001.

Mkokeli, S. and C. Paton. 'Ramaphosa SA's "prime minister" – Mantashe', *Business Day*, 20 December 2012, https://www.pressreader.com/south-africa/business-day/20121220/281479273739269.

Morobe, M. 'Towards a people's democracy: The UDF view', *Review of African Political Economy*, Vol. 40, December 1987, pp. 81–7.

Moodie, T. Dunbar. 'Becoming a social movement union: Cyril Ramaphosa and the National Union of Mineworkers', *Transformation*, Vol. 72 (73), 2010, pp. 152–80.

Moodie, T. Dunbar. 'Managing the 1987 mineworkers' strike', *Journal of Southern African Studies*, Vol. 35 (1), 2009, pp. 45–64.

Moseneke, D. *Reflections on South African Constitutional Democracy – Transition and Transformation*. Keynote address, conference: 20 Years of South African Democracy: So Where to Now? University of South Africa, 12 November 2014.

Motsepe, T. 'Five reasons why Zuma is unfit to govern', *Business Report*, 18 December 2015, https://www.iol.co.za/business-report/opinion/five-reasons-why-zuma-is-unfit-to-govern-1961637.

Munsamy, R. 'ANC's leadership race: The rise of the "Premier League"', *Daily Maverick*, 7 September 2015, https://www.dailymaverick.co.za/article/2015-09-07-ancs-leadership-race-the-rise-of-the-premier-league/#.WeSx-0x7HeQ.

Munsamy, R. 'Julius Malema and the move towards #MandelaMust Fall', *Daily Maverick*, 12 April 2015.

Munsamy, R. 'Scrum over Mandela's legacy exposes hollow heart of SA politics', *Daily Maverick*, 27 July 2016.

Myburgh, J. 'The African National Congress and the Evolution of South Africa's One Party Dominant System', *European Consortium for Political Research*, conference paper, April 2005, https://ecpr.eu/Filestore/PaperProposal/56f77ccc-91f9-40e5-8fc8-d139087ca431.pdf.

Myburgh, J. 'Who is the real ANC?' *Politicsweb*, 22 December 2016, http://www.politicsweb.co.za/opinion/who-is-the-real-anc.

Myburgh, P.-L. *The Republic of Gupta*, Johannesburg, 2017.

Namier, L. 'Men who stumbled into the war', in L. Namier (ed.), *Avenues of History*, London, 1952.

Nattrass, N. 'AIDS and the scientific governance of medicine in post-apartheid South Africa', *African Affairs*, Vol. 107 (427), 2008, pp. 157–76.

Nattrass, N. and J. Seekings. '"Two nations?" Race and economic inequality in South Africa today', *Daedalus*, Vol. 130 (1), 2001, pp. 45–70.

Nkosi, S. 'SACP split over who will lead', *Mail and Guardian*, 19 June 1998.

Paton, C. and P. Naidoo. 'Who will take on Zuma?' *Financial Mail*, 2 June 2006.

Pauw, J. *The President's Keepers: Those Keeping Zuma in Power and Out of Prison*, Cape Town, 2017.

Pearson, J., S. Pillay and I. Chipkin. *State-Building in South Africa after Apartheid: The History of the National Treasury*, Johannesburg, 2016.

Peele, G. 'Leadership and Politics: A case for a closer relationship?' *Leadership*, Vol. 1 (2), June 2005.

Phillips, L., A. Lissoni and I. Chipkin. 'Bantustans are dead – long live Bantustans', *Mail and Guardian*, 11 July 2014.

Posel, D. '"Madiba Magic": Politics as enchantment', in R. Barnard (ed.), *The Cambridge Companion to Nelson Mandela*, 2014, pp. 70–92.

Powell, I. 'Smoke and mirrors', *Mail and Guardian*, 5 January 2009, https://mg.co.za/article/2009-05-01-smoke-and-mirrors.

Powell, J. *Great Hatred, Little Room*, London, 2010.

Pye, L. 'Political Culture', in Seymour Martin Lipset (ed.), *Encyclopedia of Democracy*, London, 1995.

Qobo, M. 'The dangers of false optimism in a Ramaphosa presidency', *Daily Maverick*, 16 January 2018, https://www.dailymaverick.co.za/opinionista/2018-01-16-the-dangers-of-false-optimism-in-a-ramaphosa-presidency/#.Wnl1eyOZPMI.

Rachman, G. 'Donald Trump is more than a blip in history', *Financial Times*, 9 October 2017, https://www.ft.com/content/ecfcbf32-acca-11e7-aab9-abaa44b1e130.

Rawnsley, A. 'How long will Theresa May survive? She is the very last person to ask', *The Observer*, 3 September 2017, https://www.theguardian.com/commentisfree/2017/sep/02/how-long-will-mrs-may-survive-last-person-to-ask-lead-conservatives-election.

Rhodes, R. and Paul t'Hart (eds), *The Oxford Handbook of Political Leadership*, Oxford, 2014.

Robinson, J. 'Fragments of the past: Homeland politics and the South African transition, 1990–2014', *Journal of Southern African Studies*, Vol. 41 (5), 2015, pp. 953–67.

Roodt, D. 'The medium term budget, the SARB, and the Public Protector: A mystery solved', *Business Day*, 24 October 2017, https://www.businesslive.co.za/bd/opinion/2017-10-24-the-medium-term-budget-the-sarb-and-the-public-protector-a-mystery-solved/.

Rotberg, R. 'The need for strengthened political leadership', in Robert Rotberg (ed.), Strengthening Governance in South Africa: Building on Mandela's Legacy, *The Annals of the American Academy of Political and Social Science*, Vol. 652, March 2014, pp. 238–56.

Rotberg, R. *Transformational Political Leadership: Making a Difference in the Developing World*, Chicago, 2012.

Roux, D. 'Mandela writing/writing Mandela', in R. Barnard (ed.), *The Cambridge Companion to Nelson Mandela*, 2014, p. 209.

Runciman, D. 'Review of *How Democracies Die*', *The Guardian*, 27 January 2018.

Runciman, W. G. *Social Science and Political Theory*, Cambridge, 1969.

Russell, A. *After Mandela: The Battle for the Soul of South Africa*, London, 2010.

Sampson, A. *The Observer*, 18 February 1990.

Sampson, A. 'President select', *The Observer*, 10 June 2001.

Saul, J. and P. Bond. *South Africa: The Present as History*, Martlesham, Suffolk, 2014.

Sarotte, M. E. *The Renewal of the Russian Challenge in European Security: History as a Guide to Policy*, Transatlantic Academy, 2017, Paper series No. 9.

Seekings, J. 'The "Lost Generation": South Africa's "Youth Problem" in the early 1990s', *Transformation*, Vol. 29, 1996, pp. 103–25.

Sexwale, T. 'The death that mobilised a nation', *Sunday Times*, 13 April 2008.

Smith, D. *Young Mandela*, London, 2010.

South African Institute of Race Relations (SAIRR). *Mirror, Mirror on the Wall: Provinces Compared*, Fast Facts 12, December 2014.

Southall, R. 'The ANC has a new leader but South Africa remains on a political precipice', *The Conversation*, 18 December 2017, https://theconversation.com/the-anc-has-a-new-leader-but-south-africa-remains-on-a-political-precipice-89248.

Southall, R. 'The "Dominant Party Debate" in South Africa', *Africa Spectrum*, Vol. 40 (1), 2005, pp. 61–82.

Southall, R. 'Family and favour at the court of Jacob Zuma', *Review of African Political Economy*, Vol. 38 (130), 2011, pp. 617–26.

Southall, R. *Opposition and Democracy in South Africa*, London, 2014.

Sparks, A. *Tomorrow Is Another Country*, Johannesburg, 1994.

State Capacity Research Project (various authors). *Betrayal of the Promise: How South Africa Is Being Stolen*, 2017, http://pari.org.za/wp-content/uploads/2017/05/Betrayal-of-the-Promise-25052017.pdf, p. 4.

Steinberg, J. 'Ransacking the house apartheid built', *Business Day*, 2 February 2018.

Suttner, R. 'Did Mandela "sell out" the struggle for freedom?" *Daily Maverick*, 8 March 2016.

Taghavi, D. *Exploring Fallism: Student Protests and the Decolonization of Education in South Africa*, Masters thesis, University of Cologne, 2017.

Taylor, A. J. P. *Origins of the Second World War*, London, 1961.

Thamm, M. 'Zuma, state security and Public Protector behind attack on SA Reserve Bank court papers reveal', *Daily Maverick*, 12 September 2017, https://www.dailymaverick.co.za/article/2017-09-12-zuma-state-security-and-public-protector-behind-attack-on-sa-reserve-bank-court-papers-reveal/#.WfBcrEyQ3eQ.

Thlabi, R. *Kwhezi*, Cape Town, 2017.

Tracy, M. 'Steve Bannon's book club', *New York Times*, 2 April 2017.

Trade and Industrial Policy Strategies (TIPS). *The Real Economy Bulletin: Provincial Review 2016*, https://www.tips.org.za/images/The_REB_Provincial_Review_2016_KwaZulu-Natal.pdf.

Trewhela, P. 'Jacob Zuma, Mbokodo and the death of Thami Zulu', *Politicsweb*, 12 February 2009, http://www.politicsweb.co.za/news-and-analysis/jacob-zuma-mbokodo-and-the-death-of-thami-zulu.

University of KwaZulu-Natal. 'The unemployed in South Africa: Why are so many not counted?', 2013, www.econ3x3.org/article/unemployed-south-africa-why-are-so-many-not-counted.

Von Holdt, K., et al. *The Smoke That Calls: Insurgent Citizenship, Collective Violence and the Struggle for a Place in the New South Africa*, Johannesburg, 2011.

Van Onselen, G. 'The ANC and the DA battle for the past', *Business Day*, 27 July 2016.

Van Onselen, G. *Clever Blacks, Jesus and Nkandla: The Real Jacob Zuma in His Own Words*, Johannesburg, 2014.

Van Onselen, G. *Political Musical Chairs: Turnover in the National Executive and Administration since 2009*, South African Institute of Race Relations Occasional Report, August 2017.

Waldmeir, P. *Anatomy of a Miracle*, London, 1997.

Weeks, S. M. 'South Africa's traditional courts bill 2.0: Improved but still flawed', 4 April 2017, https://theconversation.com/.

Wimberley, H. and J. Savishinsky. 'Ancestral memorialism', in W. H. Newell and Walter de Gruyter (eds), *Ancestors*, Oxford, 1979.

Williams, J. M. *Chieftaincy, the State and Democracy in Post-Apartheid South Africa*, Bloomington, 2010.

Zamani Saul. 'The anatomy of a faction: A negative tendency', *ANC Today*, 18–24 September 2016, http://www.anc.org.za/content/anc-today-volume-15-no-30-0.

Court decisions and commissions of enquiry

Bruce, D. *Summary and Analysis of the Report of the Marikana Commission of Inquiry*, Document prepared for the Council for the Advancement of the South African Constitution (CASAC), https://www.casac.org.za/wp-content/uploads/2015/02/Summary-and-Analysis-of-the-Report-of-the-Marikana-Commission-of-Inquiry.pdf.

South African Human Rights Commission. *Marikana Commission of Inquiry Report*, https://www.sahrc.org.za/home/21/files/marikana-report-1.pdf.

High Court of South Africa. Natal Provincial Division: case number 8652/08: *In the matter between Jacob Gedleyihlekisa Zuma and the National Director of Public Prosecutions*, http://www.politicsweb.co.za/politicsweb/action/media/downloadFile?media_fileid=1077.

Supreme Court of Appeal. Judgement: *National Director of Public Prosecutions vs. Zuma*, Case no: 573/08, 12 January 2009, http://www.justice.gov.za/sca/judgments%5Csca_2009/sca09-001.pdf.

Constitutional Court of the Republic of South Africa. *Case CCT 89/17* (decided 22 June 2017).

Constitutional Court of South Africa. *Cases CCT 143/15 and CCT 171/15* (decided 31 March 2016), http://www.news24.com/SouthAfrica/News/full-text-constitutional-court-rules-on-nkandla-public-protector-20160331.

High Court of South Africa North Gauteng (Pretoria) Division, *South African Reserve Bank v Public Protector and Others*, Case no: 43769/17, Sections 4 and 5. http://www.saflii.org/za/cases/ZAGPPHC/2017/443.pdf (Southern African Legal Information Institute).

Constitutional Court ruling on the matter of impeachment criteria, http://www.saflii.org/za/cases/ZACC/2017/47.html.

For the text of the judgement see SAFLII, http://www.saflii.org/za/cases/ZACC/2017/21.html#_ftnref52.

O'Malley archive coverage of the Hefer Commission, https://www.nelsonmandela.org/omalley/index.php/site/q/03lv03445/04lv04015/05lv04120.htm.

Oxford Human Rights Hub. *South African Constitutional Court Allows Secret Ballot for Motion of No Confidence in the President*, 23 June 2017, http://ohrh. law.ox.ac.uk/south-african-constitutional-court-allows-secret-ballot-for-motion-of-no-confidence-in-president/.

Newspaper reports

Africa Check, 'The 2 ways SA's parliament can boot a president from office', 28 June 2017 (updated 5 January 2018), https://africacheck.org/factsheets/factsheet-many-motions-no-confidence-sa-president-zuma-faced/.

Africa Confidential, 'A fight to the photo finish', Vol. 58 (25), 15 December 2017, https://www.africa-confidential.com/article/id/12192/A_fight_to_the_photo-finish.

amaBhungane Centre for Investigative Journalism, 'Minister versus top spooks', 16 September 2011, http://amabhungane.co.za/article/2011-09-16-minister-vs-top-spooks.

BBC News, 'Mandela hands the baton to Mbeki', 20 December 1997, http://news.bbc.co.uk/1/hi/41252.stm.

Business Day, 'Zuma now willing to serve two terms', 5 June 2009.

Business Day, 'Supreme Court of Appeal dismisses Zuma NPA bid on corruption charges', 13 October 2017, https://www.businesslive.co.za/bd/national/2017-10-13-supreme-court-of-appeal-dismisses-zuma-npa-bid-on-corruption-charges/.

Business Day, 'Food security the target of land expropriation without compensation says Ramaphosa', 16 February 2018, https://www.businesslive.co.za/bd/national/2018-02-16-food-security-the-target-of-land-expropriation-without-compensation-says-ramaphosa/.

Business Day, 'Jacob Zuma's legal fees have cost us a bit more than we thought', http://www.businesslive.co.za/bd/national/2018-09-07-jacob-zumas-legal-fees-have-cost-us-a-bit-more-than-we-thought/.

City Press, 'The highlights and lowlights of being Public Protector', 14 April 2016, http://city-press.news24.com/News/the-highlights-and-lowlights-of-being-public-protector-20160414.

City Press, 'Security bosses reveal how Cyril dodged a coup: Security bosses reveal all', 22 July 2018, https://www.news24.com/SouthAfrica/News/security-bosses-reveal-how-cyril-dodged-a-coup-20180722-2.

City Press, 'We haven't anointed Cyril prime minister yet – Mantashe', 20 December 2012, https://www.news24.com/Archives/City-Press/We-havent-anointed-Cyril-prime-minister-Mantashe-20150429.

Daily Maverick, 'Winds of change in SA blowing strong', 15 January 2018, https://www.dailymaverick.co.za/article/2018-01-15-analysis-winds-of-anc-change-blowing-strong/#.WnrdQCOZPMI.

Eyewitness News, 'Dlamini-Zuma urges undertakers to back radical economic transformation', 19 September 2017, http://ewn.co.za/2017/09/20/ dlamini-zuma-urges-undertakers-to-back-radical-economic-transformation.

Eyewitness News, 'Ramaphosa: ANC is the parliament of the people of South Africa', 13 January 2018, http://ewn.co.za/2018/01/13/ ramaphosa-anc-is-the-parliament-of-the-people-of-south-africa.

Financial Mail, 'Soul for Sale: the ANC and business', 19 January 2007.

Independent Online, 'Court sets aside #Shaun Abrahams' appointment as NDPP', 8 December 2017, https://www.iol.co.za/news/south-africa/gauteng/ court-sets-aside-shaunabrahams-appointment-as-ndpp-12315116.

Independent Online, 'Cyril's bid to nail Zuma in ConCourt', 20 January 2018, https://www.iol.co.za/news/south-africa/gauteng/ cyrils-bid-to-nail-zuma-in-concourt-12819456.

Independent Online, 'Public protector: Watchdog or lapdog?' 26 July 2004, https://www.iol.co.za/news/politics/public-protector- watchdog-or-lapdog-217323.

Mercury (South African Press Association: SAPA), 'Mandela slams SACP and Cosatu over Gear criticism', 2 July 1998.

Mail and Guardian, 'Is Thabo Mbeki fit to rule?' 17 May 1996, https://mg.co.za/ article/1996-05-17-is-thabo-mbeki-fit-to-rule.

Mail and Guardian, 'Do not look where you fell but where you slipped', *Mail and Guardian*, 25 October 2006, https://mg.co.za/ article/2006-10-25-do-not-look-where-you-fell-but-slipped.

Mail and Guardian, 'Moment of truth for SACP', 3–9 July 1998.

Mail and Guardian, 'Watchdog or lapdog', 28 May 2004, https://mg.co.za/ article/2004-05-28-watchdog-or-lapdog.

Mail and Guardian, 'The spy who saved Zuma', 9 April 2009.

Mail and Guardian, 'Browse Mole', https://cdn.mg.co.za/uploads/2009/04/30/ special-browse-mole-report.pdf.

Mail and Guardian, 'Zuma case struck from the roll', 20 September 2006, https:// mg.co.za/article/2006-09-20-zuma-case-struck-from-the-roll.

Mail and Guardian, 'The good, the bad and the ugly: The 2000 report card', http://allafrica.com/stories/200012220171.html.

Mail and Guardian, 'Cabinet Report Card 2016', Jacob Zuma: http://cabinet. mg.co.za/2016/jacob-zuma.

Mail and Guardian, 'Motsoko Pheko "Insulted" by Malema, Vavi comments', 22 June 2008, https://mg.co.za/article/2008-06- 22-motsoko-pheko- insulted-by-malema-vavi-comments.

Mail and Guardian, 'Zuma and Cosatu: The end of the affair', 19 February 2010.

Mail and Guardian, Coverage of the Hefer Commission, https://mg.co.za/tag/ hefer-commission.

Mail and Guardian, 'Spy bosses to spill beans on Guptas', 24 March 2016, https:// mg.co.za/article/2016-03-23-ex-spy-bosses-to-spill-beans-on-guptas.

Mail and Guardian, 'Zuma case struck from the roll', 20 September 2006, https://mg.co.za/article/2006-09-20-zuma-case-struck-from-the-roll.

Mail and Guardian, 'ANC boss accuses judges of conspiracy against Zuma', 4 July 2008, https://mg.co.za/article/2008-07-04-anc-boss-accuses-judges-of-conspiracy-against-zuma.

Mail and Guardian, 'ANC Women's league believes men used Nkosazana Dlamini-Zuma', 19 December 2017, https://mg.co.za/article/2017-12-19-anc-womens-league-believes-men-used-nkosazana-dlamini-zuma.

Mail and Guardian, '"A new dawn" – President Cyril Ramaphosa's maiden SONA in full', 16 February 2018, https://mg.co.za/article/2018-02-16-a-new-dawn-president-cyril-ramaphosas-maiden-sona.

Mail and Guardian, 'Deputy Chief Justice to head state capture commission of inquiry', 9 January 2018, https://mg.co.za/article/2018-01-09-deputy-chief-justice-raymond-zondo-to-head-state-capture-commission-of-inquiry.

News24.com, 'Public protector nominee Mkhwebane on state security payroll DA claims', 6 September 2016, http://www.news24.com/SouthAfrica/News/public-protector-nominee-mkhwebane-on-state-security-payroll-da-claims-20160906.

News24.com, 'Political hyenas in feeding frenzy –Vavi', August 2010, http://www.news24.com/SouthAfrica/Politics/Political-hyenas- in-feeding-frenzy-20100826.

News24, 'Absence of the best led to Zuma election: Malema', 6 November 2015, http://www.news24.com/SouthAfrica/News/Absence-of-the-best-led-to-Zuma-election-Malema-20150611.

News24.com, 'Zuma vote: How many ANC MPs broke ranks?' 9 August 2017, https://www.news24.com/SouthAfrica/News/zuma-vote-how-many-anc-mps-broke-ranks-20170808.

New York Times, 'New Model for Africa: Good Leaders above All', March 25, 1998.

Pretoria News, 'Zuma calls Malema "leader in the making"', 26 October 2009, https://www.iol.co.za/news/politics/zuma-calls-malema-leader-in-the-making-462670.

Reuters (UK), 'South Africa's Ramaphosa warns against land invasions', 11 March 2018, https://uk.reuters.com/article/uk-safrica-politics/south-africas-ramaphosa-warns-against-land-invasions-idUKKCN1GN0K4?il=0.

Reuters (Cape Town), 'SA's Ramaphosa assures Moody's on land reform', 8 March 2018, https://af.reuters.com/article/africaTech/idAFKCN1GK0TY-OZATP.

Sunday Independent, 'SACP licks its wounds', 4 July 1998.

Sunday Independent, 'Line-up of ANC's would-be kingmakers', 28 October 2007.

Sunday Times (Johannesburg), 'Decisions, Decisions', 25 November 2007.

Sunday Times, 'Ajay Gupta threatened to kill me', 24 August 2018, https://www.timeslive.co.za/politics/2018-08-24-ajay-gupta-threatened-to-kill-me-mcebisi-jonass-shocking-revelations/.

Sunday Times, 'National security threat: CIA alerted SA to the Gupta's "dodgy deals"' in 2009', 2 September 2018.

The Sowetan, 'Marikana inquiry shown Ramaphosa emails', 24 October 2012, https://www.sowetanlive.co.za/news/2012-10-24-marikana-inquiry-shown-ramaphosa-emails/.

The Economist, 'The presidency of Jacob Zuma looms', 18 September 2008, http://www.economist.com/node/12263140.

The Sowetan, 'JZ will serve only one term as president', 14 December 2007, http://www.sowetanlive.co.za/sowetan/archive/2007/12/14/jz-will-serve-only-one-term-as-president.

Government documents

Constitution of the Republic of South Africa (Act 108 of 1996).

Department of Cooperative Governance and Traditional Affairs. *Annual Report*, 2012.

Government of South Africa. *Accelerated and Shared Growth Initiative for South Africa (Asgisa)*, hosted on the O'Malley archive: https://www.nelsonmandela.org/omalley/index.php/site/q/03lv02409/04lv02410/05lv02415/06lv02416.htm.

Public Protector South Africa. *State of Capture*, 2016. http://cdn.24.co.za/files/Cms/General/d/4666/3f63a8b78d2b495d88f10ed060997f76.pdf.

Statistics South Africa (StatsSA). *Census in Brief, 2011*, Pretoria, 2012.

Statistics South Africa (StasSA). *Mid-Year Population Estimate*, August 2017, http://www.statssa.gov.za/?p=10277.

Statistics South Africa (StatsSA). *Census 2011*.

Statistics South Africa (StatsSA). *Migration and Urbanisation in South Africa* Report 03-04-02, 2006, p. 22.

Statistics South Africa (StatsSA). *Community Survey 2016*.

The Presidency. *Report of the Presidential Review Commission on the Reform and Transformation of the Public Service in South Africa*, 1999.

The Presidency. *Towards a Ten Year Review: A Synthesis Report on Implementation of Government Programmes*. Pretoria, 2004.

The Presidency. *Twenty Year Review: South Africa 1994–2014*, Pretoria, 2014.

The Presidency (National Planning Commission). *National Development Plan*, 2011, p. 364.

The Presidency (Department of Performance Monitoring and Evaluation). *Twenty Year Report: South Africa 1994–2014*, Background Paper: Changing Public Service.

The Presidency. *Annual Address by President Zuma to the National House of Traditional Leaders*, Cape Town, 1 November 2012.

The Presidency, *Background Report: Changing Public Service*, p. 21.

Video and other visual sources

Democratic Alliance election ad 1.
https://www.youtube.com/watch?v=7ov_jfKaxa4.
Democratic Alliance election ad 2.
https://www.youtube.com/watch?v=OuocHCwGi88.
De Gaulle 'je vous ai compris'
https://www.youtube.com/watch?v=vzm0APfrflk.
Jacob Zuma's televised address to the nation after being recalled by the ANC's
national executive committee: https://www.news24.com/Video/SouthAfrica/
News/watch-live-president-zuma-addresses-nation-on-anc-recall-20180214.
Zapiro. 'High Noon', *Daily Maverick*, 6 February 2018, https://www.zapiro.
com/180206dm.

Index

criticisms of 97, 99–100
influence on ANC 37
legacy 140
   betrayal theme and 95–107
   possession theme and 91–5
politics of sublime and 5
SACP membership of 106
as state president 4
successors of 119–25
warning to SACP 156
Mantashe, G. 81, 207, 245, 247,
   280, 306
Manuel, T. 170, 185, 224, 240,
   307–8
Marais, H. 222
Marikana shootings 273–5, 340 n.22
Maseko, T. 236, 334 n.44
Masethla, B. 177
Mass Democratic Movement
   (MDM) 130
Mbalula, F. 225
Mbeki, G. 129
Mbeki, T. 4, 37, 220, 276, 295,
   296, 307–9
accusation of being neo-liberal 50
'After Mandela' syndrome's
   impact on 6
ambiguity under 44
as ANC president 121
as authoritarian centralizer 180
on centralizing government 167–72
central leadership and local
   democracy and 159–63
constitution under 39
as deputy president of ANC 131
early life of 129
fall of 189–92, 196–9
as government leader 163–5
and Hani 131
HIV/AIDS and 186–9
'I am an African' speech of 146–8,
   325 n.19
intellectual image of 141–3
Left, African nationalism
   and 153–9

making sense of 179–81
new cadre and new person
   philosophies under 80
ousting of 16
party domination as path to
   President and 42
politicization and 172–5
populism under 38
as representative individual
   138–41
revisionist vision of 143–5
rise of 132–4
'rogue democracy' under 27
role in negotiations 131
second term of 189–90
as 'Third Way' political
   leader 149–52
'Two Nations' speech of 148–9,
   325 n.19
'Unmandated Reflections' by
   134–7, 167
Zimbabwe 186–9
and Zuma 123, 176–8, 249–50,
   298–302, 306–7
struggle between 193–6
Mbete, B. 208, 248, 256
Mda, Z. 97
Medium Term Expenditure
   Framework (MTEF) 170
Mentor, V. 236, 333 n.44
Meyer, R. 270, 277, 278
Michels, R. 111
Miller, A. 214
Mkhwebane, B. 247, 248, 249
Mlambo-Ngcuka, P. 189, 196
modernization and
   neo-traditionalism 78
Mogoeng, M. 32, 245,
   246, 255
Mokaba, P. 132, 133, 274
Moodie, T. D. 267, 268, 269,
   340 n.18
moral panic about young people,
   critique of 320 n.22
Morobe, M. 318 n.27

Lightning Source UK Ltd.
Milton Keynes UK
UKHW021306060320
359884UK00005B/285